SAMS
Teach Yourself
Microsoft®
Office 2000®
in 21 Days

SAMS

201 West 103rd St., Indianapolis, Indiana, 46290 USA

Sams Teach Yourself Microsoft® Office 2000® in 21 Days

Copyright © 1999 by Sams Publishing

International Standard Book Number: 0-672-31448-7

Library of Congress Catalog Card Number: 98-87071

Printed in the United States of America

First Printing: June, 1999

00 99   4   3   2   1

Trademarks

Warning and Disclaimer

EXECUTIVE EDITOR
Jim Minatel

DEVELOPMENT EDITOR
Susan Hobbs

MANAGING EDITOR
Brice Gosnell

PROJECT EDITOR
Gretchen Uphoff

COPY EDITOR
JoAnna Kremer

INDEXER
Kevin Kent

PROOFREADER
Andrew Beaster

TECHNICAL EDITOR
Sherry Kinkopf
Don Roche

SOFTWARE DEVELOPMENT SPECIALIST
Andrea Duvall

INTERIOR DESIGN
Gary Adair

COVER DESIGN
Aren Howell

COPY WRITER
Eric Bogert

LAYOUT TECHNICIANS
Susan Geiselman
Amy Parker

Contents at a Glance

APPENDIXES

Table of Contents

About the Author

Laurie Ulrich is the author of four other books for Macmillan Computer Publishing: *Using Word 97, Using PowerPoint 97, The Office Productivity Pack,* and *The Complete Idiot's Guide to Running Your Small Office with Microsoft Office.* She is the co-author of *Special Edition Using Excel 2000,* and she has contributed chapters and served as technical editor on several other titles. Laurie is also a teacher, having trained thousands of people to use computers and business software over the last ten years. She also runs her own firm, Limehat & Company, Inc., specializing in technical documentation, Web page design, and Web site hosting. She can be reached at `laurie@limehat.com`, and invites you to visit her Web site at `www.limehat.com`.

Dedication

I dedicate this book to Joshua and Zachary Ulrich, whose faces you see on the flyer on Day 20. They are a constant source of inspiration and happiness for me, and I hope my efforts in writing this and my other books inspire them to find something they love to do and to do their best at it.

Acknowledgments

I want to thank Jim Minatel for the opportunity to write this book, and for his patience as intervening projects continued to move my deadlines in the wrong direction. I thank him also for assigning Susan Hobbs as Development Editor—she's done a terrific job and has been great to work with. I must also thank my Technical Editors, Don Roche and Sherry Kinkoph, for a very thorough job—their expertise and objectivity were welcome additions to the project.

Tell Us What You Think!

As the reader of this book, *you* are our most important critic and commentator. We value your opinion and want to know what we're doing right, what we could do better, what areas you'd like to see us publish in, and any other words of wisdom you're willing to pass our way.

As an associate publisher for Sams Publishing, I welcome your comments. You can fax, email, or write me directly to let me know what you did or didn't like about this book— as well as what we can do to make our books stronger.

Please note that I cannot help you with technical problems related to the topic of this book, and that due to the high volume of mail I receive, I might not be able to reply to every message.

When you write, please be sure to include this book's title and author as well as your name and phone or fax number. I will carefully review your comments and share them with the author and editors who worked on the book.

Fax: 317.581.4770

Email: office_sams@mcp.com

Mail: Dean Miller
         Sams Publishing
         201 West 103rd Street
         Indianapolis, IN 46290 USA

Introduction

How to Use This Book

This book is designed to help you teach yourself, in a series of 21 days, how to use Office 2000. Each of the 21 days takes you through a project that will give you hands-on experience using the Office 2000 applications, both on their own and together.

The best way to use this book is to start with Day 1 and move through the days consecutively, moving at your own pace. Some projects might take a full day, others might only take an hour or two. Some of the projects that are created on one particular day are reused on a subsequent day or days, so following a linear path will give you the best results. If you want to use the book as a reference, however, or if you want to jump in on a particular day and not do the preceding or following days' projects, you can. In order to support you no matter how you use the book, you'll find the documents, spreadsheets, presentations, and other files that are created throughout the 21 days on the CD-ROM that accompanies this book—you can use these completed versions as needed by copying them to your local drive.

To support you no matter how you use the book, you'll find the documents, spreadsheets, presentations, and other files created in the 21 days of projects on the CD-ROM that accompanies this book — you can use these completed versions as needed by copying them to your local drive. These files show you the results you should get if you work along with the procedures throughout the days' project — you can use them to compare with your results or to "play" with in experimenting with your new Office 2000 skills.

Who Should Use This Book

Anyone who wants to become an effective, efficient, and creative user of Office 2000 should use this book. The 21 days are constructed so that a beginner can follow them, but the projects delve into territory that intermediate and advanced-level users will also find useful.

Users of previous versions of Office will also find this book helpful in making the transition to Office 2000 because it provides a series of typical business projects and uses the new version of the software to get the job done.

Welcome to Office 2000

Office 2000 is the latest incarnation of the software that 90% of the Fortune 500 is using, and that the majority of businesses and home users are working with as well. Microsoft Office has always been a powerful suite of programs for business and home use—from Word to Outlook, the applications provide the key tools for generating documents, financial reports, databases, presentations, email, and a calendar.

What's new in Office 2000? Aside from an increased focus on the Web in all the applications, you'll find new programs in the suite and a new series of Office 2000 editions:

- **The Small Business Edition**—The Small Business Edition includes Word, Excel, PowerPoint, Outlook, Publisher, and the Small Business Tools, which is a group of programs for performing tasks that are important to small business—creating a business plans and reports, putting together a mass mailing, and generating charts and graphs.

- **The Professional Edition**—The Professional Edition includes everything that is in the Small Business Edition, plus Access and FrontPage, which is a program for designing and editing Web pages.

- **The Premium Edition**—The Premium Edition includes everything that is in the Professional Edition, plus PhotoDraw, which is a graphics, illustration, and photo-retouching program.

The inclusion of Publisher, FrontPage, and the new PhotoDraw make Office 2000 a truly complete suite. Virtually any business task can now be performed with Office 2000!

Conventions Used in This Book

To help you learn, each of the days in this book is constructed in the same way—each day begins with a list of the major topics that are to be covered and ends with two valuable features:

- **Q&A**—"What if I want to…?" and "What went wrong?" questions that the author has heard from clients and students in their use of Office are asked and answered.

- **Workshop**—This is a series of quiz questions and answers that are designed to help you determine if you learned the major skills imparted by the project you just completed. If you don't know an answer, you know which topic you need to review before moving on.

In addition, you'll find the following elements throughout the 21 days. These elements are designed to give you the benefit of the author's experience, offering advice and information to enrich your own experience with using Office 2000:

Tips provide alternative methods for performing commands and tasks that are discussed in the day's text, as well as quick tricks for getting things done faster and more efficiently.

Notes are interesting asides or suggestions that are more than simple tips — you'll find realistic advice and ideas for new ways to use Office 2000 applications and features.

If something can go wrong, a Caution will warn you about it and suggest ways to avoid the problem.

What's On the CD-ROM

The CD-ROM is packed with useful third-party programs and shareware to enhance your work with Office 2000. In addition, you'll find sound files, clip art images, and photographs to use in your Office 2000 documents, worksheets, presentations, and publications. You'll also find all of the completed projects that are created throughout the 21 days in this book — compare them to the documents, spreadsheets, presentations, databases, and other files you create throughout the 21 days to evaluate your progress.

You can also use these completed versions of the files to fill in any gaps should you not perform all of the tasks in all of the projects throughout the book — some of the latter projects require you to reuse files created on previous days, and you can use the files on the CD-ROM should you not have your own versions the required files. While this book is written under the assumption that you'll be working along with the projects on each day, you don't have to — the files on the CD-ROM allow you to participate at the level that works best for you.

DAY **1**

Taking a Tour of Office 2000

Office 2000 is a powerful suite of programs that enables you to perform an incredibly wide variety of tasks, from business communication to database management to graphic design. The Office 2000 suite also contains many new and improved features that users of previous versions of Office will enjoy, and that new users will appreciate finding at their fingertips. In addition, there are many tools—menus, commands, toolbar buttons, and software features—that are repeated throughout all the programs in the Office 2000 suite. This makes it possible to take what you learn in one program and apply it in another, speeding your learning process and increasing your productivity.

You will spend your first day becoming familiar with the following topics:

- Recognizing the features that are common to all Office 2000 applications
- Working with the Office Assistant and finding the help you need
- Identifying new and improved Office 2000 features

Understanding the Office 2000 Environment

The Office 2000 installation process (whether you did it yourself or your computer already contained the software) creates two ways for you to open any of the Office 2000 applications and begin working. There is no need to use both of these methods—simply choose the one that seems the simplest and most logical to you:

- From the Start menu, choose New Office Document. The New Office Document dialog box opens (see Figure 1.1), offering 12 tabs. Each tab contains several templates and wizards for the different types of files that you can create. Click a tab and then double-click the template of your choice. The selected template or wizard opens onscreen.

Start a new blank Word document

FIGURE 1.1

The General tab contains blank templates to use when you want to start from scratch in any of the Office 2000 applications.

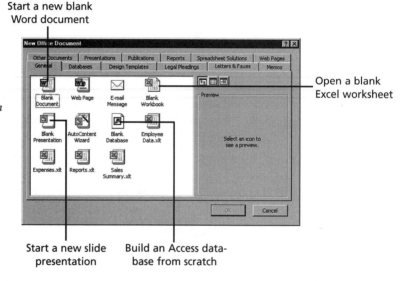

Open a blank Excel worksheet

Start a new slide presentation

Build an Access database from scratch

- From the Start menu's Programs list (see Figure 1.2), choose the Office 2000 application with which you want to work. The application opens, offering you either a blank file to work with or a dialog box in which you can make selections that begin the process of building your file.

NEW TERM The terms *application* and *program* are generally interchangeable. Microsoft Word is an application as well as a program, and it contains many smaller programs within it. Programs can be simple utilities (such as a program to compress files or perform a backup), whereas the term application is rarely used for such small programs.

FIGURE 1.2

Choose from the installed Office 2000 applications by clicking your selection from the Programs list.

NEW TERM *Templates* are files that are used as the basis for creating a new file. Template files contain default settings for the appearance and placement of text, the size and margins of the paper, and other basic formatting to enable you to create many files with similar characteristics. Templates can even contain content, text, numbers, or data that are to exist in all the files that are created with the template or that instruct you in using the template itself.

NEW TERM *Wizards* help you build a file by asking you questions that prompt you through the process. For example, a Fax Wizard asks for your name, company name, fax, and phone numbers; your answers, which are typed into dialog boxes that appear automatically when the Wizard is run, build the fax cover sheet. After running the Wizard, all you need to do is add any extra text content to the new document and send the fax.

The Office 2000 environment is designed for interaction: Each of the applications is designed to work seamlessly with the other programs in the suite. You can take text, numbers, pictures—virtually any file content—and use it in another Office 2000 file, regardless of the application. Of course, if you're running other software from another manufacturer, you can probably use much of your Office 2000 file content there, and vice versa; so the interactivity is not restricted to the programs within the Office 2000 suite.

Many common features—for example, toolbars and menus—exist in all your Office 2000 applications. This seeming redundancy is intentional; it makes it possible for you to learn one application and then apply the basics to any other application within the suite.

Note It's said that through the process of learning the basics of any one Office application, you automatically learn more than 100 things about any of the other Office applications.

Common Office 2000 Elements

Each Office 2000 application window contains a title bar that indicates the name of the application, a series of menus, and at least one toolbar. In addition, there is a workspace in which you enter the actual file content below the toolbars, and some sort of status or information bar below the workspace. Figure 1.3 shows the Word application window, with a blank document awaiting text from the user.

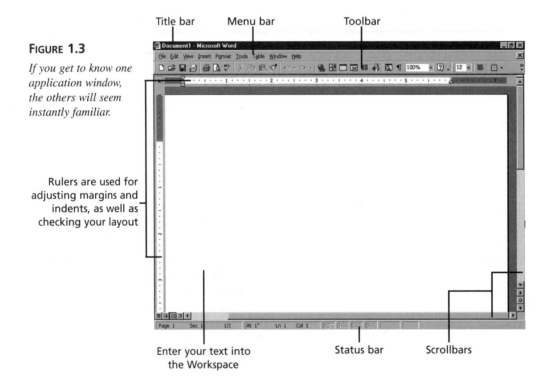

FIGURE 1.3

If you get to know one application window, the others will seem instantly familiar.

Title bar Menu bar Toolbar

Rulers are used for adjusting margins and indents, as well as checking your layout

Enter your text into the Workspace

Status bar Scrollbars

Although the workspace might look somewhat different in the various Office 2000 appli-cations, the tools that are used to perform basic tasks are very similar—whether you use the menus, the toolbar, or the keyboard to issue commands. Compare the Excel applica-tion window that is shown in Figure 1.4 to the Word window shown in Figure 1.3.

FIGURE 1.4

Common screen ele-ments and toolbar but-tons make it easy to learn all the Office 2000 applications.

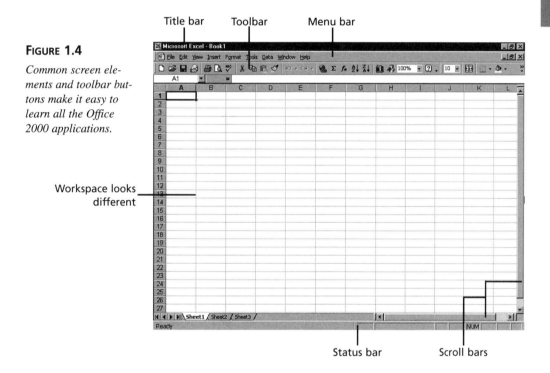

Toolbars

Within each Office 2000 application, at least one toolbar appears by default when you start a new file or open an existing file. In most applications, this toolbar is a combina-tion of the Standard and Formatting toolbars (see Figure 1.5), which you can opt to see as two separate toolbars or leave as one bar. When they are viewed as one bar, the first buttons represent the most frequently used commands: starting a new file, opening an existing file, saving a file, and printing a file.

FIGURE 1.5

Click the toolbar buttons to issue a command or open a dialog box from which the desired action can be taken.

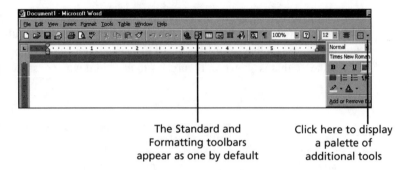

The Standard and
Formatting toolbars
appear as one by default

Click here to display
a palette of
additional tools

The Standard toolbar (or Standard/Formatting combination toolbar) also contains tools that enable you to make use of the Office 2000 Clipboard, which is an enhanced version of the Windows-based Clipboard. These buttons are described in Table 1.1.

TABLE 1.1 BUTTONS COMMON TO ALL OFFICE 2000 APPLICATIONS

Button Name	Function
New	Starts a new file based on the Blank template, a file with basic settings already in place to enable you to begin work with little or no required preparation.
Open	Opens the Open dialog box from which you can select an existing file.
Save	The first time you use Save on a new file, it opens the Save As dialog box, where you can choose a name and location for the file. Subsequent uses of Save update the file to include your latest changes and additions.
Print	Prints the open file. In some applications, it opens the Print dialog box, where you can choose which pages to print and how many copies you want.
Cut	Removes selected content and places it on the Clipboard for use elsewhere—in the same file or in a different file.
Copy	Makes a duplicate (or copy) of the selected content for use elsewhere.
Paste	Use this button to place the contents of the Clipboard in any desired location within an open file.

1

You might find other tools that appear in most or all toolbars, but those that are described in the preceding table give you the capability to build, edit, store, and create tangible evidence of your work—the basic cycle in creating a document, spreadsheet, database, presentation, graphic, Web page, or email message.

If you want to see all the tools on both the Standard and Formatting toolbars by displaying each toolbar separately, follow these steps:

1. Choose Tools, Customize to display the Customize dialog box.
2. Click the Options tab (see Figure 1.6).

FIGURE 1.6

Choose how you want to see your primary toolbars in the open application.

3. Remove the checkmark from the box next to Standard and Formatting toolbars share one row.
4. Click OK to close the Customize dialog box.

Menus

Office 2000 menus, like toolbar buttons, are very similar across the suite. They contain pictures of toolbar buttons that can be used to execute the same commands that are found in the menus, as well as showing any keyboard shortcuts that can be used in lieu of the toolbars or menus. Figure 1.7 shows the File menu in Microsoft Excel.

Tip

When a menu command is followed by a right-pointing triangle, you know that there is a submenu that provides additional choices that can issue commands directly or open a dialog box. If the command is followed by an ellipsis (…), a dialog box opens, in which options can be set for the execution of the command.

Menu   Toolbar
command   equivalent

FIGURE 1.7

Perform any command listed here and, if you want to, make note of the toolbar or keyboard equivalent for next time.

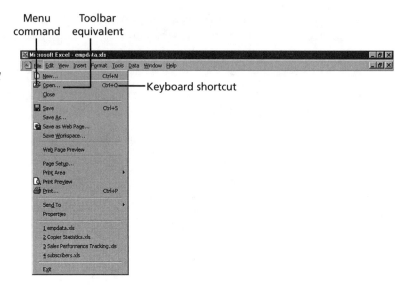

Keyboard shortcut

NEW TERM A *dialog box* is a box that opens onscreen as the result of your issuing a menu command or clicking a toolbar button. In the dialog box, you can make selections and set options for how the command or task is to be performed. The Print dialog box appears, for example, when File, Print is chosen; it enables you to choose your printer, which pages to print, and the number of copies you need.

By default, menus in Office 2000 adapt to your use. For example, if you make a selection from a menu, that selection moves to the top of the menu the next time the menu is displayed. The reasoning behind this development is that if you perform certain tasks repeatedly, it is convenient to have those tasks at the top of the menu, where they are—theoretically—easier to find.

The downside of this, for some users, is that you can't rely on finding a menu command in the same place every time you want to use it. To accommodate those users who want their menus to remain static, the option to turn off the adaptive menus is offered. Follow these steps to keep your menus static:

1. In any Office 2000 application, choose Tools, Customize.
2. In the Customize dialog box (see Figure 1.8), click the Options tab.

FIGURE 1.8

Maintain static menus by turning off the adaptive menus option.

3. Remove the checkmark next to Menus show recently used commands first.

4. Click Close to exit the dialog box.

After you turn off the adaptive menus, your menus do not change the order in which commands are displayed, and you can count on a command being exactly where you found it the last time. For the duration of this book, the adaptive menus are turned off, and any figures that show menus display them in their static condition.

In addition to the menus that are displayed on the menu bar, Office 2000 offers context-sensitive shortcut menus that can be displayed at any time by right-clicking items within your application window. Try right-clicking the items in the following list:

- **Any displayed toolbar**—As soon as you right-click any toolbar, a list of the other available toolbars is displayed (see Figure 1.9). The toolbars that are currently displayed have a checkmark next to the toolbar names. Pick a new toolbar by clicking it in the list; it is added to the window as either a floating toolbar or as an additional strip of tools surrounding your workspace.

FIGURE 1.9

The list of toolbars varies between applications, but also contains common toolbar selections.

Note

NEW TERM   Toolbars can be *floating*, which means that they appear at top of the workspace with their own title bar and close button, or they can be *docked*, which means that they adhere to the edge of the window, above or below the existing toolbars that frame the workspace.

- **Selected content**—Type some text in a Word document or PowerPoint presentation, or enter some numbers in a blank worksheet. Right-click the content, and a list of things that can be done to or with the content is displayed (see Figure 1.10).

FIGURE **1.10**

Access the formatting tools (Font, Paragraph, Bullets, and Numbering) or choose to reuse the content somewhere else (Cut, Copy, Paste).

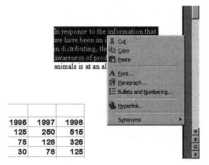

- **The title bar**—If you right-click this strip at the top of the window, options for closing the application or changing the size and position of the window are displayed in a shortcut menu (as shown in Figure 1.11).

FIGURE **1.11**

A shortcut menu can save you from having to look around for buttons or open menus to issue commands.

- **Taskbar button**—Right-click the button on the taskbar that corresponds to the application or file that you want to move, resize, or close. The same shortcut menu that appears when you right-click the title bar appears (see Figure 1.12).

FIGURE 1.12

When several files and applications are open, the taskbar offers an easy way to switch between them or close an individual file or application.

Using the Office Assistant to Get Help

Any new user will need help. Even seasoned Office users consult the built-in help files to solve problems and to figure out how to use new (or never-before-used) features. Office 2000's help comes in the form of an Office Assistant, an animated character to whom you can pose questions (see Figure 1.13).

FIGURE 1.13

The animated Office Assistant is accompanied by a bubble-like dialog box into which you type your question.

To access the Office Assistant, try the following methods:

- **Press F1**—This keyboard shortcut activates the Assistant, causing the animated character to ask you if you need help with a particular feature (whatever you might have been doing or attempting to do when you pressed F1) or if you want to pose a general question.

- **Click the Office Assistant button on the Standard toolbar**—Like pressing F1, clicking this icon while a dialog box is open or while some process is underway causes the Office Assistant to ask if you need help with that particular feature.

- **Choose Help, Microsoft *Application* Help (where *Application* indicates the name of the application that you're in at the time)**—For example, if you're in Word, the command is Microsoft Word Help. Choose this command to activate the Office Assistant, who guesses the topic with which you need help (based on what you're doing at the time) or asks you to pose a general question.

The Office Assistant works by looking at the words that you type in your question (for example, "How do I print my document?") and offering help documents that contain one or more of those key words. Figure 1.14 shows the list of possible help files that the Assistant offers when a question about printing is posed.

FIGURE 1.14

Keep your questions simple, and try to use actual terms that you see in menus and dialog boxes to help the Assistant help you.

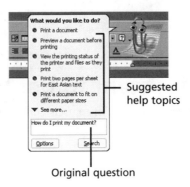

Suggested help topics

Original question

 Tip

Do you want to see a different character? To choose a character other than the default "Clippit" persona, right-click the Office Assistant character and click Choose Assistant from the shortcut menu. Look through the list of available characters, and select the one you want.

Using What's This? Help

Sometimes you need some insight right away, but you don't know what to call a particular feature or it takes too long to pose a question to the Office Assistant. Perhaps, for example, you're looking at a dialog box option or toolbar button that you're unsure of, and you want to just ask someone, "What's this?" and get a quick answer. To give you this sort of quick identification and clarification, Office 2000 offers What's This? help. When it is activated, your mouse pointer changes to include an arrow. You can now click on the dialog box option, toolbar button, or other application window element that you want to identify, and a description of the item and its use appears (see Figure 1.15).

FIGURE 1.15

If What's This? help is available for a window element, the help content appears in a yellow box.

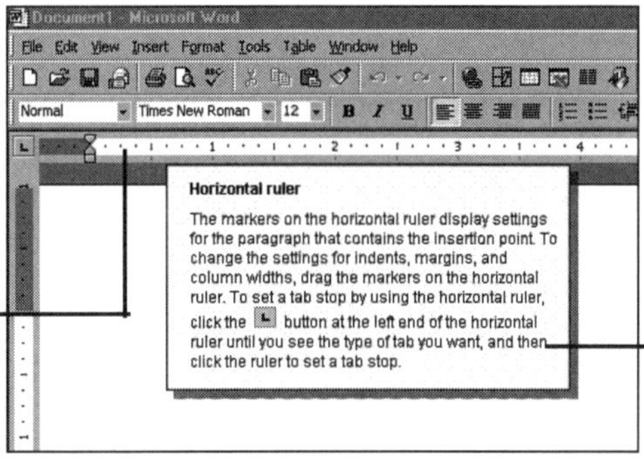
Document1 - Microsoft Word
File Edit View Insert Format Tools Table Window Help
Normal
Times New Roman
12
Horizontal ruler
The markers on the horizontal ruler display settings for the paragraph that contains the insertion point. To change the settings for indents, margins, and column widths, drag the markers on the horizontal ruler. To set a tab stop by using the horizontal ruler, click the button at the left end of the horizontal ruler until you see the type of tab you want, and then click the ruler to set a tab stop.
Element clicked
What's This? help identifies and explains the element's use

In Office 2000, there are two ways to get this type of help:

- Choose Help, What's This? from the menu.
- Press Shift+F1.

When you're in a dialog box and need some clarification of an option or feature, click the question mark button (?) in the upper-right corner of the dialog box. The What's This? mouse pointer appears, enabling you to click the item in the dialog box about which you need information. Figure 1.16 shows What's This? help in use in a PowerPoint dialog box.

FIGURE 1.16

If you're not sure what a certain option does or why it's used, invoke What's This? help in the dialog box and click on the option in question.

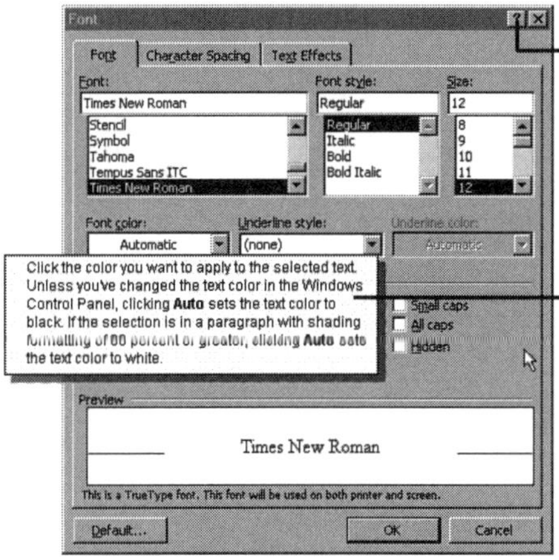
Font
Font
Character Spacing
Text Effects
Font:
Font style:
Size:
Times New Roman
Regular
12
Stencil
Symbol
Tahoma
Tempus Sans ITC
Times New Roman
Regular
Italic
Bold
Bold Italic
8
9
10
11
12
Font color:
Underline style:
Underline color:
Automatic
(none)
Automatic
Click the color you want to apply to the selected text. Unless you've changed the text color in the Windows Control Panel, clicking Auto sets the text color to black. If the selection is in a paragraph with shading formatting of 80 percent or greater, clicking Auto sets the text color to white.
Small caps
All caps
Hidden
Preview
Times New Roman
This is a TrueType font. This font will be used on both printer and screen.
Default...
OK
Cancel
Click this button to activate What's This? help in the dialog box
If help is available for the item, the help content appears in a yellow box

To turn off What's This? help, press Esc or click on a neutral area of the window or dialog box. Your mouse pointer returns to normal.

Getting More Help

If the Office Assistant's help topics don't answer your question, you can go to the
Microsoft Web site for more answers or you can call Microsoft directly for technical support at (800)936-5700. You might be directed to another phone number for help on your
specific application.

Caution	If you're running an unregistered copy of Office 2000, you are not entitled to free phone support, and you have to call their 900 number for technical support that's billed to your phone number. Currently, the charge per incident is $35. The fee applies to a single question, whether it's answered in five minutes or over the course of several calls.

Using the Web site is fast and usually effective. To access the Microsoft Web site, you
must have a connection to the Internet, and you must be connected to the Internet when
you need help.

You can access the help areas within the Microsoft Web site through the Office Assistant,
or you can use your Web browser to go to the Microsoft site. The Web address to use
with your browser is www.microsoft.com. You can look through FAQs (Frequently
Asked Questions) or send an email to a Microsoft technician and receive an answer electronically within a few days.

If you choose to use the Office Assistant to go to the specific help you need, click the
None of the above, look for more help on the Web option in the Office Assistant dialog
box (see Figure 1.17).

FIGURE 1.17

*If the application's
built-in help doesn't
do the job, follow the
Office Assistant to
the Microsoft Web
site for more help
possibilities.*

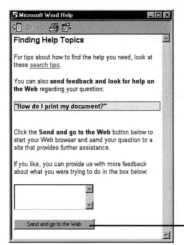

Click this button to go directly to
the Microsoft Web site and pose
your question

When you get to the Web site, you can read the resulting help files (they'll relate to your question based on the way you entered it in the Office Assistant dialog box). The help that appears when you pose the "How do I print my document?" question is shown in Figure 1.18.

FIGURE 1.18

If none of the help files are appropriate, rephrase your question and click the Search button to view other help through the Web site.

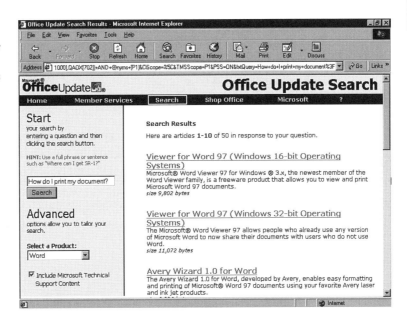

If the resulting help still does not answer your question completely, you can also send a question, via email, to one of Microsoft's technicians. The technician will respond to you via email with an answer to your question.

What's New in Office 2000

To the average user, Office 2000 doesn't look or work much differently than its predecessor, Office 97. Aside from the new combined toolbars and adaptive menus (discussed earlier in this day), the application windows don't look very different and the commands and dialog boxes look much the same as they did in the previous version of Office.

So what's the big deal? Most of the changes in Office 2000 revolve around the following areas:

- **An increased focus on the Internet and Web, and the use of HTML file formats to make all your files compatible for use on the Web**—This means that you can create Web pages from Word documents and PowerPoint presentations and post Excel and Access data to the Web. You can also collaborate online with co-workers down the hall or across the globe.

- **A friendlier help system**—The Office Assistant enables you to use *natural language* (nontechnical terms) to seek help and understand the support that's offered through installed help files and online support. A connection to the Microsoft Web site's help files, followed through your use of the Office Assistant, also makes it easier to explore all your help options; this expands the amount of information that is available to you.

- **More powerful integration tools**—The Office 2000 Clipboard supports up to 12 selections (unlike the Windows Clipboard that holds only one selection at a time). This makes it easy to take selections from Word, Excel, PowerPoint, Access, and all the other Office 2000 applications and place them on one Clipboard for use one at a time or in groups. Clipboard selections can be used in any Office 2000 program. You'll be using the Clipboard in several of your projects (including today, Day 6, "Building a Spreadsheet in an Excel Workbook," and Day 17, "Creating a Report with Office").

- **Additional programs that round out the suite**—Previous versions of Office contained the basics—a word processor (Word), a spreadsheet program (Excel), an application for building slide presentations (PowerPoint), and a database program (Access). This left the user with the need to go elsewhere for desktop publishing, graphic design, Web page development, and tools to help small businesses. Office 2000's Professional and Premium editions include FrontPage (for Web page design), Publisher (for desktop publishing), PhotoDraw (for graphic design), and Small Business Tools.

How do these changes and improvements affect you? It depends on your use of the Office programs. This book's projects, performed over a series of 21 days, give you the chance to use each of the programs in the Office 2000 suite and see how they work individually and together. What you need from the software on a daily basis dictates how much impact the new features of Office 2000 have on your daily work and home computer use.

Summary

On this, the first of the 21 days that you'll spend learning Office 2000, you learned how to open any of the Office 2000 applications, and you learned what elements they share. In addition, you learned how to find help on any Office 2000-related topic by using the Office Assistant within the suite and by contacting Microsoft through their Web site or by phone. Last, but certainly not least, you found out what new and improved features can be found in this latest incarnation of Microsoft Office, which will be especially useful to readers who might have spent any time using previous versions such as Office 97. The project in Day 2, "Creating a Letter," takes you to Microsoft Word, the most often-used of the Office 2000 applications.

Q&A

Q **If I have files that I created in Office 97, can I open and use them easily in Office 2000?**

A Yes. Backward compatibility is built in, so you can open your Office 95 and 97 files in Office 2000. You can also save your Office 2000 files in an older format for sharing with others who have not yet upgraded to Office 2000.

Q **With all the added power in Office 2000, can I really learn it in 21 days?**

A Yes. The projects in this book take you through a comprehensive set of features; you will perform basic through advanced tasks and create everything from simple letters in Word to complex reports that incorporate content created in several Office 2000 applications.

Workshop

The section that follows is a quick quiz about the day. If you have any problems answering any of the questions, see the section that follows the quiz for all the answers.

Quiz

1. How many items does the Office 2000 Clipboard hold?
2. By default, Office 2000 combines which two toolbars into one single toolbar?
3. Can these two toolbars be viewed separately?
4. Explain what is meant by *adaptive menus*.
5. How do you switch to a different animated Office Assistant character?

Quiz Answers

1. The Office 2000 Clipboard holds up to 12 items at a time.

2. By default, the Standard and Formatting toolbars are combined into one toolbar.

3. Yes. Choose Tools, Customize, and click the Options tab to turn off the default setting that combines the toolbars.

4. Adaptive menus are menus that change the order of displayed commands to place those that you've used most recently at the top of the menu.

5. To change to a different Office Assistant character, right-click the Office Assistant and click Choose Assistant.

DAY 2

Creating a Letter

Now that you know how to open a Microsoft Office 2000 application and have a general sense of the layout of an application's window, you can start using Microsoft Word. Word is probably the most used application in the Office 2000 suite—everyone needs to write a letter, a memo, a list, or a report at some time in their life, and most people create at least one of these items at least once a day. Microsoft Word is, despite its power and depth, an easy application to use. In today's project, you'll learn the following skills:

- How to get started with a blank document
- The basics of text entry and editing
- How to use the spelling and grammar-checking tools
- When and how to use Word's automatic tools to build a document
- How to save your work

Starting a Word Document

You learned techniques for opening an Office application on Day 1, "Taking a Tour of Office 2000"; now here's a review and discussion of the specific process used to start a Word document. You can open Word (which gives you a new, blank document) in one of two ways:

- From the Start menu, choose New Office Document. In the New Office Document dialog box, make sure you're on the General tab (see Figure 2.1), and then double-click the Blank Document icon.

FIGURE 2.1

Double-click the Blank Document icon to start a new document with basic settings in place.

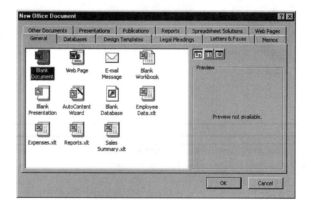

- From the list of Programs on your Start menu, choose Microsoft Word.

Either method presents you with the Word application window, complete with a blank document into which you'll type your text. Figure 2.2 shows a new blank document, awaiting your text.

The application window is blank, or so it seems—there is no text in the document yet. But a blank document isn't really empty; when you open Word from the Programs list or by choosing the Blank Document icon, you're opening a document that is based on a template. The template provides the basic setup for your letter, eliminating the need for you to do anything other than sit down and type. The Blank Document template provides the following basic setup to get you started:

- Margins set at standard measurements—1" on the top and bottom, 1.25" on the left and right.
- Single line spacing.
- 10-point text, in Times New Roman font.
- Text is set to left alignment (creating a ragged right edge for paragraphs).
- Tabs set every half-inch across the width of the page.

FIGURE 2.2

The cursor is blinking, waiting for you to begin to type.

The cursor marks where your new text is to be inserted as soon as you begin to type

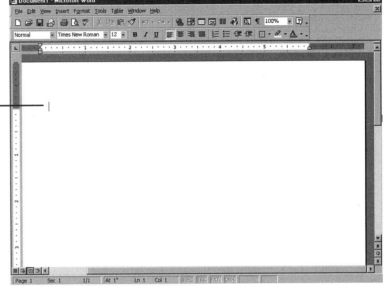

2

NEW TERM *Templates* are files that are used as the basis for creating a new file. Template files contain default settings for the appearance and placement of text, the size and margins of the paper, and other basic formatting to enable you to create many files with similar characteristics. A template can even contain some content—text, numeric, or data—that is to exist in all the files that are created with the template; or it might contain content that instructs you in using the template itself.

NEW TERM Text is measured in *points*. This measurement system enables you to choose a number (from 8 to 72) and apply it to your text, thus determining its size both onscreen and when it is printed. There are 72 points in an inch; so each character in text that is set to 10 points, for example, is slightly less than 1/6 of an inch square. When you are choosing a point size for your text (you'll learn to do that on Day 3, "Enhancing a Basic Word Document"), remember that the higher the number you choose, the bigger the text.

NEW TERM *Font* is another word for typeface. There are thousands of fonts available, and Word comes with more than a hundred fonts installed if you performed a standard installation. Fonts come in three types—serif (fonts with flourishes on the ends of the letters, such as Times New Roman or Bookman), sanserif (fonts with no flourishes, such as Arial or AvantGarde), and artistic (fancy script and graphical fonts, such as Algerian or French Script). On Day 3, you'll learn to choose different fonts for your Word text.

Typing the Letter

To begin creating your letter, simply start typing—your cursor is at the top of the space within your margins, so you don't need to do anything other than type the date (which is normally the first thing that is typed in a letter). Being a quick or accurate typist can certainly make the document creation process go faster, but it isn't essential that you type 60 words per minute or that you never make a spelling error in order to type a letter.

NEW TERM   As you type, don't press the Enter key unless you want to break off your text and force the cursor down to the next line (at the end of the date or salutation, for example). When you are typing your paragraph text, allow the text to *wrap*, which means that Word automatically flows your text onto the next line as soon as you hit the right margin. Figure 2.3 shows a letter in progress.

FIGURE 2.3

The Enter key starts a new line or adds a blank line between paragraphs.

The date has been typed, and the Enter key pressed twice

The recipient address (press Enter after each line, and twice after the last line of the address)

The salutation (press Enter twice at the end)

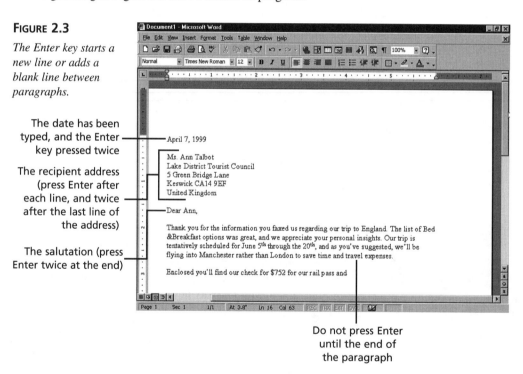

Do not press Enter until the end of the paragraph

It's a common practice to do some minor editing as you type your first draft of the letter—correcting typos as you go, using the Backspace and Delete keys. Although the next section covers large-scale editing, it's important to know what these two keys do and how to use them effectively:

- **Delete**—The Delete key removes the character to the right of the cursor. If you click it once, it removes one character, and each successive click removes additional text. If you press and hold it, it removes long strings of text—possibly more than you wanted to remove.
- **Backspace**—The Backspace key removes the character to the left of the cursor. Like the Delete key, each click of the Backspace key removes a character, and if you press and hold the key you can remove long strings of text. If you remove more than you intended to, choose Edit, Undo, and then start again.

2

If you find it difficult to remember which key to use (Backspace or Delete) as you type, remember that the Backspace backs up over your text, removing characters as it moves to the left. To decide which key to use, look at your cursor and then at the character you want to get rid of—if it's behind the cursor, Backspace over it. If it's to the right of the cursor, move forward and Delete it.

If you press Tab at the beginning of your first paragraph, Word remembers this and creates a first line indent of 1/2-inch at the beginning of all the paragraphs that follow in the current document.

Editing the Document

As you type, you're bound to make errors—too many spaces between words, no spaces between words, transposing letters, or forgetting a word altogether. You can easily correct these common errors (even seasoned typists make them) as you type, using the Backspace or Delete keys to remove extra spaces or to fix your simple typos; or you can use Word's proofing tools to correct them after you've typed your letter.

You might not spot your errors immediately—it's sometimes difficult to tell if you've placed too many spaces between words—but Word tells you when it spots a spelling or grammatical error. As soon as you complete a word, Word checks it against its internal dictionary. If it doesn't find a match, it underlines the word with a red wavy line, as shown in Figure 2.4. Grammatical errors are underlined with green wavy lines. You'll learn how to run spelling and grammar checks later today.

FIGURE 2.4

Red and green wavy lines under your spelling and grammatical errors remind you to go back and fix them.

Spelling error

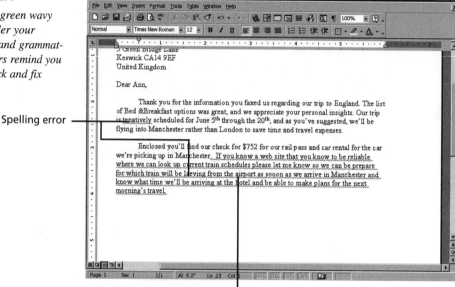

Grammatical error

Word's Show All tool is very useful for editing your document. Click this button to show all the keys you've pressed (spacebar, Tab, and Enter), not just the alphanumeric keys that comprise the text. Figure 2.5 shows the letter with Show/Hide on.

To turn Show/Hide off, simply click the Show/Hide button on the toolbar again.

FIGURE 2.5

Some users prefer to work with Show/Hide on, whereas others find it visually distracting.

Dots indicate spaces

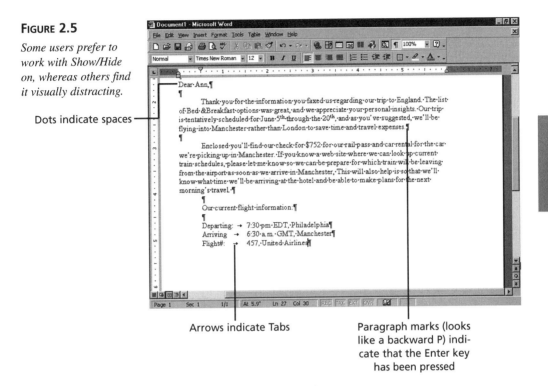

Arrows indicate Tabs

Paragraph marks (looks like a backward P) indicate that the Enter key has been pressed

Moving Around in the Document

After you've typed your document (or while it's in progress), you'll want to move around in it. Moving around can mean simply viewing different parts of your document to proofread its content, or it can mean repositioning your cursor to add, delete, or edit text.

To view different parts of your document without moving the cursor, you can use either of the following methods:

- **Use the scrollbars**—Scroll up and down with the vertical scrollbar (needed only if your letter exceeds the length of the screen), or left and right with the horizontal scrollbar (see Figure 2.6).

  If you have an Intellimouse, use the scroll button on the mouse (the roller between the left and right mouse buttons). This scrolls up and down only.

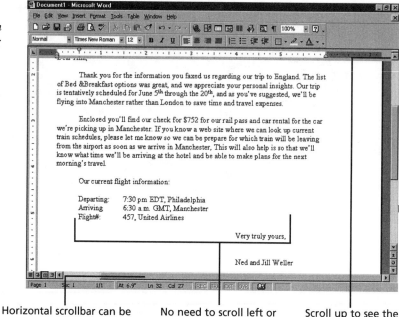

FIGURE 2.6

*Scroll in the direction
of the portion of your
document that you
need to see.*

Horizontal scrollbar can be
used if both sides of the letter
are not simultaneously visible

No need to scroll left or
right because both sides of
the text can be seen

Scroll up to see the
top of the letter

- **Adjust your view**—Click the Zoom button and choose Page Width so that
  both sides of the page can be seen, or reduce the view to 75% to see more of
  the text from all directions.

You can use your arrow keys to move up, down, left, and right, but these reposition your
cursor each time you click the keys. Normally, you reposition your cursor in order to
add, delete, or edit your text—to insert a word or sentence you forgot, to fix a typo—but
it's okay to move your cursor if you're just looking around.

The next thing you type will be inserted wherever your cursor is. The next
thing you type might be an inadvertent space or blank line if you accidentally bump the spacebar or Enter key. Always make sure that you can see
your cursor blinking in your document before you start typing or pressing
any keys—if you don't, you might find yourself making unwanted changes
to your document.

In addition to the arrow keys, there are many methods of repositioning your cursor. The most common and direct method is to simply click the mouse at the point within your text where you need to place the cursor. There are also keyboard methods to place your cursor at various places within your document; Table 2.1 contains a list of these keyboard shortcuts.

TABLE 2.1 KEYBOARD SHORTCUTS FOR DOCUMENT NAVIGATION

Keyboard Shortcut	Result
Ctrl+Home	Moves the cursor to the top of the document
Ctrl+End	Places the cursor at the end of the document
Home	Moves the cursor to the beginning of the line
End	Moves the cursor to the end of the line
Ctrl+Left arrow	Moves the cursor one word to the left
Ctrl+Right arrow	Moves the cursor one word to the right
Ctrl+Up arrow	Moves the cursor to the top of the current paragraph
Ctrl+Down arrow	Moves the cursor to the bottom of the current paragraph

When your cursor is where you need it, insert or edit your text as you choose.

Selecting Text

As you build and edit a document, you might want to make changes, the scope of which make using the Backspace and Delete keys inefficient tools. Perhaps you need to change the name in your salutation from "John" to "Mr. Smith" or move a sentence from the first page onto page two. Maybe you need to delete an entire paragraph completely. When changes of this magnitude are required, it's more efficient to use the mouse (or keyboard) to select your text and then make the change.

No matter which method you choose (mouse or keyboard) to select your text, when it is selected, the text can be deleted (press the Delete key), changed (type the replacement text), or repositioned (see the section "Using the Clipboard to Cut and Copy Text"). On Day 3, you'll learn to reformat selected text.

Caution   When text is selected, it's vulnerable. Never leave text selected onscreen unless you're going to act on it immediately. An accidental brush of the keyboard can delete a selected paragraph. As soon as you've made your change to the selected text, click somewhere in the white space on your page to deselect.

Selecting Text with the Mouse

To select text with the mouse, use one of the following methods:

- To select an individual word, position your mouse (which appears as an I-beam) within the word itself and double-click.

- To select a paragraph, point within the paragraph and click three times.

- To select a finite amount of text, point to the beginning of the text you want to select, and when your mouse pointer appears as an I-beam (which looks like the letter *I*), click and drag through the text you need to edit, move, or delete. Figure 2.7 shows a click-and-drag selection in progress.

FIGURE 2.7

Click and drag to select a few words within a sentence or a sentence within a paragraph.

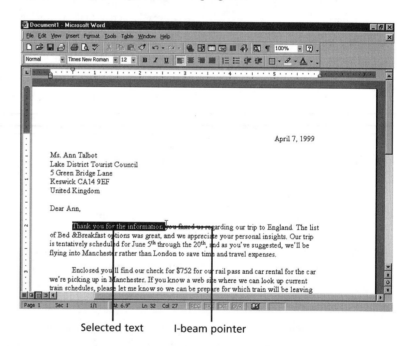

Selected text   I-beam pointer

- In the left margin, position your mouse next to the line or paragraph you want to select and click once to select the line, twice to select the paragraph, or three times to select the entire document. Your mouse appears as a right-pointing arrow, as seen in Figure 2.8.

FIGURE 2.8

Make large selections from the left margin by pointing and clicking the mouse.

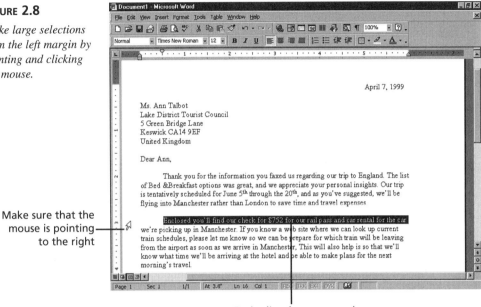

Make sure that the mouse is pointing to the right —

Entire line (not sentence) is selected

Selecting Text with the Keyboard

You can also use the keyboard to select text, which is good news for users who aren't comfortable with the mouse or who type so much or so fast that they prefer not to remove their hands from the keyboard to make selections.

To select text using the keyboard, follow these steps:

1. Using the arrow keys, position your cursor at the beginning of the text you want to select.

2. Press and hold the Shift key.

3. With the Shift key depressed, press the right arrow to select text to the right of the cursor. You can also use the left arrow to select text to the left of the cursor. Keep pressing or holding down the arrow key until you have selected all the text you need.

To select larger portions of text with the keyboard, add the Ctrl key to any of your Shift+*key* combinations. For example, Ctrl+Shift+Home selects the portion of the document that starts at your cursor's current position, all the way back to the beginning of the document. Try adding the Ctrl key to your Shift+*arrow key* combinations as well—select entire words and paragraphs instead of individual characters and lines.

Selecting Text with the Mouse and Keyboard

Suppose that you want to select the first three words in a sentence, but you released the mouse button (or Shift key, if you were using the keyboard to select) before the entire selection was made. To increase the amount of selected text, press the Shift key and click the mouse at the end of the desired string of text (see Figure 2.9). Your original selection is extended to include all the text between the original selection and where you clicked the mouse.

FIGURE 2.9

Don't start your selection all over again if you grabbed too much or too little text—use the Shift key and your mouse to adjust the amount of selected text.

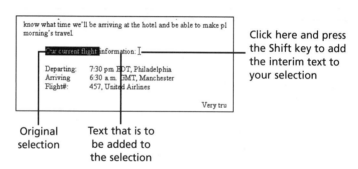

Click here and press the Shift key to add the interim text to your selection

Original selection

Text that is to be added to the selection

To reduce your selection, press the Shift key and click within your selected text at the point where you want the selection to end (see Figure 2.10). The portion of text between the end of the original selection and where you click the mouse is deselected.

When you are dragging to select text, remember that you can always drag backward, forward, up, or down to adjust the amount of text you've selected. It isn't until you release the mouse that you're committed to your selection—and you might have to adjust it with the Shift key or start dragging all over again. Remember not to let go until you have what you want!

FIGURE 2.10

If you've selected too much text and you already released the mouse button, use the Shift key and click back within your selection to reduce the amount of selected text.

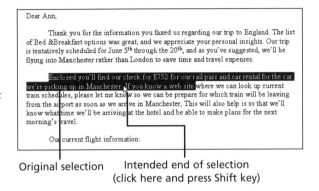

Original selection   Intended end of selection
(click here and press Shift key)

2

Tip

To select an entire sentence (from the first word to the period at the end), press the Ctrl key and click anywhere in the sentence.

Moving and Duplicating Text

In addition to replacing or editing selected text, selected text can be moved or duplicated for use elsewhere in the current document or in another document. You can even use selected text from a Word document in an Excel worksheet, PowerPoint slide, Access database, or any Office 2000 or Windows-based program.

The reasons you might have for moving text within your letter are obvious—perhaps you want to address a series of topics in a different order than you've typed them, or maybe you need to rearrange the sentences in a paragraph for clarity. On the other hand, duplicating text assumes that the text is fine as and where it is, but that you have a use for it in another location as well. Most duplications take text from one document and put it in another, but you can duplicate text and use it more than once in the same document.

 Moving and duplicating can be performed in one of two ways: with a series of commands that invoke the Clipboard or by using your mouse to drag selected text from one place to another (*drag and drop*).

Using the Clipboard to Cut and Copy Text

You can invoke the Clipboard by selecting a portion of your document text (or even the entire document) and issuing a Cut or Copy command in one of the following ways:

- Choose Edit, Cut or Edit, Copy from the menu.
- Press Ctrl+X to Cut or Ctrl+C to Copy.

- Click the Cut or Copy button on the toolbar.
- Right-click the selected text and choose Cut or Copy from the shortcut menu.

After issuing your Cut or Copy command, the selected portion of your document is on the Clipboard. As you learned in Day 1, the Office 2000 Clipboard can hold up to 12 selections (from any and all Office 2000 applications) at the same time.

To place your cut or copied selection in its new location, follow these steps:

1. Click the location at which you want your cut or copied selection to be placed.
2. Issue a Paste command in one of the following ways:

   - Choose Edit, Paste from the menu.
   - Click the Paste button on the Standard toolbar.
   - Press Ctrl+V.
   - Right-click the desired location for your selection and choose Paste from the shortcut menu.

If you have made previous cuts or copies in your current session of word, cutting or copying again opens the Clipboard toolbar (see Figure 2.11), on which an icon represents each cut or copied selection. To tell your various selections apart, point to the icons and look for a ScreenTip that will show the first few words of the selection.

FIGURE 2.11

The Office 2000 Clipboard holds up to 12 selections at a time, and they can be pasted individually or as a group.

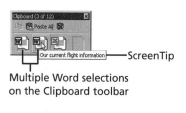

Multiple Word selections on the Clipboard toolbar

 Any item on the Clipboard can be pasted as many times as you need it, in as many locations as you want. To clear the entire Clipboard, click the Clear Clipboard button.

Moving and Copying Text with Drag and Drop

Using the Clipboard is great for moving or duplicating text from one paragraph to another, from one page to another, or to another document entirely. The Clipboard works well when the source (original location of the selection) and the target (where you're pasting it) are far apart. It works just as well when the source and target are close together (when you're rearranging words in a sentence or sentences in a paragraph, for example), but there's another way to rearrange text without having to perform three distinct steps (select, cut/copy, paste).

Drag and drop enables you to select text and literally drag it from where it is now and drop it where you want it to be. It works best in small areas, where the original location and the target are both visible at the same time. By default, drag and drop moves your text from place to place—you can, however, duplicate or copy your text by pressing the Ctrl key as you drag the selection to its new location.

To move your text with drag and drop, follow these steps:

1. With both the text you want to move and its target location visible, select the text that you want to move, and then release the mouse without deselecting the text.

2. Point within the selected text; when your mouse pointer turns to an arrow, click and drag the text.

3. When the mouse pointer (accompanied by a cursor and small box, as shown in Figure 2.12) is pointing to the desired location for your text, release the mouse button.

FIGURE 2.12

Drag and drop your text from its original spot to a new location nearby.

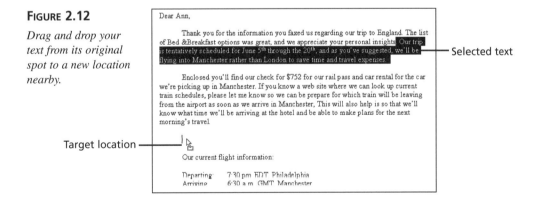

Selected text

Target location

Copying with drag and drop leaves the original text in place and deposits a duplicate elsewhere in the document. To copy with drag and drop, perform the following steps:

1. With the original text and the location for the duplicate visible, select the text that is to be copied.

2. Release the mouse without deselecting the text.

3. Press and hold the Ctrl key.

4. Point within the selected text, and wait for your mouse pointer to turn into an arrow. Click and drag a duplicate of the selection to place it in its new location. Figure 2.13 shows a copy in progress.

FIGURE 2.13

A small plus sign is appended to your drag and drop mouse pointer, indicating that a copy is being made.

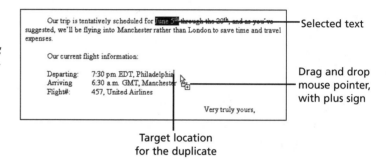

5. When the mouse is pointing to the desired location for your duplicate, release the mouse button, and then the Ctrl key.

Caution
It is essential that you release the mouse before you release the Ctrl key when you are dragging a duplicate. If you release the Ctrl key first, the copy reverts to a simple move, removing your selected text from its original location.

Tip
Are you finding that you accidentally drag and drop text when all you wanted to do was select it? You can turn off the drag and drop feature by choosing Tools, Options. In the Edit tab of the Options dialog box, remove the checkmark next to Drag and drop editing. You can find out more about customizing the way Word works in Appendix A, "Customizing Microsoft Word."

Performing a First-Time Save

As soon as you start a document and get more than five or ten minutes of work into it, save it. "Early and often" is a good phrase to describe good saving habits. You don't want to wait until your document is complete—with all edits, proofing, and formatting finished—before you save it because you risk losing all your work if your software or hardware shuts down unexpectedly.

The first time you save a file, you must choose where to save it and what to call it. By default, Word attempts to save it to a folder called My Documents, but you can redirect it to any folder you want. You can also redirect Word to save your file to a floppy disk, to another drive on your computer, or to a network to which you're attached.

Naming your file is important. As you know, Windows 95/98 enables you to give a file a name with up to 255 characters, including spaces. But you'll rarely need or want to use that many characters in your filename; rather, using short, descriptive names is a good idea.

To perform a first-time save of your document, follow these steps:

1. With your document open and active onscreen, choose File, Save from the menu; or press Ctrl+S. This opens the Save As dialog box. You can also use the Save button on the Standard toolbar.

2. Choose a location for your file if you want to save it to somewhere other than My Documents (see Figure 2.14). Click the Save in list box to select a drive, or double-click one of the other folders on your hard drive to designate that as the folder to which you'll save your file.

FIGURE 2.14

Although My Documents is the default location for saving files, you can choose any other drive or folder as the location to store your document.

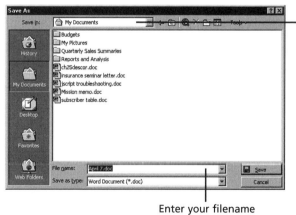

The Save in box displays your current location to save the file. You can also click the Save in list to choose a different drive

Enter your filename here by replacing the selected default name

3. In the File name box, type a name for your file. Do not type any extension—let Word apply the .doc extension for you.

4. Click Save to complete the process and close the dialog box.

Note

You'll notice that when you save a file for the first time, Word places the first few words of the document in the File name box; in Figure 2.15, for example, you see the name April 7.doc. The first words in a file are rarely useful as a filename, so you'll want to replace them with your own—more relevant—name for the file.

After you've saved your file, the name you've given it appears on the title bar, replacing the Document1 (or whatever number it was) that appeared previously. Figure 2.15 shows a saved document, with its name displayed on the title bar.

FIGURE 2.15

Save early and often to protect your work.

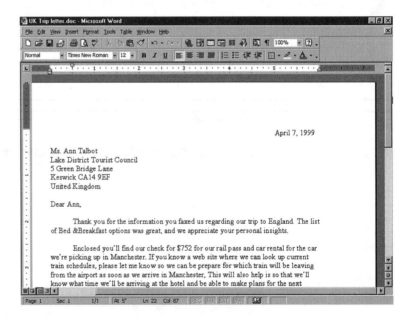

 If you continue to work on your document after saving it for the first time, resave it every five or ten minutes to save your ongoing changes and additions. Simply press Ctrl+S, or click the Save button, to resave the file with the current name (and to the current location). On Day 3, you'll learn more about the options for saving your files.

Tip

Even if you don't tend to use keyboard shortcuts—some people can't remember them or just prefer to use the toolbar or menus—it's worth committing Ctrl+S (to save) to memory. You're more likely to save often if the process of saving is fast and easy. You can use this shortcut while you're typing—no need to stop and use the mouse to click a button or menu.

Closing a Document

If you're finished working on your document and won't be going back to it for awhile, it's a good idea to close it. Why? Because having a lot of files open at the same time uses valuable system resources and potentially exposes the open files to unwanted changes. To close a document, choose one of the following methods:

- Choose File, Close from the menu.
- Press Ctrl+F4.
- Click the Close button in the upper-right corner of your Document window (see Figure 2.16).

2

FIGURE 2.16

To close the document, click the lower of the two Close sizing icons—the uppermost button closes the application, not just the document.

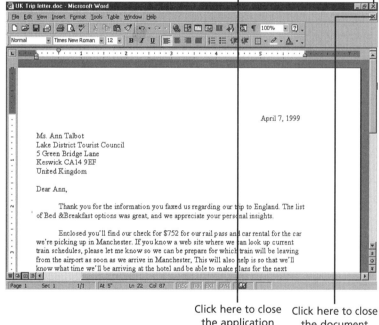

Click here to close the application   Click here to close the document

If you haven't saved your work (either for the first time or since making any changes), Word prompts you to do so before closing. Click Yes to save your changes (if you haven't previously saved the file, the Save As dialog box opens and you can choose a name and location for the file), click No to close without saving, or click Cancel to leave the file open.

Opening an Existing Document

When you want to reopen a file to continue working on it, you have several choices for accessing and opening the file:

- From the File menu, check the list of Most Recently Used files (also known as MRUs) that is found at the bottom of the menu (see Figure 2.17). If your file is among them, click it in the menu to open it onscreen.

FIGURE 2.17

The last four files you opened appear in the Most Recently Used list.

- Choose File, Open; using the Look in list box, open the drive and folder in which the file is stored. When you see your file listed, double-click it. Figure 2.18 shows a file in the My Documents folder, selected and ready to be opened.

FIGURE 2.18

Click once on the filename and click the Open button, or double-click the file's icon to open the file.

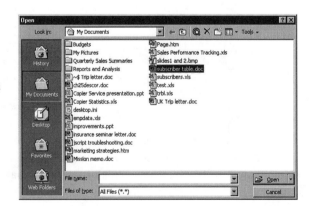

- Use the Windows Explorer. Display the contents of the folder to which you saved your file, and double-click the file icon on the right side of the window (see Figure 2.19).

FIGURE 2.19

The My Documents folder is selected in the Folder pane, and its contents are displayed on the right.

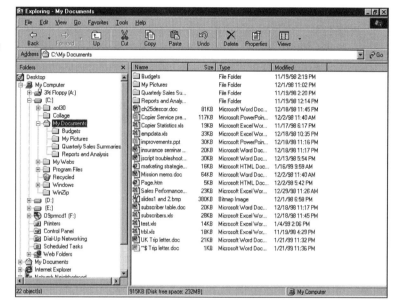

- Check the Documents list (see Figure 20.20). Click the Start button on the taskbar and choose Documents. If your file is in the list, select it to open Word and the selected document simultaneously.

FIGURE 2.20

Open files from the Documents list in the Start menu.

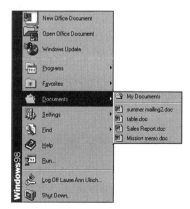

Using Proofing Tools

After your document is typed, your text is rearranged, and any simple edits are performed, you're ready to proof it. If there are any spelling errors, they appear with red underlines; grammatical errors result in green underlined text. Of course, if there are no red or green wavy underlines, you need to still proofread your document to be sure that you don't have any errors that Word's proofing tools didn't catch—misuse of homonyms, for example (there or their), or confusing or incorrect wording. A sentence can sound grammatically correct and still not make sense as it is written.

Checking Your Spelling and Grammar

You can take one of two approaches to dealing with your spelling or grammatical errors: You can address each incident individually, or you can run a global spelling and grammar check that displays each error in a dialog box and gives you options for handling each mistake.

To correct your errors individually, right-click any words that are underlined in red or green. A shortcut menu (see Figure 2.21) appears, from which you can choose an alternative spelling or wording, to Ignore the error, or to Add it to the dictionary (in the case of misspellings).

FIGURE 2.21

If you only have a few errors in your document, it might be faster to right-click each one and use the shortcut menu to make corrections.

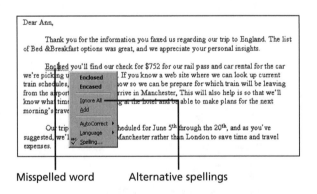

Misspelled word   Alternative spellings

If the alternative spelling or wording isn't appropriate, click in the white space or press Esc to close the shortcut menu; then deal with the error yourself by retyping the text— correctly. If you know the word is spelled correctly, you can click Ignore, Ignore All (if you know you've used the word elsewhere in the document), or Add (to place the word in your dictionary).

Tip

In the case of misspellings, if your spelling of the word doesn't come close to any words in Word's dictionary, the alternative spellings might be inappropriate—or Word might not offer any alternative spellings at all. If this happens and you don't know how to correct the word, try a "real" dictionary or choose a different word that you do know how to spell.

2

When word cites a grammatical error, it might not offer you an alternative in the shortcut menu; rather, it might merely tell you what's wrong (Fragment, Long sentence) and expect you to make the corrections yourself (see Figure 2.22). You can adjust the way Word checks your grammar by resetting the standards by which your text is measured, allowing for more colloquial content or even raising the standard to a more conservative level. See Appendix A to learn how to customize Word's spelling and grammar settings.

FIGURE 2.22

Extra punctuation inadvertently resulted in a sentence fragment. Removing the period solves the problem.

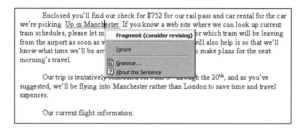

If you have a lot of errors, or if the ones you have are spread throughout a long document, you might find that it is easier to allow Word's Spelling and Grammar check program to run, showing you each error in a single dialog box and enabling you to fix the errors there. This can save you from right-clicking throughout your document and searching through pages of text for all your errors.

To run the Spelling and Grammar check, follow these steps:

1. Press Ctrl+Home to place your cursor at the top of the document.
2. Choose Tools, Spelling and Grammar. The Spelling and Grammar dialog box opens, as shown in Figure 2.23.

FIGURE 2.23

Make your corrections in the Spelling and Grammar dialog box by editing the red or green text. Click Change to make the correction happen in your document.

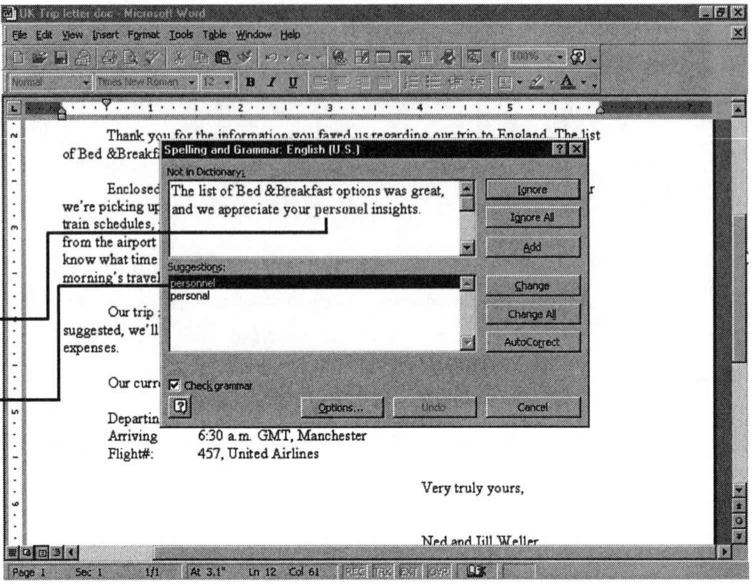

Error shown in dialog box, in context

Select a suggestion

3. As each error appears in the Not in Dictionary box, suggestions for correcting it appear in the Suggestions box below. Choose to Change to one of the suggested corrections, or click Ignore, Ignore All, or Add on the right side of the dialog box.

4. Each action (Change, Ignore, Add) moves you to the next error that was found. When all the errors have been resolved, Word informs you that the Spelling and Grammar check is complete.

Tip

The Ignore All and Change All options make it easy to correct several mistakes at once. If you've misspelled a word several times throughout a document, click Change All to fix them all. It can be a time-saver to click this button even if you don't know if the error exists again in the document—there's no harm in it even if you only made the mistake once. Of course, Ignore All saves you from dealing with repeated incidences of a word if you know it's correct as is.

You can stop the Spelling and Grammar check at any time by clicking the Cancel button.

Building Quick Fixes with AutoCorrect

AutoCorrect is an Office 2000 tool that fixes your mistakes as you type them, provided that the misspelling is in the installed AutoCorrect list of misspellings and their corrections. You can add to this list, storing the mistakes you tend to make; you can even store abbreviations and short phrases that you want Word to "fix" for you whenever you type them.

2

Note

There is only one AutoCorrect list—you don't have to build separate lists in Word, Excel, and PowerPoint. Entries you add to the list in Word are in force while you're working in any of the other Office 2000 applications, and any entries you add while using the other applications are in force while you're working in Word.

How does AutoCorrect work? As you type, each word is compared to the list of words and abbreviations stored in AutoCorrect. If the way you've spelled a word matches one of the AutoCorrect listings, the correct spelling, which is paired with that misspelling, is inserted into your document, replacing the misspelled word. For example, if you type *teh*, AutoCorrect goes back and changes it to *the* as soon as you press Enter or the spacebar after the word (indicating that the word is complete).

In addition to making automatic corrections, AutoCorrect fixes some other potential errors as soon as you make them:

- **Corrects two initial capitals**—If you hold down the Shift key too long when typing a word in title case, both the first and second letter of the word can end up capitalized. AutoCorrect goes back and reduces the second letter to lower case as soon as you finish typing the word.

- **Capitalizes the first word of sentences**—An option you might want to turn off if you create a lot of bulleted lists and outlines (in which not all first words are to be capitalized), this feature capitalizes any word that follows a period or any word typed immediately after pressing the Enter key.

- **Capitalize names of days**—Many people forget that the days of the week are to be capitalized. AutoCorrect fixes it if you do.

- **Correct accidental usage of the Caps Lock key**—If you turn on the Caps Lock by accident—or on purpose, and then forget to toggle it off after you're finished using it—Word realizes you didn't intend to be in Caps Lock mode as soon as you press the Shift key in your typing. AutoCorrect then goes back through the text typed since the Caps Lock key was pressed and switches all capital letters for lowercase letters, and vice versa.

Although AutoCorrect's installed list of words is fairly comprehensive, you might want to add to it so that it works more effectively for you.

Creating Your Own AutoCorrect Entries

To add an entry of your own (a misspelling or abbreviation), follow these steps:

1. Choose Tools, AutoCorrect to open the AutoCorrect dialog box, shown in Figure 2.24.

FIGURE 2.24

Any or all of the AutoCorrect options can be turned off if you don't want Word to make any automatic corrections to your text.

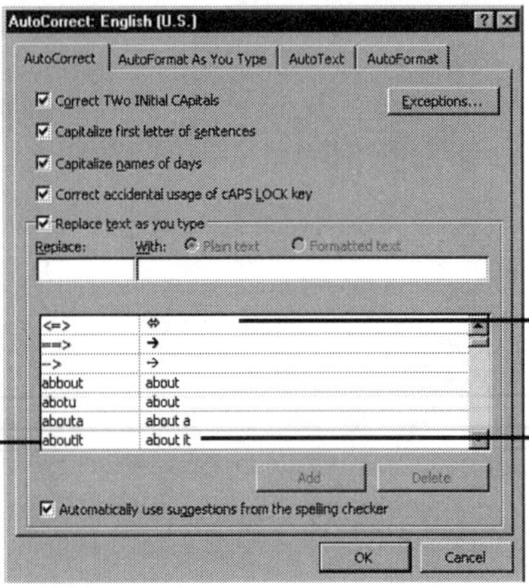

Misspellings and abbreviations

AutoCorrect also contains symbols

Correct and expanded versions

2. In the Replace text as you type section of the dialog box, click inside the Replace box, and type your misspelling or abbreviation.

3. Press the Tab key to move to the With box, and type the correction or expanded version of the abbreviation. Figure 2.25 shows a new AutoText entry in progress.

FIGURE 2.25

Someone's initials (which convert to their full name) make an excellent AutoCorrect entry.

4. Click the Add button.

5. If you have more entries to add, continue placing them in the Replace and With boxes, clicking the Add button after each new entry and its correction.

6. When you've finished adding entries, click the OK button to close the dialog box.

Your new entry now appears alphabetically in the list of AutoCorrect entries and can be changed or deleted as needed. To test your entry, type the misspelling or abbreviation in your document, and then press the spacebar or Enter key. The corrected or expanded version of your entry replaces the original text.

Changing and Deleting AutoCorrect Entries

Perhaps you realize the correction you entered to go with your AutoCorrect entry isn't spelled correctly, or you want to remove the abbreviation you entered into the AutoCorrect list. The AutoCorrect list can be edited (including the entries that were installed with Office 2000) at any time; follow these steps:

1. Choose Tools, AutoCorrect to open the AutoCorrect dialog box.

2. Scroll through the list to find the entry you want to edit or delete. You can also type the first letter of the entry to move quickly to that portion of the alphabetical list.

3. When the entry appears in the list, click on it to place it in the Replace and With boxes.

4. To edit it, click inside either the Replace or With box (whichever portion of the entry needs adjustment) and make your changes.

5. Click the Replace button.

6. To remove the entry completely, click the Delete button.

7. Continue editing and deleting any other entries as required, and then click the OK button to close the dialog box.

Tip

You can create an AutoCorrect entry automatically during your spell check process. When you right-click a misspelled word, choose AutoCorrect from the shortcut menu and then select the correct alternative spelling from the submenu that appears. This places the word and its correct spelling in the AutoCorrect list for you.

Creating AutoText Entries from Document Text

Many of the documents you create in Word will contain similar content—perhaps you end all your proposals with the same closing paragraph, or maybe your contracts contain many of the same sections and clauses. Rather than retype these blocks of text each time you need them, you can use Office 2000's AutoText feature to save you time and ensure consistency.

AutoText stores selections of document content, each with an abbreviation "trigger" that you can type to indicate that you want to insert the stored text. Your proposal closing paragraph can be stored as "proclose," for example, so that each time you type that word, the closing paragraph is inserted.

The easiest way to build an AutoText item is to use existing text—text that looks and reads exactly as you want to use it next time—in an open document. To create an AutoText entry, follow these steps:

1. In your open document, select the text that you want to save as AutoText.
2. Choose Insert, AutoText, New from the menu.
3. In the Create AutoText dialog box (see Figure 2.26), type the abbreviation you want to use as the trigger for your text.

FIGURE 2.26

Choose a short and memorable abbreviation for your AutoText.

Typing this one word saves you from typing an entire paragraph in the future

4. Click OK.

To use your AutoText entries, simply type the abbreviation you stored with the AutoText, and then press the F3 key. The abbreviation turns into the stored text block. If, as you type your abbreviation, you see your full AutoText entry displayed in a ScreenTip above your text, press Enter to insert it. This eliminates the need to press F3.

Note   Office 2000 comes with several AutoText entries for letter salutations, clos-
ings, and so forth. Choose Insert, AutoText, and then choose a category
from the menu; then select one of the stored strings of text.

You can remove your AutoText entries by choosing Insert, AutoText, AutoText to open
the AutoCorrect dialog box. The dialog box opens with the AutoText tab active (see
Figure 2.27). A list of the entries that came with Office 2000—and those that you've
built yourself—appears in the dialog box; you can click on any one of them, and then
click the Delete button to remove it.

FIGURE 2.27

*Scroll through the list
of installed and user-
added AutoText
entries.*

If you want to edit an AutoText entry, follow these steps:

1. Insert the AutoText content that you want to edit by typing the abbreviation trigger
   and pressing F3.

2. Edit the text as needed, and select it.

3. Choose Insert, AutoText, New from the menu.

4. In the Create AutoText dialog box, type the same abbreviation you gave the entry
   before.

5. Click OK. A prompt appears, asking if you intend to redefine the existing AutoText
   that is stored with that abbreviation (see Figure 2.28). Click Yes.

FIGURE 2.28

When you are redefining an AutoText entry, be sure to give it the same name it had before—otherwise, you'll be creating a new version of the AutoText and the original will not be replaced.

 Tip

When building your AutoText entries, be careful when you are selecting the text that is to become the inserted AutoText. If you select blank lines above or below the block of text (if you're selecting a paragraph), those blank lines are part of the AutoText and will be inserted each time you insert the AutoText. This can make it difficult to use a block of AutoText as anything other than a distinct paragraph in the future.

Summary

Today introduced you to the very basics of building a document in Word. With the skills you've acquired, you can type a letter, memo, or simple report and be sure that the content is accurate. You can save it for future use and access it again as needed. Day 3 discusses ways to enhance a basic document, and will culminate in the printing of the document for distribution or hardcopy storage.

Q&A

Q What if Word crashes before I've had a chance to save my work?

A Restart Word and see if a Recovered version of your file opens—if a backup (AutoRecover) version was made while you were working (Word makes a backup every ten minutes), you can probably salvage some, if not all, of your work.

Q Can I use the same name for two or more files?

A No, not if you want to save them to the same folder. Even if you save the files to different folders, you're creating a potential problem for yourself if you don't choose distinct filenames for all your files. If filenames must be similar, put numbers or letters (such as "Budget Report B") at the end of the file names.

Q **Why is it so important to let text wrap in paragraphs and not press Enter when I see the text approaching the right margin?**

A Each time you press Enter, you're creating a new paragraph. If you press Enter at the end of each line, a ten-line paragraph (for example) is really seen by Word as ten separate paragraphs. This can make it impossible to apply paragraph formats to the text because each line has to be formatted separately. The formatting topics that are covered in Day 3 will help you understand this concept more completely.

Workshop

The section that follows is a quick quiz about the day. If you have any problems answering any of the questions, see the section that follows the quiz for all the answers.

Quiz

1. What does it mean if a red wavy underline appears under your text?

2. If your text is underlined in green, what do you do?

3. True or false: You can open the last document you were working on by choosing Documents from the Start menu.

4. List two ways to close a document without exiting the Word application.

5. How do you insert an AutoText entry into your document?

6. True or false: When you save a file for the first time, type the .doc extension at the end of the filename.

Quiz Answers

1. A red wavy underline under a word means that Word cannot find a matching word in its dictionary.

2. A green wavy underline indicates a possible grammatical error. Right-click the underlined text to view a shortcut menu that shows the nature and possible solution to the problem, or choose to Ignore it if you feel the sentence is fine as it is.

3. True. The Documents menu contains a list of the last 15 files you opened. Your last Word document is on the list unless you've opened 15 other files in the meantime.

4. You can close a document by choosing File, Close, or by pressing Ctrl+F4.

5. To insert AutoText, type the abbreviation you created for the AutoText entry and press F3.

6. False. Word applies the extension for you, and the risk of your making a typo-graphical error in an attempt to type it yourself isn't worth the potential problems. An extension other than .doc on a Word document can result in Windows no longer associating Word with your document, making it difficult to open the file through the Explorer or My Computer.

WEEK 1

DAY 3

Enhancing a Basic Word Document

As you learned during Day 2, "Creating a Letter," Word's Blank Document template creates an environment that's conducive to building a solid business or personal letter, a memo, or a report. Any basic document can be typed, edited, proofed, and saved without the use of any tools outside of those you worked with on Day 2. What you are going to learn today, however, will give you the capability to take your document further—to make it more attractive and functional, and to do more with it—by covering the following topics:

- Choosing and applying fonts and styles to give a document more polish and visual impact
- Changing basic page setup options
- Adding and formatting page numbers
- Creating new versions of your documents by saving them with new names and to different folders

- Previewing the layout of your document before printing
- Printing your document—as a whole or in pieces—and utilizing a variety of output options

Applying Character Formats

The most basic change you can make to your Word document is to change the appearance of your text through the use of formatting, and by applying different fonts. Depending on your document layout, you can apply these changes to specific small areas (headings, chapter names, titles), to large sections (paragraphs, bulleted lists, entire pages), or to the entire document.

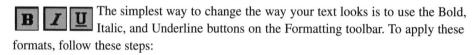 The simplest way to change the way your text looks is to use the Bold, Italic, and Underline buttons on the Formatting toolbar. To apply these formats, follow these steps:

1. Select the text you want to make bold, italic, or underlined.
2. Click the button for the effect you want to apply.

You can apply one, two, or all three formats to the selected text. To remove an effect from your text, simply select the text and click the button for the format you want to remove. Figure 3.1 shows a document with Bold and Italic formatting applied to portions of the text.

FIGURE 3.1

A simple change can make a big difference. Bold titles and italic text help draw the reader's eye to important content.

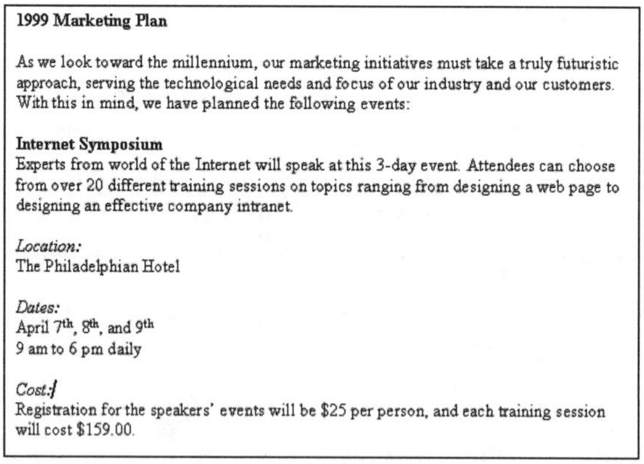

> **1999 Marketing Plan**
>
> As we look toward the millennium, our marketing initiatives must take a truly futuristic approach, serving the technological needs and focus of our industry and our customers. With this in mind, we have planned the following events:
>
> **Internet Symposium**
> Experts from world of the Internet will speak at this 3-day event. Attendees can choose from over 20 different training sessions on topics ranging from designing a web page to designing an effective company intranet.
>
> *Location:*
> The Philadelphian Hotel
>
> *Dates:*
> April 7th, 8th, and 9th
> 9 am to 6 pm daily
>
> *Cost:]*
> Registration for the speakers' events will be $25 per person, and each training session will cost $159.00.

Tip

Watch the Formatting toolbar's buttons—the buttons that you've used to format selected text appear indented while the text that is formatted with them is selected.

Tip

There are three easy-to-remember keyboard shortcuts for applying Bold, Italic, and Underline formatting to your text: Ctrl+B for Bold, Ctrl+I for Italic, and Ctrl+U for Underline.

Like these simple formats that you can apply to your text, the fonts that you use enhance your document's message by invoking a feeling. Choosing a serious, dignified-looking font makes your document appear more professional. Fonts can also be used to generate a sense of playfulness or fun, or to give your document a high-tech, graphical appearance. Figures 3.2 and 3.3 show the same document, formatted with different types of fonts. Regardless of the document's content, the fonts create an immediate mood—even before the letter is read.

3

FIGURE 3.2

If your document is to give the impression that you're conservative and reliable, choose traditional, elegant fonts.

1999 Marketing Plan

As we look toward the millennium, our marketing initiatives must take a truly futuristic approach, serving the technological needs and focus of our industry and our customers. With this in mind, we have planned the following events:

Internet Symposium
Experts from world of the Internet will speak at this 3-day event. Attendees can choose from over 20 different training sessions on topics ranging from designing a web page to designing an effective company intranet.

Location:
The Philadelphian Hotel

Dates:
April 7th, 8th, and 9th
9 am to 6 pm daily

Cost
Registration for the speakers' events will be $25 per person, and each training session will cost $159.00.

FIGURE 3.3

Evoke a sense of excitement and creativity with fonts that have a lot of visual impact.

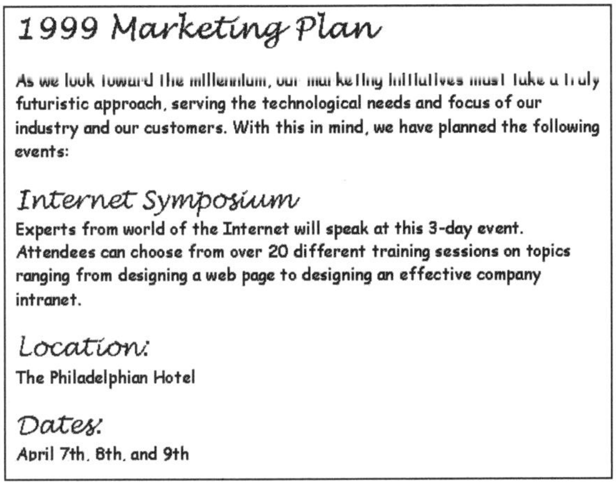

1999 Marketing Plan

As we look toward the millennium, our marketing initiatives must take a truly futuristic approach, serving the technological needs and focus of our industry and our customers. With this in mind, we have planned the following events:

Internet Symposium
Experts from world of the Internet will speak at this 3-day event. Attendees can choose from over 20 different training sessions on topics ranging from designing a web page to designing an effective company intranet.

Location:
The Philadelphian Hotel

Dates:
April 7th, 8th, and 9th

Tip

Not sure which fonts make which kind of statement? Trust your own instincts. If a font looks serious or traditional to you, it probably also does to those who read your document.

You can apply different fonts to single words, sentences, or paragraphs—or to your entire document—with a few simple steps. When using different fonts, however, keep them to a minimum—no more than two or three per document—to avoid a circus-like appearance.

Caution

It's important to use fonts that complement each other so that your readers aren't overwhelmed. Never use two different *serif* fonts (fonts with flourishes on the letters) or two different *sanserif* fonts (plain fonts with no flourishes) in the same document. Also, use fancy script and artistic fonts sparingly throughout a document, and definitely never use more than one per document.

Changing Fonts

Through one important improvement, Word 2000 makes it much easier to choose and apply fonts than it was in Office 97. You can now view the fonts graphically in the Font list box on the Formatting toolbar (see Figure 3.4).

FIGURE 3.4

Scroll through the list and select a font by its appearance, not just by name.

In Office 97, the font list listed the fonts by name only, and it wasn't until the font was applied that you could see what the font looked like.

To apply fonts from the Formatting toolbar, follow these steps:

1. In your document, select the text you want to format.

2. Click the Font button on the Formatting toolbar to display the list of available fonts.

3. Select a font from the list by clicking its name.

4. Click in the white space to deselect the text and view your results.

If you decide you don't like the font after you see it in use in your text, reselect the text and repeat steps 2 and 3 to apply a different font.

Unchanged from Office 97 is the Font dialog box (choose Format, Font from the menu), which shows a preview of the selected font before it is applied to the selected text in the document (see Figure 3.5).

FIGURE 3.5

The Font dialog box offers "one-stop shopping" for applying fonts—change the font, size, and style or apply various effects, all from one dialog box.

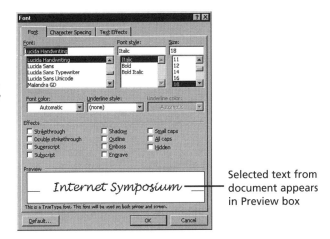

Selected text from document appears in Preview box

To apply a font from the Font dialog box, follow these steps:

1. Select the text in your document that you want to format.

2. Choose Format, Font to open the Font dialog box.

3. Scroll through the Font list, and select one by clicking it once.

4. View the Preview window, which shows your document text in the selected font.

5. After finding a font that you like (based on its preview), click OK to apply the font.

Changing Font Size

The size of your text, regardless of the font that is applied, can have a big impact on the visual effectiveness of your document. You might even find that simply increasing the size of the default Times New Roman 12-point font of your basic document can have the desired effect, and that there's no need to employ different fonts in your document. Figure 3.6 shows a document with the heading text made larger.

Font size of text is displayed on the toolbar

FIGURE 3.6

Increasing font size draws the reader's eye to important text.

Heading text is now 18 points

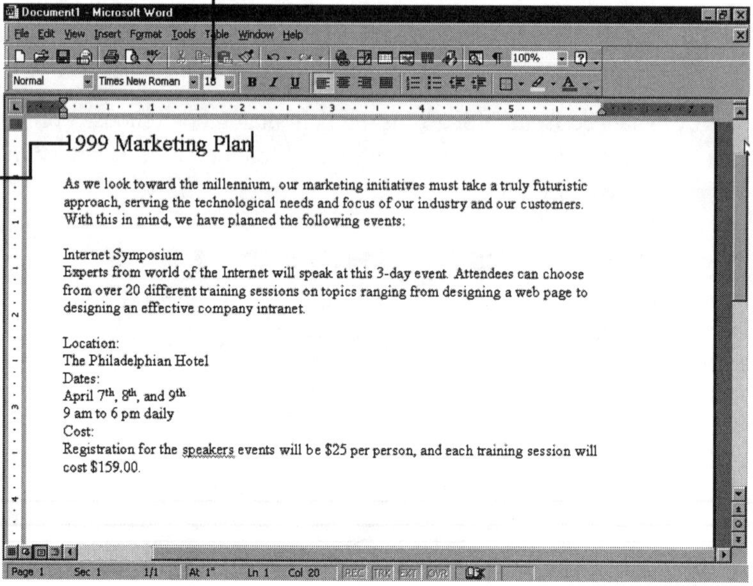
Document1 - Microsoft Word
File Edit View Insert Format Tools Table Window Help
Normal
Times New Roman
18
100%
1999 Marketing Plan
As we look toward the millennium, our marketing initiatives must take a truly futuristic approach, serving the technological needs and focus of our industry and our customers. With this in mind, we have planned the following events:
Internet Symposium
Experts from world of the Internet will speak at this 3-day event. Attendees can choose from over 20 different training sessions on topics ranging from designing a web page to designing an effective company intranet.
Location:
The Philadelphian Hotel
Dates:
April 7th, 8th, and 9th
9 am to 6 pm daily
Cost:
Registration for the speakers events will be $25 per person, and each training session will cost $159.00.
Page 1 Sec 1 1/1 At 1" Ln 1 Col 20 REC TRK EXT OVR

You can increase the size of your selected text in one of two ways:

12

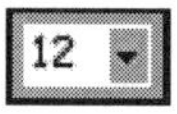

- Click the Font Size button on the Formatting toolbar, and then choose a larger point size.
- Choose Format, Font, and, in the Size section of the dialog box, select a larger size for your text. The Preview window shows you the effect. Click OK to apply the new size.

Tip

> You'll notice that as you apply different fonts in the same point size, the text does not always appear or print in the same size. For example, Courier in 10 points is not the same as Brush Script in 10 points. For very ornate fonts, you might want to apply a larger font size to achieve the same visual size of a less ornate font.

Applying a Style

So far, you've applied simple bold, italic, and underline formats; changed fonts; and changed the size of your text. Each change to the appearance of your text required that a separate command be issued—click a button, open a dialog box, make a selection from a list, and so on. Switching to a different font, making it bold, and making it bigger takes three separate steps, even if you do it all from within the Font dialog box.

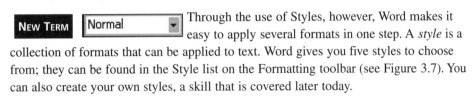

Through the use of Styles, however, Word makes it easy to apply several formats in one step. A *style* is a collection of formats that can be applied to text. Word gives you five styles to choose from; they can be found in the Style list on the Formatting toolbar (see Figure 3.7). You can also create your own styles, a skill that is covered later today.

FIGURE 3.7

Make your headings and titles stand out with Word's Heading 1, 2, and 3 styles.

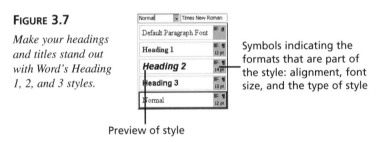

Symbols indicating the formats that are part of the style: alignment, font size, and the type of style

Preview of style

The list of styles also includes Normal and Default Paragraph Font, which are used to return text that's been formatted in a Heading style or through the other formatting tools to the basic Times New Roman 12-point format.

To apply a style to your document, follow these steps:

1. Select the text to which you want to apply the style.
2. Click the Style button on the Formatting toolbar to display the list of styles.
3. Select a style by clicking its name in the list.

It's important to note that the Heading and Normal styles are paragraph styles—you cannot apply them to specific text within a paragraph without applying them to the entire paragraph. Default Paragraph Font is a character style, meaning that it can be applied to individual words within a paragraph—and the rest of the paragraph retains whatever formatting is already in place.

Creating a Style by Example

If you find that the Heading styles that Word provides aren't appropriate for your documents, you can create styles of your own based on text that you've typed and formatted in your documents.

To create your own style, follow these steps:

1. Select existing text, or type text for the purpose of building the style.
2. Format the text as you want the style to format future text—apply fonts and sizes or use the Bold, Italic, and Underline buttons. You can also select text that has already been formatted.
3. With the text still selected, click the word *Normal* in the Style box on the Formatting toolbar (see Figure 3.8).

FIGURE 3.8

Create a style quickly and easily, using formatted text as an example.

Normal style name selected in the Style box

Selected formatted text

4. Type a name for your style. The name you type replaces the word *Normal* in the Style box.
5. Press Enter to create the style that is based on your selected text.

To use the style you've created, select other text in your document and click the Style button on the toolbar—choose the style you created from the list, and the selected text is reformatted to match the style.

Note

By default, the styles you create in a document are only available in that document. If you want a style to be available in all future documents, click the Add to template checkbox in the New Style dialog box (Choose Format, Style, and then click the New button to open the dialog box). The style you create (based on selected text) then appears in the style list in all documents that are based on the Blank Document template.

Editing Styles

The styles that came with Word, and those that you create, can be edited to better meet your needs. Suppose you decide that you like Heading 1 as it was installed, but want the text to be bigger; or maybe you created a style and want to make it Bold. You can edit these styles to change the way they work in the current document, or you can make the style changes available to all your new documents.

To make quick changes to the styles in your current document only, follow these steps:

1. Select some text to which the style in question has been applied.

2. Reformat the style as you want it to look.

3. In the Style box, click the displayed style name to select it.

4. Press the Enter key. A dialog box appears, asking you to confirm your intention to update the style (see Figure 3.9).

FIGURE 3.9

Update the existing style to match the new text example.

5. Click OK to update the style based on the new formats that are applied to the selected text.

After you update the style, all text to which that style has been or will be applied within the current document follows the formatting of the selected text. This saves you from reapplying the style to existing text, and it enables you to automatically have consistent formatting throughout your document.

Making Global Style Changes

If you want to make a change to any of the styles—installed or user-created—and have them apply to all future documents as well as the current document, follow these steps:

1. Select the text to which the style that you want to change has been applied.

2. Choose Format, Style to open the Style dialog box (see Figure 3.10).

3. The style of the selected text appears highlighted in the Styles list. If for some reason it is not selected, click it in the list.

4. Click the Modify button to open the Modify Style dialog box (see Figure 3.11).

FIGURE 3.10

The Style dialog box gives you access to all installed and user-created styles and enables you to see and edit their settings.

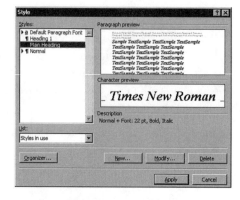

FIGURE 3.11

View a description and visual sample of the style as it is, and then modify it to meet your needs.

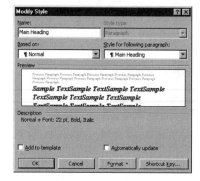

5. Click the Format button and choose Font from the list that appears (see Figure 3.12).

FIGURE 3.12

Select Font from the list of potential modifications.

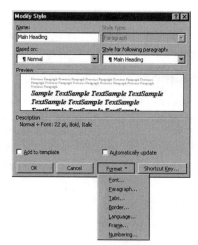

6. In the resulting Font dialog box (the same one that opens when you choose Format, Font from the menu), select the font, size, font style, and effects that you want.

7. Click OK to close the Font dialog box.

8. Back in the Modify Style dialog box, place a checkmark in the Add to template option box. This makes the style changes part of the Blank Document template; therefore, they are available in all future documents that are based on the Blank Document template.

9. Click OK to return to the Style dialog box.

10. Select any additional styles you want to edit, and follow steps 4 through 9 for each of them. When you finished editing your styles, click Close.

Resetting the Normal Style

Some users find that the default Times New Roman 12-point text doesn't work for their documents. If you want to use a different font or font size for all your future Blank Document text, you can reset the default.

To reset the default Normal font in the Blank Document template, follow these steps:

1. In an open document that is created with the Blank Document template (choose that template from the New Office Document dialog box or click the New document button on the toolbar), choose Format, Font. This opens the Font dialog box.

2. Using the Font, Font Style, Size, Color, and Effects sections of the dialog box, make any changes you require and then click the Default button in the lower-left corner of the dialog box.

3. In answer to the resulting prompt (see Figure 3.13), click Yes; this changes the default font. As is noted in the prompt, this change affects all new documents that are based on the Normal (Blank Document) template.

FIGURE 3.13

Click Yes to update the default font for all new documents.

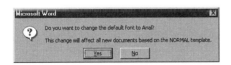

Caution

Do not change the default font for your new blank documents indiscriminately—be sure that the changes you make to this default will be appropriate in the vast majority of your documents. Otherwise, you're creating a lot of extra work for yourself when you have to reformat documents to accommodate the defaults.

Tip

The Format Painter can be used to apply formatting from one selection of text to another. Rather than repeating a series of formatting commands or applying a style from the Style list, select the text that is formatted as you want some other text to be, and then click the Format Painter. Drag through the text that you want to format to match the sample text. If you need multiple applications of the format, double-click the Format Painter button and use it repeatedly throughout your document. To turn it off, click its button again.

Adjusting Page Setup

As you learned earlier today, Word's Blank Document template is set up so that you can just start typing your document. The template's defaults, however, are set up for a basic business document—to be printed on typical letterhead (or blank sheets of paper) or viewed onscreen. What if your letterhead isn't typical? What if your paper size isn't standard? If your document has special needs, you need to adjust the page setup.

 Note

Word offers four views of your document, two of which are appropriate for editing your document and adjusting the layout of your page. The default view for all documents is Normal view, but Print Layout gives you more to work with: a vertical ruler and a graphical view of the edges of the paper in relation to your margins. To change your view, use the View menu and select the view you want to use.

 Tip

Is your ruler missing? Choose View, Ruler to bring it back onscreen in Normal or Print Layout view.

By choosing File, Page Setup, and using the Page Setup dialog box, you can easily adjust some basic features of your open document:

- **Margins**—In the Margins tab, change the top, bottom, left, and right margins of your document by typing a new measurement or using the increment and decrement triangles for each margin setting (see Figure 3.14).

Click the up triangle to
increase the measurement

FIGURE 3.14

Does your letterhead have a large logo at the top? Increase your top margin to accommodate it.

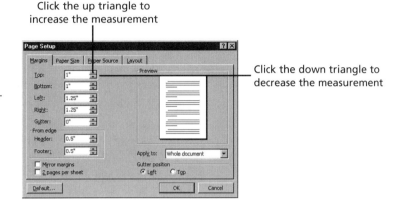

Click the down triangle to
decrease the measurement

- **Paper Size**—In the Paper Size tab, choose a paper size from the Paper size list, or type in custom width and height measurements for special paper. You can also turn your paper on its side, changing it from Portrait (the default) to Landscape Orientation (see Figure 3.15).

FIGURE 3.15

If your paper isn't the standard 8 1/2- by 11-inch, enter your special paper dimensions.

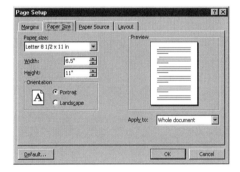

- **Paper Source**—Does your printer have more than one tray? In the Paper Source tab, choose which tray the letterhead (for page one) is to be in, and which one is to hold the subsequent pages. You'll learn more about printing later today.

- **Layout**—From the Layout tab, your document can be broken into sections, each of which can be treated differently in terms of page numbers and the headers/footers that appear on the pages of your document. On Day 5, "Improving Document Function," you'll learn to create headers and footers and to control the flow of your document through the insertion of section breaks.

3

Note

Your Page Setup changes can be applied to selected text, from the cursor forward, or to the entire document. In the Apply to list box, choose how your changes are to be applied by selecting Whole Document, This point forward, or Selected text. The last option is only available if there is text selected in the document while the Page Setup dialog box is open.

Margin adjustment is the most commonly performed page setup change. For this reason, Word gives you an alternative method of adjusting your margins. Rather than opening the Page Setup dialog box and entering exact measurements, you can increase or decrease all four margins (top, bottom, left, right) "by eye," using the rulers in your document window. To adjust your margins, follow these steps:

1. If necessary, switch to Print Layout view by choosing View, Print Layout. This adds a vertical ruler (for adjusting top and bottom margins) to your document window (see Figure 3.16).

FIGURE 3.16

The gray area on the ruler represents your margins, and the white represents the area in which you can type.

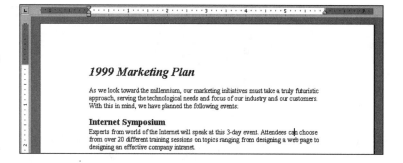

2. To adjust your top margin, point to the spot on the ruler at which the gray meets the white (see Figure 3.17). Your mouse turns to a vertical two-headed arrow.

FIGURE 3.17

Increase or decrease the margin by dragging with your mouse.

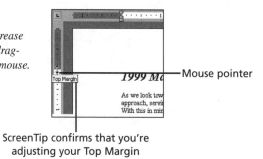

Mouse pointer

ScreenTip confirms that you're adjusting your Top Margin

3. Click and drag up to decrease the margin, or down to increase it. A horizontal dashed line appears across the page and follows you as you drag the margin up or down (see Figure 3.18).

FIGURE 3.18

Watch the measure-
ments and calibration
marks on the ruler
to see what margin
measurement you're
setting.

1999 Marketing Plan

As we look toward the millennium, our marketing initiatives must take a truly futuristic approach, serving the technological needs and focus of our industry and our customers. With this in mind, we have planned the following events:

Margin being
increased to 2"

4. As necessary, adjust your bottom, left, and right margins using steps 2 and 3. When adjusting left and right margins, drag outward (away from the center of the page) to decrease the margin, or drag toward the center of the page to increase it.

The margins you set this way might not be exact—you might end up with a 1.98" margin instead of 2". In most cases, exact measurement isn't important, so this quick and simple method might be preferable to the Page Setup dialog box. If, however, you must have exact margin measurements for your document, use the Page Setup dialog box and the Margins tab to adjust your page settings.

Tip

The margins you set for your current document apply only to that document—the next new, blank document you create will have the standard margins of 1" on the top and bottom, and 1.25" on the left and right.

Tip

If you want to change the margins—or any other Page Setup feature—for all future documents that are based on the Blank Document template, click the Default button in the Page Setup dialog box; a prompt asks you to confirm your intention to change the defaults, based on the current settings in the Page Setup dialog box.

Inserting Page Numbers

Although most business documents don't exceed a single page, some of them do—a letter with a paragraph that just won't fit on one page, a multiple-page report, a long list or memo, and so on. These documents require page numbers to help those who read keep the pages in order. Page numbers are also essential if you're printing multiple sets of a document—collating and binding is made easier if there are page numbers on the printout.

Page numbers rarely, if ever, appear on the first page of a multiple-page document. In the case of a letter, the date and salutation are clear indications of the first page, and only subsequent pages need to be numbered. You can type page numbers on your document manually, or you can let Word automatically number your pages for you. The amount of work involved in both methods of adding page numbers to the document is about the same—the difference is that if you add or delete pages in a document with pages that have been numbered manually, you have to edit the page numbers yourself. If you allow Word to number the pages for you, the page numbers update automatically when pages are added to or removed from the document.

To insert page numbers in your document, follow these steps:

1. In your open document, press Ctrl+Home to go to the top of the document. This eliminates any confusion as to where the page numbering is to start (even if you elect not to place a number on page one).

2. Choose Insert, Page Numbers.

3. In the resulting Page Numbers dialog box (see Figure 3.19), choose the placement for your page numbers by clicking the Position list box.

FIGURE 3.19

Traditionally, page numbers appear in the lower-right corner of business documents.

4. Select the appropriate alignment (Center is a good choice if you don't know how or if your document is to be stapled or bound, or if you'll be printing on both sides of the paper).

5. Remove the checkmark in the Show number on first page option.

6. Click OK to insert the page numbers and close the dialog box.

If you can't see your page numbers onscreen, switch to Print Layout view by choosing View, Print Layout, or by clicking the Print Layout View buttonto the left of the horizontal scrollbar. Your page numbers appear dimmed on the page as you scroll through your document.

 Note

> Your page numbers appear dimmed because they're on a different layer of your document than the text you've typed into your letter. The page numbers reside on the header and footer layer, where you can also add other text such as copyright information, names, or dates. On Day 5 you'll learn to create headers and footers.

Tip

> Print Layout view can be a productive view to work in for building and editing documents; this is because in addition to seeing your page numbers (if any), you also have an additional vertical ruler, which is useful in establishing document layout.

3

Saving a New Version of an Existing File

After initially saving a file, you might decide that you need to preserve the document as it stands and create a new version that you can edit and format as a separate document. You might also want to make a duplicate of the currently saved file in another folder or on a different drive.

To create a new version or a duplicate of your open file in an alternative location, follow these steps:

1. Choose File, Save As.
2. In the Save As dialog box (see Figure 3.20), type a new name for the file (replacing the name that is currently displayed in the File name box). If you only want to save the file to a new location (and keep the current name), skip to step 3.

FIGURE 3.20

Create a new version of your file by changing the name or location of your saved file.

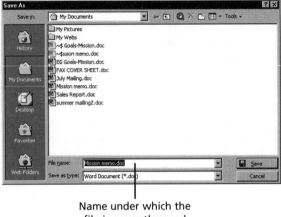

Name under which the
file is currently saved

3. If you want to save the file to a new location, select that new location from the Save in list box or double-click a different folder in the displayed list of folders.

4. When the name and location for the new version of the file are selected, click Save to create the new version and close the dialog box.

As soon as the new version of the file is created, the previous version is closed and the new version becomes the active document. You can reopen the original to continue working on that document, or you can just work with the new version.

Previewing Your Work

A complete document creation cycle culminates in the printing of a document. Before you print, however, it's a good idea to preview the document to make sure it looks the way you want it. This extra step saves paper and, in the long run, it saves time—no need to wait for the document to come out of the printer before you spot something that needs editing or reformatting.

You can view your document's overall layout in a variety of ways:

- Choose File, Print Preview. A preview window opens (see Figure 3.21), showing the document's layout.

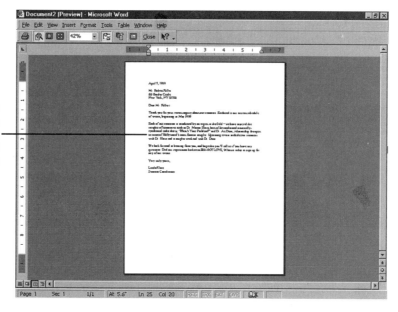

FIGURE 3.21

Eliminate surprises on paper by previewing your document first.

This short letter needs to be moved down on the page to eliminate a large amount of white space

- Click the Print Preview button on the Standard toolbar. A preview window opens (see Figure 3.21).

- While in Print Layout view, click the Zoom tool and choose Whole Page. The entire current page is displayed, with all four sides visible. You can scroll through subsequent pages to see the rest of your document, with each page in Whole Page view.

If you choose to view a Print Preview (as opposed to using the Zoom tool), your cursor is not available on the page. To activate the cursor, click the Magnifier tool. When your cursor blinks on the page, you can click within the document to reposition the cursor as needed for adding blank lines (to move text down) or deleting blank lines (to move text up). For other types of editing, exit Print Preview by clicking the Close button. Do not use Print Preview for editing text or adjusting indents, tabs, or inter-character/word spacing.

A major benefit of using Print Preview instead of zooming out to Whole Page view is that you can click the Multiple Pages button and choose to see up to 24 of your document's pages onscreen at the same time. When you click the button, drag horizontally through the palette, as shown in Figure 3.22. This can be a big help in laying out your entire document because it enables you to spot unwanted white space on specific pages, or blank pages within the document.

FIGURE 3.22

Use the pages palette to select the number of pages you want to see at the same time.

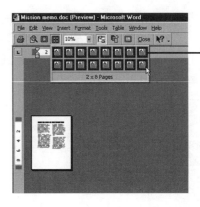

Drag to the right to select a
greater number of pages

Tip

The total number of Multiple Pages you can see depends on your monitor's resolution setting. If your monitor is set to 640x480, you can only see 12 pages at a time. If your monitor is set to 800x600 or 1024x768, you can see up to 24 pages at the same time.

If you choose to preview your document using the Zoom tool, you never lose cursor control—the document text merely becomes too small to see well enough for text editing. Like Print Preview, Whole Page view is best for adding or deleting space between paragraphs or at the top or bottom of a page.

Tip

It can be easier to adjust your margins while in Print Preview or a Whole Page zoom view—you can see the entire page and adjust all four margins from the ruler. Simply drag the gray areas of the ruler (as described earlier today) and watch your text move to fit within the new settings.

Tip

Use the Shrink to Fit button to reduce the number of pages in your document by one. If your document is flowing onto an unwanted second page, for example, clicking this button forces the entire document onto one page.

Printing Your Office 2000 Document

The final step in the process of building a document is printing it—creating tangible evidence of your efforts. Documents are printed for the purpose of distribution or hard copy storage, and sometimes for proofreading. Although the document can be proofread onscreen, some users find that they seem to spot errors more readily when reading a document on paper.

 Your document can be printed quickly from the Standard toolbar by clicking the Print button. Clicking this button sends a print job to your printer, resulting in one copy of every page of your document.

If you want to control the print job, you must select File, Print from the menu to access the Print dialog box. The Print dialog box is shown in Figure 3.23. Through this dialog box, you can control

- Which printer to use (if you're attached to more than one via a network or electronic switching device).

- How many copies to print and whether to collate several sets of a multiple-page document.

- Which pages to include in the printout—you can print all of them, a single page, or a range of pages.

FIGURE 3.23

Control the direction and scope of your print job through the Print dialog box.

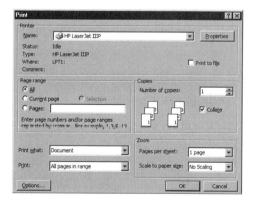

Tip

If you're printing more than one set of a multipage document, be sure to leave the Collate option on, saving yourself the trouble of putting the sets of pages in numerical order.

Printing Pages and Selections

By default, Word prints one copy of all the pages in your document. If you want to print a specific page or range of pages, you must specify that in the Print dialog box. Your page selection options are as follows:

- **All**—Every page in the document prints.
- **Current page**—The current page is defined by where your cursor was when you opened the Print dialog box.
- **Pages**—Specify which pages are to print using commas for nonconsecutive pages and dashes for ranges, for example, 3,5,7; 8–12.
- **Selection**—Use this option to print text you select with your mouse before opening the Print dialog box. If no text is selected, the option is dimmed.

In addition to specifying specific page numbers or sections of your document, you can also choose to print just the odd or even pages by clicking the Print list box (see Figure 3.24).

FIGURE 3.24

Save paper by printing on both sides of the paper.

Printing just the odd or even pages enables you to create two-sided printed output. If your multipage document is to be bound or stapled and you want text on both sides of the page, print the odd pages first, and then put the paper back in the printer (upside down, so you'll print on the blank sides) and choose to print the even pages.

Working with Printing Options

In addition to the choice and number of pages printed, the Print dialog box offers options for including information about the document in the printout and creating special print-outs. Your options are as follows:

- **Print What**—To include document information such as Properties (name of the author or when the document was written, last printed, or last modified), Styles (both the installed Heading styles and user-created styles), and AutoText entries that are used in the document, click the Print What list box. From this list you can select the type of document background data to include with your printout. The selected content appears at the end of the printed document, and can help you—and others who might use your document—to understand how your document was built.

- **Pages per sheet**—In the Zoom section of the dialog box, click the Pages per sheet list box to print up to 16 pages of text on a single sheet of paper. Use this option to show the layout of a multipage document—make decisions about rearranging your pages and see the "big picture" of a long document in a single, paper-saving print-out.

- **Scale to paper size**—Also found in the Zoom section of the Print dialog box, this option enables you to create scaled printouts that convert the amount of text in your document pages to a different size of paper than was established during Page Setup. This option makes it possible for you to retain your 8 1/2- by 11-inch setup but output to a nonstandard paper size for one print job.

Summary

Today you learned how to take a basic document and customize its content, name, and printed appearance to suit your needs. With the skills you've acquired, you can format your document text by applying styles, changing fonts and font sizes, and controlling your document's margins. In addition, you can now save a new version of your document to preserve the original, and print any document you create. Day 4, "Building a Complex Document," will show you how to control document layout with indents, tabs, and tables.

Q&A

Q Can I delete a file from within Word, or do I have to use My Computer or the Windows Explorer to do that?

A Yes, you can delete files within Word. Choose File, Open, and navigate to the folder that contains the file you want to delete. Click once on the file to select it in the dialog box, and then press the Delete key. The document is placed in the Recycle Bin after you click Yes in response to a confirmation prompt. To close the Open dialog box after your deletion, click Cancel.

Q After I've started a print job, can I stop it?

A Yes, if the job was big enough. Print jobs of one or two pages tend to happen so fast that there isn't time to stop them. If your print job is among others in a network print queue, or if the content of the printout is so large that the job takes some time to be processed by the printer, you might have time to stop it. Look for a small printer icon on the right end of the taskbar, and double-click it. The current print jobs in the queue for that printer are displayed, and you can cancel yours by clicking once on the job and choosing Document, Cancel Printing from the menu.

Workshop

The section that follows is a quick quiz about the day. If you have any problems answering any of the questions, see the section that follows the quiz for all the answers.

Quiz

1. Name three ways to make text bold.

2. Define a Heading style and discuss how one might be used.

3. True or false: Page numbers always start on the first page of a document.

4. True or false: When you save a file with a new name, the original file is deleted.

5. When performing a Print Preview, can you edit your document in any way?

6. List two ways to adjust your document's margins.

Quiz Answers

1. You can make text bold by selecting it and clicking the Bold button [040], pressing Ctrl+B, or choosing Bold from the Font Style list in the Font dialog box.

2. A Heading style is a group of formats that can be applied to text in a Word document. A Blank Document has three Heading styles in the Style list, and each can be applied to titles, chapter names, and other prominent text in your document.

3. False. Page numbering should start on the second page of most, if not all, business documents. The first or cover page need not be numbered at all because its content indicates that it is the first page.

4. False. When you save a new version of a document by giving it a new name, the original document is closed, left intact as of the last time it was saved under the original name. The new version remains open onscreen.

5. Yes, you can edit your document in Print Preview. Restrict your edits to adding or deleting blank lines—to move your document text up or down—rather than editing text.

6. You can adjust your document's margins through the Page Setup dialog box (File, Page Setup), or on the ruler by dragging the gray margin section of the ruler to increase or decrease the margin.

DAY 4

Building a Complex Document

Although most business word processing takes the form of simple letters, a great number of the remaining documents—reports, résumés, forms—are fairly complex, the types of documents that require Word's tools for controlling the layout of a document.

Today you will learn to set up and move content around in a complex document. You'll discover the following Word tools and features:

- Paragraph formatting with indents and tabs
- Creating tables to contain and display text and numeric content
- Editing and formatting tables for maximum visual effect
- Creating fill-in forms with tables

Controlling Document Layout

By default, text that is typed into a Word document starts at the intersection of the left and top margins, and continues down the page until you stop typing. Blank lines separate paragraphs, and page breaks separate pages of text. The flow of text onto a page or pages of 5 1/2- by 9-inch blocks of text (the space within standard margins) happens quite naturally.

What if you need a different overall shape for your document, though? Or what if you want to include a section of text that quotes another document? You'll need to set indents on the left and right sides of the quoted text. What if you need to type a list? Tabs can help line up several items in a list. What if you want to create newspaper columns? Converting your block text to two or three narrow columns of text on the page is easily done. Word gives you tools to move existing text up, down, or over, as well as to set up your blank document so that new text falls into the desired pattern.

Working with Indents

Indents control the horizontal placement of text in lines and paragraphs. The most common type of indent is the left half-inch indent at the beginning of a paragraph. Typing the tab key at the start of the paragraph creates the indent, and all subsequent paragraphs in the document are indented by a half-inch without any further effort from you. Figure 4.1 shows a series of indented paragraphs, a typical document layout.

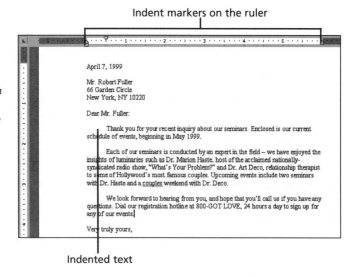

FIGURE 4.1

Use the Tab key at the beginning of a paragraph to set a half-inch tab for that and all subsequent paragraphs in the document.

When the Tab indent is set, you'll notice that the left indent marker moves on the ruler—the top triangle moves to the left by one half-inch. This triangle represents the first line in the paragraph. The bottom triangle represents the body of the paragraph.

Tip Is your ruler missing? Bring it back onscreen by choosing View, Ruler.

These indent markers do more than show you the indents that are set—they can also be used to create indents for the left and right sides of a paragraph or for any selected text. Figure 4.2 shows the ruler and indent markers.

Bottom triangle represents   Top triangle represents
body of paragraph   first line of paragraph

FIGURE 4.2

Click within or select the paragraph, and then drag the indent triangles to set indents for your text.

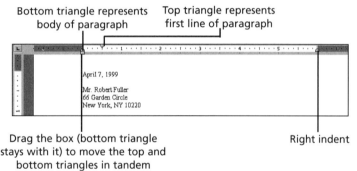

Drag the box (bottom triangle stays with it) to move the top and bottom triangles in tandem   Right indent

Like many Word tools, indents can be set in a variety of ways. In addition to using the Tab key for a simple first-line indent or dragging the ruler's indent markers, you can use the following methods to set indents:

- Use the keyboard (shortcuts listed in Table 4.1).
- Choose Format, Paragraph to open the Paragraph dialog box and set a Left, Right, or Special indent (see Figure 4.3).

4

FIGURE 4.3

Set indents to precise measurements in the Paragraph dialog box.

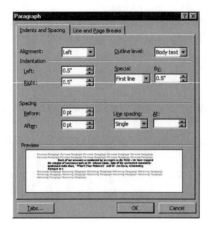

TABLE 4.1   INDENT KEYBOARD SHORTCUTS

Shortcut	Effect
Ctrl+T	Creates a hanging indent (first line on the left margin, body of paragraph indented one half-inch)
Ctrl+M	Indents the entire paragraph one half-inch from the left
Ctrl+Shift+M	Moves a left indent back one half-inch
Ctrl+Q	Removes all indents and paragraph formats

Tip

The keyboard shortcuts that create indents can be used repeatedly to increase the indent—for example, pressing Ctrl+M twice indents the cursor a total of one inch. To reverse the effect one half-inch at a time, add the Shift key to the key combination; for example, pressing Ctrl+Shift+M moves the cursor back one half-inch.

Figure 4.4 shows a variety of indents in a document.

FIGURE 4.4

You can press the keyboard shortcut or set the indent before typing the paragraph; or you can select the text after typing and then apply the indent.

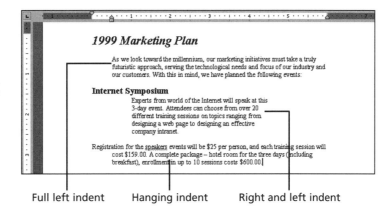

Full left indent   Hanging indent   Right and left indent

After an indent is set, you can adjust it using any of the methods for creating the indent in the first place. The simplest method of adjusting an indent (increasing or decreasing it) is to drag the indent markers on the ruler. Be sure that the text you want to move is selected when you move the indent markers—this tells Word which paragraph you intend to adjust.

Note

Word 2000 offers a new feature called Click and Type. By double-clicking your mouse anywhere in the white space of a document (within the margins), you can position your cursor at that spot. There is, therefore, no longer any need to use the space bar to move the cursor in or to set specific indents to position your cursor before you type anywhere to the right of the left margin. Unlike an indent, however, the position of the cursor is not retained in subsequent paragraphs. When you press the Enter key, your cursor returns to the left margin.

Using Default Tabs

Surely you've used the Tab key to indent a paragraph or line, and you know that a blank document has tabs set every half-inch across the page. For most documents, this represents the extent of your use of the Tab key. Figure 4.5 shows a document that contains a tabbed list created with default tabs.

FIGURE 4.5

*Default tabs are set
every half-inch, start-
ing at the left margin.*

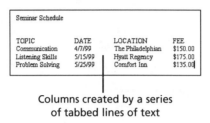

Columns created by a series
of tabbed lines of text

To use the default tabs to create a tabbed list, follow these steps:

1. On the line that is to contain the first of your tabbed text, press the Tab key to indent the first text and create the first column.
2. Type the text, and then press tab to create the second column in the list.
3. Type the next selection of text, and press Tab again as needed.
4. At the end of the first line of tabbed text, press Enter to move to the beginning of the next line.
5. Press Tab to move under the first tabbed text on the preceding line.
6. Type the text for the next line of tabbed text, pressing Tab to place text in the tabbed columns.

Setting Custom Tabs

There might be times that the tab position you need doesn't fall at one of the half-inch increments along the ruler. In these situations, you can set your own tabs to any position on your ruler; you can have as many tabs across the page as you need. You can also set as many sets of custom tabs as you want throughout a document. Figure 4.6 shows a document with two different sets of tabs set for two different tabbed lists.

FIGURE 4.6

*Tabs go into effect
wherever your cursor
is when you place the
tab stops on the ruler.
The tab stops remain
in effect until you cre-
ate a new set at anoth-
er point in the docu-
ment.*

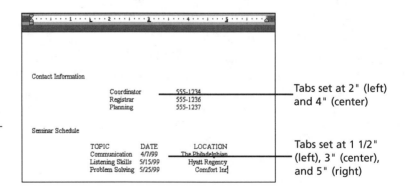

Tabs set at 2" (left)
and 4" (center)

Tabs set at 1 1/2"
(left), 3" (center),
and 5" (right)

Custom tabs can be set in two ways:

- **Use the ruler**—Click the tab button at the left end of the ruler (see Figure 4.7) to establish the alignment of the tab, and then click on the ruler to place the tab stop of your choice.

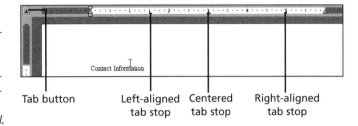

Tab button   Left-aligned Centered   Right-aligned
                    tab stop   tab stop   tab stop

- **Use the Tabs dialog box**—Choose Format, Tabs, and then create one or many tabs using the Tabs dialog box (see Figure 4.8). Enter the ruler position (such as 1.25), choose an alignment, and select a *leader* (a character that leads up to the tab stop) as needed. Tab leaders can only be set through the Tabs dialog box.

Tip

There is another type of tab that can be set from the ruler and within the Tabs dialog box—a bar tab. Bar tabs place a vertical line between columns of tabbed text; they are positioned by your choosing a ruler position that is exactly halfway between two existing tabs. If you need columns of text with vertical lines, though, you're better off using a table with visible borders to structure your text! (Tables are covered later today.)

FIGURE 4.8

For precise placement of custom tabs, use the Tabs dialog box.

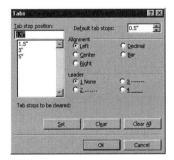

4

Tip

You rarely, if ever, need to use decimal tabs, unless you're typing scientific notation or a series of numbers with a varying amount of digits to the right of the decimal point. For currency, a right-aligned tab is best.

Typing tabbed lists with custom tabs involves the same process as typing tabbed text that use the default tab stops—press Tab to move the cursor under the tab stop, and then type the text.

After tabbed text is typed, you can adjust its placement by dragging the tab stops to the left or right on the ruler—moving, for example, a tab at 2.25" to 2.5" by dragging it one quarter of an inch to the right. When you move tab stops, the text that is typed under the stops must be selected in order for the text to move in conjunction with the tab stops. Figure 4.9 shows the adjustment of a tab stop position.

FIGURE 4.9

Even if you used the Tabs dialog box to create your tab stops, dragging them along the ruler is the fastest way to adjust them.

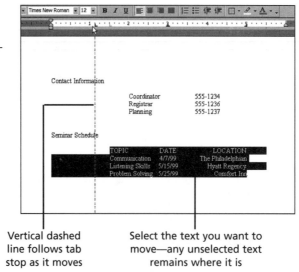

Vertical dashed line follows tab stop as it moves

Select the text you want to move—any unselected text remains where it is

To remove a tab stop, simply drag the tab marker down and off the ruler with your mouse. Any text that is typed under that tab stop moves to the left, falling under a previous tab stop or aligning against the left margin.

Tip

If you want to remove all tabs, select the tabbed text and press Ctrl+Q.

Typing Text in Newspaper Columns

Office 2000 now includes Microsoft Publisher, a great tool for building brochures, flyers, and newsletters. Therefore, Word no longer comes with an installed newsletter template—Microsoft prefers that you use Publisher to create such documents. You might, however, need to format your text into newspaper columns—the type of columns through which text "snakes," flowing down one column and beginning again at the top of the next column.

The best approach for creating columns of text is to type the text first, select it with your mouse, and then apply the columns—choosing to flow your text through two or three columns. Figure 4.10 shows text in two columns under a headline that is not part of the column text.

FIGURE 4.10

Like most formatting, it's best to type the text first, and then apply the column format to selected portions of your document.

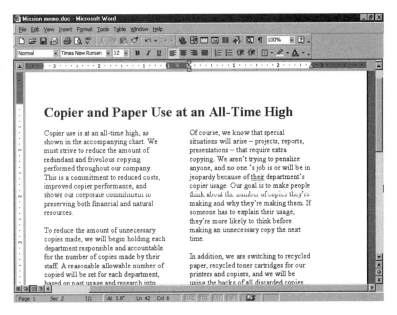

4

Avoid using more than three columns for documents that are set to Portrait orientation. Formatting four or more column results in columns of text that are too narrow to read.

To apply columns to existing text, follow these steps:

1. Type your entire document, including the text you want to place in columns. Allow all text to wrap naturally from margin to margin, pressing Enter only to create blank lines between paragraphs.

2. Select the text that you want to place in columns. Leave unselected any text that is not to be placed in columns—unselected text remains in a single column, which is the width of the page within your margins.

3. Apply your columns to the selected text. You can choose one of the following methods:

    • Click the Columns button on the Standard toolbar. In the resulting palette, drag through the number of columns you want to use (see Figure 4.11).

FIGURE 4.11

Drag, from left to right, through the number of columns you need for the selected text.

   • Choose Format, Columns. In the Columns dialog box (see Figure 4.12), choose the number of columns and select the Width and spacing for them. The Preview window shows the effect of your choices. Click OK to apply your settings.

FIGURE 4.12

By default, columns of equal width are created. You can also choose to place a vertical Line between the columns, which can be helpful to your readers.

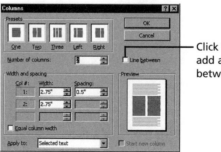

Click this check box to add a vertical line between the columns.

After you've placed your text in columns, you can change the number of columns by reselecting the text and choosing a greater or lesser number of columns for the text.

To remove the effect of columns, choose one column for the selected text from either the Columns button or the Columns dialog box.

Structuring a Document with Tables

Tables are perhaps the most powerful feature in your word processing arsenal, and Word 2000 gives you some very powerful tools for creating, editing, and formatting them in your documents. Tables give your document structure, creating confined spaces in which you can type text. Figure 4.13 shows a résumé—a document with a visually complex layout that can be easily built with tables.

FIGURE 4.13

A table's columns and rows can be positioned and sized to give your document exactly the layout you need.

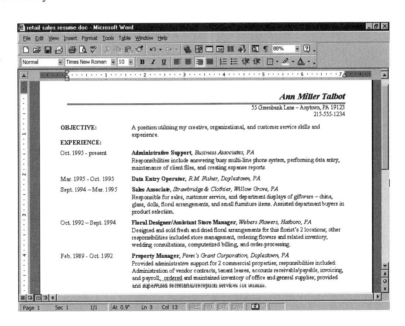

To see how a table can be used to lay out such a document, see Figure 4.14. The table borders are turned on so that you can see the structure of the table.

FIGURE 4.14

By adjusting column widths, the appearance of custom tabs or indents is achieved—with half the effort.

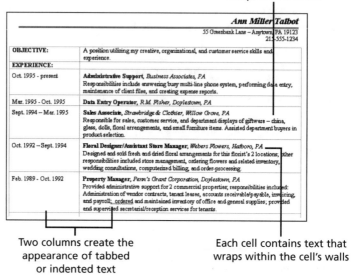

Rows become taller as more text is typed and wraps within them

Two columns create the appearance of tabbed or indented text

Each cell contains text that wraps within the cell's walls

Inserting a Table

Word gives you two ways to add a table to your document—you can draw a table or you can insert a table. You'll learn about drawing a table later today, when building fill-in forms with a table is discussed. For the purposes of a table that is used to structure a document, however, this section focuses on inserting a table.

To insert a table, follow these steps:

1. In your open document, position your cursor where you want to place the table.
2. Choose Table, Insert Table. The Insert table dialog box opens, as shown in Figure 4.15.

FIGURE 4.15

Change the default five-column by two-row table to one with dimensions that meet your needs.

3. Enter the number of columns and rows you want in your table.

4. Click OK to insert the table and close the dialog box.

Tip

By default, all the columns in your new table are of equal width. They can be adjusted later as needed.

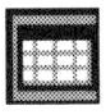

Another way to insert a table involves the Insert Table button button on the Standard toolbar. To insert a table from the toolbar, follow these steps:

1. Place the cursor in your document at the spot where you want to insert the table.

2. Click the Insert Table button. A grid appears, as shown in Figure 4.16.

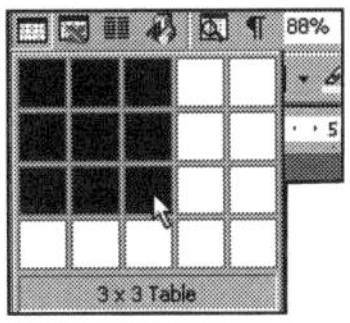

FIGURE 4.16

A table with columns of equal width is created automatically with the Insert Table button.

3. Drag diagonally through the grid, starting in the upper-left corner, until the number of selected blocks in the grid matches the dimensions that you want for your table.

After your table is inserted (using either method), borders appear: There is a thin black line around each cell in the table. It's a good idea to leave the borders on while you're entering table content and adjusting column widths—the borders help you see what you're doing. After you've typed your content and set up the columns to the widths you want, you can turn the borders off if you don't want them to print. The procedure for changing or removing table borders is discussed later today.

If you decide that you don't need your table or that you want to start the table-creation process over, click in any one of your table's cells and choose Table, Delete, Table. You can also remove individual rows, columns, or cells—with these three options, the portion of the table you want to delete must be selected before you issue the command.

Entering and Editing Table Content

Most users start working on a table by typing at least the first row of content, if only to see what adjustments (if any) are required to properly display the table cells' content. After spotting any problems—such as columns that are too narrow, or the need for an additional column or two—you can proceed to finish your text entry and formatting.

Typing Text in Table Cells

To type text into your table, follow these steps:

1. Starting in the first cell (upper left), type the text that is to go in that cell.

2. Press the Tab key to move to the next cell to the right. Type any text into that cell, and press Tab again.

3. Continue typing text in cells and pressing Tab to move to the next cell. When you reach the last cell in the row on the right, press Tab again to move to the first cell in the next row down.

4. If you enter text into all your cells and reach the last cell in the table, pressing Tab adds a new last row.

Need to move backward to the previous cell? Press Shift+Tab.

Do not press the Enter key when typing cell content unless you need more than one paragraph in the cell or the cell is to contain a list of words or short sentences. Think of each cell as a little document—the text wraps within the cell, just as text wraps on your page, as you approach the right margin.

Editing Cell Content

Cell content can be edited much like standard paragraph text—click within the text to position your cursor, use the Backspace or Delete keys to remove unwanted characters, and type new text to replace the removed text. You can also select table text with your mouse, and then type replacement text or delete the selection.

To select entire cells, columns, and rows for the purpose of editing, use the techniques that are described in the following list:

- To select an individual cell, point to the left border of the cell. When your mouse turns to a black right-pointing diagonal arrow (see Figure 4.17), click the mouse once.

FIGURE 4.17

Select a single cell before applying shading, borders, or formatting to all the text inside it.

- To select a row, move your mouse to the left margin outside the table, next to the row you want to select. When your mouse turns to a white right-pointing arrow (see Figure 4.18), click once. Drag up or down to select adjacent rows.

FIGURE 4.18

Click once to select the row, three times to select the entire table.

- To select a column, position your mouse just above the column, outside the table. When your mouse turns to a black down-pointing arrow (see Figure 4.19), click once. Drag left or right to select the contiguous columns.

FIGURE 4.19

Before making changes to a column or series of columns, select them with your mouse.

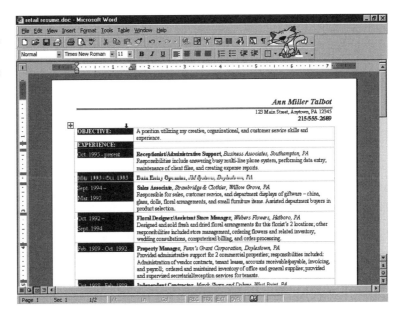

4

Tip

If you prefer to use the keyboard to make selections, use the Shift key in conjunction with your arrow keys to select cells.

Formatting a Table

After typing text into your table (or before, if you already know how you want the table laid out), you want to adjust the way your table looks. Adjusting column width helps your text flow within the table cells. You can also turn borders on and off for display and printing purposes, and you can add shading to cells.

A feature that's new to Word 2000 is the capability to move Word tables freely on the page. While in Print Layout view (View, Print Layout), point to the upper left corner cell; a small box with a four-headed arrow appears (see Figure 4.20). Point to the box and, when your mouse turns to a four-headed arrow, drag the table up, down, left, or right, adjusting its position on the page.

FIGURE 4.20

Word tables are free-moving objects that can be dragged into any position on your page.

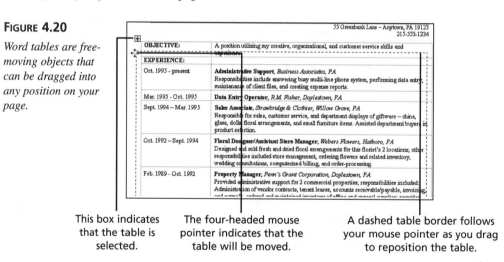

This box indicates that the table is selected.

The four-headed mouse pointer indicates that the table will be moved.

A dashed table border follows your mouse pointer as you drag to reposition the table.

If your table will appear along with nontable text, you can adjust the way the table and the nontable text coexist by choosing Table, Table Properties from the menu to open the Table Properties dialog box. Click the Table tab (see Figure 4.21), and then choose the Alignment and Text wrapping settings that meet your needs.

FIGURE 4.21

Place text alongside a table by choosing how text is to wrap around your table in the document.

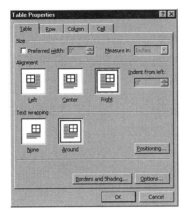

Figure 4.22 shows a table set to right alignment, with Text wrapping set to Around. The text lines up on the left side of the table and wraps under it.

FIGURE 4.22

Text can only wrap around a table if the table's width is less than that of the page within your margins.

This candidate shows great promise due to the variety of skills she's acquired without job-hopping. She obviously can perform a great number of tasks on the job and seems willing to learn new skills.	**OBJECTIVE:**	A position utilizing my creative, organizational, and customer service skills and experience.
	EXPERIENCE:	
	Oct. 1995 - present	**Administrative Support**, *Business Associates, PA* Responsibilities include answering busy multi-line phone system, performing data entry, maintenance of client files, and creating expense reports.
	Mar. 1995 - Oct. 1995	**Data Entry Operator**, *R.M. Fisher, Doylestown, PA*
	Sept. 1994 – Mar. 1995	**Sales Associate**, *Strawbridge & Clothier, Willow Grove, PA* Responsible for sales, customer service, and department displays of giftware – china, glass, dolls, floral arrangements, and small furniture items. Assisted department buyers in product selection.

Ann interviewed well, and seems to get along with coworkers. The references we called had nothing but wonderful things to say about her.

Changing Column Width

To adjust the width of your columns, you have a few choices. Choose the one that you find most effective and easy to perform:

- Point to the vertical seam on the right side of the column you want to adjust. Your mouse pointer turns to a two-headed arrow, at which point you can drag to the right to widen the column, or left to make it narrower. Figure 4.23 shows a column that is being widened with this technique.

4

FIGURE 4.23

Point to and drag the vertical seam between columns to adjust column width.

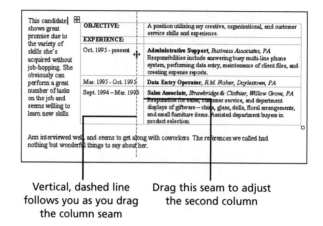

Vertical, dashed line
follows you as you drag
the column seam

Drag this seam to adjust
the second column

- Drag the Table Column markers on the ruler. While your cursor is within the table, the ruler changes to show these markers, as shown in Figure 4.24. Point to the marker above the right-hand seam of the column you want to adjust, and drag the marker to the right to widen the column or to the left to narrow it.

Column marker for
the second column

Use the ruler's calibrations
to determine your new
column width

FIGURE 4.24

Your mouse turns to a two-headed arrow when you point to the Table Column markers.

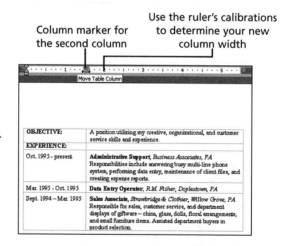

- Choose Table, Table Properties to open the Table Properties dialog box, and click the Column tab (see Figure 4.25). The active column or columns (the ones you've selected or the one in which your cursor is located) are listed in the dialog box, along with the current width measurement. Enter a new measurement in the Preferred Width box, and then click OK. The measurement is applied to the selected columns.

FIGURE 4.25

For precise column adjustments, use the Table Properties box.

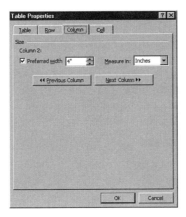

Tip

You can also right-click your table and choose Table Properties from the shortcut menu to open the Table Properties dialog box.

Tip

Although you can adjust row height by dragging the horizontal seams between rows (but only while you are in Print Layout view), it's a good idea to allow the text within your cells to determine row height. The cells grow taller to accommodate several lines of text.

4

Using Borders and Shading

When a table is used purely for document layout—to give the illusion of indents and tabs—you probably won't want the borders of the table to show when the document is printed. There are times, however, when the borders are useful—to create visual breaks between paragraphs in your cells, for example, or to direct the reader's eye to specific cells. Borders draw attention and divide the table into visual sections.

When you create a table, it has borders on all four sides of each cell. Using your mouse to select sections of the table and the Border button to choose the type of border you want from the Border palette, you can turn borders on and off throughout your table. The Border button displays a palette of borders (see Figure 4.26) that you can use to turn borders on and off in any selected cell, column, row, or block of cells in your table.

FIGURE 4.26

*Select a portion of
your table and then
select the border
option for it.*

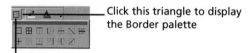

Click this triangle to display
the Border palette

The button itself applies the
border that is displayed on
the button face

Table 4.2 shows the various borders that are found on the Border button's palette. Simply click the list triangle to the right of the Border button to display the border options that are listed in Table 4.2.

TABLE 4.2   BORDER PALETTE BUTTONS

Button	Effect
	Single border outside border
	All borders
	Top border
	Left border
	Inside horizontal border
	Descending diagonal (places a diagonal line through your selected cells)
	Horizontal line (places a horizontal line through the middle of your selected cells)
	Inside border
	No border (turns off all borders in the selected cells)
	Bottom border
	Right border
	Inside vertical border
	Ascending diagonal (places a diagonal line inside your selected cells)

You can also apply borders with the Borders and Shading dialog box. This dialog box, shown in Figure 4.27, gives you options for the placement and style of border lines, including graphic borders. To use this dialog box to change your table's borders, select the table (or a section thereof) and choose Format, Borders and Shading.

FIGURE 4.27

Choose the Setting, Style, Color, Width, and position for your borders within the selected section of your table

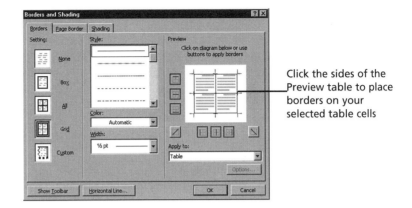

Click the sides of the Preview table to place borders on your selected table cells

Figure 4.28 shows a table with a variety of border effects—portions of the table have no borders, and borders are used in other sections to draw attention to important information in the table's cells.

This border creates an underline for the table's title

This cell contains important data

4

FIGURE 4.28

Borders can create interesting graphical effects for your table and give your content added structure on the page.

Borders have been turned off here

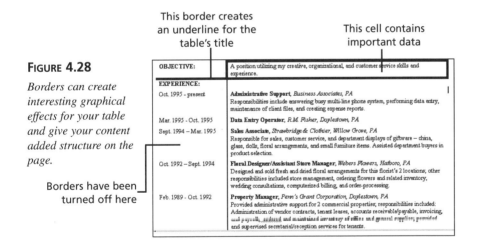

Use the Borders and Shading dialog box to apply shading to cells within your table. Select a cell or cells in your table, and then choose Format, Borders and Shading. Click the Shading tab (shown in Figure 4.29), and choose a solid Fill color or Pattern to fill in your selected cells. Patterns range from a series of shades of gray to dots, slashes, and checkerboard fills.

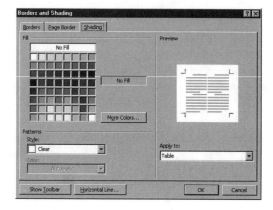

FIGURE 4.29

Choose one of 64 different colors and shades for your fill, or apply a pattern to the selected cells.

Figure 4.30 shows a table with shaded and patterned fills that are used to direct the reader to important information and to create sections within the table.

FIGURE 4.30

Create a divider by filling an entire row with shading or a pattern.

If you're applying shading to a cell that is to contain text, avoid dark colors for the fill color and don't use patterned fills. Both choices make it difficult to read the text in the cell.

If you want to choose from a variety of graphical horizontal lines (patterned, colored, or repeated pictures that form a line), click the Horizontal Line button in the Borders and Shading dialog box. The Horizontal Line dialog box opens, displaying an array of interesting lines you can apply to your cell or table.

> **Tip**
>
> If you don't want any sign of the table's cells to appear, even onscreen, you can turn off your table's gridlines. Choose Table, Hide Gridlines from the menu. Bear in mind that not viewing your gridlines makes it difficult to select table cells and make any width adjustments. It's best to turn the gridlines off only after all changes and formatting are complete.

Using AutoFormat to Quickly Format a Table

If you don't have any significant preferences as to how wide a column is or what color your borders are, you can use Word's Table AutoFormat feature to let Word format your table for you.

To use AutoFormat, click anywhere in your table and choose Table, Table AutoFormat. The Table AutoFormat dialog box opens (see Figure 4.31), offering a wide variety of preset table formats.

FIGURE 4.31

View the formats' previews and choose which of the AutoFormat's attributes to apply to your table.

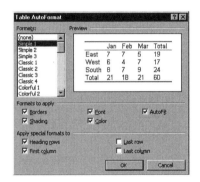

4

By default, the AutoFormat you choose applies the borders, shading, fonts, and overall layout you see in the Preview window. You can control which of these formats are actually applied to your table by checking and unchecking the Formats to apply and Apply special formats to options. As you add and remove check marks in these two sections, the Preview of the selected AutoFormat changes to show you the effect of your changes.

When you've selected an AutoFormat and adjusted it to meet your needs, click OK to apply it to your table and close the dialog box.

> **Tip**
>
> If you've already gone to the trouble of adjusting column widths in your table, be sure to turn off (uncheck) the AutoFit option in the AutoFormat dialog box. Left on, this option resizes all columns to be only as wide as the widest entry in the column.

Using Word Tables to Build a Form

Tables can be used to create fill-in forms—to be filled in on paper after printing the forms or onscreen. Forms can be created for everything from a customized fax cover sheet, to a questionnaire, to a job application. On Day 5, "Improving Document Function," you'll learn to automate your forms, controlling the user's onscreen input. Today, you'll create a simple form that can be printed out for use on paper or filled out onscreen, but with no user prompts or automation.

It's a good idea to start the form creation process with a sketch—figure out what information you'll want to provide and ask for on the form, and how you want it laid out. Planning on paper speeds the process of building the form onscreen.

After you decide on your overall layout, you can begin building the table. Depending on the layout of your form, you can probably use the structured table format you looked at earlier today—a rectangular table with columns and rows of equal dimension. Figure 4.32 shows a fax cover sheet form, suitable for use onscreen or on paper.

FIGURE 4.32

Use a standard rectangular table to give structure to a simple form such as a fax cover sheet.

Turn off the borders around the cells on the left to achieve the look of a real form

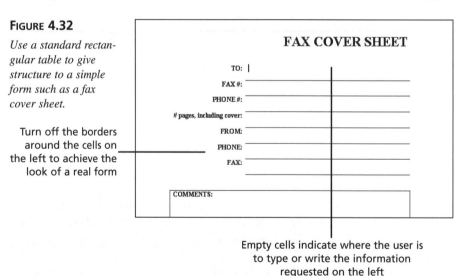

Empty cells indicate where the user is
to type or write the information
requested on the left

If, however, your form design won't fit neatly into a box of columns and rows, you can draw a table to fit your exact layout needs. Figure 4.33 shows a more free-form layout, which is much easier to create with Word's table drawing tools.

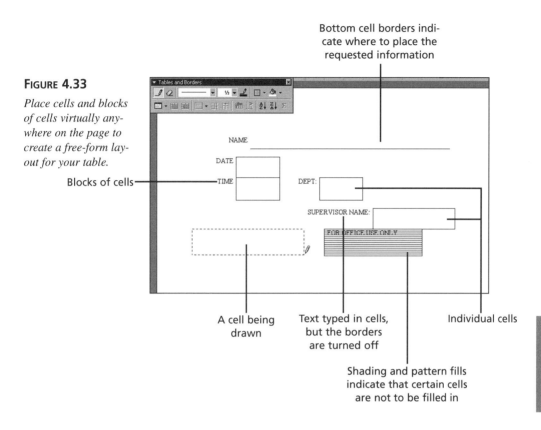

Bottom cell borders indi-
cate where to place the
requested information

FIGURE 4.33

*Place cells and blocks
of cells virtually any-
where on the page to
create a free-form lay-
out for your table.*

Blocks of cells

A cell being
drawn

Text typed in cells,
but the borders
are turned off

Individual cells

Shading and pattern fills
indicate that certain cells
are not to be filled in

To draw a table, you'll want to display the Tables and Borders toolbar, which is activated by clicking the Tables and Borders button on the Standard toolbar. The toolbar contains the tools that are described in Table 4.3.

TABLE 4.3   THE TABLES AND BORDERS TOOLBAR

Button Name	Icon	What the button does/how to use it
Draw Table		Draws individual cells. Click and drag to draw a cell anywhere on your page. Draw adjoining cells by clicking and dragging from any corner of the existing cell. Create two or more new cells by adding horizontal and vertical lines within existing cells.
Eraser		Remove cells and cell walls by clicking the table borders.

continues

TABLE 4.3   CONTINUED

Button Name	Icon	What the button does/how to use it
Line Style		Click the list box to see a variety of lines— single, double, triple, and graphic styles such as zigzags and patterns.
Line Weight		Choose the thickness of your line from this list. After selecting a thickness, click on one of your cell walls with the Draw Table tool. The thickness you choose can also be applied to the next cells you draw in the current document.
Border Color		Click the button to see a palette of colors. To apply the chosen color, click the walls of your drawn cells. If you choose the color before drawing the cells, the next cells you draw will be bordered in the selected color.
Borders		Just like the Border tool on the Formatting toolbar, this one displays a palette of borders—top, left, right, bottom, no border. Click the triangle to the right of the button to display the palette, and choose the border you want to add. If the button in the palette is already on, clicking it removes the border from the active cell.
Shading Color		Click the triangle to the right of the button to see a palette of colors with which to fill your cells. The selected color can be applied to the active cell, to another cell you click on after choosing the color, or to the next cell you draw.
Insert Table		Use this tool to build a standard fixed-width table. The tool works just like the one on the Standard toolbar.
Merge Cells		If you want to make two or more cells into one large cell, select them and click this button. If there is text in any or all of the cells, the text is jumbled into the single merged cell.
Split cells		Convert a single cell into several cells. A dialog box opens, from which you can select how many columns and rows you want to create from your single cell.

Button Name	Icon	What the button does/how to use it
Alignment		Choose how the text is to align within the selected cell. Click the triangle to the right of the button to see a palette of alignment options.
Distribute Rows Evenly		Select a series of rows and click this button to make them all equal in height.
Distribute Columns Evenly		Select a series of columns and click this button to make them all equal in width.
Table Autoformat		This button opens a dialog box from which you can choose preset table formats. The formats include border, shading, alignment, and color styles.
Change Text Direction		Click this button to turn horizontal text into vertical text. Each click of the button shows you a different directional change—stop clicking when the text appears as you want it.
Sort Ascending		Put your selected cells in alphabetical (A to Z) or numerical (lowest to highest) order.
Sort Descending		Put your selected cells in Z to A order. If they contain numeric content, they are sorted highest to lowest.
AutoSum		Taken from Excel's Standard toolbar, this tool totals the cells above or to the left of your active cell.

You can type text outside your cells by adjusting the settings for your table. Choose Table Properties from the Table menu or right-click the cells around which you want to place text. Choose Table Properties from the shortcut menu and, in the Table tab, click the Around option (see Figure 4.34).

FIGURE 4.34

You can place text around your free-form table's cells if you set the Table Properties to wrap text Around.

Figure 4.35 shows a form with accompanying paragraph text that wraps around the table cells.

FIGURE 4.35

Place instructional text around your form's cells to assist users in completing the form.

Table cells —

Nontable paragraph text —

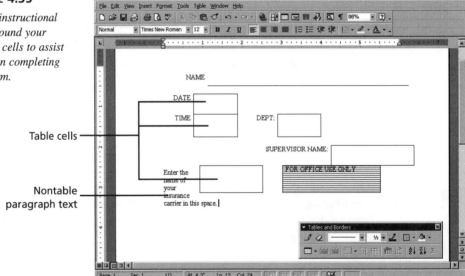

Summary

Today you learned about Word 2000's tools for controlling the placement and flow of text over the pages of your document through the use of indents, tabs, margins, and tables. Day 5 will build on your table skills, and you'll learn to automate forms with user-interactive fields, break your document into sections, and control the appearance of each section through the use of headers and footers. In addition, you'll learn to create your own templates from documents you create, enabling you to build many documents from one common foundation.

Q&A

Q Can I set lots of different indents throughout my document?

A Of course. Your indents go into effect from the point where your cursor is active when the indents are set. As you move down your document, you can set new indents for each paragraph of your document, if needed.

Q Why might I use a dot leader tab?

A Leaders are characters that lead up to tabbed text. They help guide the reader's eye from one side of a tabbed list to the other. You see them used in Tables of Contents, where they visually connect topics with page numbers on the other side of the page.

Q Can I turn existing text into a table without cutting and pasting the text into the table cells?

A Yes. Tabbed lists can easily be converted to a table. Select the tabbed text and choose Table, Insert Table, or click the Insert Table button once. A table is formed from the text, and the tabs you typed when the list was created are used to determine individual cells. For each line of tabbed text, a row is created, and for each tab across the page, a column is built.

4

Workshop

The section that follows is a quick quiz about the day. If you have any problems answering any of the questions, see the section that follows the quiz for all the answers.

Quiz

1. Name two ways to set a half-inch left indent.
2. In a blank document, default tabs are set at what intervals across the page?
3. How many custom tabs can you set in any one document?
4. Describe at least two ways to build a table in your Word document.
5. True or false: You can hide the fact that your document was built with a table by turning off the table's borders.

Quiz Answers

1. To set a left half-inch indent, you can drag the top triangle indent marker one half-inch to the right, or you can press Tab at the beginning of the paragraph. You can also choose Format, Paragraph, and set a left indent of 0.5 in the Paragraph dialog box.
2. Default tabs are set to every half-inch across the full width of the page.
3. You can set an unlimited number of custom tabs in any document. You can set as many as you need across the width of the page and you can, conceivably, set a different group of tabs for every line on the page.
4. You can build a table by Inserting one from the Table menu or by using the Insert Table button on the toolbar. You can also Draw a table one cell at a time with the Draw Table button.
5. True. When tables are used to determine document structure, they are often hidden in the printed version of the document. To turn off the default table borders, select the entire table (or the portion for which you don't want borders) and click the Borders button. Choose No borders from the palette. You can also set borders to None in the Borders and Shading dialog box, which is found by choosing Format, Borders and Shading. Again, the table or a portion thereof must be selected before you open the dialog box and turn off your borders.

DAY 5

Improving Document Function

Day 4, "Building a Complex Document," showed you how to control the appearance of your documents with indents, tabs, and tables. Tables, as you discovered, can be used to give your document structure and to create forms for people to fill in onscreen or on paper. Today builds on these tools—as well as on the skills you acquired in Days 1, "Taking a Tour of Office 2000," 2, "Creating a Letter," and 3, "Enhancing a Basic Word Document"—by covering the following topics:

- Turning table cells into interactive fields
- Inserting section breaks within your document
- Using headers and footers to add more information to your document's pages
- Using one document as the foundation for another by turning it into a template

Automating a Form with Fields

Forms that are created with tables rely on common sense to tell the form users where to enter their information, whether the information is written on a printed form or typed into a form onscreen. Figure 5.1 shows a form that relies on table borders to indicate where user entries are to be placed.

FIGURE 5.1

The bottom borders on the cells in the right-hand column indicate where to enter data.

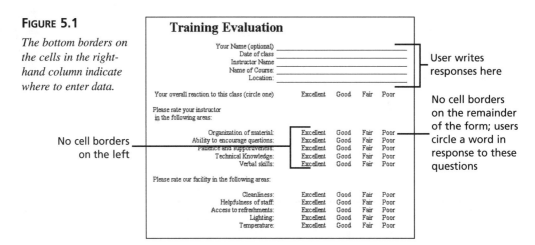

The limitation of such forms is that they rely on the user's vocabulary and interpretation of the questions to elicit answers. What if you need the responses on the form to meet specific requirements? What if there are only three possible responses? You can waste space on the form listing them, and then hope that the person filling out the form can see them and read the instructions to limit their response to one of the three approved responses. Or you can provide a field within the form that offers just those three responses and requires that the user choose one and only one of them.

NEW TERM A *field*, in the context of a form, is a space to enter data or make a selection. The data that is entered or the selection that is made within the field is stored as part of the entire form, which in some cases is used to build a larger database. *Field* has similar definition in terms of a database (as you'll learn on Days 8, "Building an Excel Database," and 13, "Setting Up a Database"), in which a field is a component of a database record. For example, if the record in a database stores someone's Name, Address, City, State, and Zip, each of those components is a field.

There are three types of fields that you can add to your form:

- **Text box**—The user is prompted to type text, any text, into a field box. This type of field is best used for things such as names and addresses—things only the user knows.

- **Check boxes**—This option is great for choosing one or more from a series of options (use in "check all that apply" situations) or for choosing Yes or No in response to a question. The text that accompanies each check box indicates to the user what checking or not checking the box means in the context of the form.

- **List boxes**—When you want to control the responses your users give, this is your best option. For example, if the user must indicate which department he or she works in, a list of departments drops down, and the user can select one from the list. This prevents people from saying that they work in "Accounting" when the correct department title is "Financial Services."

Consider the following uses for forms with interactive fields:

- **Fax cover sheets**—Use fields for the recipient and sender names, phone numbers, and reply boxes (Urgent, For Your Review, Please Reply).

- **Memorandums**—Use fields for the date, the cc: names, and any data that the user might select from a list of options.

- **Surveys**—Forms that ask opinions are a great use for fields. Use check boxes to indicate a selection from multiple choices or true/false questions.

- **Applications**—People not understanding the nature of a question can be the biggest stumbling block to an appropriate answer. Giving the user choices in a list box assures consistency and gives the user a contextual resource for interpreting your questions.

Inserting Fields

After you've decided which questions or sections on your form might be improved by the use of an interactive field, you can begin to insert fields into the appropriate cells.

To add fields to your table form, follow these steps:

1. Create your table form, including the text that poses questions or indicates what information goes where. Figure 5.2 shows such a form, ready for the insertion of fields.

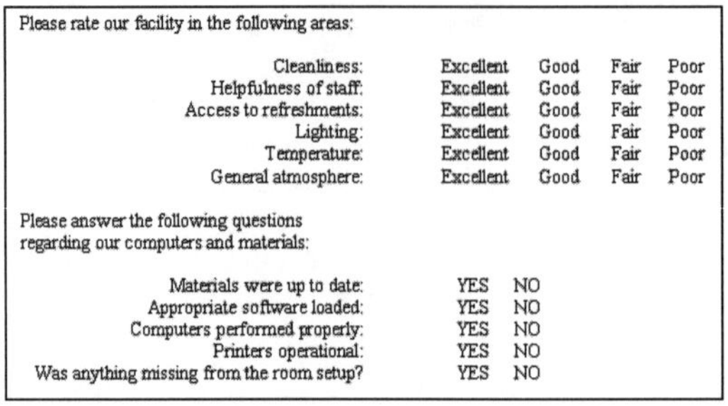

FIGURE 5.2

Create a document that can serve as a questionnaire/form by building tables.

Please rate our facility in the following areas:

	Excellent	Good	Fair	Poor
Cleanliness:	Excellent	Good	Fair	Poor
Helpfulness of staff:	Excellent	Good	Fair	Poor
Access to refreshments:	Excellent	Good	Fair	Poor
Lighting:	Excellent	Good	Fair	Poor
Temperature:	Excellent	Good	Fair	Poor
General atmosphere:	Excellent	Good	Fair	Poor

Please answer the following questions
regarding our computers and materials:

	YES	NO
Materials were up to date:	YES	NO
Appropriate software loaded:	YES	NO
Computers performed properly:	YES	NO
Printers operational:	YES	NO
Was anything missing from the room setup?	YES	NO

2. Display the Forms toolbar by right-clicking one of the currently displayed toolbars and choosing Forms from the list (see Figure 5.3).

FIGURE 5.3

You can also choose View, Toolbars to see this list of available toolbars.

3. Click in the first cell that is to contain a field.
4. On the Forms toolbar (see Figure 5.4), click the button for the type of field you want to insert.

FIGURE 5.4

All the tools you need to create and customize your fields are available on the Forms toolbar.

(Table 5.1 identifies the tools on the Forms toolbar.)

TABLE 5.1 THE FORMS TOOLBAR BUTTONS

Button Name		Description/How to use it
Text Forms Field	ab	Click this button to insert a text box—a field into which the user can type their response to a question.
Check Box Form Field	☑	Add one of these check boxes after text (such the word *yes* or *no)*.
Drop-Down Form Field		When you want your users to pick a response from a list, click this button.
Form Field Options		Click this button to open a dialog box that enables you to control how the selected field is to work—what type of data is to be accepted in the field or which items to offer in the list box.
Draw Table		If you forgot to add a cell to your table, click this button and draw the cells you need. You can also use this tool to subdivide one of your existing cells.
Insert Table		Although you should have your table created before starting this process, you can use this tool to build the table from scratch, indicating the number of columns and rows you want.
Insert Frame		If you need to place a box around something on your document and turn it into a movable object, select the content and then click this button. After an item is framed, it can be moved anywhere on the document.
Form Field Shading	a	Click this button to shade the fields you've created. This button is on by default, making it easier to see the fields you've added to your document.
Protect Form	🔒	Protecting a form prevents users from changing your field settings. Be sure this button is off before trying to add or edit fields, and then turn it on before you save and distribute your form for electronic use.

5. After inserting the field you want, click the Form Field Options button [108] to set up the field. Figure 5.5 shows the drop-down Form Field Options dialog box, with the list of options that the field will display being set up.

Items already added

FIGURE 5.5

Establish the settings for your field in the Field Options dialog box.

Use these Move arrows to change the order of selected items in the list

Type the items you want to see in your drop list here and click the Add button

To remove an item, select it from the list and click this button

6. Click OK in the Field Options box to return to your table and continue adding and setting up fields. To add a check box field (for Yes/No responses), click the Check Box Form Field button, and then set up the field by clicking the Form Field Options button. The Check Box Form Field Options dialog box appears in Figure 5.6.

FIGURE 5.6

Choose the default value for your check box (on or off).

Choose the point size (if not the default Auto) for the check box

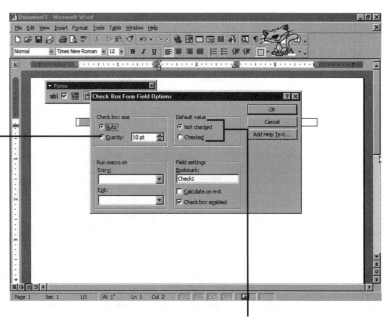

Is the box on (checked) or off (unchecked) by default?

7. When your fields are set up, click the Protect Form button to prevent users from changing your field settings when they use the form.

8. Save the form and place it in a publicly accessible folder on your network or distribute it via email or some other means to those who might need to use it.

Although the form shown in Figure 5.2 doesn't show the portion of the form where the user enters their name and other particulars, you can assume that the form has them. Try to create that portion of the form (add it at the top of the page); see Figure 5.7, which shows a table that requires Text fields and the Text Form Field dialog box.

Create this small (two columns, two rows) table, formatted as shown, for the user to enter text

FIGURE 5.7

Create space for the form user to enter his or her name and the name of the course taken. This portion of the form uses text fields.

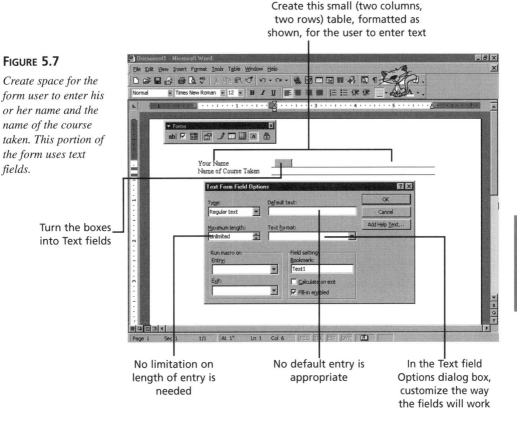

Turn the boxes into Text fields

No limitation on length of entry is needed

No default entry is appropriate

In the Text field Options dialog box, customize the way the fields will work

5

Creating Help for Form Users

Many people don't follow instructions, and might answer a question incorrectly because they didn't understand it. Unless you crowd your form with instructions, you run the risk of receiving incomplete forms. Having help available makes it less likely that questions will be skipped, and more likely that those that are answered are answered appropriately.

If you want to assist your users in working with the form, you can create your own help prompts. Follow these steps:

1. Click on the inserted field for which you want to create a help prompt. If your form is protected, click the Protect Form button [113] to toggle the protection off.

2. Using the Forms toolbar, click the Form Field Options button [108].

3. In the Field Options dialog box, click the Add Help Text button. This opens the Form Field Help Text dialog box, shown in Figure 5.8.

FIGURE 5.8

Help your users by supplying instructional text that they can access easily while using the form.

4. Choose how you want help displayed:

   - **On the Status Bar**—When the field is active on a protected form, the user sees your help text (up to 138 characters) on the Status Bar at the bottom of the Word application window.

   - **When the Help (F1) key is pressed**—A good choice if your users know to press F1 for context-sensitive help. When the field is active, pressing F1 displays your help text.

5. Type your help text in the Type your own box on one or both of the tabs, and click OK to return to the Field Options dialog box. Figure 5.9 shows help text in the Help Key (F1) tab.

FIGURE 5.9

It's your form, and you have the best idea of what people need to know to use it. Create your own help text for the most effective assistance.

6. Click OK to close the Field Options dialog box and return to your form. Remember to protect your form before saving and distributing it—unless the form is protected, none of the help you've just created appears, and the form won't work.

Figure 5.10 shows the help that appears when a check box field is activated by a user.

FIGURE 5.10

Make sure your help text is as short and simple as possible.

Breaking a Document into Sections

NEW TERM Documents that exceed a single page of text contain *page breaks*—points at which the text reached the bottom margin and flowed onto a subsequent page. These breaks happen naturally as you type. You can also force them (by pressing Ctrl+Enter) to make the next text you type appear at the top of the next page. These forced breaks enable you to control the flow of text, keeping a single topic from being split over two pages or keeping a certain document element on its own page. Word gives you another type of break, called a *section break*, which enables you to break a document into pieces—by chapters or topics, for example—and treat each piece of the document differently.

Why break your document into sections? For increased flexibility throughout the document. Each section of your document can have different page numbers, different headers and footers, different margins, and different page orientation (portrait or landscape).

5

NEW TERM   *Headers* and *footers* are text that appear at the top (header) or bottom (footer) of each page in your document. By default, your headers and footers are consistent throughout your document, but through the use of section breaks, you can have different headers and footers for each section in your document.

Like page breaks, some section breaks can occur naturally. If you change your margins and choose to apply the change to a selection of text (rather than to the whole document), a section break is inserted automatically. The same thing happens if you change the orientation of a single page in your document. These automatic section breaks can be ignored as you work on your document, and they rarely affect your page numbering or headers and footers if you inserted these elements after incurring the section breaks.

Adding your own section breaks, however, gives you real control over your document's appearance. To force a section break in your document, follow these steps:

1. Position your cursor at the point in your document where you want to create the section break.

2. Choose Insert, Break to open the Break dialog box (see Figure 5.11).

FIGURE 5.11

Force a section break by choosing how and where to insert one.

3. Choose from the following list of Section break types:

   - **Next page**—When this type of section break is selected, a page break is inserted as well, and the new section begins on the inserted page.
   - **Continuous**—The section break is added at the cursor, and no page is added to your document.
   - **Even Page**—A new section is created for your next even page. If the section break is inserted on an even page, the next odd-numbered page is left blank.
   - **Odd Page**—A new section is created for your next odd page. If this section break is inserted on an odd page, the next even-numbered page is left blank.

4. Click OK to insert the selected section break and close the dialog box.

To see which section you're in, check the bottom of your application window. As you click to position your cursor at different points throughout your document, the section you're in at the time is displayed on the status bar (see Figure 5.12).

FIGURE 5.12

According to the status bar, the cursor is active in Section 2.

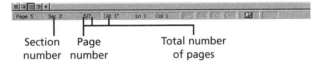

Section number   Page number   Total number of pages

Adjusting Section Page Numbers

One of the most common reasons for inserting a section break is to have different page numbers for a given section or sections of the document. Perhaps Section 1 is the cover page and table of contents, and therefore doesn't have any page numbers. Maybe Section 2 needs lowercase Roman numerals for page numbers and Section 3 needs standard Arabic numbers. Only with section breaks is this level of differentiation between conceptual parts of a document physically possible.

To change the page numbering in different sections of your document, follow these steps:

1. Position your cursor where your page numbering (regardless of number format) is to begin.

2. Choose Insert, Page Numbers, and open the Page Numbers dialog box (see Figure 5.13).

FIGURE 5.13

It's easier to start by numbering the whole document and then change the numbering in specific sections.

5

3. Choose the Position and Alignment for your numbers (don't worry about the format of your numbers for right now).

4. Click OK to insert the page numbers and close the dialog box.

After numbering the document, you can change the numbering in individual sections. For each section that requires different page numbers, follow these steps to change the type and starting number for the section:

1. Consult the status bar to see which section you're in; then go to the beginning of the section for which you want to reformat your page numbers.

2. Choose Insert, Page Numbers, and click the Format button in the Page Numbers dialog box.

3. In the Page Number Format dialog box (see Figure 5.14), choose a Number format.

FIGURE 5.14

Choose from Arabic (1,2,3), letters of the alphabet, and upper- and lowercase Roman numerals for your section's page numbers.

4. If your document has chapters and you've applied Heading styles to the chapter titles, click the Include chapter number option, and choose the Heading style you used.

5. If don't want the page numbers to continue from the preceding section, click the Start at box and type the page number with which your section is to begin.

6. Click OK to return to the Page Numbers dialog box, and click OK in that dialog box to apply your changes.

For each section in your document for which you need to change the format or starting number of your page numbers, repeat the preceding steps.

Adding Headers and Footers

Headers and footers serve a variety of purposes in a document. Sometimes they contain copyright information, which is important to the author or publisher who wants to make sure that every page is attributed to them. If your document has separate chapters throughout, you might want to have the chapter titles appear in the header. Typical header/footer content is displayed in Figure 5.15, which shows a footer that includes the copyright, page number (plus total number of pages in the document), and the date. Because the footer is active, the Header and Footer toolbar is displayed.

FIGURE 5.15

Headers and footers visually frame your pages, and they contain important information for your readers.

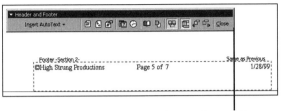

The Header and Footer toolbar appears whenever the header or footer in the document is active.

To add a header or footer to your document, follow these steps:

1. Choose View, Header and Footer. It doesn't matter where your cursor is in the document—by default, the header or footer content appears on all pages until you add section breaks and remove the header/footer content from specific sections.

2. The Header and Footer toolbar appears onscreen, and your document layer is dimmed, displaying the Header area in a dashed box (see Figure 5.16). If you weren't already in Print Layout view, note that you are switched to that view as soon as you view your header/footer.

FIGURE 5.16

Note the Center tab on the ruler. The header box is preformatted for your header content.

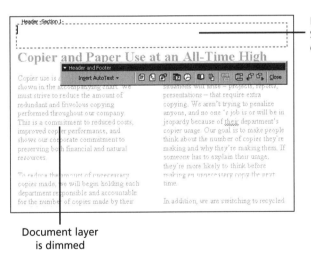

Header area for Section 1 of the document

5

Document layer is dimmed

3. Type your header content, and then click the Switch Between Header and Footer button ▣ to display the footer area.

4. Type your footer content, and then click Close on the Header and Footer toolbar. The toolbar disappears and your document returns to normal display (see Figure 5.17).

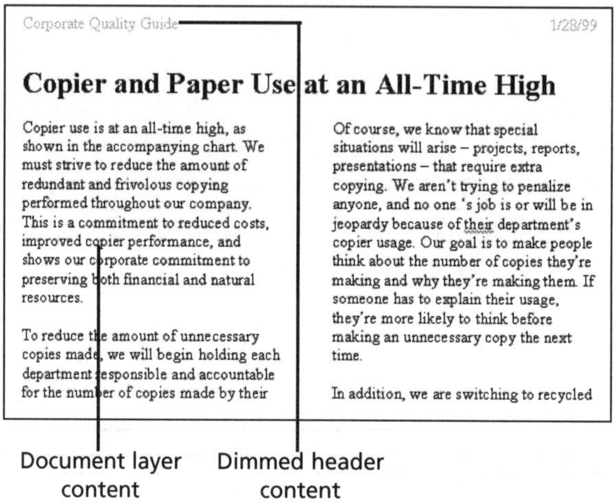

Document layer content   Dimmed header content

You can add your own text to the header and footer or use the Header and Footer toolbar buttons to insert automatic content. Table 5.2 describes the Header and Footer toolbar's buttons.

TABLE 5.2   HEADER AND FOOTER TOOLBAR BUTTONS

Button Name		Description/How you use it
Insert AutoText	 Insert AutoText ▾	Choose from an installed list of typical header and footer content, such as Author, Page Number, and Date.
Insert Page Number	 #	Click this button to automatically insert the current page number on each page. As you add or delete pages from your document, the numbers that appear on each page update accordingly.
Insert Number of Pages	 🗂	Use this button to add the total number of pages in the document to the header or footer content.
Format Page Number	 🗗	If you want to switch to a different number format, click this button to open the Page Number Format dialog box.

Insert Date		The system date is added to your header or footer when you click this button. Each time you open the document, that day's system date replaces the previous date content in the header/footer.
Insert Time		Insert the system time into the header or footer each time you open the document.
Page Setup		Click this button to open the Page Setup dialog box, which includes settings for the vertical distance between the header and footer and the edge of the paper.
Show/Hide Document Text		If you find it visually distracting to see the dimmed document text, click this button to hide it. When it is hidden, click this button to redisplay it.
Same as Previous		Click this button to break the connection between the previous section's header and footer and the current section. Click this button to break the link between sections before you make any changes to the current section's header and footer content, or before you make changes that apply to all sections.
Switch Between Header and Footer		As the name indicates, this button switches your view from header to footer and back again.
Show Previous		When working in a multisection document, use this button to go to the previous section's header or footer.
Show Next		Click this button to see the next section's header or footer content.
Close		This button closes the Header and Footer toolbar and puts all changes you've made into effect.

5

Tip

To keep your header or footer content visually separate from your document text when it is printed, keep the header/footer content to one line, and consider adding a border below the header text and above the footer text using the Border button on the toolbar.

> **Tip**
>
> If you have a lot of text to add to your header or footer, you might want to increase the header and footer margins. To do this, choose File, Page Setup, and then adjust the From edge measurement for the Header or Footer. The default is a half-inch, which is sufficient for most single-line headers and footers.

Saving Your Document as a Template

A *template*, as defined earlier in this book, is a document on which other documents are based. When you start the Word program, you are given a blank document that is based on the Blank Document template. This template contains the basic settings for a standard document—margins, line spacing, fonts, and tabs. Your documents can become templates, making their content and formatting the foundation for future documents, speeding up the process of building a document that's similar to one you've already created, and—if they are created for other users to work with—providing instruction in the form of sample text. Figure 5.18 shows a document designed to be saved and used as a template—its content instructs the potential user and sets the stage for a quick document completion.

FIGURE 5.18

A template document contains only the content that every document based on it will need, plus any sample or instructional text to assist the user.

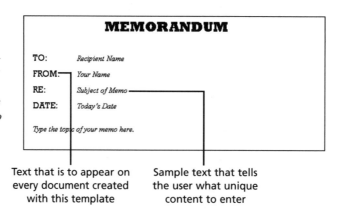

Text that is to appear on every document created with this template

Sample text that tells the user what unique content to enter

The difference, beyond content, between a template and a normal document is the file type; this is something you can establish when you save the document. The process of saving a document as a template is as important as the template's content—if you don't do it properly, you won't have access to the template in the future.

To save your document as a template, follow these steps:

1. Either start with an existing document or create one that contains the common and sample content you'll need to build future documents.

2. Choose File, Save As. If the document has already been saved as a regular document, this opens the Save As dialog box, freeing you to continue with this procedure.

3. Click the Save as type list box (see Figure 5.19) and select Document Template (.dot) from the list.

FIGURE 5.19

Merely typing .dot *at the end of your filename does not turn it into a template. You must select the Document Template format.*

4. Notice that the Save in box automatically changes to display the Templates folder. You must save to this folder (or a subfolder of it) in order for your template to be available for future use.

5. Type a name for your template. Don't type the file extension; let Word add that for you.

6. Click Save. The dialog box closes, and the template's name appears on the title bar.

To use this new template, choose File, New, and click the General tab in the New dialog box. Your template appears in the tab (see Figure 5.20); when you double-click it, a new document opens, containing the content and formatting of your template.

5

FIGURE 5.20

Find your new template on the General tab in the New dialog box.

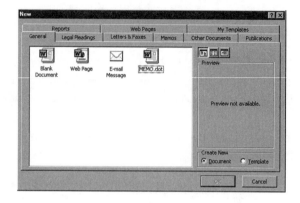

Figure 5.21 shows a new document created from the template you built in this procedure; note that the title bar says Document2. The template is not open, but a new document that is based on it is.

FIGURE 5.21

Use your template to build a new document. Changes that are made to the new document do not affect the template in any way.

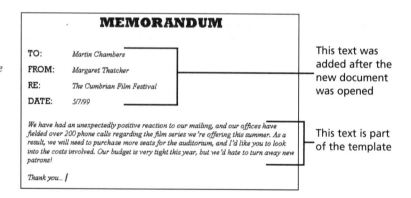

Editing a Template

Your templates can be edited like any other document—open the template (File, Open, and navigate to the Templates folder) and make any changes to content or formatting that you need. Save the file (File, Save or Ctrl+S), and the changes are updated. Your template, with your changes, is ready to be used immediately.

Creating a Template Category

In the preceding section, you saved your template to the Templates folder, which caused the template to appear on the General tab in the New dialog box. If you only create a few templates in your life, this might be adequate—you won't have any trouble remembering which template is used for which type of document. If, however, you create a lot of templates—for proposals, letters, memos, reports—you will want to categorize them. Maybe you'll want to place all your templates in one category to merely differentiate yours from the templates that came installed with Word.

To create your own template category, follow these steps:

1. When you save the template for the first time (or save it again after any edits), click the Create New Folder button in the Save As dialog box.

2. Enter a name in the New Folder dialog box (see Figure 5.22), and click OK.

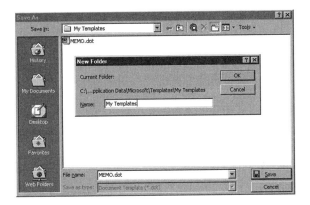

FIGURE 5.22

Name your template folder something that makes sense on a tab in the New dialog box.

3. The folder is created and automatically selected as the Save in location for your new template.

4. If this is a first-time save for your template, name your template in the File name box.

5. Be sure that Document Template (.dot) appears in the Save as type box.

6. Click Save.

Test your new template and category by choosing File, New from the menu to open the New dialog box. Click your new tab, and double-click the template you saved to that category (folder). Figure 5.23 shows the category you created in the New dialog box.

5

FIGURE 5.23

Using a short, relevant folder name keeps your tabs under control.

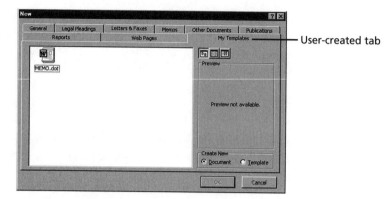

User-created tab

Summary

Today you learned how to automate your forms with check, list, and text box fields. In addition, you learned to break your document into sections, and how to apply different page numbering and header/footer content to the entire document and to specific sections within it. As the culmination of all five days of Word-based instruction, today ended with the topic of templates—how to turn your documents into templates, and how save them to useful categories for future use. Day 6, "Building a Spreadsheet in an Excel Workbook," will take you into the world of Excel 2000 and show you the basics of building a spreadsheet to store text and numbers.

Q&A

Q How can I work with forms after people have filled them in electronically?

A Your users fill them in onscreen and save the forms with a new name—perhaps they save with their names, or they might use some naming convention that meets your identification needs. The documents can then be sent back to you via email, or they can be placed in a network folder to which everyone has access.

Q How many sections can I have in a document?

A As many as you need. Remember, however, that sections only need to be added if you're changing the setup of an individual page or range of pages. If there is no difference between pages within your document beyond text content, there is no need to insert section breaks.

Q Can I delete a template or a template category?

A Yes. You can use the Windows Explorer to do either or both of these things. You can also use Word's Open dialog box—navigate to the Templates folder, right-click the template you want to delete, and choose Delete from the shortcut menu. To delete an entire templates folder, right-click the folder and choose Delete, again from the shortcut menu. Be sure, however, that your folder doesn't contain any templates you didn't want to remove!

Workshop

The section that follows is a quick quiz about the day. If you have any problems answering any of the questions, see the section that follows the quiz for all the answers.

Quiz

1. List the three types of fields that can be added to a form.

2. Why must a form be protected?

3. True or false: In a document with more than one section, you must apply page numbers to each section individually.

4. True or false: Headers and footers appear on every page of your document unless you remove them from certain sections.

5. To which folder must all templates be saved in order to use them in the future?

Quiz Answers

1. You can add check boxes, drop-list boxes, and text boxes to your forms.

2. A form must be protected (by clicking the Protect Form button on the Forms toolbar) to activate the fields for use and to prevent the people that use the forms from changing the field settings.

3. False. Page numbers span all sections by default. You must reformat the page numbers in certain sections in order to have different numbering throughout your document.

4. True. Like page numbers, your header and footer content appears on every page of your document unless you edit your document sections otherwise.

5. All templates must be saved to the Templates folder or to a subfolder that you create within that folder. If not, your templates won't be available through the New dialog box.

5

DAY 6

Building a Spreadsheet in an Excel Workbook

You're probably familiar with the sheets of paper (usually green) that accountants and bookkeepers use to store their numeric information. These manually built and maintained sheets are the electronic spreadsheet's predecessors. Excel 2000's workbook (comprised of one or more individual worksheets) is Microsoft's response to the needs of users who need to store text and numbers, perform calculations, sort lists of information, and create charts to graphically represent their data. The manual spreadsheet has come a very long way. Today, and in Days 7 through 9, you'll be learning to use Excel's major features. Today covers the following topics:

- Building a basic worksheet
- Editing worksheet content
- Creating names for cells and ranges to speed navigation in the workbook
- Using text and numeric formatting for increased visual effectiveness
- Applying Borders and Shading to sections of the worksheet

Entering Worksheet Data

When you start the Excel 2000 program, a blank workbook appears, ready to accept your entries. Each workbook contains three worksheets (Sheet1, Sheet2, and Sheet3), and each of these sheets contains 256 columns and 65,536 rows. As Figure 6.1 shows, cell A1 is active, and a full set of tools is at your disposal to help you build your worksheet.

FIGURE 6.1

Click in any cell and start typing your worksheet title.

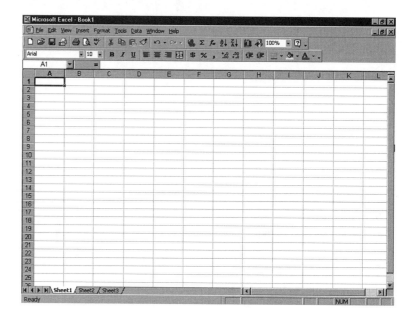

Most worksheets contain a title—something typed in cell A1 or in some other cell close to the top of the worksheet. This title helps you and—more importantly—anyone else who views the sheet know what to expect in the data. The worksheet shown in Figure 6.2 contains a title typed in cell A1, which describes the content and purpose of the data that will follow.

FIGURE 6.2

The entire title is typed in cell A1. It overflows into the adjoining cells because these cells contain no content of their own.

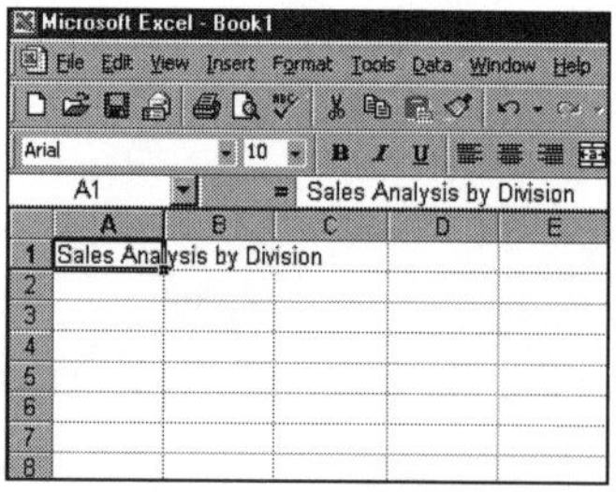

Before you get too far into the process of building your worksheet, take the time to familiarize yourself with the parts of an Excel 2000 worksheet by reviewing Figure 6.3.

FIGURE 6.3

In addition to the tools that are common to all Office 2000 applications, you'll find tools for formatting numeric content and performing calculations.

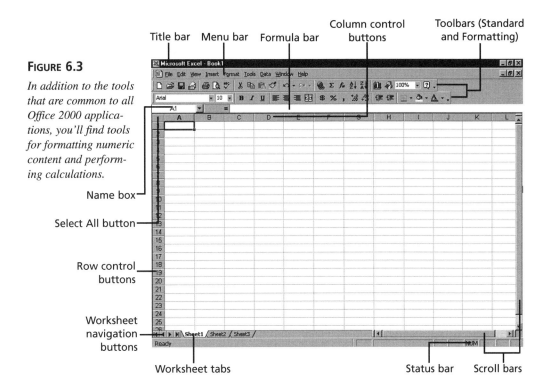

When you're building a worksheet for the first time, certain tools are especially helpful. They're labeled in Figure 6.3 and described in the following list:

- **Formula bar**—Whatever you type in a cell appears in the cell, and in the Formula bar as well (see Figure 6.4). You can use the Formula bar to edit existing content (you will learn about other ways to edit worksheet content later).

6

FIGURE 6.4

The Formula bar displays the selected cell's content.

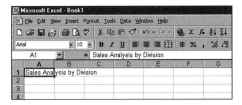

- **Name Box**—If you're not sure where you are, check the Name Box. The address of the active cell appears here, as shown in Figure 6.5.

FIGURE 6.5

*The Name Box is espe-
cially useful when the
active cell is not cur-
rently in view.*

Cell M50 is active, but
not within the dis-
played range of cells

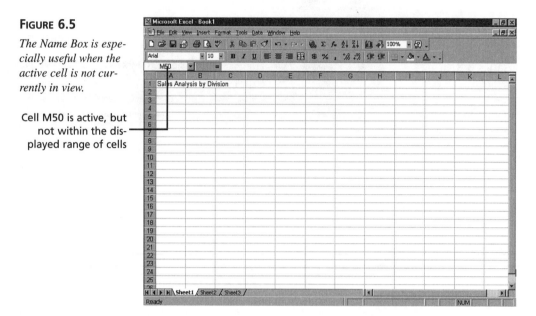

- **Select All button**—To quickly select the entire worksheet (for the purpose of delet-ing all your entries or to make some global formatting change to your content), click this button first.

- **Column and Row control buttons**—These gray buttons enable you to select an entire row or column. Click the letter at the top of a column to select all 65,536 cells in that column, or select the number at the left end of the row to select all 256 cells in that row. Figure 6.6 shows column E selected.

- **Status bar**—Make sure that the letters *NUM* appear in the status bar to indicate that your Numlock is on. It's a good idea to enter your numeric content from the numeric keypad rather than the number keys at the top of your alpha keyboard.

As you continue to enter your worksheet content, be sure to create column headings and row labels that clearly illustrate the nature of your worksheet's content. Figure 6.7 shows a worksheet in progress, with headings and labels that make it clear what data is to be contained in the worksheet.

FIGURE 6.6

Delete, edit, or format the width or contents of an entire column by clicking the letter at the top of the column.

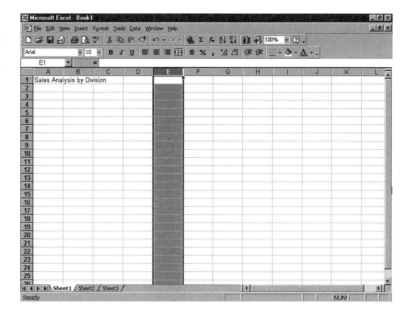

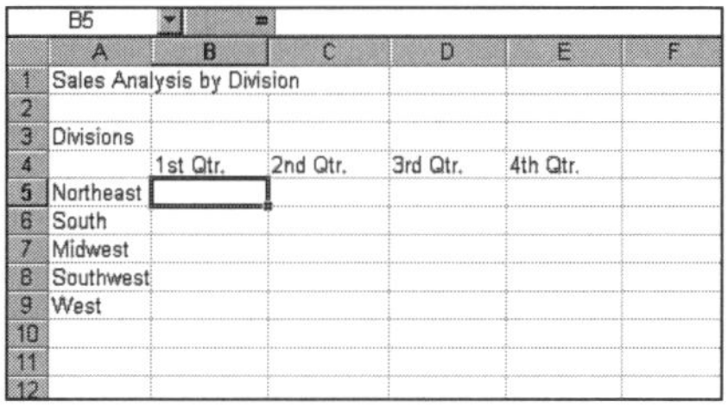

FIGURE 6.7

Use abbreviations to keep column headings and row labels short enough to be visually manageable.

Navigating an Excel Worksheet

Assuming that you have a general layout for your worksheet in mind, the need to move around in your worksheet and get to specific cells to make and edit entries is paramount. Table 6.1 lists a variety of navigation tools and methods that can simplify and speed up your data entry process.

TABLE 6.1   NAVIGATING AN EXCEL WORKSHEET

Navigation Technique	Effect
Arrow keys	Move one cell left, right, up, or down
Tab key	Moves one cell to the right
Shift+Tab	Moves one cell to the left
Enter	Moves down one cell

continues

TABLE 6.1 CONTINUED

Navigation Technique	Effect
Ctrl+Home	Returns to cell A1 of the active worksheet
Ctrl+End	Moves you to the last cell containing data in the active sheet. If the worksheet is blank, it takes you to the last cell in the sheet.
Home	Moves to the first cell in the row that contains the currently active cell
Page Down	Moves down one screenful of rows
Page Up	Moves up one screenful of rows
Alt+Page Down	Moves one screenful of columns to the right
Alt+Page Up	Moves one screenful of columns to the left
Ctrl+Right Arrow	Moves to the last cell in the current row
Ctrl+Left Arrow	Moves to the first cell in the current row
Ctrl+Down Arrow	Moves to the last cell in the current column
Ctrl+Up Arrow	Moves to the first cell in the current column
Ctrl+G or F5	Opens the Go To dialog box, into which you can enter the address of the cell to which you want to go
Type a cell address in the Name Box	After typing the address, press Enter to go to that cell
Click a sheet tab	To go to one of the other sheets in your workbook, simply click that sheet's tab

Using techniques from the preceding table, find the most expeditious method to follow these steps:

1. Start in cell A1.
2. Move to cell D8.
3. Select cell M15.
4. Go back to cell A1.
5. Select cell J500.
6. Select cell Q15.
7. Go to cell Q1.
8. Return to cell A1.

Understanding Worksheet Defaults

As you type your worksheet content, Excel's defaults affect the way your entries are displayed in the cells. Just as a blank document has settings in place to facilitate simple document creation, Excel has defaults that make it fast and easy to build a worksheet:

- Text content is automatically left-aligned in the cell.
- If the adjacent cells are empty, text that exceeds column width overflows into the empty cells.
- If the adjacent cells have their own content, the active cell's excess text is truncated (chopped off).
- Numeric content is automatically right-aligned in the cell.
- Any content other than numbers and correctly placed decimals, commas, and dollar signs results in Excel viewing the content as text.
- The default font and size for your entries (both text and numbers) is Arial, 10 points.
- The column width adjusts automatically to accommodate wide numeric entries. The columns do not widen automatically for text entries.

Figure 6.8 shows some simple worksheet content with Excel's defaults in use.

FIGURE 6.8

Allow Excel's defaults to work for you as you enter your basic content. After your content and formulas are entered, you can go back and reformat your work to be more visually dynamic.

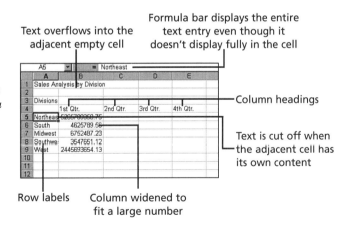

Text overflows into the adjacent empty cell

Formula bar displays the entire text entry even though it doesn't display fully in the cell

Column headings

Text is cut off when the adjacent cell has its own content

Row labels

Column widened to fit a large number

6

Tip

You needn't bother typing commas and dollar signs when your entries represent currency. Use the Currency button to automatically insert commas and dollar signs in your selected cells. You'll learn more about formatting numeric content later today.

Selecting Cell Ranges

NEW TERM You already know how to select a single cell—click in the cell or use one of the navigation techniques listed in Table 6.1. After a cell is selected, the next thing you type becomes that cell's content. You also know how to select the entire worksheet or an entire row or column. But what if you need to select a specific block (also known as a *range*) of cells? Imagine that cells B5 through D8 need to be edited or that you want the numbers in those cells displayed as currency. You can click in each cell individually and make your changes, but that is very time consuming. It is much easier to select the block of cells as a unit and then perform your task.

To select a range of cells, follow these steps:

1. Click in the first cell in the desired block of cells.

2. Drag your mouse across and down (or down and across) through the cells you want to include in your selected range. Figure 6.9 shows a selection in progress.

FIGURE 6.9

Select any size range of cells by dragging through them with your mouse.

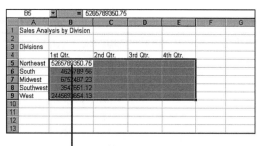

First cell in the range
remains white during the
selection process and when
the selection is complete

3. When the desired range of cells is selected, release your mouse. Note that the first cell in your range (where you started) remains white.

Selecting Cells with the Keyboard

If you're not comfortable with your mouse yet or you're so busy making entries that you don't want to take your hands off the keys to make a selection, you can use the keyboard to select a block of cells. Follow these steps:

1. Use any method to select the starting cell of the desired range.

2. Press and hold the Shift key on your keyboard.

3. Use your Arrow keys to select cells to the right, left, above, or below the starting cell. As long as the Shift key remains down, the cells that you move through with your Arrow keys are selected.

4. When the desired range is selected, release the Shift key.

 Tip   You can also use the mouse and keyboard together to select a range of cells. Click in the first cell in the range, and then press and hold the Shift key. Click in the last cell in the range, and the entire block of cells is selected. Release the Shift key after completing the selection.

Selecting Noncontiguous Ranges

So far, you've selected individual cells and simple blocks of cells; such selections are made for the purposes of editing cell content or applying a format to one or more cells simultaneously. But what if you want to make changes to cells in more than one area of your worksheet? Perhaps your column headings and row labels need to be in a different font, or you want to delete them all at once in favor of some other entries. To save yourself the time of editing or deleting the headings in one step and the rows in a second step, use the following method to select both ranges at the same time:

1. Using the mouse or keyboard, select the first range. Release the mouse or Shift key to end the selection process.

2. Press and hold the Ctrl key.

3. Using the mouse, click in the starting cell of your next range—the range can be anywhere on your worksheet.

4. Click and drag through your desired range of cells. Note that the original range remains selected as you're selecting the second range.

5. Continue (as needed) to select other contiguous and noncontiguous ranges of cells. As long as the Ctrl key is pressed, your currently selected ranges remain selected.

6. When you have selected all the ranges you need, release the Ctrl key.

After your ranges are selected, you can apply any formats you want, or you can press the Delete key to remove the content from all the selected cells. If you want to edit the cells' content, see the section "Editing a Block of Cells" later in this day.

6

Changing and Deleting Worksheet Content

Rarely, if ever, will you enter your worksheet content and not have to edit any of it. Typos, changes in data since you originally gathered it for your worksheet, and a variety of other factors can result in the need for you to change the content of one or more of your worksheet's cells.

> **Tip**
>
> After you've entered your basic worksheet content, always save your work before doing your editing and reformatting tasks. This can save you from losing your work and not having an original version of the file to go back to in the event of a power outage or system failure.

Editing a Single Cell's Content

Editing individual cell content is simple—click in the cell and type your new content. The original content is removed and replaced by your new entry. If, however, a cell contains a sentence or some other, longer string of content, you might want to change only some of it. To make minor edits in a cell, leaving some of the current content intact, follow these steps:

1. Click in the cell you want to edit. The cell's contents are displayed on the Formula bar as well as in the cell itself.

2. To edit the cell's content, choose one of the following methods:

   - **Click your mouse in the Formula Bar**—Your mouse pointer turns into an I-beam, as shown in Figure 6.10. Use the Backspace or Delete keys to remove the current content and type corrections. You can also select text within the cell content by clicking and dragging through it with your mouse.

FIGURE 6.10

To edit rather than replace cell content, edit your cell on the Formula Bar.

Active cell

| A1 | X ✓ = Sales Analysis by Division |

	A	B	C	D	E
1	Sales Analys				
2					
3	Divisions				
4		1st Qtr.	2nd Qtr.	3rd Qtr.	4th Qtr.
5	Northeast	5265789350.75			
6	South	4625789.56			
7	Midwest	6752487.23			
8	Southwest	3547651.12			
9	West	2445693654.13			
10					

Content of active cell displayed on the Formula bar

- **Double-click the cell**—This activates your cursor directly in the cell, enabling you to delete individual characters, words, or phrases and type corrected content.

- **Press F2**—This key also activates your cursor in the cell, as shown in Figure 6.11.

FIGURE 6.11

While your cursor is blinking in your cell, you can use your arrow keys to move around in the content; use the Backspace and Delete keys to remove numbers or text.

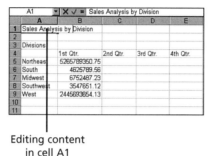

Editing content
in cell A1

3. Edit the cell content (in the Formula Bar or within the cell) and press Enter to confirm your changes.

 Tip

> Pressing Enter moves to the cell below the one you've just edited. To confirm your changes and remain in the cell, click the green checkmark button on the Formula Bar.

Editing a Block of Cells

A block or range of cells can also be deleted, either in one quick action (press Delete while a range is selected) or by editing each cell's content in the selected range, one cell at a time. With a range (or a group of noncontiguous ranges) selected, follow these steps to edit the individual cells:

1. Visually locate the first cell in the range (it will be white). If you have two or more ranges selected, the white cell is in the last range you added to your overall selection.

2. Type the new content for that cell (you can also edit the cell's content through the Formula Bar).

3. Press Enter. The next cell down in the range is activated, enabling you to edit that cell (see Figure 6.12).

6

FIGURE 6.12

Select a range of cells to edit, and use the Enter key to move from cell to cell within the range.

B6	▼	=	4625789.56	
	A	B	C	D	E

	A	B	C	D	E
1	Sales Analysis by Division				
2					
3	Divisions				
4		1st Qtr.	2nd Qtr.	3rd Qtr.	4th Qtr.
5	Northeast	53668762.75			
6	South	4625789.56			
7	Midwest	6752487.23			
8	Southwest	3547651.12			
9	West	2445693654.13			
10					
11					
12					

4. Continue to press Enter after editing each cell (you can skip cells by pressing Enter without making any changes).

5. When the desired changes have been made to cells in your ranges, click outside of the selected cells to deselect the ranges.

Tip

You can also use this technique for making new entries—select a range of currently empty cells and begin making entries, pressing Enter after each one. This makes it easy to control the group of cells into which your entries are placed, without your having to click in individual cells with your mouse.

Tip

When you are editing a selected range of cells, you can edit individual cell contents without replacing them entirely by pressing F2 when the cell is active. This activates the cursor in the cell for making adjustments to the current cell content. Press Enter to accept the edits and move to the next cell in the range.

Moving and Copying Ranges

Even with the most thorough planning for your worksheets, you're bound to want to move something or duplicate a cell or range for use in another worksheet, or even another workbook. You can't possibly think of every contingency, and it's usually after you've started (or even finished) building your worksheet that you realize that things need to be moved or copied.

Bear in mind that it's not the cells you're moving or copying, but their content. You have a fixed number of cells per worksheet, and copying cells or ranges merely duplicates the content in another location—it doesn't increase the number of total cells in the sheet.

Tip

Don't forget to save your work before you make any major changes in the location of your current worksheet content!

Moving Cells and Ranges

When you choose to move cell or range content from one place to another, you have two choices, depending on the distance you want to move them. If the distance between the current location and the target location is short, and if the current and target spots are visible simultaneously, you can use your mouse to drag the cells to their new location. If the distance is long and you can't see both the current and target locations at the same time, you'll want to use the Clipboard to methodically move the content from place to place.

To use your mouse to move content a short distance, follow these steps:

1. Select the cell or range of cells to be moved.

2. Point to the edge of the selected cell or range. Your mouse turns to a left-pointing arrow, as shown in Figure 6.13.

FIGURE 6.13

Grab the selected cells by the edge, and drag your content to its new location.

A3		≡	Divisions		
	A	B	C	D	E
1	Sales Analysis by Division				
2					
3	Divisions				
4		1st Qtr.	2nd Qtr.	3rd Qtr.	4th Qtr.
5	Northeast	52658762.75			
6	South	4625789.56			
7	Midwest	6752487.23			
8	Southwest	3547651.12			
9	West	2445693654.13			
10					
11					

3. Click and drag your mouse until the cell or range is in the desired location. Release your mouse.

If you attempt to move cell content to a location that already has content, you are prompted to confirm your intention to replace the content of the cells in the target location (see Figure 6.14). Click OK to replace the target cells with content from the cells you moved.

6

FIGURE 6.14

Consider carefully if you want to both move content and replace content in the desired location.

To use the Clipboard to move cell content, follow these steps:

1. Select the cell or range that contains the content you want to move.
2. Choose Edit, Cut, or press Ctrl+X.
3. Click in the cell at the beginning of the target range for your content. If you're moving a single cell, click in the target cell.
4. Choose Edit, Paste, or press Ctrl+V.

If your selection was the first and only item placed on the Clipboard, your cut content can be pasted only once. If, however, your Clipboard toolbar is displayed (due to an accumulation of more than one Clipboard selection), you can paste the selection repeatedly in the current worksheet or in any other workbook or Office 2000 file. Figure 6.15 shows the Clipboard toolbar with a series of Excel selections on it.

FIGURE 6.15

Paste any item on the Clipboard toolbar an unlimited number of times while Office 2000 is open.

Cut selection on the Clipboard toolbar

 Note

You probably recall from Day 2, "Creating a Letter," that the Clipboard is a name for your computer's memory when it is used to store selected content for use in another location. The Office 2000 Clipboard holds up to 12 cut or copied selections, but the Windows 95/98 Clipboard holds only one selection at a time. You can use the 12 selections only within Office 2000.

Copying Cells and Ranges

Copying cell content creates a duplicate of the selected cells and enables you to use the content in another place—somewhere else in the same worksheet, in another worksheet in the current workbook, in another workbook, or in another file in another application. As with moving cell content, you have two methods available to you; the choice you make depends on the relative locations of the selected content and the target location.

You can use your mouse to copy content when the selected content and target location are visible at the same time. Follow these steps:

1. Select the content you want to copy.

2. Press and hold the Ctrl key.

3. Point to the edge of the selected cell or range of cells. The mouse pointer changes to a left-pointing arrow with a small plus sign next to it, as shown in Figure 6.16.

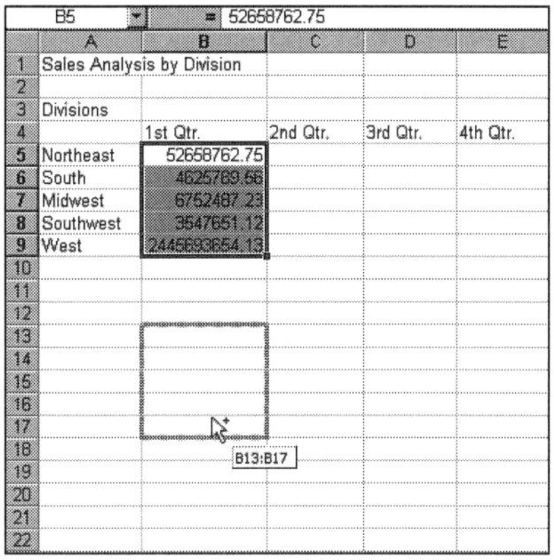

FIGURE 6.16

The Ctrl key turns a move into a copy.

4. With the Ctrl key still pressed, click and drag the content to the desired location.

5. Release the mouse, and then the Ctrl key. Your content now appears in both the original location and the target cells.

Caution If you release the Ctrl key before releasing the mouse, your copy process reverts to a simple move. Always release the mouse first.

When the selected cell content and the desired target for it are not simultaneously visible, you must use the Clipboard to copy and paste it. Follow these steps:

1. Select the cell or range of cells to be copied.

2. Choose Edit, Copy, or press Ctrl+C.

3. Click in the first cell in the target range of cells. If you're copying a single cell, click in the cell that you want to contain your copied content.

4. Choose Edit, Paste, or press Ctrl+V. Your content is pasted and appears in both the original location and the target.

6

Tip   You can invoke the Clipboard commands (Cut, Copy, and Paste) by right-clicking the selected content and choosing Cut or Copy from the shortcut menu. To paste, right-click the desired location (typically a blank cell) and choose Paste from the shortcut menu.

Naming Ranges

Naming cells and ranges makes it easier to find parts of your worksheet without remembering the address of the cell that contains what you're looking for—and it makes it easier to build formulas. Named ranges can also assist others who might use or view your worksheet to identify content—they can refer to the data by a logical name rather than a cell address. You'll learn about the use of named ranges in formulas later—for now, you'll learn about naming ranges to assist you in navigating the worksheet and finding worksheet content quickly.

Names that are applied to cells and ranges appear in the Name Box in your worksheet window. Figure 6.17 shows a name that was applied to an individual cell on a worksheet.

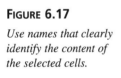

FIGURE 6.17

Use names that clearly identify the content of the selected cells.

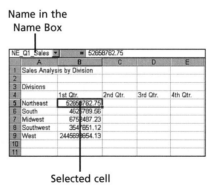

Name in the Name Box

Selected cell

Applying Names to Individual Cells and Ranges

To assign your own name to an individual cell or range of cells, follow these steps:

1. Select the cell or range of cells.

2. In the Name Box, click the displayed cell address, as shown in Figure 6.18.

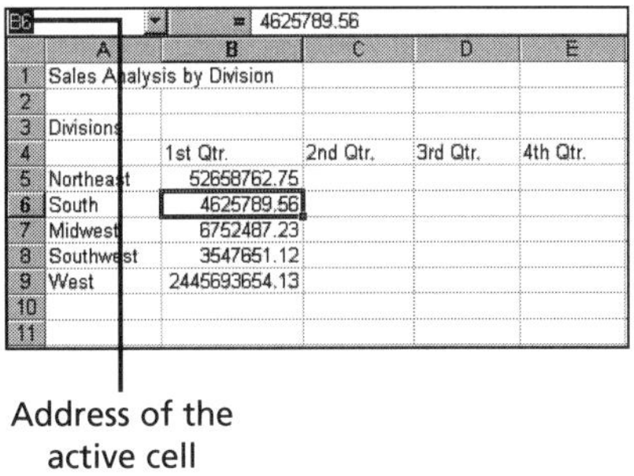

FIGURE 6.18

A cell address doesn't tell us much about the selected cell. Replace the address with a concise and relevant name for the cell's content.

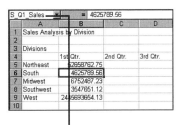

Address of the active cell

3. Type a name for the selected cells. Your name cannot contain spaces or any punctuation. If you need the appearance of a space, type an underscore (see Figure 6.19).

FIGURE 6.19

When using abbreviations in a cell or range name, use common, simple abbreviations to make it easier for you to remember and for others to interpret.

South Sales for the First Quarter is abbreviated in this range name.

4. Press the Enter key to confirm the typed name.

After a cell or range has been named, that name appears in the Name Box whenever the cell or exact range is selected. You can change the name at any time by selecting it in the Name Box and typing a new name.

Removing a Name

Although it's easy to change the name you've applied to a cell or range, the process of deleting a name is a little more complex. To delete a name and revert to the cell address as the sole display in the Name Box for a selected cell or range, follow these steps:

1. Select the cell or range and see that the name you applied is displayed in the Name Box.

2. Choose Insert, Name, Define.

6

3. In the Define Name dialog box (see Figure 6.20), the range of cells you selected is displayed in the Refers to box. Select the name you want to delete from the list—you can verify that it's the right name by checking the Refers to box to see that the range address hasn't changed.

FIGURE 6.20

Verify that you've selected the correct range for deletion by checking the Refers to box.

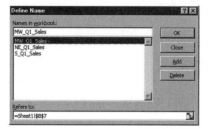

4. Click the Delete button in the dialog box. The name disappears from the list.

5. Click OK to close the dialog box.

After it is deleted, a range name can be brought back through the use of Edit, Undo.

Tip

If you prefer a methodical approach, you can use the Define Name dialog box to create your names as well. Select the cell or range, and choose Insert, Name, Define. Type a name for the cell or range, and then click Add. Click OK to close the dialog box.

Note

If you want to use your existing column and row labels for names, select the block of cells that includes the labels and the data they identify. Choose Insert, Name, Create, and then choose which columns or rows to use in creating names. This feature is only effective if your column and row labels contain text—if your row or column labels are numeric, the feature doesn't work.

Using Custom Lists

Custom Lists are preset lists of words that you can use for quick column headings or row labels. You can use the lists that are installed with Excel 2000, or you can create your own custom lists to make building your worksheet easier.

The installed group of custom lists includes:

- Days of the week

- Months of the year

- Fiscal quarters (Q1, Qtr 1, QTR1, Quarter 1)

- A series of dates

To use a custom list, follow these steps:

1. Type any word from the list, such as Monday or October.

2. Point to the fill handle in the lower right corner of the cell that contains the custom list text. Your mouse turns to a black cross (see Figure 6.21).

FIGURE 6.21

Custom lists make it quick and easy to fill a range of cells with related words or phrases.

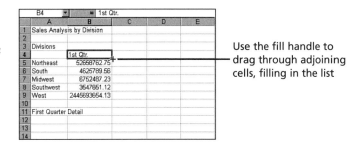

Use the fill handle to drag through adjoining cells, filling in the list

3. Drag your mouse through the adjoining cells that you want to fill with the remaining words in the custom list. If you drag through more cells than there are words in the list, the list begins again from the beginning (see Figure 6.22).

FIGURE 6.22

Create two years' worth of fiscal quarters by dragging through eight cells.

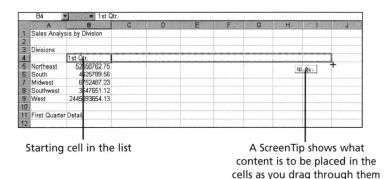

Starting cell in the list

A ScreenTip shows what content is to be placed in the cells as you drag through them

6

4. When the desired range of cells has been filled, release the mouse.

Creating Your Own Custom Lists

The cutom lists that Excel offers might be all you ever need—worksheets that track sales or other data over time will be adequately supported by column headings or row labels that list the days of the week or the months of the year. If, however, you find yourself typing the same series of words or phrases in many of your worksheets—the names of your company's divisions, a list of salespeople, a group of product names—you'll want to create your own custom lists.

To build a custom list, follow these steps:

1. Type the list in a series of cells, as shown in Figure 6.23. This list was already part of your worksheet.

FIGURE 6.23

If you already have a worksheet that contains the list, open it and select the cells to save yourself the t rouble of typing them again for this procedure.

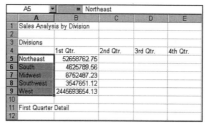

2. Select the cells that contain the list.

3. Choose Tools, Options, and then click the Custom Lists tab (see Figure 6.24).

FIGURE 6.24

A list of the installed and any user-created lists appears in the Custom lists box.

Range of selected cells from the active worksheet

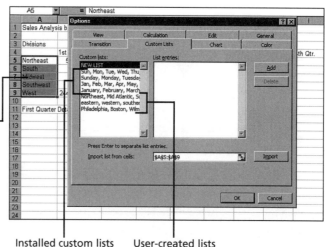

Installed custom lists   User-created lists

4. Click NEW LIST in the Custom lists box. A cursor appears in the List entries box.

5. To use the selected list in your worksheet, click the Import button. This imports the cells in the range that appears in the Import list from cells box.

6. Make any necessary spelling corrections or additions to the list as it appears in the List entries box, and click Add.

7. Click OK to close the dialog box.

Test your list to make sure that the words and phrases are in the correct order if you start with the first one in the list. If they aren't in the right order, or if there are any spelling errors you missed when creating the list, choose Tools, Options, and then click the Custom Lists tab. Select your list and edit any of the words in the List entries box. Click Add to update the list, and click OK to close the dialog box. Figure 6.25 shows a list being changed.

FIGURE 6.25

You might not spot an error until you use the list for the first time.

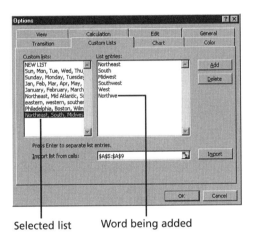

Selected list   Word being added

Creating Numeric Patterns with the Fill Handle

The fill handle can be used for more than completing custom lists—you can also use it to complete a series of numbers (such as a 1,2,3 list) or a series of incremental numbers (such as 50, 100, 150). To create a numeric pattern, follow these steps:

1. Type the first two numbers in the pattern into any two adjoining cells.

2. Select the two cells, and point to the fill handle in the second cell (see Figure 6.26).

FIGURE 6.26

The remaining cells are filled with numbers that follow the pattern you establish in your sample cells.

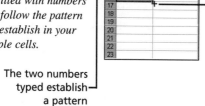

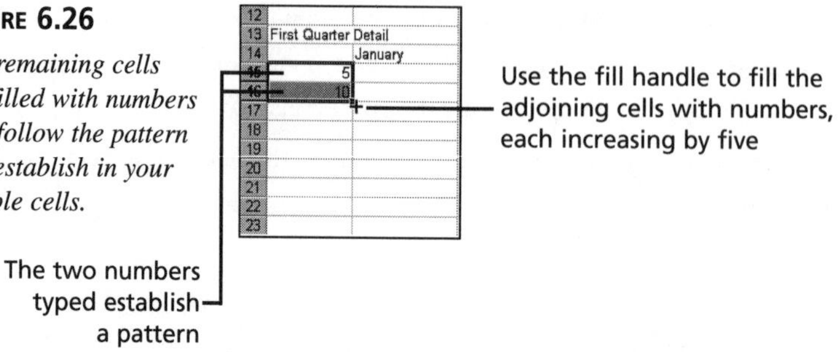

Use the fill handle to fill the adjoining cells with numbers, each increasing by five

The two numbers typed establish a pattern

3. Drag the fill handle through the adjoining cells in which you want to enter the completed pattern. Figure 6.27 shows the pattern you started completed through six cells.

FIGURE 6.27

For a monthly sales breakdown in five-day increments, set up a numeric pattern for 5, 10, 15, 20, 25, and 30 days.

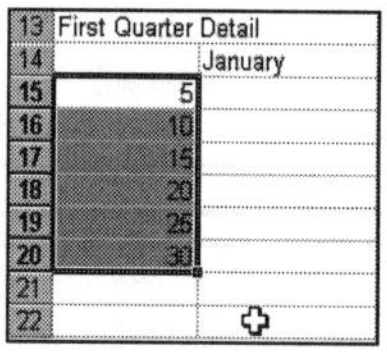

4. When the series is complete, release the mouse.

Formatting Your Worksheet

After you enter and edit your worksheet content, the next step is to make your worksheet more visually effective. This can mean simply making it more interesting to look at, or it can mean making the content more informative. Good formatting achieves both goals, as is shown in Figure 6.28.

Although some formatting is a good thing, too much formatting can defeat your purpose. Avoid using too many different fonts (typefaces) in one sheet, and keep your use of shading and borders to a minimum. Use formatting to clarify the nature of your data and to simplify the process of reading your worksheet. You don't want people to be distracted by your formatting while they're trying to read and interpret your information.

FIGURE 6.28

Format your text for visual impact, and format your numbers to make clear what kind of data is stored in your worksheet.

Shading draws attention to important information

Title format sets the tone for the worksheet

Enlarged text in column headings and row labels make the data stand out

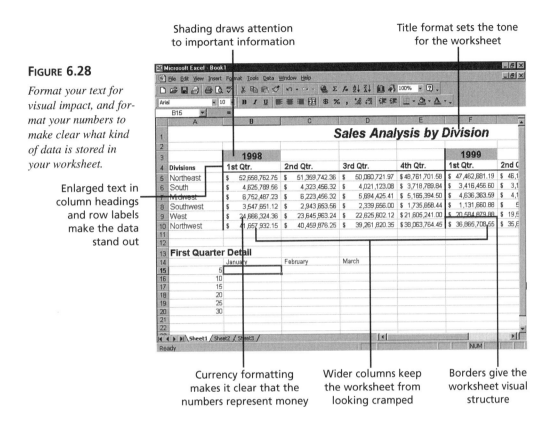

Currency formatting makes it clear that the numbers represent money

Wider columns keep the worksheet from looking cramped

Borders give the worksheet visual structure

Adjusting Column Width

As was discussed earlier today, Excel widens the column automatically to fit the content as you type numeric content into your cells. Text entries do not affect column width. Because Excel's automatic adjustments for numbers—and lack of any adjustment for text—can leave your worksheet looking cramped or leave some text hidden, it's important to adjust your columns' width to give your worksheet more visual space. Figure 6.29 shows a worksheet in progress, with columns just wide enough for your numbers and missing text where columns weren't wide enough for the entry.

By adjusting column width to give a roomier look, the numbers are easier to read, and all the text is showing. Figure 6.30 shows the same worksheet with widened columns.

6

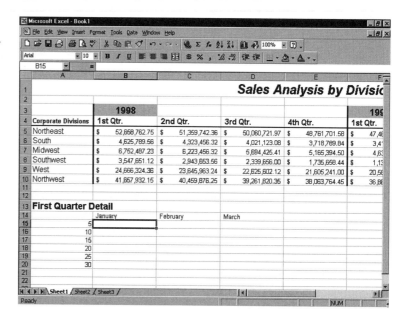

To widen an individual column, follow these steps:

1. Click the column control button at the top of the column you want to widen.

2. Point to the seam between the selected column and the unselected column to its right. Your mouse pointer turns to a two-headed arrow.

3. Drag to the right to widen the column. If you want to make a column narrower, drag to the left. Figure 6.31 shows a column being widened.

FIGURE 6.31

A vertical line and a ScreenTip follow your mouse pointer to give you a preview and measurement of your new column width.

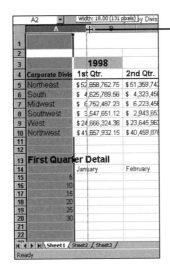

Look for two-headed arrow to appear before dragging

Tip

If you want to widen a column to match the width of the widest entry in that column, double-click the right seam on that column's control button.

To widen several columns at once (to a uniform width), follow these steps:

1. Select the columns by dragging through their contiguous control buttons. If you want to select noncontiguous columns, use the Ctrl key and click the control button for each column you want to select.

2. Point to the right seam on any one of the selected columns' control buttons. Your mouse turns to a horizontal two-headed arrow (see Figure 6.32).

6

FIGURE 6.32

Adjust any one of the selected columns, and all the selected columns are widened at the same time.

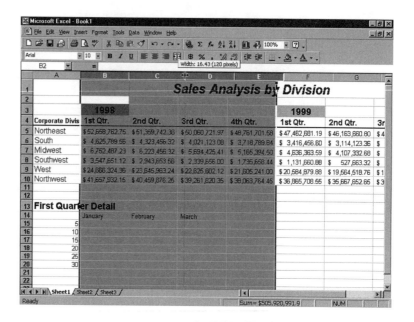

3. Drag to the right to widen the selected columns. If you want to narrow the columns, drag to the left.

When you release the mouse, all the selected columns are of a uniform width. This is a useful technique for adjusting columns that contain similar information—you emphasize their similarity by applying a uniform width to them.

Applying Character Formats

Character formatting can be applied to text or numbers; this is normally done to improve a worksheet's appearance. Making text bigger, changing the font of certain text within a worksheet—these simple changes can give your worksheet a polished, professional look.

Excel gives you two ways to apply character formats:

- **The Formatting toolbar**—You can use these tools to change the font and size of the text, change the alignment of text, and apply Bold, Italic, and Underline styles (see Figure 6.33).

FIGURE 6.33

The Formatting tool-bar's buttons represent the most commonly used formats for your worksheet.

- **The Format Cells dialog box**—Choose Format, Cells, and then click the Font tab to change the appearance of text (see Figure 6.34); use the Alignment tab to change the way text and numbers align within the cells (see Figure 6.35).

FIGURE 6.34

The Font tab in the Format Cells dialog box gives you a wide variety of tools for changing the appearance of text.

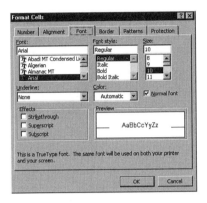

FIGURE 6.35

Adjust the position of your content within the cells using the Alignment tab in the Format Cells dialog box.

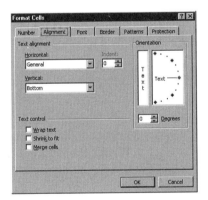

Does it matter which approach you take (toolbar versus dialog box)? Not really. The Fonts tab of the Format Cells dialog box shows you a preview of the effects your changes will make, and it gives you more tools, all in one place. Using the toolbar is faster, however, and makes it less likely that you'll apply too many formats in your worksheet—the extra effort involved in using multiple tools seems to inhibit undesirable "overformatting."

6

To format the worksheet in its basic, unformatted state (shown in Figure 6.36), use the Formatting toolbar.

FIGURE 6.36

Don't let your worksheet be needlessly boring. This vanilla worksheet needs some help to be more interesting and informative.

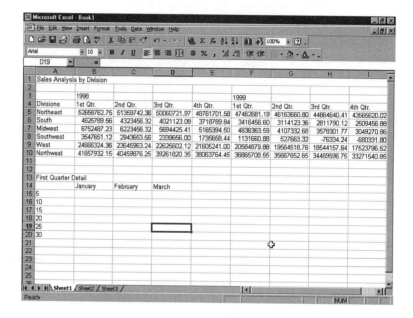

Follow these steps:

1. First, select cell A1, which contains the worksheet title. Continue your selection to include the range of cells from A1 to I1 (the width of the worksheet cells).

2. Click the Merge and Center button. The title is centered within one large cell across the selected cells.

3. Select your column headings and click the Center alignment button.

4. Click the Bold button to make the column heading text bold.

5. Add your title to the selection, and increase the font size to 12 points by clicking the Font Size button and choosing 12 from the list.

6. Select the row labels and click the Bold button and then the Italic button.

The results of this formatting procedure appear in Figure 6.37.

FIGURE 6.37

Emphasized titles, headings, and labels make it easier to read the worksheet and quickly assess its content.

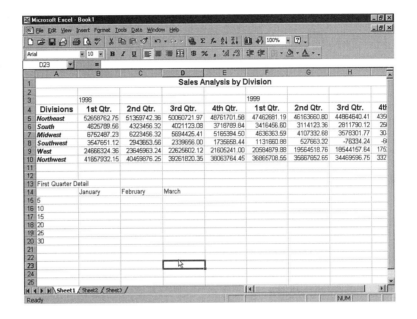

Formatting Numeric Content

Number formats serve a more functional purpose than do character formats. Applying Currency formatting, for example, can clarify the nature of your numbers, showing that the numbers represent dollars rather than units. Applying the Percentage format can make it easier to interpret .1532 as 15%. These changes don't just dress up your worksheet—they increase its effectiveness as a data analysis tool.

To apply number formats, you can use the Formatting toolbar or the Format Cells dialog box (Format, Cells). As in the case of character formatting, the tools that are offered on the Formatting toolbar represent the most commonly-applied formats, in their default settings. For most worksheets, these buttons suffice for your numeric formatting needs.

If, however, you need to adjust how a format is applied, or if you want to choose from more types of formatting than are offered on the Formatting toolbar, you'll want to use the Format Cells dialog box. To open and use the dialog box, follow these steps:

1. Select the cells you want to format.

2. Choose Format, Cells, and click the Number tab.

3. Select a Category. Each category offers a set of options on the right side of the dialog box, plus a sample of how the effects will appear (see Figure 6.38).

6

FIGURE 6.38

Reduce or increase the decimal places, and choose how negative numbers are to be displayed.

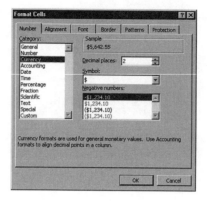

4. Adjust the settings for your selected category, and click OK to apply them to your selected cells.

Using your worksheet, apply the following formats using both the Formatting toolbar and Format Cells dialog box where needed:

1. Select the range of cells that contain numeric content.

2. Show that these numbers represent money by clicking the Currency Style button on the toolbar.

3. Reduce the number of decimal places displayed. You can use the Decrease Decimal button or you can open the Format Cells dialog box, choose Currency, and reduce the decimal setting to zero.

Figure 6.39 shows your worksheet after you apply the changes in steps 1 through 3.

Tip

Although most of the buttons on the Formatting toolbar function as toggle buttons (one click on, a second click off), the Currency, Percent, and Comma buttons do not turn off with a second click. You must use the Format Cells dialog box to convert numbers back to General (no special numeric formatting) or to switch to a different format.

Tip

Create your own numeric cell formats in the Format Cells dialog box. Click the Custom category and type the format you want using pound signs (#) for numbers, and inserting your own dashes, slashes, and decimals as needed. For example, to create a custom format for your company's product numbers, enter ####-###-# in the Type box. This format can then be applied to cells into which you'll enter your product numbers, causing an entry of 12345678 to appear as 1234-567-8 without your having to type the dashes.

FIGURE 6.39

Simple formatting and minor adjustments make the worksheet much clearer.

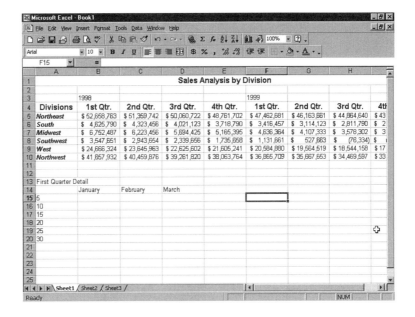

Using Borders and Shading

Apply borders and shading sparingly, to give your worksheet a more "graphical" look and to give it some visual structure. Figure 6.40 shows your worksheet with borders and shading applied.

FIGURE 6.40

A shaded row breaks the worksheet into sections, and a border around an important cell draws the reader's attention.

6

Like character and numeric formatting, you can apply border and shading effects from either the Formatting toolbar or the Format Cells dialog box. The dialog box gives you more options, whereas the toolbar gives you quick access to a simple set of tools.

Applying Borders to a Cell or Range of Cells

To apply a border to a cell or range of cells, follow these steps:

1. Select the cell or range to which you want to apply the border.

2. Click the triangle to the right of the Borders button on the toolbar. A palette of borders displays, as shown in Figure 6.41.

FIGURE 6.41

*Choose from borders
for the inside, outside,
left, right, top, or bot-
tom of the selected
cells*

3. Click the buttons in the palette for the borders you want to apply. To apply more than one border, you must redisplay the palette.

To apply borders from the Format Cells dialog box, follow these steps:

1. Select the cells to which you want to apply borders.

2. Choose Format, Cells, and then click the Border tab.

3. Choose the sides of the cells to which you want to add a border by clicking the border buttons that surround the sample (see Figure 6.42).

Click these buttons to choose
which sides of the cells are
to have borders

FIGURE 6.42

*The same buttons you
see in the Borders
palette are displayed
in the Format Cells
dialog box. The capa-
bility to preview your
results can be useful.*

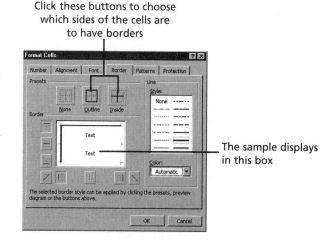

The sample displays
in this box

4. Choose a border Style if you want something other than a hairline border.

5. If necessary, choose a Color for your borders.

6. Click OK to apply the borders and close the dialog box.

Applying Shading to Cells

Shading can have a dramatic effect on your worksheet—even if you only use shades of gray, you're essentially adding color to your worksheet by deviating from the white background. Figure 6.43 shows shading applied in a variety of ways.

FIGURE 6.43

Separate parts of the worksheet with shading, and draw attention to important information.

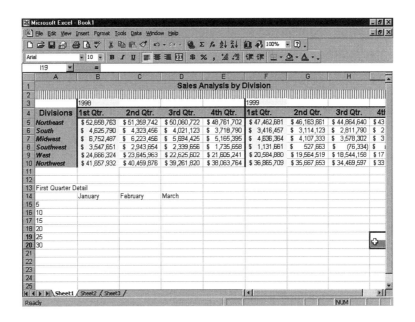

 To apply shading, you can use the Fill Color button on the Formatting toolbar, or you can use the Patterns tab in the Format Cells dialog box.

To apply a quick solid color fill, follow these steps:

1. Select the cell or cells that you want to fill with color. The color appears behind any cell content.

2. Click the triangle to the right of the Fill Color button. A palette of 40 different colors, plus a No Fill option, appears (see Figure 6.44).

6

3. Click the color you want to apply. The palette closes, and your fill is applied to the selected cells.

To access the solid colors, plus a series of patterns that can be applied to the background of your cells, follow these steps:

1. Select the cells you want to shade.

2. Choose Format, Cells, and click the Patterns tab (see Figure 6.45).

FIGURE 6.45

Using the Format Cells dialog box, you have access to more fill options, and you can view a sample prior to applying the fill to your cells.

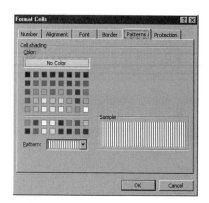

3. Click a color to fill your cells. The color displays in the Sample box.

4. If you want to also apply a pattern to the cell (or apply a black and white pattern), click the Patterns list box. A palette of patterns appears (see Figure 6.46).

5. Choose a pattern by clicking it in the palette. The selected pattern appears in the Sample box.

6. When your desired color or pattern is chosen, click OK to apply it to your selected cells and close the dialog box.

FIGURE 6.46

Use pattern fills in empty cells, rows, and columns to separate sections of a worksheet or to indicate that certain cells are not to be used.

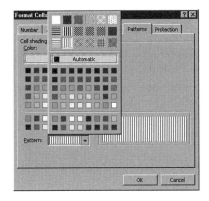

Avoid using dark colors and patterns in cells that have content—it is too hard to read them. Dark shaded fills also present problems when you photocopy or fax your printed worksheets. Use light shades for cells with content, and pattern fills only in empty cells.

Summary

Today introduced you to Excel 2000 and showed you how to build, edit, and apply simple formats to a basic worksheet. Day 7, Adding Worksheet Depth and Power," will take you a few steps further—taking advantage of Excel's multiple worksheets and the use of formulas, functions, and complex calculations.

Q&A

Q Can I save my Excel 2000 worksheet for use in other spreadsheet programs, such as Lotus 1-2-3?

A Yes. You can choose from a variety of .WKS and .WK1 formats through the Save As dialog box. Click the Save as type list, and choose the format that will work best in the other program. You'll also see .DBF formats, for use with older DOS-based database software.

Q I received an odd result when I typed a large number into my cell. After typing 1200000000000 into a cell, Excel displayed 1.2E+12. What does this mean?

A Excel interpreted your number as an exponent, and the result literally means that the cell contains 1.2 plus 12 more digits. To see your entire number as you typed it, widen the column.

6

Q I typed a number and it didn't right-align as I thought Excel does by default. What went wrong?

A If you type anything other than the numbers from 0 to 9, commas, a decimal point, or a dollar sign into a cell, Excel perceives the entry as text and aligns it to the left side of the cell. In addition, the number might fail to work in any formulas. Avoid typing anything other than numbers into your cells and rely on Excel's numeric formatting to insert commas, decimals, and dollar or percent signs for you.

Workshop

The section that follows is a quick quiz about the day. If you have any problems answering any of the questions, see the section that follows the quiz for all the answers.

Quiz

1. How many cells are in each worksheet?

2. How many worksheets are there in a new workbook?

3. True or false: Excel automatically widens its columns to match the width of your entries.

4. Describe two ways to take content from one cell and place it in another.

5. Name two ways to edit cell content.

6. If you're in cell A1, what's the fastest way to get to cell M150?

7. Describe two ways to draw visual attention to a cell or range of cells in your worksheet.

Quiz Answers

1. There are 16,777,216 cells in each worksheet (multiply 256 columns by 65,536 rows).

2. A new, blank workbook has three worksheets, named Sheet1, Sheet2, and Sheet3. You'll learn how to rename them on Day 7.

3. False, sort of. Excel automatically widens columns to accommodate numeric entries of up to 11 digits. It does not widen to accommodate text entries.

4. You can move content from one cell to another by dragging it or using the Clipboard to Cut and Paste it.

5. To edit a cell's content, you can click in the cell and use the Formula Bar, or you can double-click the cell and edit the content directly in the cell.

6. To get to a cell that's not currently onscreen, press Ctrl+G to open the Go To dialog box. Enter the desired address and click OK.

7. You can draw a reader's eye to a particular cell or range of cells by applying shading to the cells, by placing a border around the cells, or by making the text or numbers bold.

6

DAY 7

Adding Worksheet Depth and Power

After Day 6, "Building a Spreadsheet in an Excel Workbook," you understand the basics of worksheet creation: entering and editing text and numeric data, and formatting your worksheet in order to improve its overall appearance and visual impact and make the worksheet more informative. Today focuses on more advanced worksheet features, taking advantage of Excel's tools for working with the three-dimensional aspects of a workbook and creating formulas. Specifically, today you will learn the following skills:

- How to name, insert, and delete your individual worksheets
- How to use and build your workbook's sheets as a group
- How to build formulas and use Excel's AutoSum and Functions to manipulate your numeric data
- How to use Relative, Absolute, and Mixed references to build and edit complex calculations
- How to combine numbers from two or more worksheets and workbooks in one formula

Naming Worksheets

A new workbook opens with three sheets: Sheet1, Sheet2, and Sheet3. Many users never go past Sheet1 and never need to change its name because the filename they choose when they save the workbook says all they need to about its contents. There are times, however, when you need to use more than one sheet, so—for the sake of clarity and distinction—you need to name the sheets.

Naming a sheet is simple: Double-click the sheet's tab, type a new name, and press Enter to confirm the new name. Sheets can be renamed as many times as needed. Figure 7.1 shows Sheet1 in the process of being renamed.

FIGURE 7.1

Choose a short—but clear and relevant— name for your sheet tab. If others use your workbook, avoid using abbreviations and other insider jargon.

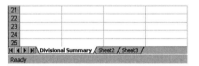

Inserting and Removing Sheets

If you're going to need more than one sheet in your workbook, stop and think about how many sheets you need, what you want to call them, and the order in which they are to appear. Planning ahead can save you a lot of work later on. Figure 7.2 shows a series of tabs that make clear what type of data can be found on the individual sheets; it also clarifies the function of the workbook as a whole.

FIGURE 7.2

The worksheets in a single workbook need to be related in terms of content and function. If your worksheets are unrelated to each other, consider placing them in different workbooks.

If the three worksheets that came with your workbook aren't enough, you can add more by choosing Insert, Worksheet. The new worksheet appears to the left of the sheet that was active at the time that you added the new worksheet. You needn't worry, however, about where the new sheet falls in relation to your existing sheets—it is easy to reorder sheets as needed.

To change the order of your worksheets, follow these steps:

1. Click and drag the sheet tab that you want to move. A small page icon is appended to your mouse pointer, and a triangle follows your mouse movements (see Figure 7.3).

FIGURE 7.3

Rearrange your work-sheets by dragging their tabs to the left or right.

2. When the triangle is pointing to the desired location for your selected sheet, release the mouse.

 Tip

After you've named and added new sheets, you might find that you can't read more than two or three of the tabs—some of them might be completely hidden. To reveal more of your sheet tabs, drag the handle at the left end of the horizontal scrollbar to the left; it decreases the width of your scrollbar and gives you more room for your sheet tabs.

To remove a worksheet, click the sheet's tab to select it, and then choose Edit, Delete Sheet. A prompt appears, asking you to confirm your intention to delete the sheet and any data in it (see Figure 7.4). Click OK to delete the sheet.

 Note

If your Office Assistant is onscreen when you delete your sheet, the confirmation prompt appears in the Assistant's dialog box. Otherwise, a standard Office prompt box appears.

7

FIGURE 7.4

Don't be too quick to click OK and delete your sheet; there might be data on the sheet that you forgot about—and it is deleted along with the sheet. In addition, after it is deleted, your sheet cannot be brought back through the use of Undo.

Tip

A quick way to check for any worksheet content prior to deleting the sheet is to press Ctrl+End, which takes you to the last cell (if any) that contains data. If no cell contains any data, you are taken to the last cell in the worksheet.

Tip

To move through your sheet tabs quickly (especially if you have more tabs than can be viewed simultaneously), use the sheet navigation buttons to the right of the sheet tabs. The triangles enable you to go (in order) to the first sheet, previous sheet, next sheet, and last sheet in the workbook.

Creating Identical Worksheets

So you've added all the sheets you need, and they're all named appropriately. If you haven't entered your data yet and the sheets will contain similar content, you can save yourself a great deal of time by creating the similar sheets all at once. How? By grouping the sheets and then entering the content that is common to all the grouped sheets.

The first hurdle in this process is deciding what the common content is. Titles, column headings, and row labels are often the same between worksheets in a workbook. If, for example, your workbook consists of five sheets (one for each division of your company), each of the five sheets is likely to have the same general layout, headings, and labels.

Rather than typing this common content into each sheet one at a time or using the Clipboard to copy and paste it into each sheet, you can group the blank sheets and then type the common content once. While sheets are grouped, all entries, edits, and formats that are applied are automatically applied to each sheet in the group.

Grouping Worksheets

You can use the Shift key to group your sheets. The Shift key enables you to click the first and last sheet in the intended group, and it assumes that all the interim sheets are part of the group. Figure 7.5 shows such a grouping.

FIGURE 7.5

Group a series of contiguous sheets by pressing the Shift key and clicking the first and last tabs in the group. The first and last sheets, and all sheets in between, are part of the group.

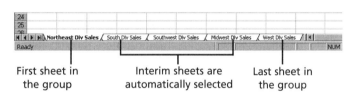

First sheet in the group

Interim sheets are automatically selected

Last sheet in the group

If your intended group is not made up of contiguous sheets, you can use the Ctrl key to select random sheets. Press the Ctrl key and then click the tabs of each sheet that you want in the group. Figure 7.6 shows a group of noncontiguous sheets.

FIGURE 7.6

Gather random sheets for your group with the Ctrl key.

Tip

To select and group all the sheets in your workbook, right-click on any one of the sheet tabs and choose Select All Sheets from the shortcut menu.

When sheets are grouped with either method, the worksheet tabs are white. You only need to work on one sheet in the group—remember that your entries, edits, and formats apply to all the sheets in the group, so you only need to enter your content and perform your edits and formatting tasks once. It doesn't matter which sheet you choose to work on.

7

Building Grouped Worksheet Content

As you enter your group content, remember that only the content that is to appear on all the sheets in the group needs to be entered. Don't enter anything that is specific to one sheet in the group. On your division tabs, for example, don't enter anything that pertains to only one of the divisions while the sheets are still grouped.

While you are working on one of the grouped sheets, build your title, column headings, row labels, and any other common content. After entering your content, go through the sheet and apply any required formatting (for example, change fonts and sizes or apply borders and shading), doing anything you want to do to the appearance of all the sheets in the group.

Figure 7.7 shows the common content for a group of sheets that track the sales for five divisions in one company.

FIGURE 7.7

Enter content and apply formats that are appropriate for all the sheets in the group.

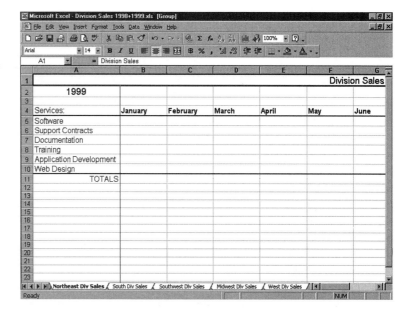

Ungrouping Worksheets

When you're ready to start entering specific data on individual sheets, you can break your group apart. Choose one of the following methods to ungroup your sheets:

- Click on a sheet tab that's not in the group. The grouped tabs turn gray again, and only the sheet that you've clicked remains white.

- If there are no sheets that aren't part of the current group (and, therefore, you can't use the first method), right-click any one of the sheet tabs and choose Ungroup Sheets from the shortcut menu (see Figure 7.8).

FIGURE 7.8

Before entering content that doesn't belong on all the sheets in your group, ungroup the worksheets.

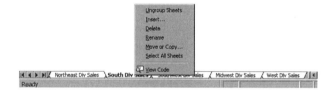

If you later realize that you neglected to enter some of the common content, you can always regroup and enter what you forgot. Similarly, if, while the sheets were grouped, you entered anything or applied any formats that you don't want applied to all the sheets, you can edit the ungrouped sheets individually to remove any unwanted content or formats.

Using AutoSum to Add Columns and Rows

So far, this discussion of Excel has not covered the most commonly performed task in any spreadsheet—the totaling of a series of numbers that are stored in your worksheet's cells. In Excel, this process requires the use of a feature called AutoSum, and is primarily an intuitive procedure. When you click at the foot of a column or at the end of a row of numbers and invoke Excel's AutoSum feature, Excel "guesses" which cells you want to total. You can redirect the process if the guess is incorrect; in most cases, however, Excel guesses correctly, based on the position of the cell that contains the total in relation to the cells that contain numbers.

To use Excel's AutoSum feature, follow these steps:

1. To total a column or row of cells, click at the end of the column or row, in the cell that is to contain the total.

7

2. Click the AutoSum button on the Standard toolbar. A dashed border appears around the cells that Excel assumes you want to total (see Figure 7.9).

FIGURE 7.9

If there are numbers in the cells above or to the left of the cell that contains the total, Excel assumes that you want to total those numbers.

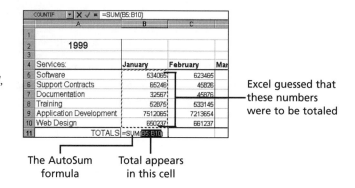

Excel guessed that these numbers were to be totaled

The AutoSum formula

Total appears in this cell

3. If Excel's assumption is correct, press Enter or click the AutoSum button again to perform the calculation.

The total appears in the cell, and a formula is built. The formula for a total appears in Figure 7.10.

The AutoSum formula appears on the Formula Bar

FIGURE 7.10

A simple total is calculated quickly and easily with AutoSum.

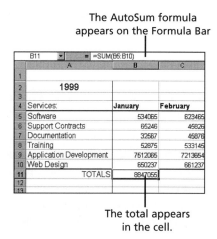

The total appears in the cell.

Redirecting an AutoSum Formula

What if Excel's guess as to which cells you want to total is wrong? When you click the AutoSum button, if the dashed border doesn't encompass the correct group of cells, you can redirect it by dragging through or clicking in the cells that you do want to total.

To redirect an AutoSum formula to a different range of cells, follow these steps:

1. Click in the cell that is to contain your total.

2. Click the AutoSum button. Observe the dashed border around the cells that Excel assumes you need totaled.

3. Using your mouse, click and drag through the contiguous range of cells that you want to total. The AutoSum formula is edited to include the range you select (see Figure 7.11).

FIGURE 7.11

Redirect Excel's AutoSum formula to include a different range of cells.

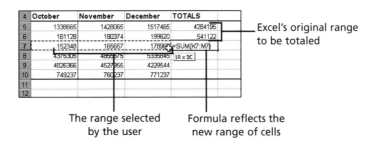

The range selected by the user

Formula reflects the new range of cells

4. Press Enter to perform the AutoSum on the newly selected range of cells.

> **Tip**
>
> Your range of cells that are to be totaled can be anywhere—in a distant block of cells somewhere on the same worksheet, on a different worksheet in the workbook, or in another workbook altogether. Formulas that include data from different workbooks and worksheets are discussed later today.

When using AutoSum, you aren't restricted to contiguous ranges of numbers. Your AutoSum formula can include single noncontiguous cell addresses as well as multiple random ranges of contiguous cells. To edit an AutoSum formula to include single and random ranges of cells, follow these steps:

1. Click in the cell in which you want the total to appear.

2. Click the AutoSum button.

7

3. Ignoring Excel's assumed range of cells, click in the first single cell that you want to include in your total.

4. Press and hold the Ctrl key, and continue clicking in other single cells. The single cell addresses are added to the formula, each separated by a comma (see Figure 7.12).

FIGURE 7.12

Using the Ctrl key, you can gather as many individual cells as you want in your AutoSum formula.

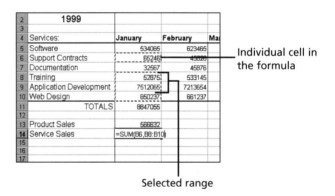

	1999		
Services:		January	February
Software		534065	623465
Support Contracts		65246	45826
Documentation		32567	45876
Training		52875	533145
Application Development		7512065	7213654
Web Design		650237	661237
	TOTALS	8847055	
Product Sales		=SUM(B5,B7)	
Service Sales			

5. If you want to include a range of cells in your formula, continue holding the Ctrl key and drag through any range of contiguous cells. The range appears, with a colon between the first and last cell address in the range (see Figure 7.13).

FIGURE 7.13

Add a range of cells to your collection of random cells.

	1999			
Services:		January	February	Ma
Software		534065	623465	
Support Contracts		65246	45826	
Documentation		32567	45876	
Training		52875	533145	
Application Development		7512065	7213654	
Web Design		650237	661237	
	TOTALS	8847055		
Product Sales		566632		
Service Sales		=SUM(B6,B8:B10)		

Individual cell in the formula

Selected range

6. When all the cells that you want to total are represented in the formula, press Enter.

Tip

To create totals for a series of columns or rows, select the cells in which the consecutive totals are to appear, and click the AutoSum button; the totals for each column or row appear in the cells automatically.

Editing an AutoSum Formula

After you press the Enter key to perform an AutoSum calculation, the formula can still be edited to reflect changes in the range or group of cells that you want to total. You don't necessarily need to delete the current formula and start over, although that is one approach if the required changes are extensive.

To edit an existing AutoSum formula, follow these steps:

1. Click in the cell that contains the formula, and edit the formula on the Formula Bar (see Figure 7.14). The formula itself does not appear in the cell unless you double-click the cell.

Formula on the
Formula Bar

FIGURE 7.14

The Formula Bar gives you more room to maneuver as you edit your AutoSum formula.

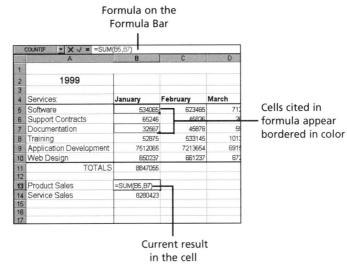

Cells cited in formula appear bordered in color

Current result
in the cell

2. Type any additional cell addresses or edit the addresses that are included in the formula.

3. Press Enter to put your changes into effect and recalculate.

Updating an AutoSum

The primary benefit of using cell addresses in formulas rather than actual numbers is that you can update the result by changing the content of the cells that are used in the formula. For example, if your result totals the range of cells from B5 through B10 (`=SUM(B5:B10)`), if you change the number in cells B5, B6, B7, B8, B9, or B10, the result is recalculated and updated automatically.

7

To update the results of a formula by editing the content of a cell or cells that are included in the formula, follow these steps:

1. Click in the cell that contains your total. The formula is displayed on the Formula Bar (see Figure 7.15). Note the cell addresses that are included in the formula.

FIGURE 7.15

Use the Formula Bar's display to remind you which cells are included in the formula.

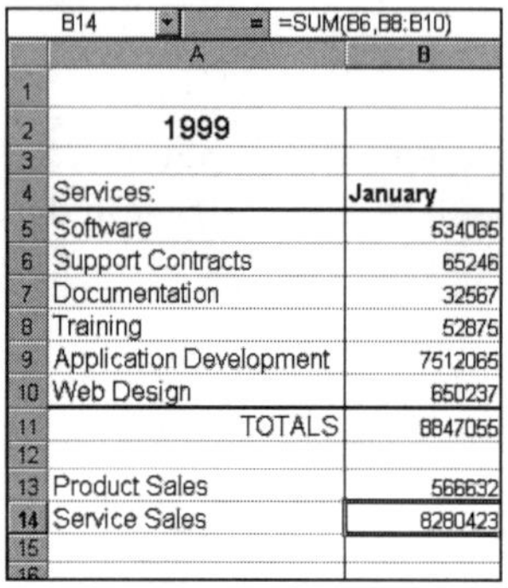

2. Go to the cell that you want to edit. Click in the cell and type the new number.

3. Press Enter. Note that the result in the cell that contains the AutoSum formula updates automatically.

4. Continue editing any of the other cells that are in the AutoSum formula, pressing Enter after each cell is edited.

Building Simple Formulas

NEW TERM   The AutoSum feature invokes a *function*; a function is an established mathematical procedure that adds up the numbers in the cells that are included between the parentheses, as in the case of the formula =SUM(B5:B10). The word SUM tells Excel to add the cells (you'll learn about other functions later). For now, you want to create your own formulas—formulas that combine mathematical operations (addition, subtraction, multiplication, division) and incorporate real numbers as well as cell addresses into the formula.

To start, all formulas need an equal sign (=). This tells Excel that what follows is a formula. The AutoSum process inserts this sign for you, but when you build your own formulas, you must type the equal sign yourself.

To build a formula, follow these steps:

1. Click in the cell that is to contain the result of the formula.

2. Type the equal sign. Think of this as telling Excel, "This cell will be equal to...".

3. Click in the first cell that contains a number that you want to use in your formula. The cell address is placed in the formula, as shown in Figure 7.16.

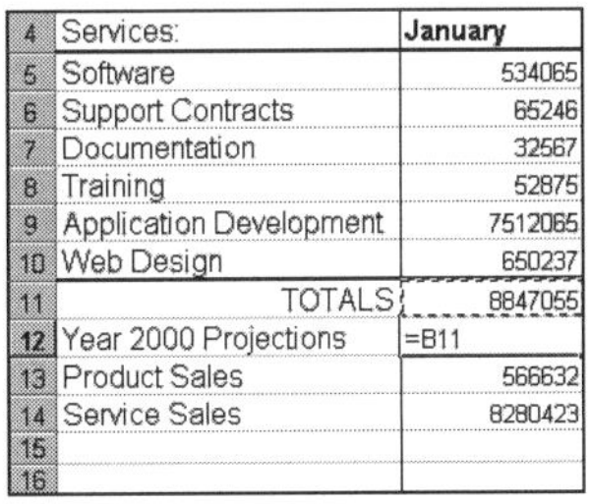

FIGURE 7.16

Don't type the cell addresses for your formula—it wastes time and creates a large margin for error. Click in the cells to include them in your formula.

4	Services:	January
5	Software	534065
6	Support Contracts	65246
7	Documentation	32567
8	Training	52875
9	Application Development	7512065
10	Web Design	650237
11	TOTALS	8847055
12	Year 2000 Projections	=B11
13	Product Sales	566632
14	Service Sales	8280423
15		
16		

4. Type a mathematical operator, such as +, −, * (for multiplication), or / (for division).

5. Click in another cell or type a number that you want to add to, subtract from, multiply, or divide the first cell by. This second cell address or number becomes part of the formula, as shown in Figure 7.17.

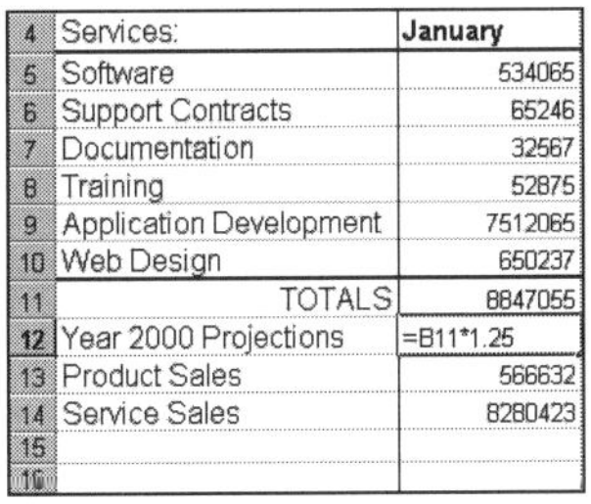

FIGURE 7.17

*You can gather as many cells or type as many numbers as you want, separating each separated with an operator such as +, −, *, or /.*

4	Services:	January
5	Software	534065
6	Support Contracts	65246
7	Documentation	32567
8	Training	52875
9	Application Development	7512065
10	Web Design	650237
11	TOTALS	8847055
12	Year 2000 Projections	=B11*1.25
13	Product Sales	566632
14	Service Sales	8280423
15		
16		

6. For a simple calculation, press Enter to end the process and perform the calculation.

Controlling the Order of Operations

NEW TERM If your formula contains more than one operation, you might have to concern yourself with a mathematical concept known as *order of operations*. This concept is based on the order in which certain mathematical operations are performed. Excel follows these standard rules and applies them to your formulas.

7

When you're simply adding or subtracting numbers, you can gather as many cells as you need; for example, the formula =B5+B7-C5 adds B5 and B7, and then subtracts C5 from that. It works just fine the way you created it, in the order in which you gathered the cells and typed the operators.

If, however, you perform any multiplication or division, you must bear in mind the following order of operations:

- An operation that is in parentheses is performed first.
- Multiplication is performed after anything in parentheses.
- Division is performed after multiplication.
- Addition is performed next.
- Subtraction is the last operation performed.

 Tip

> To help you remember this order of operations, remember the sentence that I was taught in grade school: *Please My Dear Aunt Sally*, or *P* (parentheses), *M* (multiplication), *D* (division), *A* (addition), and *S* (subtraction).

To control the order of operations, you must use parentheses. The use of parentheses tells Excel to perform the operation that is within the parentheses first. In the formula =(B5+C5)*D5, cells B5 and C5 are added together, and their sum is multiplied by D5. Without the parentheses, however, Excel would have multiplied C5 by D5, and then added B5 to the result of that operation. If you look at it with real numbers, consider the two different results:

- (5+3)x6=48 (with parentheses, 8 is multiplied by 6)
- 5+3x6=23 (without parentheses, 5 is added to 18)

If you have several sets of parentheses, the operations are performed before any surrounding operations. Consider, for example, =(B5+C7)*B10+(G7+G10). In this formula, the operations that are in parentheses are performed first, followed by multiplication, and finally by the addition of the result of G7 plus G10. Figure 7.18 shows a formula with parentheses that control the order of operations in a worksheet.

FIGURE 7.18

Use parentheses to dictate the order of operations.

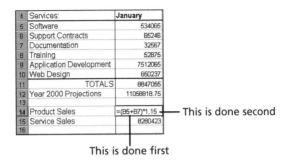

4	Services:	January
5	Software	534065
6	Support Contracts	65246
7	Documentation	32567
8	Training	52875
9	Application Development	7512065
10	Web Design	650237
11	TOTALS	8847055
12	Year 2000 Projections	11058818.75
13		
14	Product Sales	=(B5+B7)*1.15
15	Service Sales	8280423
16		

This is done second

This is done first

Using Excel's Built-in Formulas

As you've seen today, you can create virtually any formula that you need. By clicking in cells, typing numbers, and adding parentheses to control the order in which your operations are performed, you can make just about anything happen in your Excel worksheet—mathematically, that is. The only potential limitation that you might encounter is your own knowledge of accounting or mathematics. What do you do if you don't know how to construct a formula to achieve a certain result?

To help you handle more complex operations, Excel has an extensive set of functions. You've already used one today—the SUM function, created through the use of the AutoSum button. The word *SUM* at the beginning of your AutoSum formulas invokes the SUM function, and tells Excel to add up all the cells in the formula. Excel offers hundreds of other functions, however, many of which you'll never use (or even think of a reason to use); but most of them have realistic applications in any worksheet. Today, you will use a few of the more common functions, such as

- **AVERAGE**—Although you might know that an average is obtained by totaling a series of numbers and dividing by the number of numbers in the series, it is time-consuming to build that formula yourself. The AVERAGE function does it for you.

- **COUNT**—Sure, you can count the number of items in a column, but why do it manually if the COUNT function can do it for you?

- **COUNTIF**—How about counting the number of cells in a range that meet a certain criteria? COUNTIF compares your criteria to the range of cells that you specify and tells you how many cells match the criteria.

7

Averaging a Range of Cells

In your division sales worksheet, you can average the sales for each month and for each sales representative by using the AVERAGE function. You can type the function and the parentheses and drag through the range of cells yourself, or you can invoke the function automatically and use the Function dialog box to set the range and perform the calculation.

Typing a Function Formula Manually

Building a function requires two things: that you know the name of the function, and the information that Excel needs to perform the function properly. In the case of the AVERAGE function, the word AVERAGE is the name of the function, and the range of cells to be averaged is the information that Excel requires.

To average a month's sales in your division sales worksheet, follow these steps:

1. Click in the cell that is to contain the average result.

2. Type the following: =AVERAGE(

3. Click in the first cell in the range of cells to be averaged, and drag through the entire range of cells.

4. When the range appears in the formula, type a right parenthesis, and press Enter. The average is calculated and appears in the cell.

Tip

You don't have to bother typing the final right parenthesis—the formula works even if you don't—but it's good practice to insert it. Many formulas won't work if you have an uneven number (any incomplete pairs) of parentheses, and you need to get into the habit of watching out for this common oversight.

Caution

Be careful when typing a function formula; a typographical error in the name of the function, any additional spaces between arguments (parts of the formula), or the omission of a comma, colon, operator, or other required element results in an error message instead of the expected result.

Using the Paste Function Dialog Box

If you'd prefer to be coached through the process of building your AVERAGE formula, follow these steps to display the Paste Function dialog box:

1. Click in the cell that you want to contain your average result.

2. Click the Paste Function button on the Standard toolbar.

3. The Paste Function dialog box opens (see Figure 7.19).

FIGURE 7.19

Select the AVERAGE *function from the Most Recently Used category, or choose the All category and scroll to find* AVERAGE *listed alphabetically.*

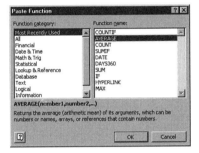

4. Click the Most Recently Used category, and view the functions in the Function name list.

5. Select AVERAGE, and click OK to begin building the function.

6. As shown in Figure 7.20, the formula is started for you on the Formula bar (and also in the cell, but the dialog box might be obscuring it).

FIGURE 7.20

The function name and a set of parentheses appear automatically when you choose your function.

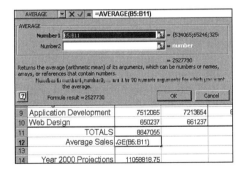

7

7. If you need to adjust the range that Excel has selected for your function, click the Shrink button at the end of the Number1 box. This reduces the dialog box to a title bar and enables you to drag through the range of cells that you want to average (see Figure 7.21).

FIGURE 7.21

Shrink the dialog box or drag it aside to expose your work-sheet's cells. Drag through the cells you need for the formula.

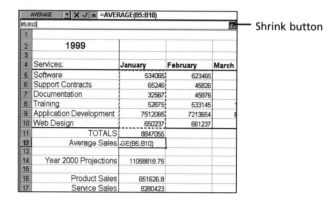

Shrink button

8. Drag through the cells that you want to average, and press Enter.

9. The dialog box reopens. Click OK to close the dialog box and perform the calculation.

Note

The Number2 box in the Paste Function dialog box offers you the capability to select an additional range of cells to average. You can select up to five ranges.

NEW TERM   This process is a lot longer and more complex than just typing the function formula and dragging through the range of cells, but it serves to familiarize you with the process of building a function that isn't as simple as AVERAGE. Each box (such as Number1 or Number2) in the function dialog box represents an *argument*, or component of the function formula. Arguments are separated by commas, and these commas are placed in the formula for you if you go through the function dialog box. If you type the function yourself, you have to type them yourself, and omitting one or placing one in the wrong place prevents the formula from calculating properly.

Counting Cells in a Range

With COUNT, as with AVERAGE, it's easier to type the function manually than to go through the paste dialog box. To count the number of cells in a range, follow these steps:

1. Click in the cell in which the COUNT result is to appear.
2. Type the following: =COUNT(
3. Click and drag through the range of cells to be counted.
4. Type the right parenthesis) at the end of the formula.
5. Press Enter to perform the function.

Why use COUNT? If your range spans many rows or columns, it's easier to use the function than to subtract the first row number from the last or to figure out (in the case of columns) how many control button letters fall between your first and last columns. Also, if you add rows or columns within the range, the count increments automatically if you use the COUNT function to calculate it.

Counting with Criteria Applied

COUNTIF takes a simple COUNT and makes it an intelligent function. You can use it, for example, to count the number of sales representatives with sales exceeding $500,000. Follow these steps:

1. Click in the cell in which your COUNTIF result is to appear.
2. Type the following: =COUNTIF(
3. Drag through the range of cells that are to be counted.
4. Type a comma after the last cell in the range.
5. In quotes, type your criteria. In this case, type ">500,000".
6. Type the right parenthesis). The resulting formula appears in Figure 7.22.

FIGURE 7.22

The comma separates the range argument from the criteria argument in the function.

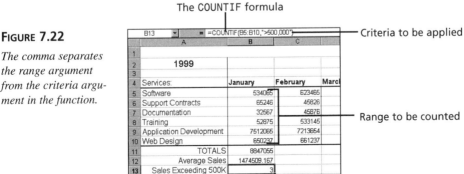

The COUNTIF formula

Criteria to be applied

Range to be counted

7

7. Press Enter. The number of sales reps with sales exceeding $500,000 is displayed in the cell.

If you edit any of the cells in the range and the number of reps with sales exceeding $500,000 changes, the COUNTIF result automatically updates.

Repeating Formulas through a Range of Cells

Imagine a series of columns, each of which needs a total at its foot. Below each total, you also need an average. With the skills you've acquired today, coming up with both of these numbers is easy. What makes the process even easier is the fact that you need only to perform the two calculations once—on the first column in the series. Using the Fill Handle (you used it to fill in custom lists of days and months), you can fill the formulas across the columns, saving yourself the repetitive task of calculating a total and average for each column.

To repeat a formula through adjacent cells, follow these steps:

1. Click in the cell that contains the formula that you want to repeat throughout a series of cells.

2. Point to the cell's Fill Handle (see Figure 7.23), and drag through the cells in which you want to repeat the selected formula.

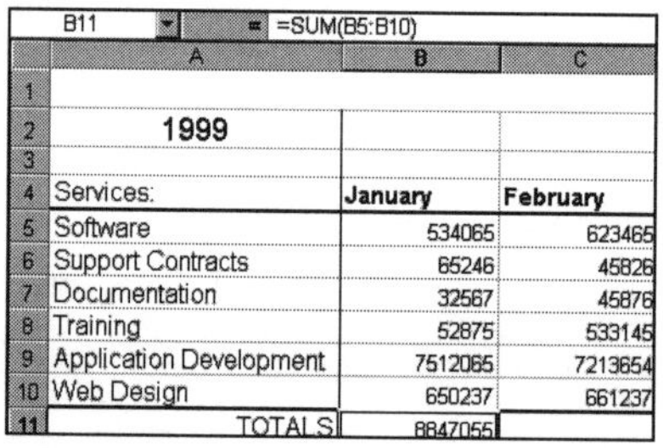

FIGURE 7.23

Although you normally drag through a row or down a single column, you can drag and copy your formula through any configuration of adjoining cells.

3. At the end of the series, release the mouse. The formula is placed in each of the cells in your series, updated to include the cell addresses that are appropriate for the new location of each repeated formula.

Understanding Relative Addressing

To understand what has happened to the repeated versions of your original formula, click in any of the cells that now contain totals; notice that the cell addresses in the formula have changed to reflect the new location of the formula. If the original formula totaled cells B3–B8, for example, the total at the foot of column C totals cells C3–C8. This phenomenon is known as *relative addressing*—the formulas are updated relative to their new positions.

Figure 7.24 shows a series of cells containing a formula that was copied from cell B11.

FIGURE 7.24

Relative Addressing allows formulas to update to match their new location.

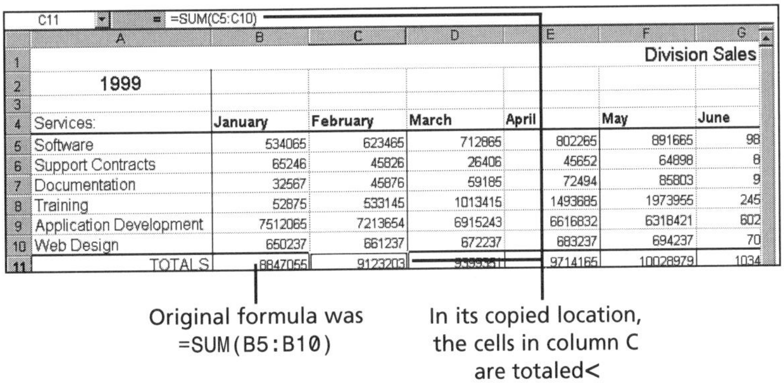

Original formula was
=SUM(B5:B10)

In its copied location, the cells in column C are totaled<

Using Absolute References

NEW TERM What if you want to copy a formula through adjacent cells but don't want some or all of the cell addresses to update in the new versions of the formula? An *absolute reference* gives you the control you need. Absolute references are cells in a formula that do not update when a formula is copied to a new location. Figure 7.25 shows a worksheet with formulas containing an absolute reference.

FIGURE 7.25

Designate one or more cells as absolute references, and the cell addresses don't update when the formula is copied to adjacent cells.

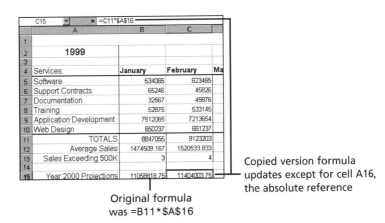

Copied version formula updates except for cell A16, the absolute reference

Original formula was =B11*A16

7

Sometimes you want to use a specific cell in every repetition of a formula; for example, you do so when one cell contains a multiplier or amount that is to be used in every repetition of the formula. If you don't make that cell absolute, the formulas cite empty cells or cells that contain text as the cell addresses update to match the new locations of the formula. Storing static data in one cell also makes it easier to update the results of all the repeated formulas; in Figure 7.26, the content of cell A16 has changed, so the results in row 15 have changed accordingly.

FIGURE 7.26

Rather than use a real number in the formula, cite a cell that contains the number. When you want to change the formula, you only need to change that one cell in order to change all your formulas' results.

Changed from 1.25 to 1.30

B15				=B11*A16			
	A	B	C	D	E	F	G
1							Division Sales
2	1999						
3							
4	Services:	January	February	March	April	May	June
5	Software	534065	623465	712665	802265	891665	98
6	Support Contracts	65246	45826	26406	45652	64898	8
7	Documentation	32567	45876	59185	72494	85803	9
8	Training	52875	533145	1013415	1493685	1973955	245
9	Application Development	7512065	7213654	6915243	6616832	6318421	602
10	Web Design	650237	661237	672237	683237	694237	70
11	TOTALS	8847055	9123203	9399351	9714165	10028979	1034
12	Average Sales	1474509.167	1520533.833	1566558.5	1619027.5	1671496.5	17239
13	Sales Exceeding 500K	3	4	4	4	4	
14							
15	Year 2000 Projections	11501171.5	11860163.9	12219156.3	12628414.5	13037672.7	134469
16	1.3						
17	Product Sales						

Formulas now show a 30% increase

To create a formula with an absolute reference, follow these steps:

1. Click in the cell that is to contain the formula.

2. Begin your formula with the equal sign (=), and click in the first cell that you want to include in the formula. If this cell or any subsequent cells are to be absolute references, press the F4 key as soon as you click in the cell. Dollar signs appear in front of the column letter and row number for the cell's address (see Figure 7.27).

FIGURE 7.27

Dollar signs in front of the column letter and row number indicate that the cell is an absolute reference, so the address does not change when the formula containing it is copied to other cells.

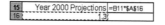

15	Year 2000 Projections	=B11*A16
16	1.3	

3. Continue to create your formula and press Enter when your formula is complete.

If a range of cells is to be the absolute reference, both the first and last cells need to be designated as absolute references. You can type the dollar signs manually; or you can click on the Formula Bar in front of the first address and press F4, and then click in front of the last address and press F4 again.

Creating 3D Formulas

Three-dimensional formulas are formulas that include cells from two or more worksheets or workbooks. The process of including cell addresses from several sheets or books is simple and doesn't deviate much from the basic formula-building skills you've learned today.

Formulas that draw data from two or more places enable you to summarize several sheets on a separate sheet or to bring data from an entirely different workbook into your data, giving both the source workbook and your current workbook added dimension.

Combining Worksheets in a Single Formula

A single workbook has not just width and height, but also depth—the three sheets (or more, if you've added any extras) give the workbook a third dimension. Formulas that draw from two or more sheets in a workbook also have depth. To create a 3D formula in a single workbook, follow these steps:

1. Click in the cell that you want to contain your formula.

2. Begin your formula by typing an equal sign (=), and click in the first cell that you want to include in the formula. If that cell is in another sheet, click that sheet's tab and then click in the cell within that sheet. Figure 7.28 shows the beginning of the formula.

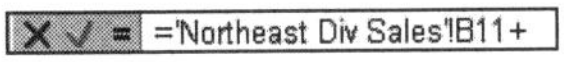

FIGURE 7.28

| ✗ ✓ = | ='Northeast Div Sales'!B11+ |

In this case, the first cell in the formula comes from another sheet.

7

3. As needed, type in your operator and click in another cell on the same or a different worksheet in the current workbook.

4. When your formula is complete, do *not* go back to the sheet that contains the formula unless you need to select another cell from that sheet for the formula. Press Enter to complete your formula.

You can click on as many sheets and in as many cells as you need for your formula, typing operators between cell addresses and inserting parentheses to control the order of operations. In short, do nothing differently than you do when building a formula that includes cells from a single sheet.

Combining Data from Different Workbooks in a Formula

If your formula requires data that you have stored in another workbook, you must open that workbook in order to include one or more of its cells in your formula. Like the process of including cells from multiple sheets, including cells from multiple workbooks doesn't deviate too much from the procedure that you use to create a simple formula that draws from a single sheet. To build your multiworkbook formula, follow these steps:

1. Make sure that the additional workbook you want to use is open.

2. Switch back to the workbook that is to contain the formula (to access that workbook, use the Window menu or click its button on the Taskbar).

3. Click in the cell that is to contain the formula.

4. Begin your formula with the equal sign (=); if the first cell of the formula is in the current workbook, click in it.

5. Type in the operator. To select a cell in the other workbook, switch to that workbook by selecting it from the Window menu.

6. In that workbook, click the sheet that contains the cell you need. The workbook name appears in square brackets, and the sheet name appears followed by an exclamation point (see Figure 7.29).

FIGURE 7.29

The formula shows the workbook and sheet name for all the cells that come from external sources.

Workbook filename

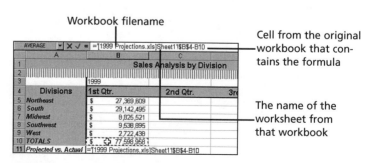

Cell from the original workbook that contains the formula

The name of the worksheet from that workbook

7. Click in the cell you want, and then type in your next operator or press Enter if the formula is complete.

Tip Excel's Functions (such as AVERAGE and COUNT) can utilize data from two or more worksheets or workbooks: Simply gather your function's arguments by selecting cells from other worksheets (click the worksheet tab and then click in the cells you need) or workbooks (select the workbook from the File menu and then click in the desired cells).

Summary

Today you learned how to increase the power and functionality of your worksheets through adding, naming, and grouping worksheets, building formulas, working with functions, and creating formulas that draw data from more than one worksheet or workbook. These skills complete your basic understanding of using Excel to store financial information. Day 8, "Building an Excel Database," will demonstrate how to use Excel as a tool for storing, sorting, and filtering data. Through the creation of a database, you'll learn how data is built and stored, and how Excel can be used to display and extract specific information from the data.

Q&A

Q If I have a formula that draws data from a different worksheet or workbook, what happens to the formula's result if I delete or move the data in the external location?

A If you delete the data, the formula returns an error message, such as #REF!, that tells you that the formula refers to something that's missing or that isn't a number. If you move the data, the formula updates to reflect the new location of the data.

Q Is there any way to display my formulas, rather than the results of the formulas, in the cells?

A Yes. Choose Tools, Options, and then click the View tab. In the Window options section of the Options dialog box, place a checkmark in the box next to Formulas. This setting applies only to the active workbook.

7

Q If I have formatted my numeric data to display no decimals, are the decimals still included in any calculations that refer to those cells?

A Yes. Even if a cell's content is hidden through formatting, the actual cell content (visible on the Formula Bar when the cell is active) is included in any calculations. For example, if your cell contains the number 7.32 and only 7 is showing, 7.32 is used in any formula that refers to that cell.

Workshop

The section that follows is a quick quiz about the day. If you have any problems answering any of the questions, see the section that follows the quiz for all the answers.

Quiz

1. When naming a worksheet, can you use spaces and punctuation?

2. Name the one item common to all formulas in Excel.

3. What function do you use to total a column of numbers?

4. List the prescribed order of operations for any formula.

5. True or false: You press F8 to turn a cell address into an absolute reference.

6. Describe two ways to ungroup a series of grouped worksheets.

7. True or false: To group a series of contiguous worksheets, you press and hold the Alt key as you click the tabs.

Quiz Answers

1. Yes, you can use spaces, punctuation, and all alphanumeric characters in your worksheet names.

2. The equal sign (=) is common to all Excel formulas and functions.

3. The SUM function is used to total a series of cells. The AutoSum button on the standard toolbar automatically invokes this function, or you can type it yourself to construct the formula manually.

4. The standard order of operations for any equation (not just in Excel) is Parentheses, Multiplication, Division, Addition, Subtraction.

5. False. The F4 key is used to mark a cell address as the absolute reference.

6. To ungroup a group of sheets, click on the tab of any sheet that is not in the group, or right-click one of the grouped sheet's tabs and choose Ungroup sheets from the shortcut menu.

7. False. The Shift key is used to select a group of contiguous sheets. Click the first tab in the series, and then—with the Shift key pressed—click the last sheet in the series. The first and last sheets, and all interim sheets, are grouped. To select non-contiguous sheets, use the Ctrl key.

7

DAY **8**

Building an Excel Database

On Day 6, "Building a Spreadsheet in an Excel Workbook," and Day 7, "Adding Worksheet Depth and Power," you learned to use Excel for storing numeric (and mostly financial) information—columns and rows of text, numbers, and formulas that document sales, products sold, and pricing information. Today you learn how to use Excel as a database tool. Unlike Access, Excel is not a database management program. It is, however, a great tool for maintaining lists: address lists, lists of products, personnel, contact information, service and repair histories—any data you maintain in list format. Today you'll learn to build, maintain, and use the data that you store in an Excel list database through coverage of the following topics:

- Understanding database concepts and terminology
- The basics of setting up a database for greater effectiveness and efficiency
- Techniques for entering records quickly and accurately
- Methods for efficient editing and deletion of records
- Sorting and filtering database records to make use of your entered data
- Creating a PivotTable for 3D views of the data

Understanding Database Concepts

A database is a collection of data, a tabular list of information. The phonebook is a database. Your daybook or personal organizer is a database. Your mind is a database, full of memories and information. Excel provides a simple tool for putting all that information—memories, dates, names, places—in a logical list format for easy retrieval and documentation.

It's important to understand the structure of databases in general, and of an Excel list database specifically. A database is a collection of records. Think of the phonebook: Each listing in the phonebook is a *record*, and each record is broken down into *fields*. In the phonebook, the fields in each record are

- Last Name
- First Name
- Address
- City
- Phone Number

The phone company keeps more information on each person who is listed, but only the fields that were listed previously are actually printed in the book. Excel gives you that capability as well; you can break each of your records down into as many as 256 fields, but you can choose to display or print only those that you need.

How many fields does each record require? As many as you need to properly view and search through your records. Why not have a single field for each person that lists the entire string of information about them? Because the more you break a record down into small parts, the more flexibility you have to look at and manipulate the data.

For example, if you have a field called Address that contains the house number, street, city, state, and zip code all in one string, how do you search for all the records for people living in a specific city? How do you sort the records by zip code to print bulk mailing labels? You can't—at least not easily. By breaking Address into Street address, City, State, and Zip, you can look for people on certain streets in certain towns. You can put everyone in New Jersey together, and then sort them by zip code. The more detailed your database is, the more you can do with it.

Building a List Database in Excel

An Excel database places each record in a row, and the fields are set up in the columns on the worksheet. Figure 8.1 shows the field names for a database, with one record entered.

Fields

FIGURE 8.1

Use up to 256 of your worksheet's columns to break your records into usable fields.

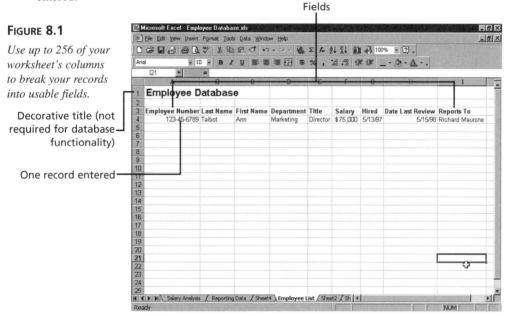

Decorative title (not required for database functionality)

One record entered

 Caution Your list database can have as many as 65,535 records (65,536 rows per sheet, less one row for your field names) and cannot span worksheets in a workbook. If you need more than 65,000 records, consider Access for your database needs.

Setting Up Fields

The first step in building a database is to decide how many fields you need and what to call them. The names and number of fields depend on the type of data you're storing and how you plan to sort it and search through it for specific records.

For a personnel database, which you are building today, you need the following fields:

- Employee number (social security number)
- Last Name
- First Name
- Department
- Job Title
- Salary
- Date Hired
- Date of Last Review
- Reports To (name of manager/supervisor)

In "real life," you can probably think of other pieces of information that might be stored about an employee—perhaps the number of vacation days they've earned, or the number of sick days they took last year. For the purposes of this exercise, however, you are making a more simplified database. The techniques that you use to build it will enable you to create as complex a database as your real requirements dictate.

To create your fields, follow these steps:

1. Click in the first cell of the row that you've chosen to be your fields row. If your worksheet has a decorative title, the fields row needs to be at least two rows below it to keep the sheet from looking too crowded (see Figure 8.2).

FIGURE 8.2

Add a decorative title and choose your fields row.

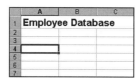

2. Type the name of your first field. Widen the column as necessary to fit the field name and the anticipated width of your entries into that field or column. Figure 8.3 shows your first field, with the column widened appropriately.

FIGURE 8.3

You can abbreviate field names, as long as the abbreviation still clearly explains the nature of the data in the field.

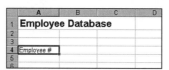

3. Press Tab and type your next field name. Repeat the column width adjustment.

4. Continue to press Tab as you enter field names and move across the field names row in your worksheet. When you've entered your last field, press Home to return to the first field.

5. Click the column control button at the top of your first field column. The entire column is selected.

6. Choose Format, Cells, and then click the Number tab.

7. In the Category list, choose Custom. The Type box opens on the right side of the dialog box (see Figure 8.4).

FIGURE 8.4

The Custom Number category enables you to create your own mask, or overlay, for the selected cells (in this case, the entire Employee Number column).

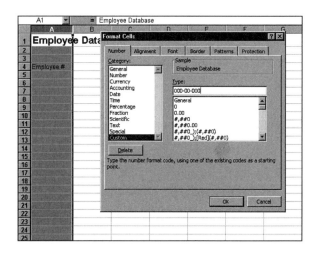

8. Select the content that is in the Type box and type the following: 000-00-0000

9. Press Enter. The dialog box closes and the column is formatted for numbers that fall into the pattern of a social security number.

10. Click the control buttons for the two date fields (drag through them to select both columns).

11. Choose Format, Cells; from within the Number tab, select the Date category.

12. Select the date format that you want to use (use 3/14/98, as shown in Figure 8.5).

FIGURE 8.5

With your data entry task in mind, select a date format that seems natural to you and the way your organization typically stores or writes the date.

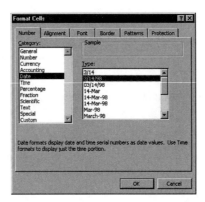

13. Click OK or press Enter to close the dialog box.

14. Select the Salary column by clicking the control button at the top of that column.

15. Click the Currency button on the Formatting toolbar. The entire column is now formatted for currency.

Your fields are now set to accept data and display that data in formats that match the nature of the fields. Text fields normally don't require any special formatting, so leave those fields alone.

Entering Your Records

Your first field in the first record is the employee's social security number. Because you created a custom format for this column, you don't need to type the dashes in the numbers. To enter the social security number 123-45-6789, for example, simply type those numbers. The column's formatting inserts the dashes for you, breaking the number into three parts. Figure 8.6 shows the first record's Employee Number entry.

FIGURE 8.6

Achieve consistency in your records by formatting your columns for the type of entries that are to be placed in them.

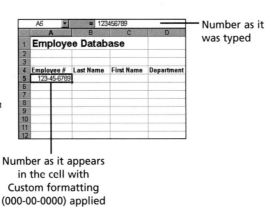

Number as it was typed

Number as it appears in the cell with Custom formatting (000-00-0000) applied

As you enter text into the remaining fields for your first record, press Tab between each field and type your content as you go along. At the end of the row, press the down arrow, and then Home, to return to the first field in the next row down.

As you type your individual records, there will probably be repeated content; for example, in your database, there will be more than one person in the Accounting department, and perhaps more than one Administrative Assistant in that department. Excel's AutoComplete feature makes these repetitions easier to enter and assures the sort of consistency you need as you build a database.

Using AutoComplete to Speed Your Data Entry

As you enter your data, Excel checks the previous entries in the current column and looks for similarities. For example, if your previous records included people in the Accounting, Marketing, and Sales departments, typing A, M, or S as you begin a new record's content in the Department field causes Excel to offer one of these full words in an AutoComplete ScreenTip. Figure 8.7 shows such a "guess" being made by Excel as you enter the second record.

FIGURE 8.7

To accept the AutoComplete "guess," press Enter. Otherwise, just ignore it and keep typing your entry.

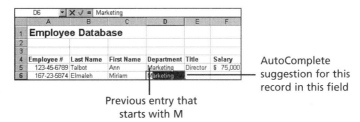

AutoComplete suggestion for this record in this field

Previous entry that starts with M

Continue to build the database, entering record after record. Note one important rule: Do *not* leave any blank rows within your data records. Do not skip a row, and do not delete the contents of an entire row without deleting the row itself (which pulls up the row below it to fill in the blank).

Tip

To quickly build a new record that is very similar to the record directly above it, press Ctrl+'. The content from the cell above is inserted automatically.

> **Caution**
>
> When entering repeated content (such as department names in the sample database), be sure to use consistent terminology and abbreviations. For example, if you enter `Acctg.` for one record, you must use that same abbreviation for the rest of the employees in that department. Failure to maintain this level of consistency makes it difficult to search later for everyone in Accounting—you have to do a custom filter for *Acc* (the common portion of the entry), or you must do separate filters for each way you entered the text.

AutoComplete has some minor limitations, especially when it comes to longer entries that have a common beginning: The AutoComplete suggestion won't appear until after you type the last of the common content. To quickly select a previous entry for a new record or to edit an existing record, right-click the cell in which you want to enter or edit content, and then choose Pick From List. Choose the content that you want from the list that appears.

Don't concern yourself with the order of your records—you can sort them later. To give you some sample data to work with, Figure 8.8 shows a 20-record employee database; you can use these employees to finish your database for today.

FIGURE 8.8

A completed 20-record employee database.

Employee #	Last Name	First Name	Department	Title	Salary	Hired	Last Review	Reports To
			Employee Database					
123-45-6789	Talbot	Ann	Marketing	Director	$ 75,000	5/13/97	5/15/98	Richard Maurone
167-23-5874	Elmaleh	Miriam	Human Resources	Director	$ 68,500	4/20/96	4/15/98	Linda Kline
152-66-7890	Kline	John	Accounting	Manager	$ 62,000	3/29/95	4/1/98	Barbara Weller
124-56-9861	Frankenfield	Craig	Sales	Coordinat	$ 38,000	3/6/98	3/15/98	Zachary Ulrich
139-17-0412	Patrick	Adrienne	Sales	Manager	$ 65,000	2/11/93	2/15/98	Zachary Ulrich
136-04-6535	Mattaliano	Joan	Marketing	Coordinat	$ 35,000	1/20/92	2/1/98	Richard Maurone
136-92-2658	Costanza	Lee	Human Resources	Admin As	$ 28,500	12/28/90	1/15/99	Linda Kline
135-79-8781	Maio	Lou	Accounting	Director	$ 78,250	12/5/98	12/15/98	Barbara Weller
134-67-4904	Balsamo	Anthony	Marketing	Coordinat	$ 32,000	11/12/88	11/15/98	Richard Maurone
133-55-1028	Martin	Robin	Operations	Director	$ 82,000	10/21/87	11/1/98	Martin Chambers
132-42-7151	Fuller	Robert	Operations	Manager	$ 72,500	1/28/99	n/a	Martin Chambers
131-30-3274	Reilly	Mike	Marketing	Coordinat	$ 27,500	9/5/94	9/15/98	Richard Maurone
130-17-9397	Schiller	Jo Ann	Sales	Represer	$ 45,000	8/13/94	8/15/98	Zachary Ulrich
129-05-5520	Miller	Pam	Sales	Represer	$ 52,000	7/22/83	8/1/98	Zachary Ulrich
127-93-1644	Chambers	Rosemary	Marketing	Coordinat	$ 38,750	6/29/92	7/1/98	Richard Maurone
126-80-7767	Kissell	June	Accounting	Admin As	$ 32,500	6/6/98	6/15/98	Barbara Weller
125-68-3890	Pederzani	Bruce	Operations	Admin As	$ 35,000	5/14/97	5/15/98	Martin Chambers
124-56-0013	Ulrich	Lilly	Human Resources	Coordinat	$ 34,500	4/22/79	5/1/98	Linda Kline
123-43-6136	Graham	Alice	Marketing	Coordinat	$ 36,000	3/30/95	4/15/98	Richard Maurone
122-31-2260	Cramer	Martha	Sales	Coordinat	$ 32,500	3/7/97	3/15/98	Zachary Ulrich

Editing Your Database

Editing your database records is no different than editing any other type of worksheet content. Your editing can take three forms:

- Editing specific cells to fix spelling errors, change amounts, or adjust dates
- Inserting records
- Deleting records

You already know how to edit the content of an individual cell, so this section concentrates on inserting and removing records. In an Excel database, each record is stored in its own row. Therefore, to delete a record, you can take one of two approaches:

- **Click the row control button and press Delete**—The contents of the row are deleted, and you can insert a new record in the blank row.
- **Choose Edit, Delete**—The row and its contents are deleted simultaneously, and the row beneath it is moved up. This approach eliminates the potential for accidentally leaving a blank row within the database.

When making these deletions, you can use Undo if you find that you've deleted the wrong data.

To insert a record, pick one of the following methods:

- **Go to the end of the database (Ctrl+Down Arrow) and add the record as a new last row**—You can always re-sort the data to put the record in alphabetical or some other relevant order. Be sure that you're in the first column (usually A) when you press Ctrl+Down Arrow so that you are in the first field when you begin to enter the inserted record.
- **Click on an existing record (in any cell within that record), and then choose Insert, Rows**—A new, blank row appears above the row that contains the active cell. Enter your record data in the new row.

Again, when inserting rows, don't worry about where you add the new record. It's not important to enter your records in alphabetical order or to insert new records where they belong alphabetically. You can sort the database at any time, as you learn in the next section.

Using Your Database

You probably want to do more with your data than simply store it in your worksheet; for example, you might need to print a list of the items in your database or generate a report that shows a select number of your records that meet some criteria. In the case of your employee database, you might want to generate a list of employees for another department to use in setting up email accounts for everyone in the office, or you might want to provide a list of everyone in a particular department.

Excel provides very simple—yet powerful—tools for creating these reports. Using Excel's sorting and filtering tools, you can print or display a list of everyone in the database or just the few that contain specific data in one or more of their fields.

Sorting Database Records

Sorting a database changes the displayed order of the records. It does not extract any particular records or suppress the display or printing of any others. You can sort your Excel database by any field, or by any group of fields. Most lists are sorted alphabetically, but you can also sort by a field that prioritizes or ranks the records (such as the Salary field or the Date Hired field in the sample employee database).

Sorting by a Single Field

If you merely want to place your entire list in order by one field (for example, Last Name to place the employees in alphabetical order, or Date Hired to place them in date order), follow these steps:

1. Locate the field by which you want to sort.

2. In that column, click in any cell other than the field name (see Figure 8.9).

FIGURE 8.9

Click in a cell in the column that corresponds to the field on which you want to sort.

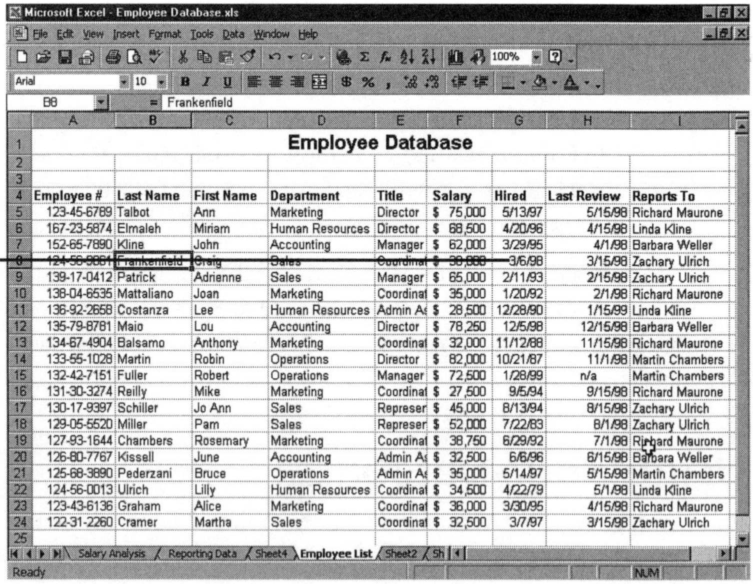

A cell in Date
Hired column
is selected, so
the list will be
sorted by date

3. Click the Sort Ascending or Sort Descending button on the Standard toolbar. The records are sorted by the field that you selected, in the order that you specified.

Figure 8.10 shows your Employee Database, sorted by Date Hired in ascending order (with the earliest-hired listed first).

FIGURE 8.10

Put your database records in any order you need by sorting a single field.

Field sorted   Records in Date
                      Hired order

Caution

The importance of not leaving blank rows within your range of records cannot be stressed enough. If you attempt to sort a database that has one or more blank rows within it, the entire database will not be sorted.

Sorting by Multiple Fields

If you want to sort by more than one field, open the Sort dialog box. First, click in any cell other than a field name, within your data records. Then choose Data, Sort. The dialog box (see Figure 8.11) offers you the capability to sort by up to three different fields.

FIGURE 8.11

Sort your database by one, two, or three different fields using the Sort dialog box.

When you open the Sort dialog box, check the My list has option setting; be sure that Header row is selected. This is important because if this option is not selected, Excel sorts your field names right along with your records.

Assuming that Header row is selected, you can see that one of your field names is already selected in the Sort by list box. The field that is displayed is one of the following: the field by which you last sorted (when doing a single-field sort), the first field in your database if the data has never been sorted before, or the field that contains the cell that was active when you began the sort.

To build your multiple field sort in the Sort dialog box, follow these steps:

1. Click the Sort by list box and choose the first field by which you want to sort. This field needs to be one with very few unique records, such as Department or Reports to in the sample database.

2. Choose the order for the sort—Ascending (the default) or Descending.

3. Click the first Then by list box, and choose the second field by which to sort. The number of unique records in this field is less important than in the first-level sort field.

4. Choose Ascending or Descending for your second-level sort.

5. Click the second Then by list box and choose the third field by which to sort. This field can be entirely unique, such as Employee Number or Last Name. Note that although you are sorting by three fields in this procedure, you *can* sort by only two fields, using only the Sort by and first Then by boxes.

6. When your sort order for the last field is selected, click OK to perform the sort. Figure 8.12 shows the Sort dialog box, prepared to do your three-level sort.

FIGURE 8.12

Choose your multiple-field sort order by selecting the field with the least amount of unique records first, followed by fields with increasing numbers of unique data.

The number of unique records in a field is important because if you want to sort by more than one field, the first field that is chosen must have a lot of duplicate data so that the second- and third-level sorts can sort within the groups created by the first-level sort. Figure 8.13 shows the result of your three-level sort.

FIGURE 8.13

Your data, sorted first by Department, by Salary, and then by Last Name.

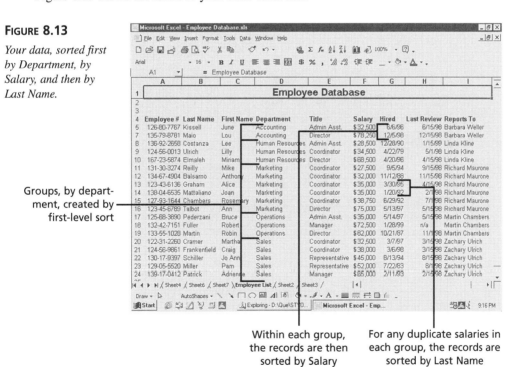

Groups, by depart-
ment, created by
first-level sort

Within each group,
the records are then
sorted by Salary

For any duplicate salaries in
each group, the records are
sorted by Last Name

You can sort your records as many times as you need, in as many different ways as you need. To quickly clear a two or three-level sort and return your list to alphabetical order, simply do a single-field sort by Last Name.

| **Caution** | If the Header row option is not selected when you open the Sort dialog box, you were either in a field name cell when you opened the dialog box or you had a range of cells or rows selected. Close the dialog box. click in a single cell within your data, and try opening the dialog box again. Unless the Header row option is selected, you won't have access to your field names to select the fields by which to sort. |

Filtering Excel Data

Just as sorting shows all your records in the order that you specify, filtering your data shows only the records that you want to see, based on the criteria that you present to the database.

If you sort by Salary, all the records are shown in Salary order. If, however, you want to see only those employees who earn more than $50,000, you need to filter the database, applying the criteria `Salary > 50,000`.

Using AutoFilter

Excel gives you a powerful and flexible tool, known as AutoFilter, to use in applying your criteria to one or many fields in your database. Figure 8.14 shows your employee database filtered to show only those employees in the Marketing department who earn $35,000.

FIGURE 8.14

Filter the Department and Salary fields to create this display of your database.

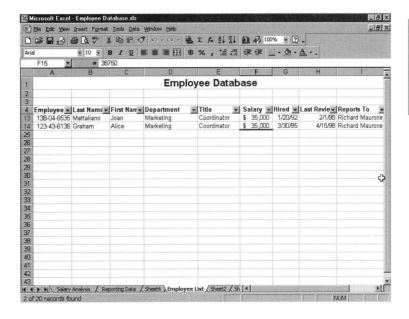

To activate AutoFilter and filter your database, follow these steps:

1. Click in any cell (other than a field name) within your data. Do not click in a blank cell at the end of your records or above your field name cells.

2. Choose Data, Filter, AutoFilter. Each of your columns changes to include a list triangle next to the field names (see Figure 8.15).

FIGURE 8.15

You can sort by one or all of your fields by clicking the AutoFilter list triangles next to the field names.

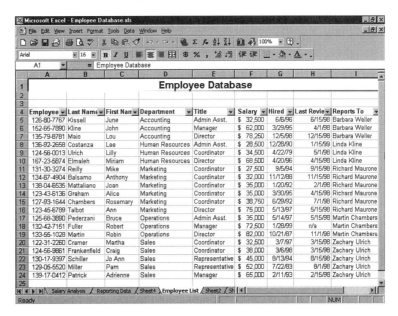

3. Click the list triangle next to the first field by which you want to filter the data. A
   list descends, displaying all the entries for that field in your database (see Figure
   8.16).

4. Click the entry by which you want to filter, such as Accounting in the Department
   field to see only those employees who work in Accounting.

5. Continue to click the list triangles next to any additional fields by which you want
   to filter the data. After each selection, your list of displayed records becomes shorter and shorter because the criteria are applied to the displayed records (the result of
   your previous filters) only.

As you filter on more and more fields, the list of records is reduced because you're
honing in on a more specialized list of records (as shown in Figure 8.17).

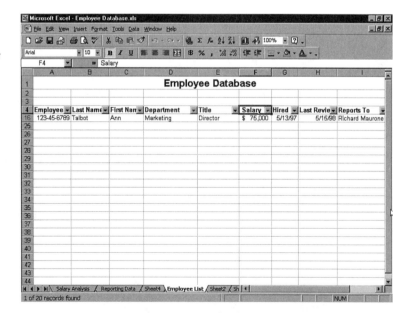

Tip

You can tell at a glance which fields you've filtered by—the list triangles turn blue for the fields that you've used, and the row numbers for the resulting records also turn blue, signifying that the records match your filter criteria.

Tip

To see just the records with the highest or lowest values in a particular field, choose Top 10 from that field's AutoFilter list. In the Top 10 AutoFilter dialog box, choose to Show the Top or Bottom entries, choose the number of entries you want to see, and then select Percent (in lieu of Item) to see the records whose entries for that field make up the highest percentage of the total for the database.

If you've filtered on more than one field, you can bring all your records back onscreen by choosing Data, Filter, Show All; this turns off all filters in all fields. To turn off just one of your filters (for an individual field), click that field's list triangle, and choose (All) from the list.

Creating Custom Filters

In addition to the list of entries made into the selected field, you can choose Custom (see Figure 8.18) to create your own specialized filter.

FIGURE 8.18

Customize your filter by choosing Custom from the list under any field in your database.

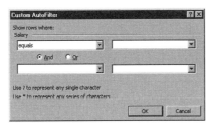

NEW TERM The Custom AutoFilter dialog box offers a list of *Boolean* expressions—greater than, less than, and so on—to which Excel compares the data in your selected field. It is only through a Custom AutoFilter that you can filter for salaries in excess of a certain amount or for people who were hired after a certain date.

To create a custom filter, follow these steps:

1. Click in the field by which you want to filter the data. For this procedure, choose the Salary field.

2. Choose Custom from the AutoFilter list.

3. In the Custom AutoFilter dialog box (see Figure 8.19), choose the Boolean expression that you want use in applying your criteria. In this case, it is greater than.

FIGURE 8.19

Choose from twelve different Boolean expressions in the Custom AutoFilter dialog box.

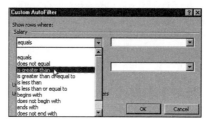

4. In the list box to the right of the expression, enter the comparison value, such as 60,000, to filter for employees with a Salary that is greater than $60,000.

5. If you want to set up another criterion, such as And less than 80,000, click the And option and select another Boolean expression, and then enter another comparison value. Figure 8.20 shows this second-level filter.

FIGURE 8.20

Create a range for your criteria by selecting greater than and less than with two different comparison values.

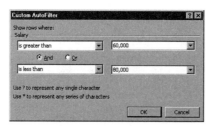

6. Click OK to perform the filter and close the dialog box. Figure 8.21 shows your database, filtered for employees who earn more than $60,000 but less than $80,000.

FIGURE 8.21

Custom AutoFilters give you great flexibility in creating your filter criteria.

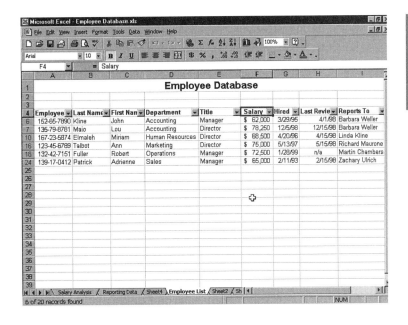

> **Tip**
>
> If you want to filter on a field that contains text, you can use the Contains expression and enter just a portion of the text. For example, to find everyone in Accounting, choose Contains and then enter the comparison value Acc. If you haven't used consistent entries for the Department name, this finds them all, based on common content. The Begins With and Ends With expressions enable you to specify where in the data the portion of the text appears.

After you've filtered your data, you can print the displayed records or return to a normal view of your data by turning off AutoFilter. While your list is filtered, only the displayed records print. To turn AutoFilter off, choose Data, Filter, AutoFilter, which toggles the AutoFilter view. After turning AutoFilter off, the list triangles disappear and, if all your records were not showing (by virtue of your last filter), they all return in the order in which they were last sorted.

>
>
> **Tip**
>
> It's a good idea to turn AutoFilter off before saving and closing your file, especially if you share your database worksheet with other users. If you close the file with the filters on (and with only some of your records displayed as a result of the filters), the file opens in AutoFilter mode for the next user, and the "missing" records might cause that user some confusion.

Hiding Database Columns and Rows

You can choose to hide rows or columns in any worksheet, not just in a list database. Following is a good example of why you might want to do it in a list database, however: You might need to hide, for example, the confidential Salary data in your Employee Database.

Hiding a column or row removes it from your onscreen display and any printouts you make of your worksheet. It doesn't remove the data in the column or row, however, and you can unhide the content at any time.

Hiding a Column

You can hide your column by selecting it (by clicking the column's control button) and choosing Format, Column, Hide. The selected column disappears. You can also use this method to hide several contiguous columns or a group of noncontiguous columns.

An alternative method might appeal to users who feel comfortable with the mouse. To hide your column or columns by reducing their width, follow these steps:

1. Click the control button for the column that you want to hide. The entire column is selected.

2. Point to the seam between the selected column's control button and the control button to its right (see Figure 8.22). Your mouse pointer turns to a two-headed arrow.

FIGURE 8.22

The process of hiding a column starts out just like the process of changing a column's width.

Title	Salary	Hired
Admin Asst.	$ 32,500	6/6/96
Manager	$ 62,000	3/29/95
Director	$ 78,250	12/5/98
Admin Asst.	$ 26,500	12/28/90
Coordinator	$ 34,500	4/22/79
Director	$ 66,500	4/20/96
Coordinator	$ 27,500	9/5/94
Coordinator	$ 32,000	11/12/88
Coordinator	$ 35,000	1/20/92
Coordinator	$ 35,000	3/30/95
Coordinator	$ 38,750	6/29/92
Director	$ 75,000	5/13/97
Admin Asst.	$ 35,000	5/14/97
Manager	$ 72,500	1/26/99
Director	$ 82,000	10/21/87
Coordinator	$ 32,500	3/7/97
Coordinator	$ 38,000	3/6/98
Representative	$ 45,000	8/13/94
Representative	$ 52,000	7/22/83
Manager	$ 65,000	2/11/93

3. Click and drag the column to the left, as though you are reducing its width. Drag the seam until you meet the seam on the other side of the column (see Figure 8.23).

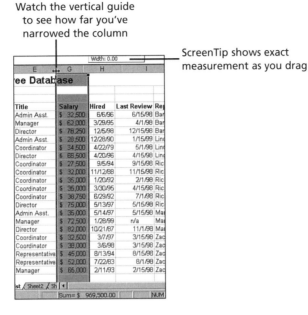

Watch the vertical guide
to see how far you've
narrowed the column

ScreenTip shows exact
measurement as you drag

FIGURE 8.23

*Drag the seam until
the measurement in
the ScreenTip reads*
Width: 0.00 *inches.*

4. Release the mouse. Your column is hidden (see Figure 8.24).

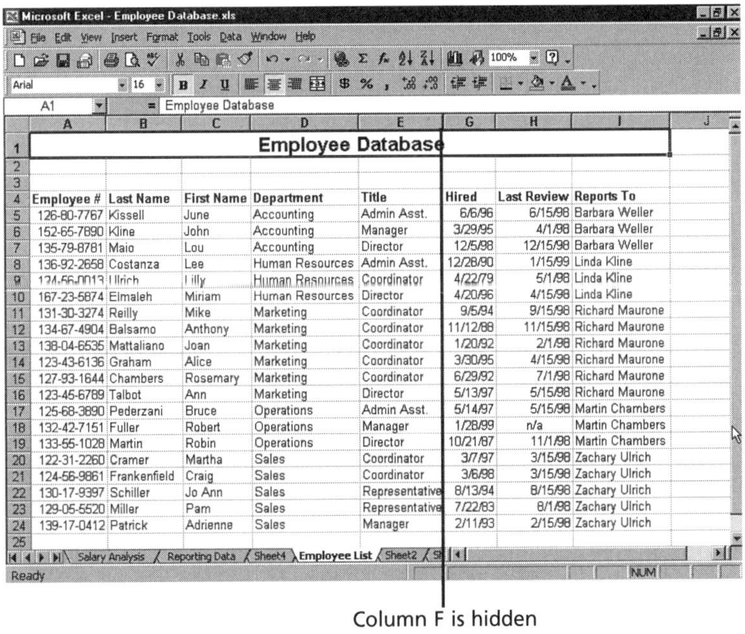

FIGURE 8.24

*Note the missing letter
in the series of column
control buttons.*

Column F is hidden

Tip

Of course, you can hide as many columns as you want in a single step. Select a series of columns by dragging through their contiguous column control buttons; then perform the preceding procedure on the outermost column, dragging its seam to meet the column to the left of the selected group.

To unhide a column, you can choose one of the following methods:

- Select the columns on either side of the hidden column and choose Format, Column, Unhide. The hidden column returns to view.

- Point to the seam where the hidden column is supposed be; when your mouse pointer turns to a split two-headed arrow (see Figure 8.25), drag to the right to reveal the hidden column.

FIGURE 8.25

A split two-headed arrow indicates that you're pointing to a hidden column.

Title	Hired	Last R
Admin Asst.	6/6/96	
Manager	3/29/95	
Director	12/5/98	1
Admin Asst.	12/28/90	
Coordinator	4/22/79	
Director	4/20/96	
Coordinator	9/5/94	
Coordinator	11/12/88	1
Coordinator	1/20/92	
Coordinator	3/30/95	
Coordinator	6/29/92	
Director	5/13/97	
Admin Asst.	5/14/97	
Manager	1/28/99	n
Director	10/21/87	
Coordinator	3/7/97	
Coordinator	3/6/98	
Representative	8/13/94	
Representative	7/22/83	
Manager	2/11/93	

Hiding a Row

In a database, hiding a row means hiding a record. Perhaps your list contains a record that will be deleted and, although you're not ready to delete it now, you don't want it to appear on the report that you're about to print. For whatever reason, you can hide a row using either of the following methods:

- Select the row by clicking its control button, and drag the seam on the bottom of the button up to meet the row above it. The height ScreenTip says 0.00 inches (see Figure 8.26). Release the mouse, and the row is hidden.

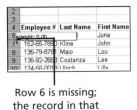

FIGURE 8.26

Watch the ScreenTip measurement. When the width reaches 0.00 inches, your column is hidden as soon as you release the mouse.

Row 6 is missing; the record in that row is hidden

- Select the row and choose Format, Row, Hide. The row disappears.

Either of these methods can be applied to multiple rows, although the latter method works best if you want to hide noncontiguous rows.

To unhide a single hidden row, select the rows on either side of the hidden row and choose Format, Row, Unhide. The row reappears. If you have hidden several rows, select the entire worksheet (click the Select All button or press Ctrl+A) and choose Format, Row, Unhide.

> **Tip**
>
> Worksheets can be hidden as easily as rows and columns can. Click the sheet tab that you want to hide (making it the active sheet), and choose Format, Sheet, Hide. When a sheet is hidden, you can return it to the display by choosing Format, Sheet, Unhide.

Creating a PivotTable Report from a List Database

A PivotTable Report is so named because the report spins (pivots) the data on an axis that you choose—the axis being one or more of your data fields. Figure 8.27 shows a PivotTable report based on your Employee Database. The Salary field is the axis for the report.

FIGURE 8.27

Create a three-dimensional report on your database with a PivotTable.

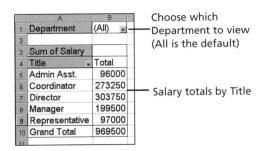

Choose which Department to view (All is the default)

Salary totals by Title

PivotTables make it easier for you to analyze your data from a variety of perspectives. By selecting the axis for your table, you are selecting the most important data for you at the time. In Figure 8.27, the Salary field was the most important—how much do you pay out to different departments? In Figure 8.28, the number of employees reporting and to whom they report is what matters.

FIGURE 8.28

Select the Reports To person, and see how many people report to him or her.

Select the Reports To *name*

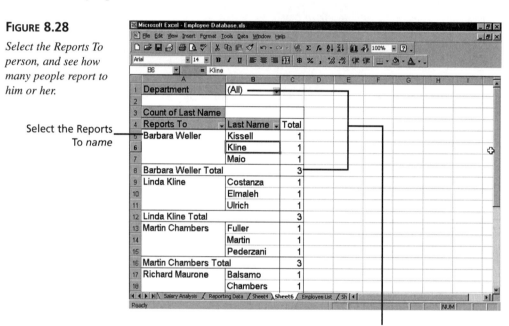

Data changes to show Department and number of people in various positions that report to the selected person

To create a PivotTable from your Employee Database, follow these steps:

1. Click in any cell in the data on your list.

2. Choose Data, PivotTable and PivotChart Report.

3. The PivotTable Wizard opens (see Figure 8.29). Accept the defaults (Microsoft Excel list or database and PivotTable) by clicking the Next button.

FIGURE 8.29

The PivotTable Wizard coaches you through the process of building your pivot table.

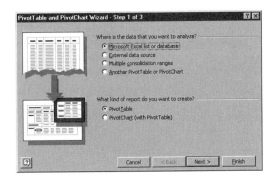

4. Check to see that the entire range of your list is shown in the Step 2 of 3 dialog box. You see a moving dashed border around your entire list (you can move the dialog box out of the way and scroll around to make sure that your entire list is selected). Figure 8.30 shows your list selected, with its range displayed in the dialog box.

FIGURE 8.30

The Wizard assumes that you want to use the active worksheet's database.

5. Click Next to display Step 3 of 3 (see Figure 8.31). Select the New Worksheet option; this places your PivotTable on a new sheet in the workbook rather than on the existing worksheet.

FIGURE 8.31

To keep your database worksheet intact, choose to create the pivot table on a new worksheet in the current workbook.

6. Click the Layout button to set up your PivotTable.

7. In the Layout dialog box (see Figure 8.32), drag the field boxes onto the white layout boxes as follows:

FIGURE 8.32

The Layout dialog box enables you to drag your fields onto the pivot table form, designing the final PivotTable report.

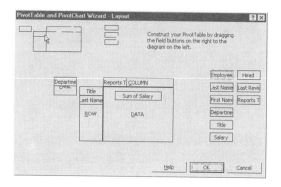

- Drag Department into the Page box.
- Drag Salary into the Data box.
- Drag Title and Last Name into the Row box.
- Drag Reports To into the Columns box.

8. When all your fields are in position, click OK.

9. In the final box of the PivotTable Wizard, click the Finish button. Figure 8.33 shows the resulting report.

FIGURE 8.33

See only the fields that you want to see, and choose the most useful perspective on the data when designing your PivotTable report.

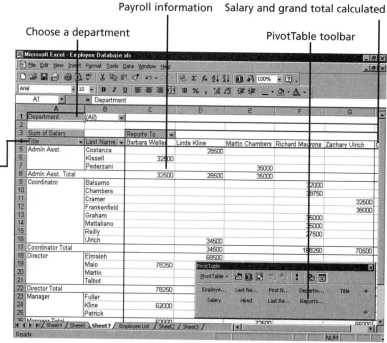

After the PivotTable is created on a new sheet, you can name the sheet if you plan to keep it in the workbook, or you can delete the sheet and create a different PivotTable. You can create several PivotTable Reports per workbook, although having more than two per workbook creates large files.

Summary

Today concentrated on the use of Excel for storing lists of data, demonstrated through the creation, editing, and manipulation of an Employee Database. Changing the order of displayed records through various sorting techniques was covered, as was the use of AutoFilter for viewing certain records based on user-defined criteria. Day 9, "Creating and Using Charts," will show you how to use Excel for creating bar and pie charts (the two most commonly used chart types), based on Excel spreadsheet data.

Q&A

Q If I decide that I need some of Access's functionality for my database, can I use my Excel list database in Access?

A Yes. There is no need to reenter your records in Access. You can use the Clipboard to copy the Excel data and then use Access's Edit, Paste Append command to insert your records into a new Access table database. You'll learn more about using Access on Day 13, "Setting Up a Database."

Q Can I store more than one list in a single workbook?

A Yes. Each list needs to be self-contained on a single worksheet, and you can have separate lists on each sheet in the workbook.

Q Can I save my worksheet after filtering the records and save only the displayed records?

A No. Filtering a database to show only certain records is a temporary measure—all the records are still there, your filter just hides those that don't meet your filter criteria. If you save your file while it's in AutoFilter mode, there is no change to the content of the file.

Workshop

The section that follows is a quick quiz about the day. If you have any problems answering any of the questions, see the section that follows the quiz for all the answers.

Quiz

1. How many records can be stored in a single database?

2. True or False: Sorting your database shows only the records that match the active cell.

3. Describe two ways to hide one or more columns in your list database.

4. Name two important rules for structuring an Excel list database.

5. True or False: You can only filter your database on three fields.

Quiz Answers

1. You can store up to 65,535 records in any one worksheet. This is based on the assumption that your field names are in Row 1, and that the records begin in Row 2. With a total of 65,536 rows per worksheet, this leaves 65,535 for the database.

2. False. Sorting shows all the records in the database; it merely changes the order in which they're displayed.

3. You can hide one or more columns by narrowing them (by dragging their control buttons) to the point at which the columns have 0.00 inch width, or you can choose Format, Column, Hide while the columns you want to hide are selected.

4. The two primary rules for building a database are the creation of field names in the first row of the database, and having no blank rows within the list of records.

5. False. You can filter your database on as many fields as needed, potentially every field in the database.

WEEK 2

DAY 9

Creating and Using Charts

They say a picture is worth a thousand words—if you can express an idea or share information quickly and easily with a single image, why not do it? This old adage is as true when it comes to numbers as it is with regard to words. A chart is worth a thousand numbers—it takes your numeric data and turns it into easily understood and visually dynamic pictures that show sales, productivity, turnover, trends, frequency, and data comparisons. Why look at rows and rows of numeric data when a simple image tells the story quickly?

Excel's charting tools make it easy to convert columns and rows of numbers (along with their headings and labels) to many different types of charts. In today's project, you'll be displaying data from a worksheet in a column chart, and then taking a smaller portion of the data and showing each cell as one slice in a pie chart. The skills you acquire in building, editing, and formatting these two charts will give you a solid foundation for any further charting needs you might have in your use of Excel 2000. Today's project will cover the following topics:

- Charting concepts and terminology
- Tips for selecting the right chart for your message
- Techniques for choosing the data for your chart
- Building Excel charts
- Customizing your chart
- Enhancing your chart with graphics
- Integrating the other Office 2000 applications with your chart—using Excel charts in a PowerPoint presentation, using Access table data to build a chart

Charting Basics

Not all of us are familiar with charting—the terminology and concepts that go into building and interpreting charted data. Figure 9.1 shows a simple column chart, and Table 9.1 explains several of the chart's elements.

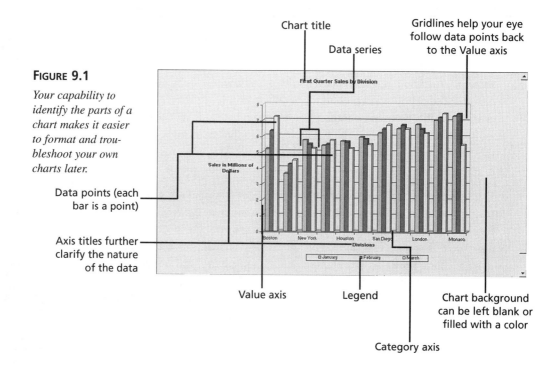

FIGURE 9.1

Your capability to identify the parts of a chart makes it easier to format and troubleshoot your own charts later.

TABLE 9.1 CHARTING TERMINOLOGY

Term	Definition
Data point	Each cell in your charted range that contains a number becomes a data point, plotted on the chart.
Data series	Any logical group of data points—the numbers in a row or column in the charted section of your worksheet.
Value (vertical) axis	In bar, column, line, and area charts, the value axis shows a range of the amounts represented by your data points.
Category (horizontal) axis	The category axis shows the groups of data plotted. The text displayed on this axis comes from your column headings or row labels.
Legend	Differentiates and identifies the data in your chart by color or pattern.

9

Your chart's elements can all be formatted—moved, resized, font sizes changed, colors added, or removed—to suit your needs for the particular chart. After it is created, your chart can add dimension to your other Office 2000 files—for example, you can use it in a Word document or a PowerPoint slide presentation. These topics will be covered in Day 17, "Creating a Report with Office."

Choosing the Right Type of Chart

Different types of charts convey different messages about the data that is charted in them. Your message, for most charts, is one of the following types:

- **Show trends over time**—Data over a series of chronological weeks, months, quarters, or years, is best shown in a line chart. A good second choice is a bar or column chart.
- **Make visual comparisons**—Pie charts are the best choice for comparisons, although a pie is limited to showing just one data series per chart. If you need to compare several series, use a bar, column, or area chart.

Some charts show both comparisons and trends. The chart in Figure 9.2 compares the data in each series, as well as showing trends over time.

FIGURE 9.2

Within each series, compare the height of the bars. Over the entire chart, see the trends for each category.

Compare columns
within the series

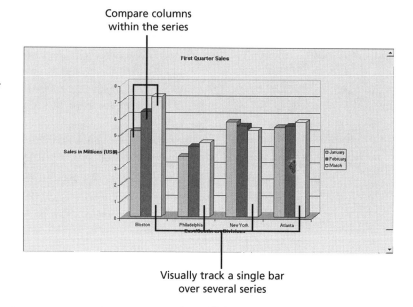

Visually track a single bar
over several series

The type of chart you choose for your data isn't carved in stone—you can change types later or simply delete the chart and start over with a different type of chart if the one you started with is not effective for displaying your data.

Selecting Worksheet Content for the Chart

The first step in the chart creation process is to select the data that is to be plotted on the chart. It's important to select only the data that you want, and to eliminate things such as titles, extra blank rows and columns, or any data you don't need in the chart. Figure 9.3 shows a worksheet with a range selected for charting.

 To select your range of cells, simply drag through them with your mouse, or use the Shift and arrow keys on your keyboard. When the range you want to chart is selected, click the Chart Wizard button.

Tip

You can use data from an Access table for your chart by copying and pasting the data into an Excel worksheet. Find out how to build an Access table on Day 13, "Setting Up a Database."

The column headings become
your category axis labels

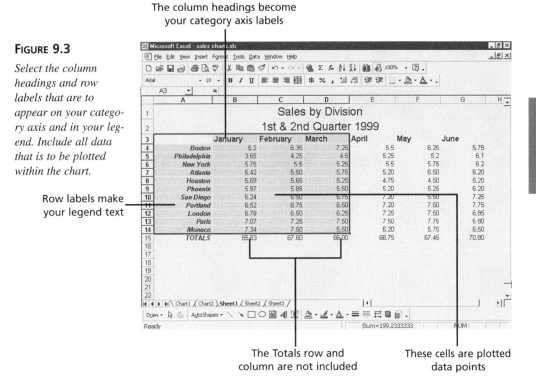

FIGURE 9.3

Select the column headings and row labels that are to appear on your category axis and in your legend. Include all data that is to be plotted within the chart.

Row labels make
your legend text

The Totals row and
column are not included

These cells are plotted
data points

Creating a Column Chart

Using the data in Figure 9.3, create a 3D Column chart that shows the sales for 11 divisions over a three-month period (one fiscal quarter). The range that you need to plot is also shown selected in the figure.

After your worksheet range is selected, click the Chart Wizard button on the Standard toolbar. You can also choose Insert, Chart from the menu to invoke the Chart Wizard. The Chart Wizard is a program that, through a series of dialog boxes, helps you choose your chart type, verify the range of cells you want to chart, and add chart elements such as axis and chart titles.

To use the Chart Wizard to create your chart, follow these steps:

1. With step 1 in the Chart Wizard, select your chart type from the list on the Standard Types tab. For this procedure, choose the Clustered Column with 3D Visual Effect (shown in Figure 9.4).

FIGURE 9.4

Choose a simple chart type to display your data effectively.

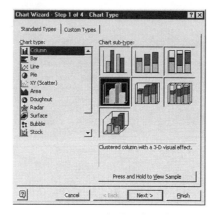

2. Click Next to move to Step 2 of 4.

3. Step 2 displays the chart using the selected data (see Figure 9.5). Verify the range of worksheet cells to be plotted in the chart.

FIGURE 9.5

View the sample chart in Step 2 of 4.

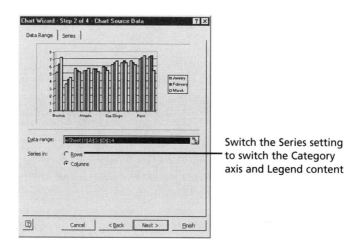

Switch the Series setting to switch the Category axis and Legend content

4. Note that the Division names are displayed on the Category axis. If you want to change this so that the years move to this axis, switch to Series in Rows.

5. Click Next to move to Step 3 of 4.

6. Step 3 of 4 offers six tabs, each of which gives you options for customizing your chart. Because the chart's defaults are appropriate for most situations, you'll change only following settings:

   • **Titles**—Add the Chart title `Sales by Division` (see Figure 9.6). A Value axis title indicates that the numbers represent dollars.

FIGURE 9.6

The Category text is clear enough—you need a title for the whole chart and for the Value axis.

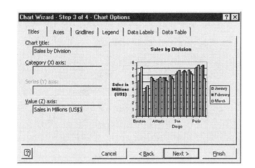

   • **Legend**—In the Placement section, click the Bottom option (see Figure 9.7).

FIGURE 9.7

Bottom placement of the Legend leaves more horizontal room for your seven-department data series.

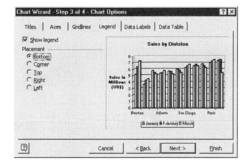

7. Click Next to apply your changes to the building chart and move to Step 4 of 4.

8. Choose to place the chart in As new sheet, and name the sheet tab `Division Sales Chart` (see Figure 9.8).

Figure 9.8

Placing the chart on its own sheet gives it plenty of room.

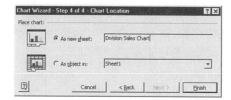

9. Click Finish to end the Wizard and create your chart on its own sheet.

After your chart is built, it remains linked to the worksheet data that was used to create it. If you edit the cell content within the plotted range, the chart updates automatically—bars and columns change in height and pie slices become thicker or thinner, depending on the new numeric values that are entered into the worksheet cells.

Tip

To switch back to your data, right-click the chart and choose Source Data. The worksheet data that was used to build the chart is displayed and selected; also, the Source Data dialog box appears, from which you can change the range of cells used to create the chart.

While your chart is active, the Chart toolbar is displayed, offering tools for editing various chart features (see Figure 9.9).

Figure 9.9

Reformat your chart's elements quickly with the Chart toolbar.

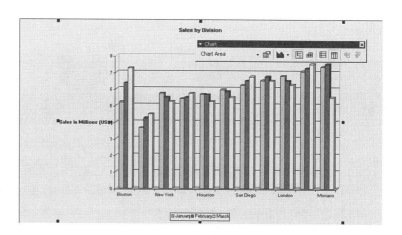

In addition, the Chart menu appears on the menu bar; from the Chart menu, you can make formatting changes to any chart element. You'll learn about these tools after you create your pie chart.

Building a Pie Chart

As was stated previously, a standard pie chart can only plot one data series at a time. Each pie slice represents a single data point, enabling you to compare individual points in a single data series. If you tried to plot more than one data series in a single pie, you'd have more than one slice of the same color, and you'd be unable to easily interpret the data.

Tip

If you must have a pie-like chart, and you have more than one data series to plot, try a doughnut chart.

You can use a portion of your sales data for the pie, as shown in Figure 9.10.

FIGURE 9.10

Select the row labels and a single column of data from the worksheet.

Row labels are used to identify each pie slice.

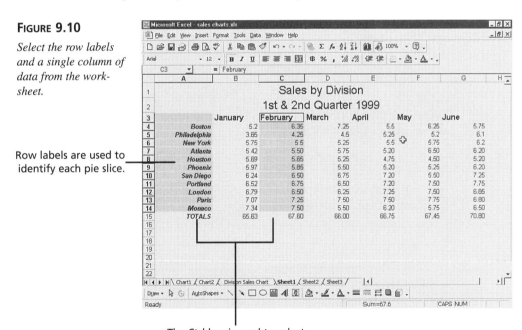

The Ctrl key is used to select noncontiguous sections of the worksheet.

After selecting this range within the worksheet, invoke the Chart Wizard by clicking the button on the Standard toolbar. Follow these steps to complete your pie chart:

1. In Step 1 of 1, click Pie in the list of Chart types. A list of subtypes appears on the right side of the dialog box, as shown in Figure 9.11.

FIGURE 9.11

A variety of two and three-dimensional pie options is displayed.

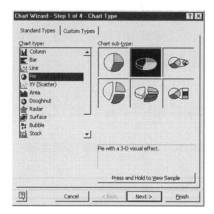

2. Select the Pie with a 3D visual effect (the second pie on the top row), and click Next to move on to Step 2 of 4.

3. The pie is displayed, using your data, and you can verify your selected range by clicking Next to proceed. If there aren't 11 slices in the pie and 11 items in the legend, drag the dialog box to the side and reselect the appropriate cells. Reposition the dialog box, and click Next to proceed.

4. In Step 3 of 4, enter a chart title. For your chart, `February Sales by Division` is a good choice.

5. Click the Legend tab, and remove the check mark next to Show legend. A pie needn't have a legend if you turn on Data Labels, as you will do in the next step.

6. Click the Data Labels tab. Click to select the Show label and percent option. The chart sample in the dialog box shows how your changes will affect the chart (see Figure 9.12).

7. Click Next to move to Step 4 of 4.

8. Click the As new sheet option, and replace `Chart2` with `February Sales Chart`.

9. Click Finish to create your chart and close the Chart Wizard dialog box.

FIGURE 9.12

Don't waste space on the chart with a legend. Data labels are much more effective on pie charts.

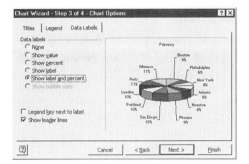

Tip

If you want to quickly create charts for each individual month, copy and paste the February chart onto separate sheets—one for each month you want to chart. Using the Chart toolbar, redefine the range for each of the copies of the February chart, selecting a different month's data for each chart. The charts are redrawn to reflect the new data, and you need only change the chart titles to correctly identify the content of each chart.

Tip

If your chart is on its own sheet, you might find that when it is pasted to another worksheet it appears much too large and needs to be resized. To create a copy of a chart that is on its own sheet, right-click the chart sheet tab and choose Move or Copy from the shortcut menu. This technique for copying chart sheets is covered in detail later today.

The pie chart that shows February's data now appears on its own sheet, as shown in Figure 9.13.

FIGURE 9.13

Each slice is labeled, and the percentage that each one represents is calculated and displayed on the chart.

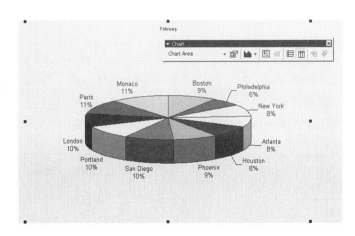

9

Exploding a Pie Slice

After your chart is created, you can make changes to its appearance. General formatting techniques (that can be applied to any chart) will be discussed later; for now, concentrate on things you do only to a pie chart.

Exploding a pie slice means moving one of the slices away from the main pie. Doing so draws attention to that particular slice. To move a slice away, follow these steps:

1. On your pie chart sheet, click anywhere on the pie itself. Handles appear on the perimeter of the pie, as shown in Figure 9.14.

FIGURE 9.14

Select the entire pie first, and then select a single slice.

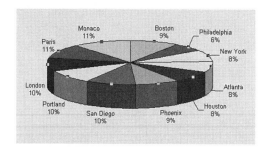

2. Click once again on the slice you want to explode. Handles appear around that slice only (see Figure 9.15).

FIGURE 9.15

Click once on a particular slice to select it for formatting or to move it away from the center of the pie.

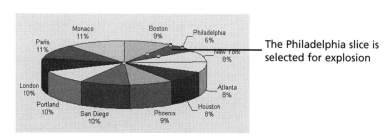

The Philadelphia slice is selected for explosion

3. Drag the selected slice away from the center of the pie. Don't drag it too far, though, or the entire pie image shrinks—you want to drag it away just fractions of an inch, as shown in Figure 9.16.

FIGURE 9.16

Drag the slice just far enough from the pie to make it stand out.

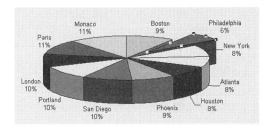

It's a good idea to explode only one slice per pie. This enables those who view your chart to concentrate on just one part of the data. If you need to discuss multiple slices, copy the chart's sheet (creating multiple sheets with the same chart on them), and explode a different slice on each of the copied sheets. To copy a sheet, follow these steps:

1. Right-click the sheet tab for the sheet you want to copy.

2. From the shortcut menu, choose Move or Copy.

3. In the Move or Copy dialog box (see Figure 9.17), leave the current workbook selected in the To book box and choose the sheet that is to come after your copied sheet.

FIGURE 9.17

Create a duplicate sheet and use the repeated chart to discuss and highlight a different portion of the pie.

4. Place a check mark in the Create a copy box, and click OK.

In the copied sheet, drag the exploded slice back to the center of the pie, and explode a different slice. Later today, you'll learn to add callouts (text boxes with lines pointing to chart elements), which can be added to your pie charts to offer information about the exploded slice.

Adjusting Your 3D View

Excel's default setting for the angle of your 3D charts is appropriate for most charts—the chart is angled just enough to show the sides and top of the bars and columns, making a real 3D effect.

Pie charts, however, can usually benefit from some adjustment of the 3D view. To change the vertical and horizontal angles of your pie's display, follow these steps:

1. With your pie selected, choose Chart, 3D View. The 3D View dialog box opens, as shown in Figure 9.18.

FIGURE 9.18

Get a new perspective on your 3D chart by adjusting the Elevation and Rotation.

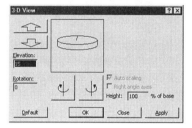

2. Adjust the Elevation by entering a new number or by clicking the up and down arrow buttons.

3. Adjust the Rotation by entering a new number or by clicking the left and right curled arrows.

4. You can make the pie thicker by increasing the Height number.

5. Click OK to put your changes into effect and close the dialog box.

Figure 9.19 shows your pie chart with an Elevation of 40 and a Rotation of 80.

FIGURE 9.19

Changing the pie's rotation can bring the smaller slices closer to the front of the display, making it easier to see them.

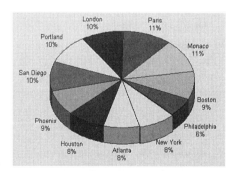

Formatting and Customizing a Chart

Excel's chart defaults are appropriate for most charts—you will, however, need to make minor changes to accommodate both cosmetic and functional preferences. To make these changes, you can use the Chart toolbar or the Chart menu. Table 9.2 discusses the Chart toolbar's tools.

TABLE 9.2 CHARTING TOOLS

Tool Name/Icon		Function
Chart Objects	Chart Area	Choose the portion of your chart that you want to reformat. The button displays the currently selected portion of your chart—click the drop-down list to make an alternative selection.
Format Selected Object		The element that was selected from the Chart Objects list (or by clicking directly on an element in the chart) can be formatted with this button. Click the button to access tools specific to the selected element.
Chart Type		If you decide to change to the two-dimensional version of your selected chart type, or to switch to an entirely different chart type, click the list triangle and make your selection. The chart automatically reformats in the selected chart type.
Legend		Click this button to turn the legend on or off.
Data Table		Another toggle switch, click this button to view the Data Table (a display of your selected worksheet range) below the chart. If the table is displayed, click this button to turn it off.
Series in Rows		If your data is currently in Series in Columns format, click this button to switch the focus of your chart by swapping the current Category axis labels and the legend text.
Series in Columns		If your data is currently in Series in Rows format, click this button to switch the Category axis labels and legend data.
Angle Text Downward		A great option if your Category axis labels are too wide; put them on a 45-degree angle, running downward.
Angle Text Upward		Place your Category axis labels on a 45-degree angle, running upward.

The Chart menu contains the same tools, and is similarly context-sensitive. When you have selected a chart element (by clicking directly on the element in your chart), choose Chart, Format Selected Object where Selected Object is the selected element. The resulting dialog box contains tools for formatting that element.

Tip   If the Chart toolbar isn't displayed, right-click any displayed toolbar and choose Chart from the list of available toolbars.

Changing Chart Colors

The color of your chart's bars, columns, slices, or lines is important. Although Excel's default colors are usually fine, you might want to change them to avoid clashing with your stationery colors or to eliminate a situation in which adjacent bars, columns, or slices are too similar in color. To change the color of selected columns within your chart, follow these steps:

1. With the chart sheet displayed, click once on one of the columns in the series you want to recolor. The entire series is selected (see Figure 9.20).

FIGURE 9.20

To recolor an entire series, click just one of the bars or columns in that series.

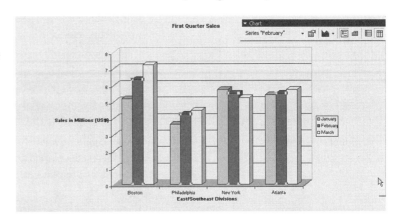

 2. On the Chart toolbar, click the Selected Object button (now called the Format Selected Data Series button).

3. The Format Data Series dialog box opens, offering five tabs for reformatting the appearance of your data series. Click the Patterns tab, and then select a different Border or Area color (see Figure 9.21).

4. Click OK to put your changes into effect and close the dialog box.

Tip
If you're printing your chart in black and white, your colors are printed as shades of gray. To avoid shades of gray that are visually identical, apply a pattern fill by clicking the Fill Effects button in the Format Series dialog box. Choose from Gradient, Texture, Pattern, and Picture fills for the selected data series.

FIGURE 9.21

Keep your printout and any onscreen displays of your chart in mind as you choose new colors for your chart's data series.

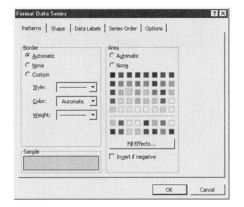

Caution
Nearly 15% of the male population is colorblind, and a small percentage of the female population is, too. If you're not sure of your chart's potential audience, avoid using green and red together—they're the colors that most colorblind people confuse and see as a muddy shade of grayish brown.

Adding Callouts and Graphic Elements to Enhance a Chart

The formatting changes you make to your chart need to either improve your chart's appearance or make it easier to understand—preferably, both effects will result from whatever changes you make. To make your chart simple to interpret and to give it a polished appearance, consider adding callouts and graphics to drive your message home. Figure 9.22 shows a chart with these items added.

Callouts consist of a text box and an
arrow that points from the box to
the element you're identifying

FIGURE 9.22

*Callouts identify
potentially confusing
items, and graphics
make your chart more
visually accessible.*

Choose a clip art
image that matches
the tone and content
of your chart

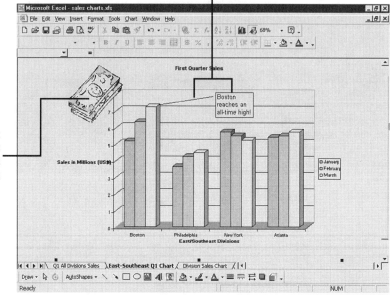

Adding a Callout to Identify Chart Elements

Callouts are like a whispered aside, some parenthetical information that the readers of
your chart might find useful and informative. You can add as many as you want, but to
avoid a circus-like appearance for your chart, avoid using more than two or three per
chart. To create a callout, follow these steps:

1. If it isn't already displayed, choose the Drawing toolbar by right-clicking the
   Standard or Formatting toolbar. Select Drawing from the shortcut menu.

2. On the Drawing toolbar, click the AutoShapes button. From the menu,
   choose Callouts, and choose a callout from the resulting palette (see
   Figure 9.23).

FIGURE 9.23

*Choose from cartoon
bubbles and simple
rectangle-and-line
combinations for your
chart's callouts.*

3. With your mouse, point to the object that the callout defines or explains. Click on or near the object, and drag away from the object. Release your mouse to set the position of the callout box and the length of the arrow line that points from the box to the chart element. Figure 9.24 shows a callout being drawn.

FIGURE 9.24

When drawing a call-out, start dragging on or near the item to which the callout will point. Drag away to create the line and text box.

Callout points to this bar (dragging started here)

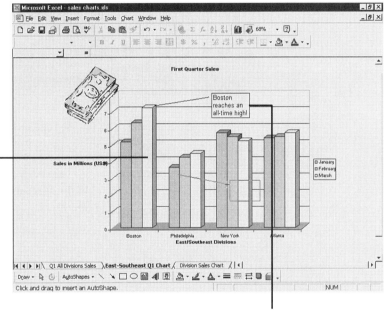

Text box positioned so that it doesn't obscure the height of any other bars

4. Begin typing in the callout's text box (the cursor is active in the box as soon as you release the mouse). Type the content of the callout box, allowing word wrap to confine the text to the box.

You can move your callout text box or change the length of the arrow line by clicking on the callout and dragging any one of its handles. Figure 9.25 shows a selected callout and identifies the use of various handles.

FIGURE 9.25

Drag the callout handles to move or resize it.

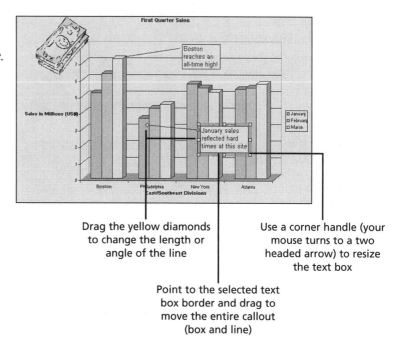

Drag the yellow diamonds
to change the length or
angle of the line

Use a corner handle (your
mouse turns to a two
headed arrow) to resize
the text box

Point to the selected text
box border and drag to
move the entire callout
(box and line)

Tip

To avoid lengthy callout text, use short, punchy phrases such as *Turnover rates down 1998* instead of *Turnover rates were much lower in 1998*.

Using Clip Art Images with a Chart

Although clip art doesn't add real information to your chart, it does add visual impact. Depending on the forum in which your chart is to be shared (simple printouts, a slide presentation, published in a report), the use of clip art can keep people interested and draw attention to your chart. Some venues won't be appropriate for the use of clip art—a report to the sober board of directors, for example—whereas other situations call for something humorous or a familiar image to put the finishing touch on your chart.

Adding clip art to a chart is the same as adding clip art to any worksheet within your workbook—or to a Word document or PowerPoint slide, for that matter. It's a simple process. To add clip art to your Turnover Rates chart, follow these steps:

1. With your chart sheet displayed, click the Insert Clip Art button The Insert ClipArt dialog box opens, as shown in Figure 9.26.

FIGURE 9.26

The Office 2000 ClipArt collection is extensive—you'll have no trouble finding an appropriate image to use in your chart.

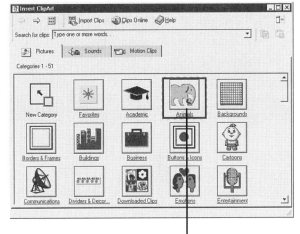

Each icon represents a
clip art category, or
group of similar images

2. From the Pictures tab, select a category by clicking one of the icons—for your project, choose People.

3. The People category is displayed. Select the Working toward goals image (see Figure 9.27) by right-clicking the image and choosing Insert. If you don't have this image (perhaps you didn't install all the clip art), choose some other appropriate image.

FIGURE 9.27

From your chosen category, select an image.

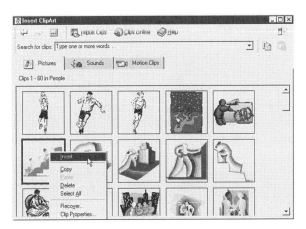

4. Click the Close button in the Insert ClipArt dialog box, and view your inserted image on the chart. It probably will require resizing and repositioning, as shown in Figure 9.28.

FIGURE 9.28

Clip art images are usually too big, and might cover important chart content; resize and move the image as needed.

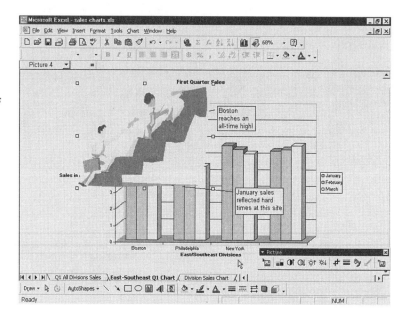

5. Using the image handles (see Figure 9.29), drag inward to shrink the picture to a manageable size, and then drag the entire image to an appropriate spot on or near the chart. Be sure not to obscure any chart data, titles, labels, or the legend.

Tip

For an interesting visual effect, select your chart's walls; then click the Insert Clip Art button and select a clip art image. The image you insert covers the walls of your chart. Beware, however, of making the chart illegible or too visually busy for some business environments.

FIGURE 9.29

Clip art should enhance—not over-whelm—the chart. Keep the images small and out of the way.

Drag a corner handle to resize and maintain the current horizontal and vertical proportions.

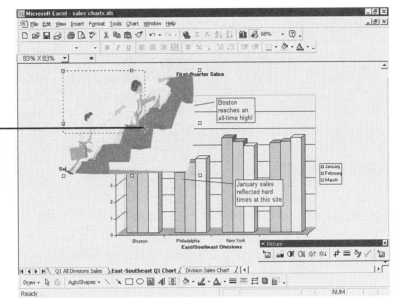

Figure 9.30 shows your chart with callouts and clip art, ready for publication on paper, distribution for viewing onscreen, or for addition to a Web page (you'll find out how to do that on Day 19, "Distributing Data Through a Web Page").

FIGURE 9.30

Informative callouts and an unobtrusive use of graphics give your chart a polished, professional appearance.

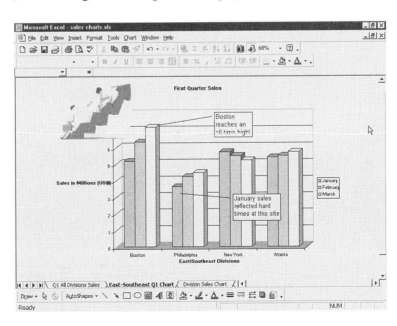

Summary

Today you learned how to take your Excel worksheet data and convert the appropriate parts of it into a chart. By creating both a column and a pie chart from portions of the same data, trends and comparisons are made quickly and easily, proving that a simple graphical image can convey as much information as several columns and rows of numeric data. Day 10, "Automating Word and Excel with Macros," will take you to the next level in your use of both Excel and Word by demonstrating the power of automation—the recording, editing, and use of macros to perform repetitive document and worksheet building tasks.

Q&A

Q Can I place more than one chart on a single worksheet?

A Yes, if it's a regular worksheet. If it's a sheet that was created specifically to contain a chart (through Step 4 of 4 in the Chart Wizard), however, you can only place one chart on the sheet. If you're working with a standard worksheet, you can place as many charts as you need on the sheet.

Q Can I use my Excel charts in Word and PowerPoint documents?

A Yes, and on Day 17 you'll be placing an Excel chart in both a Word document and a PowerPoint presentation. Simply use Edit, Copy to place the chart on the Clipboard; then use Edit, Paste to deposit it in any other Office 2000 file. Establishing a link between the chart and the target file will be covered specifically on Day 17.

Q When I create a chart and then change the type, there are times when the chart becomes unusable—it is either resized strangely, or the chart subtype isn't what I expected. What can I do?

A It is often easier to delete a chart and start over with a different type than to change chart types, especially if the change is a radical one (such as going from a column chart to a pie, or from a pie to line chart). If sizing is the only conversion problem, however, try resizing various elements in the chart after you've changed types—reducing font sizes or expanding the chart area. These minor "tweaks" can restore the chart to a more appropriate appearance.

Workshop

The section that follows is a quick quiz about the day. If you have any problems answering any of the questions, see the section that follows the quiz for all the answers.

Quiz

1. When selecting worksheet data for your chart, what items are not to be included?

2. The Chart Wizard can be invoked by what two methods?

3. True or false: A column chart can only show trends over time.

4. True or false: To change the color of a series of bars or columns in a chart, you must select each one individually and apply the new color.

5. When you edit the worksheet data that was used to build your chart, does the chart update to reflect the new data?

Quiz Answers

1. When selecting data for your chart, don't include worksheet titles, blank rows or columns, or too many data series for the type of chart you're building.

2. You can invoke the Chart Wizard by clicking the Chart Wizard button or by choosing Insert, Chart.

3. False. A column chart (or a bar chart, for that matter) can also show comparisons. Bar and column size within and between series can be visually compared, and if the series are displayed over a span of time, trends can also be shown.

4. False. To change the color of a data series, select one of the bars or columns; the entire series is selected automatically. The color you then select is applied to all the bars or columns in the series.

5. If the worksheet and the chart are in the same workbook, the chart automatically changes whenever the cells that are plotted within it are edited.

DAY 10

Automating Word and Excel with Macros

NEW TERM *Macros* are programs that you write by recording your steps through a process, such as formatting a document or creating a new file based on a particular template. Why record yourself? To save time and achieve consistency. By recording your steps and turning them into a macro, you can run the macro (and have the steps performed automatically) by pressing a keyboard shortcut, clicking a toolbar button, or making a selection from a menu (it's up to you how the macro is invoked). Your most time-consuming and complex procedures can now be automated, potentially saving you hours of work and assuring you that the steps are performed in the same order every time.

You don't need to be a programmer to write or use macros; in fact, you don't need to know any programming language at all. You only need to know the steps that are required to perform a certain task in the Office 2000 application, and the order in which the steps are to be performed. After that, you can record yourself performing the steps, thus building the macro. Today will show you how to automate repetitive tasks in Word and Excel; specifically, the following topics will be covered:

- Choosing which tasks to automate
- Recording macros in Word and Excel
- Testing macros
- Editing and deleting macros
- An introduction to the Visual Basic Editor window

Deciding Which Tasks to Automate

As software has evolved throughout the past decade, the list of things that the software can do has grown considerably. Many of the things for which users once had to create macros are now part of the software—Word's AutoText and AutoCorrect features are perfect examples of such processes. Clicking Excel's Currency button to automatically apply dollar signs, commas, and decimal places to numbers in cells is another example of automation that's already part of Office. To add further automation, you can create macros to do the things you want the software to do for you. Some ideas for things you can automate include

- **Applying styles and formats**—If you find yourself choosing a certain font, in a certain size, in a certain style over and over again, it's time for a macro.
- **Inserting files and graphics**—Do you have to insert your logo into your document's header on every new document? Create a macro that does it for you.
- **Create a new document based on a particular template**—Do you use the same template repeatedly? Save the time it takes you to find it each time you need it—create a macro that automatically finds it and opens a new document based on it.
- **Print jobs**—If you print the same range of pages in a long document or complex workbook each time you work with the file, create a macro that opens the print dialog box, selects the pages to print, and prints your pages exactly as you need them.

When deciding which of your tasks to automate, it's important to consider the following:

- Does the macro save you a lot of work and time?
- Is the procedure really done the same way every time?

Unless your answer is yes to both questions, you probably don't need a macro; or you might need to automate only a portion of the procedure—the portion that is the same every time it's performed.

Note   Macros are application-specific—you can't use a Word macro in Excel or an Excel macro in Word. You can, however, create a Word macro in one document and use it in other Word documents, and Excel macros that are stored in the Personal Macros Workbook are usable in all Excel workbooks. You'll learn more about this later today.

10

Creating Word Macros

Building a macro in Word is a simple process, but it requires some preparation. Before you record your macro, be sure that you've set the stage for the procedure you want to record. If, for example, your macro applies a format to selected text, be sure that the text is selected before you start recording. Why? Because your mouse can only be used to click on toolbar buttons and menus when the macro is recording—you won't be able to drag through your text.

After you've made any required preparations, follow these steps to begin recording your macro:

1. If you're not in one now, open a Word document based on the Blank Document template. By doing so, you ensure that the macro is available to all documents that are based on that template.

2. Select Tools, Macro, Record New Macro. The Record Macro dialog box opens, as shown in Figure 10.1.

FIGURE 10.1

Change the default Macro1 text to a name that indicates the purpose or function of your macro.

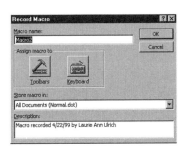

3. Type a name for your macro. Your macro name cannot have any spaces in it. If you need the appearance of a space, use an underscore, as in `Format_Chapter_Title`, which you'll use for this new macro.

4. Choose how your macro will be invoked in the future—by a toolbar button or keyboard shortcut. For this example, you want to choose Keyboard, so click that button in the dialog box.

5. The Customize Keyboard dialog box opens (see Figure 10.2), with the cursor blinking in the Press new shortcut key box. Press the keys that you want to assign to this macro; in this case, choose Alt+H, which is currently unassigned.

FIGURE 10.2

Press the keyboard shortcut keys that you want to assign to your macro. Word tells you if the shortcut is already assigned to another command.

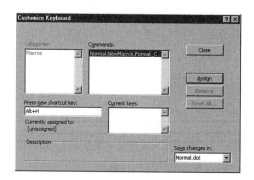

6. Click Assign, and then click the Close button. The Stop Recording toolbar appears onscreen (see Figure 10.3).

FIGURE 10.3

As long as the Stop Recording button is onscreen, you know the macro is recording.

Stop button

Click the Pause button to put the recording process on hold momentarily

The mouse pointer in macro recording mode

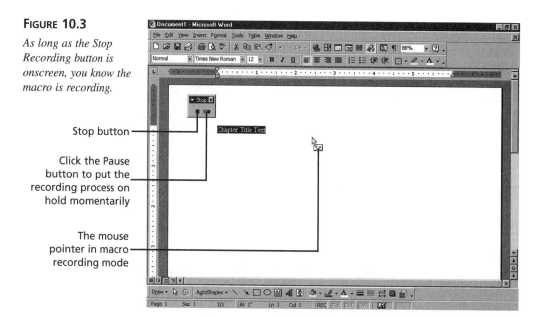

Don't click the Stop button until you've performed all the steps that are required for your macro. The next section will show you how to record a macro that applies a series of formats to selected text.

 Tip

> Don't worry if you make slight errors while recording your macro—spelling errors that you backspace through and correct, accidentally applying the wrong font and then choosing the right one immediately thereafter—the macros are performed so quickly that the inclusion of these erroneous steps won't be noticed. If you make mistakes that you don't fix while recording, you can edit many of them in the macro program itself, as you'll learn later today.

Speeding Document Formatting with Keyboard Shortcuts

When the Stop Recording toolbar is displayed, note that your mouse pointer turns to an arrow with a cassette icon. This indicates that the macro is recording. While that mouse appears, you can only use your mouse to click toolbar buttons and menus—you cannot select text or click in your document to reposition your cursor.

To proceed with the macro and record the process of applying a series of formats to selected text, follow these steps:

1. Choose Format, Font from the menu.

2. In the Font dialog box, choose Font, Font Style, Size, and then apply any Effects and Font Color you want. Figure 10.4 shows the formats you want to apply with this macro.

FIGURE 10.4

Apply all the formats at once through the Font dialog box. Your selections become part of your macro.

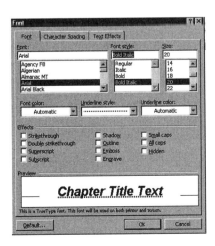

3. When your formats are selected, click OK to close the dialog box.

 4. Click the Stop button on the Stop Recording toolbar. The macro stops recording.

As soon as you stop recording, your macro is created. You can use it immediately, which is a good idea—test the macro right away to make sure it works as you intended it to. Later today, you'll learn what to do if your macro doesn't work properly.

To test your macro, select some text that is unformatted, and then press the keyboard shortcut you assigned to the macro (Alt+H). Figure 10.5 shows the result.

FIGURE 10.5

Test your macro by invoking the assigned keyboard shortcut.

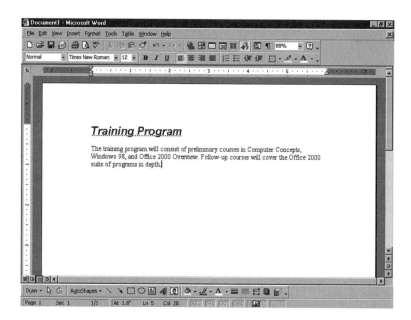

Inserting Files and Objects

If your macro will insert a file or a graphic, make sure you know where the item is—there is no sense in recording yourself searching for the folder that contains the file. After you've found the item you want to insert and have made a mental note of where it's stored, you can follow these steps to create the macro that will insert it on command:

1. Click to place your cursor where you want to insert the clip art image.

2. Select Tools, Macro, Record New Macro. In the Record Macro dialog box (see Figure 10.6), type the name Insert_Lion (your macro will insert one of the Office ClipArt images of a lion).

FIGURE 10.6

It's a good practice to create a macro name that doubles as a description of what the macro does.

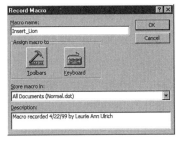

3. Click the Toolbars button to assign this macro to a toolbar. The Customize dialog box opens.

4. Click the Commands tab. Your macro is displayed on the right side of the dialog box. Drag the command name `Normal.NewMacros.Insert_Lion` up to the toolbar, releasing the mouse when the I-beam pointer is where you want the new button to be (see Figure 10.7).

10

FIGURE 10.7

Place the macro button among the existing toolbar's tools.

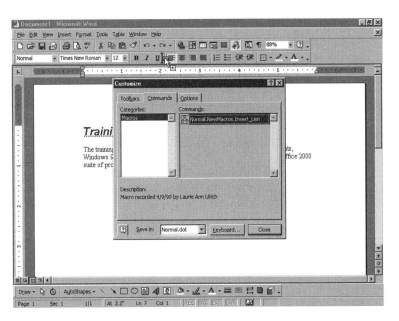

5. Click the Modify Selection button and choose Change Button Image. A palette of button faces appears, as shown in Figure 10.8.

FIGURE 10.8

Choose a face for your macro button.

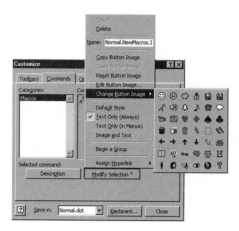

6. Select an image by clicking on it in the palette.

7. Click the Modify Selection button again, and select Text Only (under Menus) from the list. Your button now contains only the image you selected from the button face palette, as shown in Figure 10.9.

FIGURE 10.9

The macro name takes up too much room on the button—remove it by choosing Text Only (in Menus).

Macro button with no text

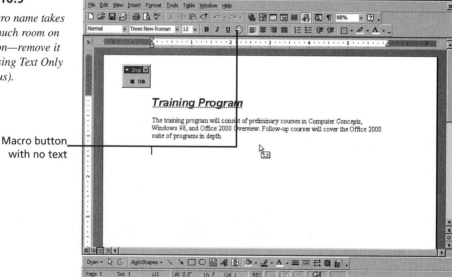

8. Click the Close button, and the dialog box closes. The Stop Recording toolbar is displayed.

9. Choose Insert, Picture, ClipArt. In the Insert ClipArt dialog box, select the Animals category (see Figure 10.10).

FIGURE 10.10

Select one of the many Office 2000 clip art images to be inserted by your macro.

10. Right-click the lion (which is the first image in the top row of images). Choose Insert from the shortcut menu (see Figure 10.11).

FIGURE 10.11

You can also drag the image out of the Insert ClipArt dialog box and onto your document.

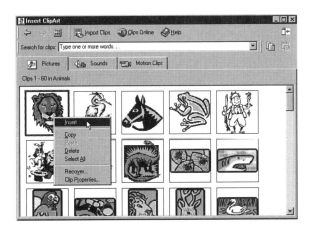

11. Click the Close button in the upper-right corner of the Insert ClipArt dialog box. The lion clip art appears in your document.

12. Click the Stop button to end the macro.

After inserting the image, you can resize it as needed with your mouse.

 Tip

> You can use this same procedure for inserting a nongraphic file, such as another document or a worksheet. Instead of Insert, Picture, ClipArt, choose Insert, File, and then select the file that you want to insert from the Insert File dialog box.

By default, all your Word macros are available in all new documents that are based on the Normal template, so you can use them in any document.

Automating Excel

If your use of Excel includes the performance of the same tasks on the same worksheets on a regular basis, you might benefit from automating some of the lengthier or more repetitive tasks. Creating macros to apply customized formats or to insert specific worksheet content can save you time and effort, as well as increase consistency between worksheets. When it comes to numeric data, consistency is extremely important.

Like Word macros, Excel macros should only be created if the task that is to be automated is performed repeatedly, and if it is performed exactly the same way each time. If the result of the macro has to be edited each time the macro is used, the macro has failed to save you time and energy.

Applying Formats with Keyboard Shortcuts

Creating an Excel macro is very similar to creating a macro in Word—the macro is named; the keyboard shortcut is assigned; and the recording process begins. Your first Excel macro will apply a custom format to selected cells; use the following steps to record the macro:

1. In an Excel worksheet, select the cells that are to be formatted.

2. Choose Tools, Macro, Record New Macro. The Record Macro dialog box opens, as shown in Figure 10.12.

3. Give your macro a name. Use underscores if you need to create the appearance of spaces. Name your macro for this procedure `Special_Currency`.

4. Click in the Shortcut key box. The use of the Ctrl key is assumed, so type the letter that will create the complete shortcut. Type an x in this case, to create a Ctrl+X shortcut for this macro.

FIGURE 10.12

Enter a name for your macro and choose how it is to be invoked.

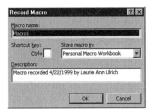

Tip

To avoid using a keyboard shortcut that's already assigned (such as Ctrl+Z for Undo or Ctrl+B for Bold), add the Shift key when you press the keys you want to assign to your macro. There are very few existing Ctrl+Shift+*letter/number* shortcuts, so you're not likely to run into a conflict.

10

Caution

Excel won't warn you if you've chosen a shortcut that's already assigned to another macro or to an Excel command, nor does it warn you if your shortcut overrides the existing assignment.

5. Choose where to store the macro. Your three choices are as follows:

- **This Workbook**—If you make this choice (the default), the macro you create is only available in the current workbook.

- **New Workbook**—Make this choice if you want the macro to be available in all new workbooks, but not in any existing workbooks.

- **Personal Macro Workbook**—This choice makes the macro available in all new and existing workbooks.

6. Click OK to close the dialog box and begin recording the macro. The Excel version of the Stop Recording toolbar opens, as shown in Figure 10.13.

7. Choose Format, Cells, and then click the Number tab.

8. Choose the Currency category, and change the decimal places to zero (0).

9. Click the Font tab, and change the Color to blue (any medium to dark shade).

10. Click OK to close the Format Cells dialog box.

11. Click the Stop button to end the recording process.

Figure 10.13

When recording a macro that applies formatting, you can build it in a blank worksheet that is opened purely for creating the macro.

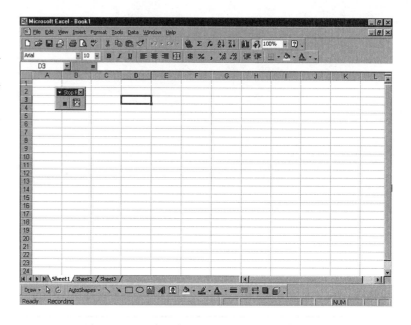

When you press Ctrl+Z, the macro applies Currency format with no decimals, and the cell content turns blue. Such a macro can be used to save time in customizing the standard currency format, and to apply a font format at the same time—changing the numbers to blue helps draw attention to them in a worksheet.

Inserting Worksheet Content Automatically

Another useful Excel macro can be created to insert worksheet content. Excel's Custom Lists feature already does this to a certain extent, but it requires that simple text or numeric data be entered into contiguous cells in list format. A macro that inserts very specific content, including formulas and cell formatting, can be a significant time-saver when you are building worksheets with similar content. The following procedure creates a macro that builds a series of column headings, row labels, and formulas.

To build this macro, follow these steps:

1. Click in the cell in which the inserted content is to begin.
2. Choose Tools, Macros, Record New Macros. The Record Macros dialog box opens.
3. Name the macro Setup_Worksheet.
4. Assign the keyboard shortcut Ctrl+Shift+W by clicking in the Shortcut key box and pressing Shift+W. Figure 10.14 shows the addition of the Shift key to the shortcut in the dialog box.

FIGURE 10.14

To avoid using only Ctrl+key shortcuts, add the Shift key—and make a lot more keyboard shortcuts available to you.

5. Click the Store macro in list, and choose to place the macro in the Personal Macro Workbook. This makes the macro available in all your Excel workbooks, both new and existing.

6. Type a description for the macro, appending your text to the existing text. For macros that insert data or make other changes to a workbook, it's a good idea to explain what's happening in case someone else uses your macro.

7. Click OK to close the dialog box and start recording.

8. Type the content that you want your macro to insert. Figure 10.15 shows the content you'll be inserting with this macro.

10

FIGURE 10.15

This content appears exactly as you enter and format it each time it is inserted through the use of the macro.

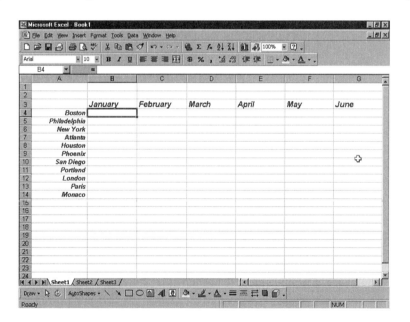

9. Apply formatting as needed to the cell content.

10. When the content looks the way you want it to whenever it is inserted by the macro, click the Stop button to end the recording and close the Stop Recording toolbar.

When you use this macro (or a similarly constructed macro) in other workbooks, the data appears in the cells into which you entered the content while you were recording the macro. For example, if you typed a series of column headings in cells B2–B5, whenever you use the macro, the text is inserted in those same cell addresses—even if there is already content in them when you invoke the macro.

> **Tip**
>
> When you exit the Excel program for the first time after having creating and storing a macro in the Personal Macros Workbook, you are prompted to save the Personal Macros Workbook so that the macro you stored in it will be available the next time you open Excel. Be sure to answer Yes to the prompt.

Editing Macros in Word and Excel

If your macro doesn't work, it might be easier to delete and rerecord it—perhaps you left out a step while recording it, and without that portion of the procedure, the macro fails to perform as expected. If you're not a Visual Basic programmer, you probably want to take this path of least resistance and just start over.

This book assumes that you aren't a programmer and that the level of Visual Basic interaction you want to have is minimal. Therefore, later in this section, you'll learn to make simple edits using Microsoft's Visual Basic Editor window and the macros you created today. Your editing tasks will be limited to changing the value that is entered into a cell and adjusting font sizes for macros that format cells.

Deleting Macros

You might want to delete a macro even if it's working properly; perhaps you've found a way to incorporate more steps into the macro, and you need to rerecord it with the same keyboard shortcut (in Excel, you can't assign a new macro to an existing shortcut). Maybe the task that the macro performs is obsolete, and you want to record a new one (with the same shortcut keys) to perform the updated version of the task.

Regardless of your reason for deleting a macro, the method is simple. The only catch is that you must be in the workbook in which the macro you want to delete is available. If, when naming and setting up your macro, you chose to store it in the current workbook or a new workbook, you must have that workbook open. Any Excel macros that you stored in the Personal Macros Workbook are available for deletion, regardless of which workbook you have open at the time. Word macros that were created in any document based on the Blank Document template are all available for deletion, just as they're all available for use in any Blank Document-based file. Assuming that you're in the workbook or document in which the macro you want to delete is available, follow these steps to delete the macro:

1. Choose Tools, Macro, Macros. The Macro dialog box opens (see Figure 10.16), showing a list of the macros you've created.

FIGURE 10.16

View a list of your macros, and then delete the ones you no longer need.

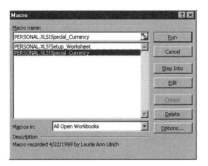

2. Click the name of the macro you want to remove, and then click the Delete button in the dialog box. If an Excel macro was stored in the Personal Macros Workbook, a prompt appears (see Figure 10.17), indicating that the Personal Macros Workbook is hidden and must be "unhidden" in order for you to delete that macro. If no prompt appears, click OK to close the dialog box and skip the following steps. By default, Word lists all macros from all documents and templates.

FIGURE 10.17

The Personal Macros Workbook must be available in order for you to access (and delete or edit) one of the macros stored in it.

3. If you must unhide the Personal Macros Workbook, close the Macros dialog box and choose Window, Unhide. The Unhide dialog box opens (see Figure 10.18). Click the Personal.xls workbook, and then click OK.

FIGURE 10.18

Choose to unhide the Personal Macros Workbook so that you can see a list of its universally-available macros.

4. Reopen the Macros dialog box by choosing Tools, Macro, Macros. Select the macro to be deleted, and click the Delete button. A prompt appears to confirm your intention to delete—click Yes in response.

Caution

There is no "undelete" for a deleted macro—if you delete it, it's gone. Be careful when deleting macros with similar names, and check the macro description carefully (assuming you created a description when you created the macro) to be sure that you're deleting the right macro.

Working with the Visual Basic Editor

If your macro doesn't work properly, you can try to fix it manually by editing the Visual Basic programming code that was created when you recorded the macro. The recording process builds an actual program; the steps you take are converted to Visual Basic commands. For non-programmers, however, it's best to restrict your editing to corrections such as changing the text that the macro inserts or changing the formatting that is applied by the macro. Figure 10.19 shows the Visual Basic Editor window, with the macro you created to enter and format Excel worksheet content displayed.

FIGURE 10.19

*View your macro in its
Visual Basic format.*

Name of macro

Description

Shortcut key you
assigned when you
created the macro

Visual Basic code
for each step the
macro performs

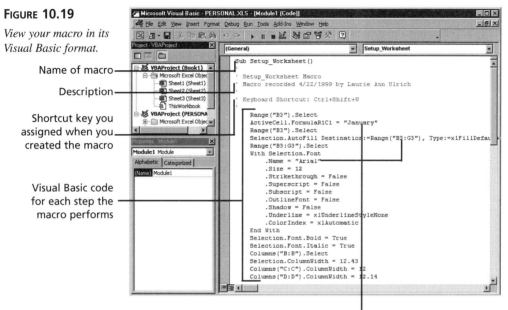

Text in quotes represents mouse
actions, entered content, or commands
you issued while recording the macro

To edit the Visual Basic code, simply click the program text and insert new text; or, using the mouse, select and replace text that you want to change. Figure 10.20 shows the previous macro's code being adjusted so that the font size that is applied by the macro is increased to 22 points.

FIGURE 10.20

It's a good rule of thumb for non-programmers to restrict their edits to the code that's in quotes, or to easily identified content.

Portion of code being edited

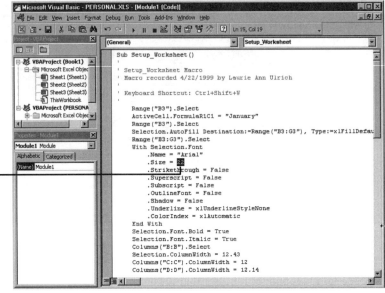

Summary

Today you learned how to automate procedures in Word and Excel. By recording macros, you can take any set of two or more consecutive actions and turn them into an automated task that is performed at the press of a keyboard shortcut or the click of a toolbar button. Tomorrow you will move on to Outlook, where you'll learn to send, receive, and respond to email messages.

Q&A

Q Is there any limit to the number of macros I can record?

A No. You can create as many as you need, assuming that you don't run out of keyboard shortcut key combinations or toolbar buttons.

Q Excel restricts macros to keyboard shortcut triggers. Can an Excel macro be assigned to the toolbar?

A Yes. You can assign an Excel macro to the toolbar by choosing Tools, Customize, and then clicking the Commands tab. Choose Macros from the Categories list, and drag the Custom Button command up to the toolbar (similar to the process of assigning a Word macro to the toolbar). A dialog box appears, from which you can select which macro to assign to that button.

Q What if I want to remove a toolbar button for a macro I've deleted?

A To remove any toolbar button, press and hold the Alt key on your keyboard, and then drag the button you want to remove down and onto the workspace. Release the mouse, and then the Alt key. You can also rearrange toolbar buttons while the Alt key is pressed. Be aware that merely deleting the macro's button does not delete the macro—you must do that through a separate procedure.

Workshop

The section that follows is a quick quiz about the day. If you have any problems answering any of the questions, see the section that follows the quiz for all the answers.

Quiz

1. Name the two ways that a Word macro can be invoked.

2. True or False: While recording an Excel macro, you cannot use your mouse within the cells of the worksheet.

3. If you want your Excel macro to be available to all workbooks, what do you do?

4. Can you assign two different macros to the same keyboard shortcut?

Quiz Answers

1. You can invoke a Word macro through a keyboard shortcut or by clicking a toolbar button, whichever method you assigned to the macro prior to recording it. In addition, you can choose the longer and methodical method—choose Tools, Macro, Macros, select the macro from the list, and click Run.

2. False. You have full use of your mouse while recording an Excel macro. While recording a Word macro, however, your mouse use is restricted to the toolbars and menus.

3. To make your Excel macros available to all workbooks, you must choose to store it in the Personal Macros Workbook. In the Record New Macros dialog box, choose this option instead of This Workbook or New Workbook.

4. No, you cannot assign two macros to the same keyboard shortcut, at least not within the same application. You can have the same keyboard shortcut for a macro in Word and also for a macro in Excel, but two macros in the same application cannot share a keyboard shortcut.

10

DAY 11

Sending Email Messages

Days 1–10 have shown you how to use two of the core programs in Office 2000—Word, for use in creating documents, and Excel, for use in creating spreadsheets that store financial data and lists of database records. The third core program for many users is Outlook, Office 2000's email and calendar application, which enables you to communicate via email and keep track of your schedule.

Very few offices can even imagine operating without email. Most home computer users have email as well, and users of all types have come to rely on the capability to send messages and attached files to co-workers, friends, and family members. Outlook provides a simple environment in which to send, receive, respond to, and forward email messages within a local area network or to the outside world via the Internet. In addition, Outlook provides a comprehensive calendar and to-do list feature, which help to keep you on track and on time. You'll cover the calendar and task list features on Day 12, "Managing Your Time with the Calendar." For today, you'll learn about the following email-related topics:

- Navigating the Outlook environment
- Creating email messages
- Sending file attachments with email
- Formatting email message content
- Handling incoming mail—responding, storing, and forwarding messages
- Working with message options
- Maintaining an email address book

Understanding the Outlook Workspace

When you launch the Outlook application, the Outlook Today window (see Figure 11.1) opens onscreen. Through this window, you can view your incoming mail and mail you've sent, you can access your calendar, and you can view your list of tasks.

FIGURE 11.1

Use the Shortcuts panel on the left to view different areas of the Outlook program.

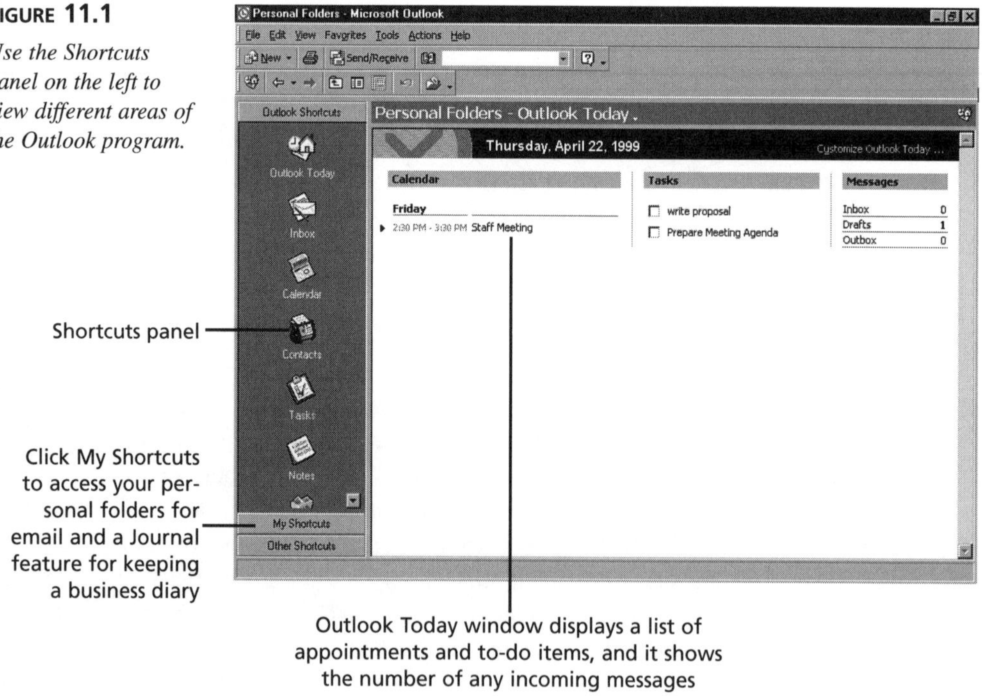

Shortcuts panel

Click My Shortcuts to access your personal folders for email and a Journal feature for keeping a business diary

Outlook Today window displays a list of appointments and to-do items, and it shows the number of any incoming messages

The most common tasks you'll perform in Outlook are sending and receiving mail and making entries into your calendar and to-do list. The first button on the toolbar is a New button that changes into a New Mail Message button when you're viewing your Inbox and a New Appointment button when you're in your Calendar. Other context-appropriate toolbar buttons appear as you move through different areas of Outlook. For this reason, you'll spend very little time using Outlook's menus—for most users, this fact shortens the learning curve considerably. Figure 11.2 shows the Inbox window and the Standard email toolbar.

FIGURE 11.2

While you're in your Inbox, tools that are related to sending and responding to email messages appear on the toolbar.

Reply and
Forward buttons

The list of messages
(read and unread)
in your Inbox

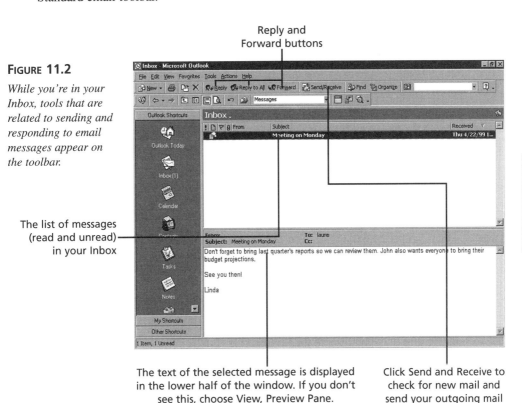

The text of the selected message is displayed
in the lower half of the window. If you don't
see this, choose View, Preview Pane.

Click Send and Receive to
check for new mail and
send your outgoing mail

Creating an Email Message

To begin using Outlook, you'll create an email message. You can address an email to someone in your office through your company's local area network, or to someone outside your office via the Internet. For the purposes of this project, you'll be sending email to Internet email users.

To start an email message, follow these steps:

1. Open Outlook by choosing it from the Start menu's Programs list. You can also choose New Office Document from the Start menu and then double-click the Email Message icon in the New Office Document dialog box.

 2. In the Outlook window, click the New Mail Message button. An Untitled Message window opens, as shown in Figure 11.3.

FIGURE 11.3

Address your message to the recipient, give your message a Subject, and type the body of the message from within the Untitled Message window.

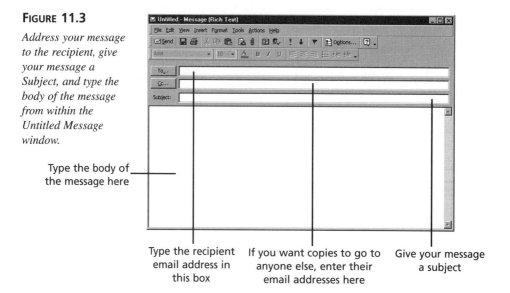

Type the body of the message here

Type the recipient email address in this box

If you want copies to go to anyone else, enter their email addresses here

Give your message a subject

3. Your cursor is blinking in the To box. Click the To button to open your Address Book (it might be empty if you installed Office 2000 yourself, or if you're not on a local area network set up by your company). This opens the Select Names dialog box. If you know the exact email address of your recipient, you can also type it into the To box. To type more than one address, separate each one with a semi-colon (;).

 Tip

When you type an email address, it's essential that the address be exact. If you're emailing someone via the Internet, the address must contain four parts—their name, the @ sign, their domain name, and the extension, for example, jsmith@company.com.

4. From within the Select Names dialog box (see Figure 11.4), select one of the addresses in the Contacts list and click the To button to add that person as a recipient. You can add as many addresses as you want—just click Add after selecting each one.

FIGURE 11.4

Choose your recipient from the Address Book and have Outlook insert his or her name in the To box automatically.

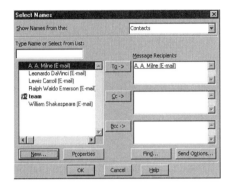

5. Click OK to return to your message window.
6. Press Tab to move to the Cc box, into which you can type the address of anyone to whom you want to send a copy of the message.

> If you want to send a copy of the message to someone and not have their address appear to the other recipients of that same message, place their address in the Bcc (blind carbon copy) box. If you don't see a Bcc box in your message window, choose View, Bcc Field.

7. Press Tab again to move to the Subject box. All messages need a subject that reveals the message topic. Keep the subject text short and clear. Figure 11.5 shows the subject line for a message about an upcoming meeting.

11

FIGURE 11.5

Let your recipient know what to expect in the body of the message by entering a relevant subject.

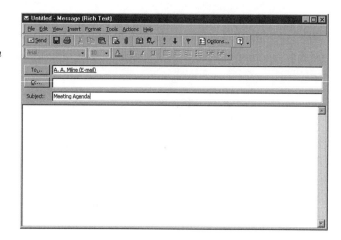

8. Press Tab again to move the cursor to the large white box that will house the body of your message. Simply begin typing, allowing text to wrap against the right margin, just as if you were writing a letter in Word (see Figure 11.6).

FIGURE 11.6

There is no limit to the length of your email message, although users who prefer short, quick messages might not read longer messages (those exceeding a page of text).

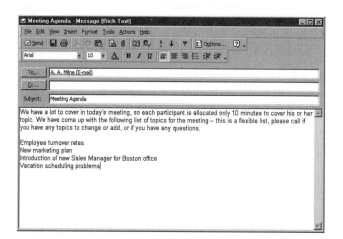

9. When the body of your message is complete, click the Send button. Your message is sent to the recipient either via your company's local area network or through a connection to the Internet.

Tip

For large groups of recipients that you email often as a group, you might want to create a distribution list, which is discussed later today.

How does your message get from your computer to the recipient? Your message is sent to your mail server, which is either a local computer at your company site or a server hosted by your Internet Service Provider. If your connection to the Internet is via phone line, the connection must be live and you must be connected to your ISP in order to send your mail.

When the recipient checks his or her server for mail (either by logging into the network or dialing their ISP), your message is waiting in their Inbox. The recipient need not be using Outlook as their email program, although for some of the features you'll learn about today it helps if they are—formatting and other Outlook-based features are stripped away by the message's trip over the Internet. For simple messages (and messages with attached files), however, it doesn't matter if the recipient is using Outlook.

Formatting Message Text

Most email messages you send contain no special text formatting. If you need to send someone a complex or visually exciting document, you're better off creating that document in Word and attaching the file to a brief introductory email message, which is covered later today. In addition, unless your recipient is also using Outlook and is on your local email network, any formatting—font, size, and style changes—might not appear in the message when the recipient receives it.

For messages you're sending over your local network to fellow Outlook users, however, you can apply all sorts of text formatting. Virtually all the text formats that Word enables you to apply are available through Outlook. Figure 11.7 shows an email message with different fonts, font sizes, and bulleting applied to the text.

11

FIGURE 11.7

Use text formatting to draw attention to important parts of your email text and to make your messages more visually interesting.

Font and size changed

Bold applied to important text

Bullets applied to list

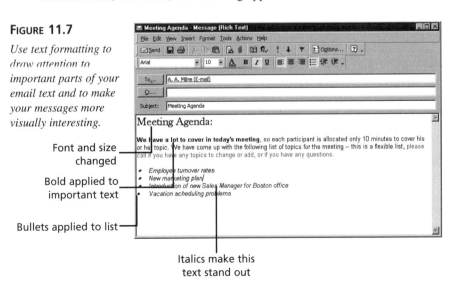

Italics make this text stand out

Before you can apply text formatting to the body of your message, your message must be displayed in Rich Text view. If you're not currently in that view, choose Format, Rich Text from within the new message window. This displays the Formatting toolbar. After this toolbar is available, follow these steps to format your message text:

1. Using your mouse or the Shift and arrow keys, select the portion of the text that you want to format.

2. Choose Format, Font. The Font dialog box opens, as shown in Figure 11.8.

FIGURE 11.8

Like a pared-down version of Word's Font dialog box, Outlook offers the basic tools for formatting text.

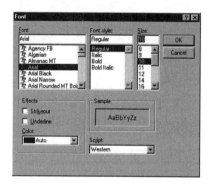

3. Choose a font, font style, size, and any effects or colors you want to apply to your selected text. View the Sample to make sure you like the formats you've chosen.

4. Click OK to apply the formats to the selected text.

B **I** For quick formats such as Bold or Italic, or for an increase in font size, use the Formatting toolbar shown in Figure 11.9.

FIGURE 11.9

Save time by applying various font and paragraph formats from the toolbar.

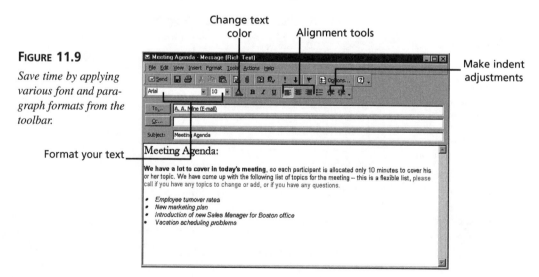

Caution Don't be like the boy who cried wolf: If you rely on formatting to draw attention to important message text, use formats sparingly. If every message that comes from you has formatted text throughout (use of color, large text), your recipients might stop noticing the formatting, and it won't have the impact you intended.

 Tip If the Font command is dimmed in your Format menu, choose Format, Rich Text. The Font command is now available, as is a set of toolbar buttons (for selecting fonts and applying styles) in the Formatting toolbar.

Attaching Files to Messages

As was stated previously, it's not a good idea to create incredibly long email messages. Most email users prefer messages (short, informative notes) to long letters. If you need to send someone a long letter, don't type it into a message—attach a new or existing Word document to the email message.

Of course, Word documents aren't the only kind of files that can be attached to email messages—and attaching files to avoid a long email message isn't the only reason to attach a file. You can attach any kind of file to an email message, and it arrives with the message in the recipient's mailbox.

To attach a message to your email, follow these steps:

1. Create your message with recipient addresses, a subject, and the body of your message. It's a good idea to mention the attachment in your message—the content of the attachment, the reason for its inclusion, and what you want the recipient to do with it.

2. Click the Insert File button on the Standard toolbar. The Insert File dialog box opens, as shown in Figure 11.10. Navigate to the folder that contains the file you want to attach, and double-click it.

FIGURE 11.10

Locate the file you want to attach to your message, double-click it to attach it to the message, and close the Insert File dialog box.

3. The attached file appears below your message as an icon (see Figure 11.11). If the recipient is also an Outlook user, the attachment appears as an icon inside their message as well. For non-Outlook users, the appearance of the attachment depends on their email software.

FIGURE 11.11

You can attach as many files as you want. Each one appears as an icon below the message.

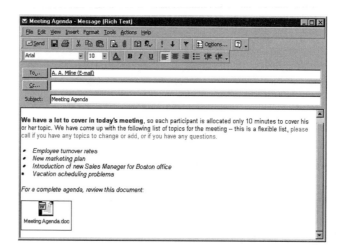

4. When your message is ready, click the Send button. The message and the attached file are sent to your recipient.

Tip

You can attach as many files as you want to an email message, with each one appearing as a separate icon in the body of the message if you're in Rich Text view, or as an icon in a separate section below the document if you're in Plain Text view. You can also attach any type of file to your message—if the file is currently stored on your computer (or on your network drive), it can be attached to an email message, regardless of format.

If you decide to delete an attachment before sending the message, simply click the icon and press the Delete key on your keyboard. You can then send the message without an attachment, or you can attach a different file to the message.

Caution

If you choose to attach more than one file to your message, keep the size of the files in mind. Some online services place a 3MB cap on attached files, and some users cannot accept multiple attachments. Even where there is no restriction, large attachments tie up the recipient's computer for a long time, which is rarely appreciated. To avoid these potential problems, compress your files into one zipped file (using a program such as PKZIP or WinZip) and attach that single file to your message. The recipient can unzip the file when it is received.

11

If you receive an Outlook message with an attachment, double-click the attachment's icon in the message—the file opens in whatever application was used to create it or in the application that your computer associates with the file type. You can also save the file to your local drive if you want to edit it or if you might need it again in the future. If you want to save the attached file without opening it first, choose File, Save Attachments. You can then open the saved file at your convenience without spending any time doing so while reviewing your email.

Tip

Want to see what the attached file is before deciding whether to save or open it? Right-click the attachment's icon and choose Quick View from the shortcut menu.

Understanding Message Options

When you send your message, you often have no idea how it will be perceived by your recipient—will he or she see it as important and read it right away? Unlike voice mail messages or live conversation, where you can clearly express your level of interest or excitement about a topic, in an email message, you have a short subject line in which to convey any urgency and reveal the subject of the message.

Outlook gives you tools that tell you when your message was received and, if the recipient is on your local network, when it was actually read. In addition, you can attach priority icons that indicate that the message is very important (or not important at all), and you can flag a message for certain actions to be performed by the recipient. These extra items make your needs and intentions clear to the recipient.

Requesting a Read Receipt

If someone claims never to have received your email, you must usually take their word for it. If, however, you request a read receipt, you'll know when they received and opened your message on their mail server. This, of course, only works if they're using Outlook on the same network as you are—if they receive the email via the Internet, you can't tell when they read the message.

To request a read receipt, follow these steps:

1. At any point during the creation of your email message, click the Options button , or choose View, Options. The Message Options dialog box opens (see Figure 11.12).

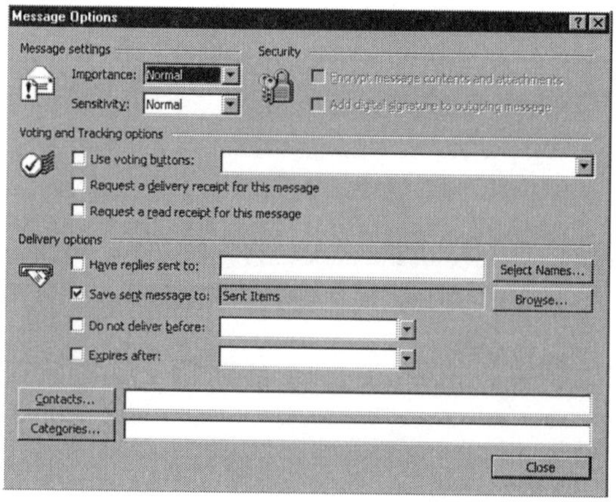

FIGURE 11.12

Ask for a receipt that shows you when your message was received and read by the recipient.

![Message Options dialog box showing Message settings with Importance and Sensitivity set to Normal, Security options, Voting and Tracking options, and Delivery options including Save sent message to Sent Items.]

2. Turn on the Request a read receipt for this message option by clicking the check box next to it.

3. Click Close to close the dialog box and continue creating your message.

When the recipient reads your message, you receive a message from your mail server, indicating the time that the message was read.

> **Tip**
>
> If you know your recipient is on vacation and you want to delay the sending of your message (but you want to send it now), use the Do not deliver before option, also found in the Message Options dialog box. Click the list box to scroll through calendars and choose the date on which you want the message to be delivered.

Setting Message Priority

The capability to mark a message as highly important is quite useful. Email doesn't allow for facial expression or tone of voice to communicate urgency—you must therefore rely on the message itself to convey this. Outlook enables you to mark a message's importance level as High, Normal, or Low.

To set the priority of your message, follow these steps:

1. In your message window, click the Options button. The Message Options dialog box opens.

2. Click the Importance list box in the Message settings section of the dialog box (see Figure 11.13).

FIGURE 11.13

If your message is urgent and requires immediate action, indicate this to your recipients by setting the priority to High. A red exclamation point accompanies your message to their inbox.

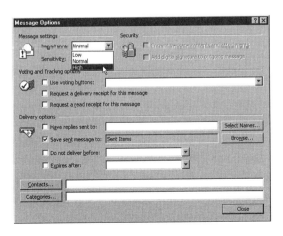

3. Choose the importance level for your message. Choosing High causes a red exclamation point to appear next to your message in your recipient's Inbox. If you choose Low importance, a down-pointing arrow appears in the Inbox.

4. If the message is Confidential, Personal, or Private, indicate this (and choose the appropriate adjective) in the Sensitivity list box, also found in the Message settings section.

5. After making your selections, click Close.

Again, only if your recipient uses Outlook do the importance and sensitivity marks appear with the message in their Inbox.

 Tip

You can also use the Importance: High button on the Standard toolbar in your message window to mark a message as important. For Normal or Low, you must use the Message Options dialog box.

 Caution

Marking all your messages as high priority can backfire—people might start ignoring your priority markings. Use the feature sparingly, so that if someone sees that red exclamation mark, they know that your message is truly important.

Using Flags to Indicate Required Actions

 For messages that are going to fellow Outlook users, you can insert a *flag*, or simple instruction, for the recipient. Flags can be set to tell the recipient how to handle the message, and what (if anything) they need to do beyond simply reading it. Your flag options are as follows:

- **Call**—When an email response won't do, use this flag to indicate that you need a live conversation about the message topic.

- **Do not Forward**—If you're afraid the recipient might share the message with others by forwarding it, use this flag to tell them not to.

- **Follow up**—This implies that some action is required, and that the nature of the action is explained or somehow obvious in the message itself.

- **For your information**—This tells the reader to do nothing more than read the message—it requires no action beyond remembering the message content.

- **Forward**—The message is to be sent on to someone else whose identity can be found in the message body.

- **No response necessary**—Similar to For Your Information, this requires no action.

- **Read**—This one is pretty obvious.

- **Reply**—If you want the recipient to give you a response, choose this flag.

- **Reply to All**—Many recipients forget to include the other recipients in their response. This flag reminds them to keep everyone "in the loop."

- **Review**—This flag is best used for long messages or messages with attached files. It tells the recipient that careful study of the content of the message or the attachment is advised.

To attach one of these flags to your message, follow these steps:

 1. While creating your message, Choose Actions, Flag for Follow Up. The Flag for Follow Up dialog box opens, as shown in Figure 11.14. You can also click the Flag button to open the dialog box.

FIGURE 11.14

Choose a flag to indicate to your recipient what action you want them to take regarding your message.

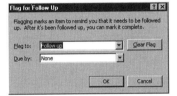

2. Click the Flag to list box, and choose the flag that you want to accompany your email message.

3. If the flagged action is to be performed by a certain date, click the Due by button and scroll through the calendar to find the date. Click the date by which you want the action completed (see Figure 11.15).

FIGURE 11.15

Give the recipient a deadline for taking the action indicated by your flag.

4. Click OK to close the dialog box and apply the flag to your message.

A boxed strip appears in your message window, as shown in Figure 11.16. The flag and any due date you applied appear in the strip, as well as in the recipient's copy of the message.

FIGURE 11.16

To make sure the recipient knows what you want him or her to do with the message, the flag you selected appears prominently in a strip above the message address.

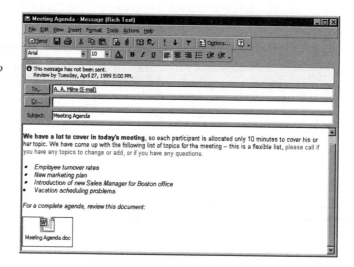

To remove a flag before sending the message, reopen the Flag for Follow Up dialog box and click the Clear Flag button.

Getting Your New Mail

Depending on your email system—a local area network or an Internet connection through an ISP—the methods you'll use to get your new incoming mail will vary.

If you're on a LAN (local area network), your system administrator will have set your Inbox up so that new mail is automatically placed in your Inbox whenever you log in to Outlook. In addition, as long as you're logged in, your local copy of Outlook checks the network server for new mail. If you want to check for it immediately, choose Tools, Send/Receive. Any outgoing mail is sent to the server for distribution to local users' mailboxes and to the outside recipients via the Internet. Your new mail (mail sent to you) is pulled from the server and appears in your Inbox.

Tip   If you're working from your home computer or a laptop while on the road, connect to a phone jack and choose Tools, Remote Mail. Click the Connect command and, using the dialing instructions that are built into your installation of Outlook, you can connect to your company's server and download your email.

If you aren't on a LAN and get your mail from the Internet only, you can choose Tools, Send/Receive, Internet Email. However, just like a LAN user, when you log in to Outlook, your Inbox contains your latest new mail (and any previously received mail).

Replying to Messages

When your new message appears in your Inbox, you might not need to do anything beyond reading it. If, however, you want to respond, you can do so by clicking one of two buttons in the message window:

- **Reply**—This opens an Untitled Message window, which is automatically addressed to the person who sent you the message. If you were not the sole recipient of the message, the other people who received it are not included in your response.

- **Reply to All**—For most messages, this is the best choice. Unlike Reply, which sends the response only to the person who sent you the message, Reply to All addresses the response to everyone who received the original message. To maintain effective teamwork, it's a good idea to use Reply to All so that no one is left out of the conversation and everyone stays up-to-date.

To respond to your message, click one of the Reply buttons (Reply or Reply to All) and enter the body of your message. Figure 11.17 shows a reply window, with the original message subject appearing both on the window's title bar and in the Subject box. RE: appears before the original subject text, indicating that the reply message is regarding this original message.

11

FIGURE 11.17

Your cursor is automatically placed at the top of the message box, above the sender's original text. Type your response and click Send.

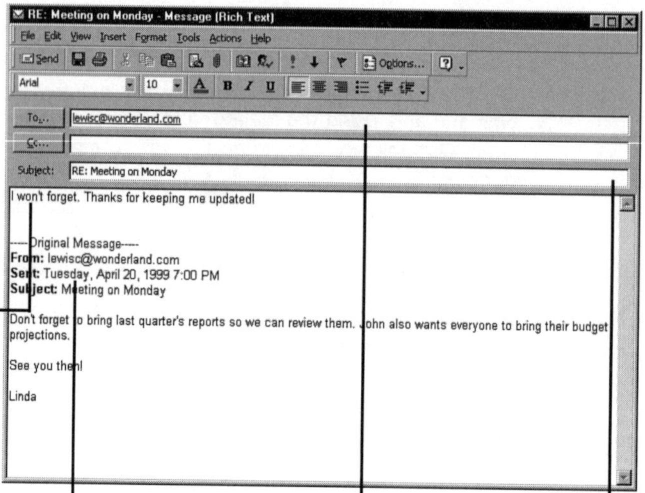

Your response is typed here

Original message to which you're responding appears below your response   Message is addressed to the sender automatically   Subject of original message is repeated in the Subject line, with RE: added at the beginning

Your sent responses, like all your sent mail, are stored in your Sent Items folder, where you can review them at any time.

Tip

It might be helpful to periodically check your Sent Items folder to see if there are messages you've sent to which you haven't had any responses. It's easy to forget what you've sent out, and checking the Sent Items folder can refresh your memory.

Forwarding Email to Others

There might be times when a message you receive really needs to be seen by someone else—perhaps the sender was responding to another message and used Reply instead of Reply to All, leaving some people out when sending their response. Whatever your reason for forwarding a message, it's simple to do if you follow these steps:

1. In the message you want to forward, click the Forward button.
2. A FW: titled message window opens (see Figure 11.18). Enter the email address of the person or people to whom you want to forward the message.

FIGURE 11.18

*The subject of the origi-
nal message is turned
into the subject of the
forward, and is preceded
by FW:.*

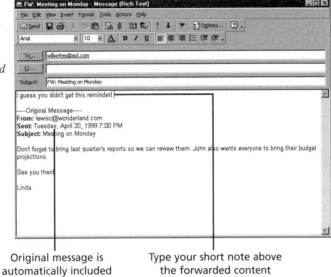

Original message is
automatically included

Type your short note above
the forwarded content

3. Press Tab three times to place your cursor in the message box, just above the
   Original Message.

4. Type a message that tells the recipient why the message is being forwarded to
   them. "You should see this," or, "What do you think about this message that Bob
   sent to me?" are good examples. They indicate that the message is being forwarded
   (in case the recipient doesn't notice or understand the *FW* that is added to the
   Subject).

5. Click Send to forward the message and your note.

Tip

If you forward a message and realize that you didn't send it to everyone you
wanted to, simply reopen the forward message from the Sent Items folder
and forward it to the forgotten recipients. This is faster and easier than creating a brand-new forward message, and it assures you that your content is
the same for all recipients.

11

Saving Messages

If your message is longer than a few words or lines, you might not finish it in one sitting. It's a good idea to devote as much care to the content and appearance of your longer, more detailed email messages as you do to a document you create in Word. If you're not ready to send a message, you can save it and then come back to it when you have time to do a thorough job and finish your message.

To save your message-in-progress as a draft, choose File, Save, or click the Save button in your Untitled Message window. No dialog box opens, and you receive no notification that the file has been saved.

To access draft versions of messages, go to the My Shortcuts panel and click the Drafts icon (see Figure 11.19). Double-click the draft you want to finish editing.

FIGURE 11.19

Click the Drafts icon to view your messages-in-progress.

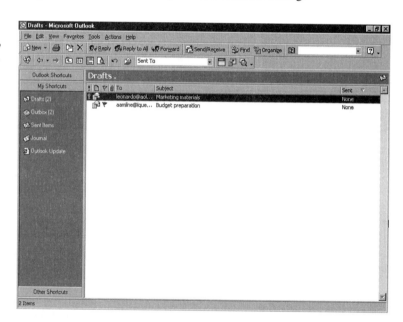

It's easy to forget about your messages-in-progress. Make it a point to check the Drafts folder every day to be sure you've completed all your email messages. If you think you'll forget to check the Drafts folder, display your Folder list (View, Folder List) and the number of messages (displayed in blue, in parentheses next to the folder) reminds you that you have unfinished messages.

With Outlook you can also save email messages as documents—choose File, Save As in your Untitled Message window. A Save As dialog box opens (See Figure 11.20), where you can give the file a name and choose a folder in which to store it. The file is saved in .RTF (Rich Text) format, which can be edited in Word.

FIGURE 11.20

If you might have use for some or all of the text in one of your messages, save the message as a text file. The file and its content can be edited and printed in Word.

Storing Your Email Messages

11

You already know you can save an email message that isn't ready to send, keeping it as a Draft. This isn't the only type of storage (long- or short-term) that Outlook offers. You can also store mail you've received and mail you've sent. You create your own folders to categorize your mail and then copy and move mail from folder to folder, just as you might copy and move files using the Windows Explorer or My Computer programs.

Creating New Folders

In the default view of Outlook, you can't see your folders. You need to display them before you can add a folder, and certainly before moving messages from one folder to another. To display your Outlook folders, choose View, Folder List. A pane opens between the Shortcuts panel and the main window, as shown in Figure 11.21.

FIGURE 11.21

Display your Folder List and click the plus sign next to Outlook Today to see a full list of your folders.

The plus sign indicates the presence of subfolders

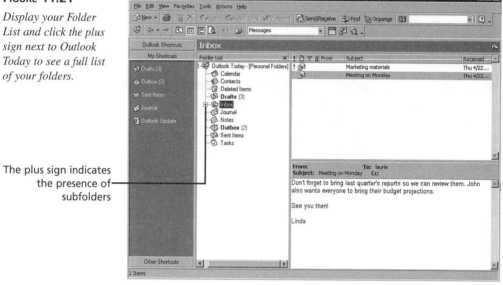

The complete folder list (shown in Figure 11.22) contains your Inbox, Outbox, and Sent Items folders, as well as others such as Calendar, Contacts, and Tasks.

FIGURE 11.22

When your complete folder list is displayed, the plus sign turns to a minus.

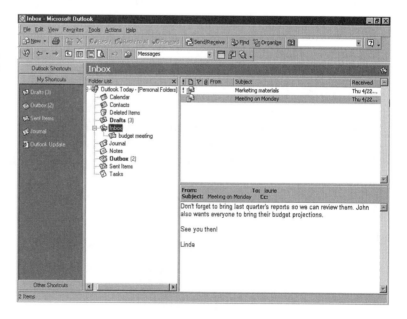

You can create subfolders in any or all of these folders. By completing the following
steps, you can create subfolders for your Inbox and Sent Items folders to categorize your
mail.

1. In the Folder List, click once on the existing folder to which you want to add a
   subfolder. In this case, click once on the Inbox.

2. Choose File, New, Folder. The Create New Folder dialog box opens, as shown in
   Figure 11.23.

FIGURE 11.23

*Give your folder a
name that makes it
clear what type of
messages can be found
inside it.*

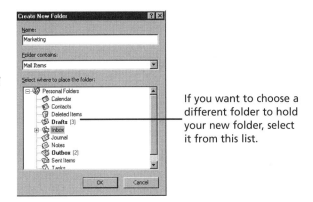

If you want to choose a
different folder to hold
your new folder, select
it from this list.

3. Type a name for your folder. For this procedure, name the folder Meetings. Mail
   pertaining to meetings will be placed in this folder.

4. Click OK. The folder is created, and the dialog box closes.

5. A prompt appears, asking if you want to add a shortcut to the new folder on the
   My Shortcuts panel. Click Yes if you want to add it.

> Don't restrict your use of new folders to the Inbox. You can create new fold-
> ers to hold and categorize your Tasks and Calendar. You'll learn more about
> creating to-do items and appointments on Day 12.

The subfolder is visible in the Folder List, and the folder in which you created it has a
minus sign next to it. If you want to collapse this view of your subfolder, click the minus
sign and the subfolder is hidden.

Moving Mail Between Folders

Moving mail is a simple task, and it might remind you of the process of moving files and folders within the Windows Explorer or My Computer windows. To move mail from one folder to another (out of the Inbox and into the Meetings folder you created, for example), you simply drag the messages from the displayed view of the folder they're in to the folder icon of the folder in which you want to place them. Figure 11.24 shows mail from the Inbox in transit to the Meetings folder.

FIGURE 11.24

Drag mail from one folder to another.

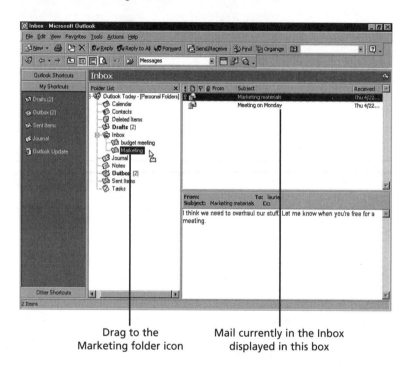

Drag to the
Marketing folder icon

Mail currently in the Inbox
displayed in this box

If you prefer a more methodical approach, you can follow these steps to move mail from one folder to another:

1. Click the folder that contains the mail you want to move.

2. Click once on the message that is to be moved. If you want to move multiple messages, press the Ctrl key and click on each message. When the group of messages is selected, release the Ctrl key.

3. Choose Edit, Move to Folder. The Move Items dialog box opens (see Figure 11.25).

FIGURE 11.25

Use a more methodical approach—use the Move Items dialog box to move your selected messages to a different folder.

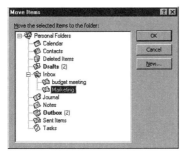

4. Click once on the folder to which you want to move the selected messages. Click OK to close the dialog box and execute the move.

You can also create a new folder from within the Move Items dialog box. Click the folder that will contain your new folder, and click the New button. The Create New Folder dialog box (seen previously) opens, and you can name the new folder there.

Deleting Mail and User-Created Folders

Deleting mail in Outlook is considered by some users to be too easy—no confirming prompt appears. It does save you, however, from losing mail that you delete in error: When mail is deleted, it goes to the Deleted Items folder. Items in the Deleted Items folder can be retrieved and put back where they came from until you empty the Deleted Items folder.

To delete a message in any folder, simply click the message once to select it and press the Delete key on your keyboard, or click the Delete button on the Standard toolbar.

After it is deleted, the message moves to the Deleted items folder; you can then permanently delete it by selecting the message and again pressing Delete or clicking the Delete button. A prompt appears to confirm you intention to permanently delete the item.

Caution

Be careful when deleting items in the Deleted Items folder—you might delete a message you didn't intend to delete, and only while it's still in the Deleted Items folder can it be retrieved and placed back in its original folder. After items are deleted from the Deleted Items folder, they are completely removed from your computer—they don't go to the Recycle Bin, and there is no way to get them back.

11

Tip

When you're absolutely sure that all the items in the Deleted Items folder can be deleted, right-click the folder and choose Empty Deleted Items Folder. You can do this on the Deleted Items icon in the Outlook Shortcuts panel or the Folder List.

Working with the Address Book

If you don't know a recipient's address, or if you are simply tired of typing it out each time you send them an email, you can add their name and email address (as well as a regular mailing address and phone number) to your Outlook contact list. The Address Book is pivotal to your other Office 2000 applications, as well as to the Small Business Tools programs (see Appendix C, "Working with Small Business Tools"). The contacts you build into your Address Book might become the recipients of a mass mailing you set up through Word or the Direct Mail Manager (a Small Business Tools feature), or they might end up in a database you work with in Excel or Access.

Adding an Address Book Entry

You can add a contact to your Address Book at any time from anywhere within the Outlook application. The dialog box that results might look different, depending on the way you opened the Address Book, but the contacts you create all end up in the same place and are accessible from anywhere in Outlook or any of the Office 2000 applications.

Choose one of the following methods to open the Select Names dialog box (shown in Figure 11.26):

FIGURE 11.26

Open the Address Book from within a message window or from Outlook's Tools menu.

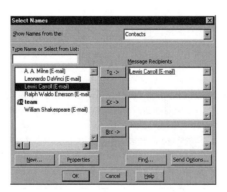

- Press Ctrl+Shift+B.
- Choose Tools, Address Book from within an Untitled Message window.

If you click the Outlook Shortcuts button on the Shortcuts panel and then click the Contacts icon, you can open the Address Book by clicking the New Contact button or by pressing Ctrl+N.

Figure 11.27 shows the Untitled Contact dialog box, a five-tabbed box into which a contact's name, address, phone, and email information can be typed. All the information is stored in the Address book, and the email address is furnished through the Select Names dialog box when you click the To or Cc buttons in a new message window.

FIGURE 11.27

Store as much or as little information as you want to about your contacts.

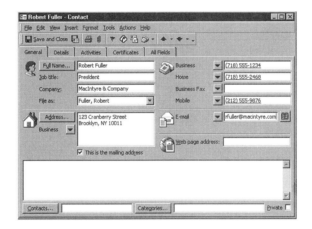

Creating Distribution Lists

When you email to the same group of people repeatedly, it can become tiresome to type their email addresses or select them from the Select Names dialog box every time you need to send them a message. Manually accruing the list of recipients also increases your margin for error and risks leaving someone out of the message—which means that you have to resend the message to the person who's been left out, or that one of the other recipients has to forward your message to them.

A distribution list is a group of email addresses stored under a single name, such as *Project Team* or *Budget Committee*, that describes what the people on the list have in common. To create a distribution list, follow these steps:

1. From anywhere in Outlook (you needn't be in the Inbox), choose File, New, Distribution List. You can also press Ctrl+Shift+L.

2. The Untitled Distribution List dialog box opens, as shown in Figure 11.28. Give your distribution list a Name.

FIGURE **11.28**

In the Members tab, name your list and click Select Members to begin building your list.

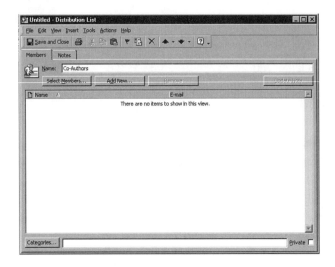

3. Click the Select Members button. The Select Members dialog box opens (see Figure 11.29). If the members of your list are in your address book, select them from the list of Contacts and click Add for each one.

FIGURE **11.29**

Choose which email addresses are to receive the messages that are addressed to your distribution list.

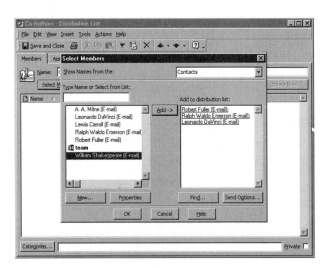

4. If you want to include people who are not currently in your address book, click the New Contact button and add them as contacts, including their email address. Click OK in the New Contacts dialog box after entering the contact information; you return to the Select Members dialog box, where you see your new contact listed. Click his or her name and then click Add to add him or her to your distribution list.

5. When the list is complete, click OK. You return to the Distribution List dialog box, where you see your selected members listed.

6. Click the Save and Close button. The list is created, and you can use it immediately to address an email to everyone in your list.

You can edit a distribution list at any time. Members can be added or deleted, or changes in their email addresses can be made. To edit a distribution list, follow these steps:

1. In a new message window, choose Tools, Address Book, and then click once on the distribution list you want to edit.

2. Click the Properties button. The Co-Authors Properties dialog box opens (see Figure 11.30), showing the name of the list and the members. Select individual members by clicking their names, and then click Remove to take them out of the list; or Select Members to select new people for the list.

FIGURE 11.30

Edit your exiting distribution list by adding or removing members.

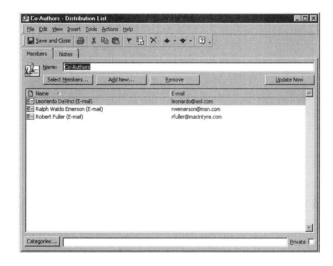

11

3. When your edits are complete, click OK.

Summary

Today introduced you to the email portions of Microsoft Outlook's total set of tools. You learned to send email and read your incoming mail, respond to and forward your new mail, and store incoming and sent mail in folders that better categorize your mail for future use. Tomorrow will focus on the schedule maintenance and to-do list portions of Outlook.

Q&A

Q How long can I keep my mail?

A If you're saving it to your local hard drive (as opposed to storing it on a network drive), you can keep your mail as long as you want—it's not tying up anyone's space but your own. Messages take up very little space unto themselves. Most users keep unnecessary mail (mail on topics that have been resolved) for 30 days and then delete it. It's a good idea to save mail that pertains to ongoing issues so that you have an audit trail of what you said and what was said to you.

Q Is it possible to send a copy of a message and not have that recipient's name appear in the address as viewed by the other recipients?

A Although misuse of blind carbon copies (bcc) of messages is an example of poor email etiquette, you can send a message to someone and have none of your other recipients know about it. In your Untitled Message window, choose View, Bcc. A place to type blind carbon recipients' email addresses appears below the existing Cc box.

Workshop

The section that follows is a quick quiz about the day. If you have any problems answering any of the questions, see the section that follows the quiz for all the answers.

Quiz

1. When you look at the mail in your Inbox, how can you tell which mail has been read and which mail hasn't?
2. What's the difference between a Reply and a Reply to All?
3. Is it possible to know if the recipient has read a message you've sent?
4. True or False: Email sent via the Internet retains all its Outlook-based formatting when it is received by the recipients.
5. Explain the importance of entering a Subject for your outgoing mail.

Quiz Answers

1. Unread mail is in bold type, and the message's envelope icon appears closed and is colored yellow.
2. Using the Reply command sends your response only to the person who sent you the message. Any other recipients of the message do not receive a copy of your response. Using Reply to All automatically addresses your response to everyone who received the original message.

3. Yes, you can tell if the recipient has read your message by using the Request a read receipt for the message option in the Message Options dialog box. Click the Options button in your outgoing message window to open this dialog box.

4. False. A trip over the Internet is likely to strip away formatting such as text color and character formats. In addition, requests for receipts and priority symbols and flag information might also be lost.

5. The Subject line on a new message tells the recipient what your message pertains to and gives them a chance to prioritize their incoming mail, determining which mail gets read first. In addition, the Subject line is used when categorizing mail into different folders—if the Subject clearly describes the topic of the message, the message need not be reopened to determine in which folder it is to be stored.

11

WEEK 2

DAY 12

Managing Your Time with the Calendar

Day 11, "Sending Email Messages," introduced you to the usefulness of
Outlook for communicating via email—sending, responding to, and attaching
files to messages that you send to people in your office or across the globe.
Today turns to the other side of Outlook: the Calendar and Task List features.
These tools enable you to store information about your schedule—where you're
supposed to be, when you're supposed to be there, and what you need to do on
any given day. Outlook gives you several views of your schedule, enabling you
to look at a single day for very specific information, a week to see the short
term, or an entire month to get the big picture of your appointments and events.
Today you'll learn about the following topics, which will enable you to build
and maintain your schedule through Outlook:

- Viewing your calendar from a variety of perspectives for maximum
  efficiency
- Creating appointments and marking important events on your calendar
- Understanding Outlook's options for setting up recurring, private, and
  other special appointments

- Setting up a to-do list to track your personal and business-related tasks
- Creating and maintaining a contacts list to facilitate email and mass mailings

Understanding Calendar Views

When you observe anything, you find out more about it by looking at it from a variety of perspectives. Get very close to something, and you see the details. Step back and look at it from a distance, and you see how it relates to the items surrounding it. Your calendar is something that you can and need to observe from a variety of perspectives, and Outlook enables you to do that quickly and easily with four different views.

To access Outlook's Calendar program and experience these views, open the Outlook application and click the Calendar icon on the Shortcuts pane (see Figure 12.1).

FIGURE 12.1

Use the Calendar shortcut to access your electronic schedule.

Click this icon to open the Calendar

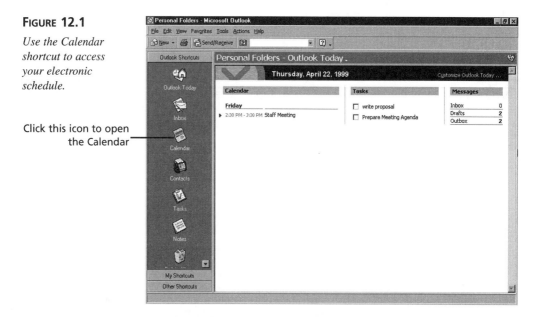

The calendar opens in Day view, a view of your calendar that shows the current date in an hour-by-hour view. Figure 12.2 shows Day view and identifies the other onscreen features of this perspective on your schedule.

The Date Navigator
calendars show the
current and next months

Click the right
arrow to move
forward

FIGURE 12.2

*The first time you open
the Outlook Calendar,
you see an hourly view
of the current date.*

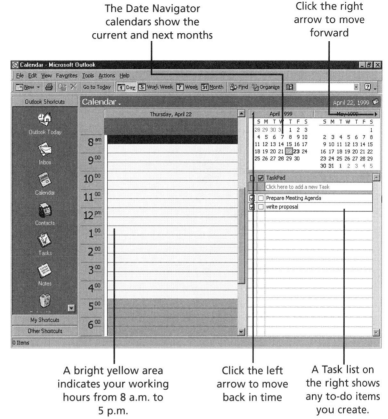

A bright yellow area
indicates your working
hours from 8 a.m. to
5 p.m.

Click the left
arrow to move
back in time

A Task list on
the right shows
any to-do items
you create.

To see a Day view of any particular date, click on the desired date in the Date Navigator in the upper-right side of the window. Figure 12.3 shows a particular date selected.

Outlook gives you three more views in addition to Day view. These views give you the capability to step back from your schedule and view it in the context of a week or an entire month.

FIGURE **12.3**

Click the left- and right-pointing triangles in the Date Navigator to move backward and forward through the months and years.

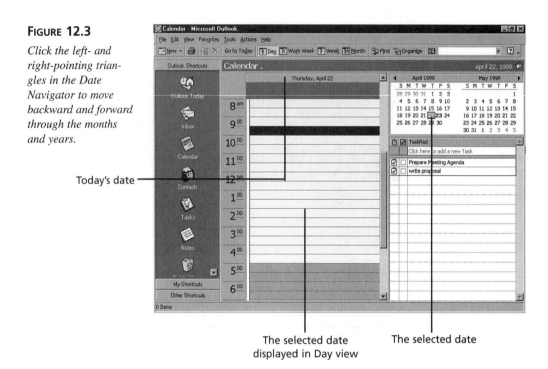

Today's date

The selected date
displayed in Day view

The selected date

Viewing Your Calendar by the Week

Outlook gives you two different week views—a Work Week of five days (Monday–Friday) and a normal Week, which shows all seven days of the week. Figure 12.4 shows the Work Week view.

FIGURE 12.4

If you use Outlook to schedule only work-related appointments, use Work Week view to see only Monday–Friday of any given week.

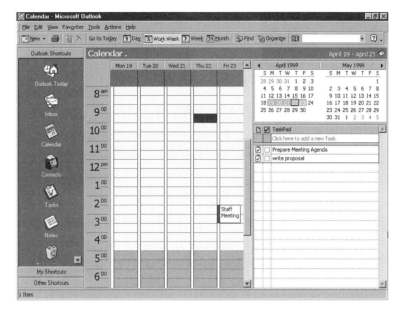

Many users track their personal commitments through Outlook as well; for these people, viewing an entire week—including the weekends—is useful. Figure 12.5 shows the Week view, with room for Saturday and Sunday appointments and events.

FIGURE 12.5

See an entire seven-day week in Week view.

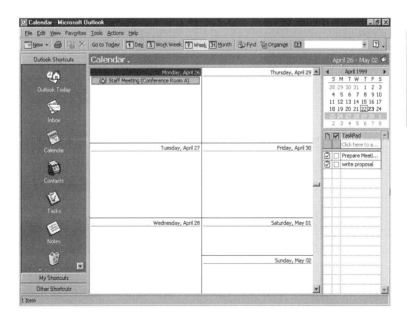

12

Tip   To see a particular week in either Work Week or Week view, click the
            Monday of that week on the Date Navigator.

Viewing an Entire Month at a Time

If you need to see the "big picture" of any month, click the Month view button. The Date
Navigator calendars and Task List disappear, showing you a full-screen view of the current month. You can use the vertical scrollbar to move through time, either backward or
forward (see Figure 12.6).

FIGURE 12.6

*See any month in the
past or future, or
scroll to a particular
spot and see portions
of two months at a
glance.*

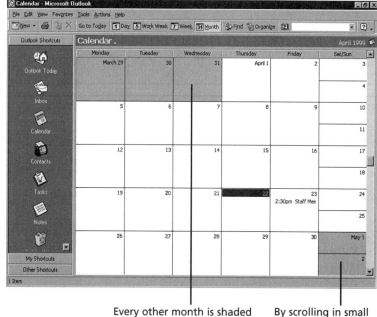

Every other month is shaded
gray to help you visually
distinguish months

By scrolling in small
increments, see the end
of one month and the
beginning of another

 Tip   To see the current date in any view, click the Go to Today button on the
            toolbar.

Entering Appointments and Events

When you're ready to start building your calendar, you can do so from any of the views—Day, Work Week, Week, or Month. Just as a particular view helps you to better interpret your activities and free time, using that same view to create an appointment or event can help you to plan your time more effectively.

Creating Appointments in Day View

Day view enables you to pick the starting and ending times for the appointment before you even create it; it is for that reason that many users prefer this approach.

To create an appointment or event in Day view, follow these steps:

1. In Day view, select the date of your appointment by clicking on the date on the Date Navigator calendars.

2. With that date displayed in Day view, click on the time that your new appointment or event is to start.

3. Drag down until the range of times representing the duration of your appointment or event is selected (see Figure 12.7).

FIGURE 12.7

Drag through the yellow lines to set the duration of your appointment.

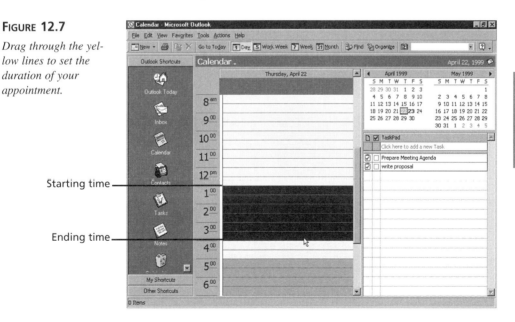

Starting time

Ending time

4. Click the New Appointment button or press Ctrl+N to open the Untitled
   Appointment window, as shown in Figure 12.8.

FIGURE 12.8

*The Untitled
Appointment window
displays the starting
and ending times for
your appointment.*

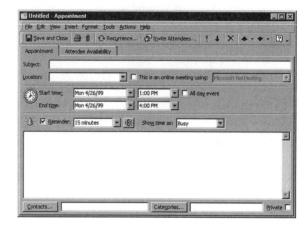

5. Type a Subject for your appointment.

6. Press Tab to move to the Location box and enter a location for your appointment.
   You can skip this step if the location is obvious or unnecessary for the specific
   appointment or event.

7. As necessary, adjust the starting and ending dates and times for the appointment
   by clicking the list triangles in the boxes that display the current settings (see
   Figure 12.9).

FIGURE 12.9

*Click the date triangle
to display a calendar.
Select an alternative
date for the appoint-
ment as needed.*

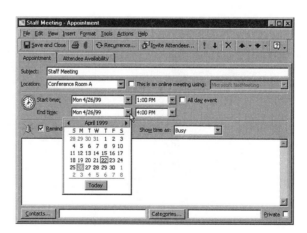

8. To make the appointment an event, place a checkmark in the All day event box. The times for the appointment disappear, as shown in Figure 12.10.

FIGURE 12.10

An all day event has starting and ending times.

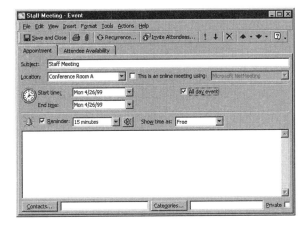

9. Adjust the Reminder settings as necessary. A reminder is automatically set for 15 minutes prior to the appointment, but you might need more time if the appointment requires travel or last-minute preparation.

10. Click in the large white box to type more information about the appointment or event—enter notes for what to bring to the meeting, preparations you need to make for the event, or a list of topics that are to be discussed, as shown in Figure 12.11.

FIGURE 12.11

Type any extra information you need to remember about your appointment or event. You can view or edit this content later by double-clicking the appointment in your calendar.

12

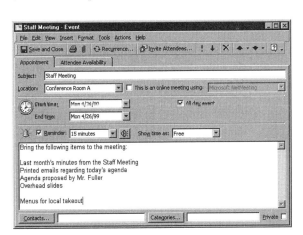

11. Click the Save and Close button to close the dialog box and enter the appointment or event into your calendar.

Your appointment is displayed in Day view (the view you were in when the appointment was created). If you can't read the full subject as you typed it, widen the hourly view by dragging the divider between the hours and the Date Navigator/Task List panels as shown in Figure 12.12. The Date Navigator can be set to display only one month at a time, allowing more room to display your hourly view of the day.

FIGURE 12.12

Point to the divider and drag to the right when your mouse turns into a two-headed arrow.

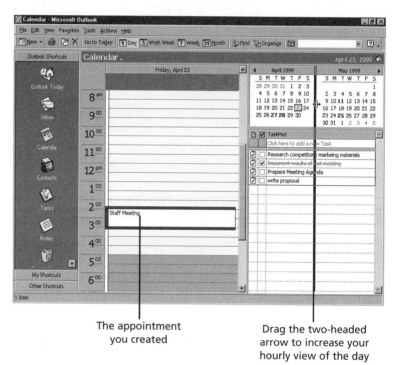

The appointment
you created

Drag the two-headed
arrow to increase your
hourly view of the day

Creating Appointments in Weekly and Monthly Views

If you're looking at your calendar in Work Week, Week, or Month view, there is no need to switch to Day view to create an appointment. Simply double-click anywhere in the empty block for the date of the appointment or event you want to create (see Figure 12.13); the Untitled Appointment dialog box opens automatically.

FIGURE 12.13

Double-click the date block to create an appointment for that date.

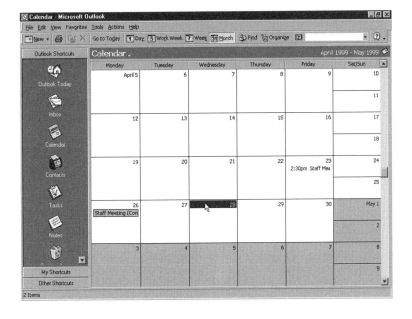

Note

When you create an appointment from within Week or Month view, the Untitled Event dialog box opens instead of the Untitled Appointment dialog box. This is because neither of these views offers a list of times during the day—each block is seen as an entire day, with no hourly or half-hourly breakdown. To create an appointment from within the Untitled Event dialog box, simply remove the checkmark from the All day event box and use the Start and End time boxes to set the starting and ending times for the appointment. You'll also notice that the dialog box's title bar changes to Untitled Appointment when you turn off the All day event option.

12

Caution

If there is already an appointment in the block, be careful to double-click above or below it when you are creating a new appointment. If you double-click the existing appointment, you open a dialog box from which you can edit the existing appointment.

Figure 12.14 shows an appointment in Work Week view, and Figure 12.15 shows an appointment in Month view.

FIGURE 12.14

View your appointment in a five-day context in Work Week view.

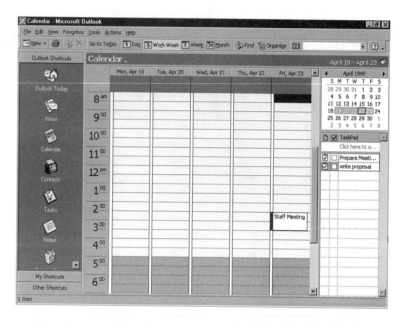

FIGURE 12.15

Your appointment's position within the entire month is seen in Month view.

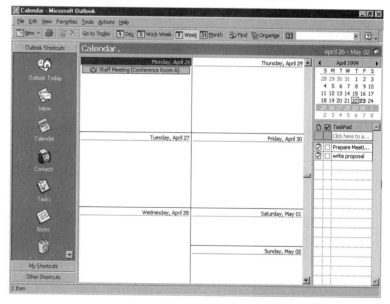

Working with Appointment Options

A simple appointment or event consists of a date, a subject, starting and ending times (for appointments only—events last all day), and a description, which is optional if the subject explains the appointment or event adequately. Beyond these basics, there is nothing you need to do when building an appointment or event unless you have specific needs such as the following:

- **A special reminder**—By default, a reminder is set to appear, and a reminder sound to play, 15 minutes before the scheduled appointment or event. You can change this from as few as zero minutes (no reminder) to two days, and you can choose a different sound to accompany your visual reminder. Figure 12.16 shows a reminder set to one hour reminder and the Reminder Sound dialog box.

FIGURE 12.16

If your computer has sound capabilities, you can choose to accompany your visual reminder with a sound.

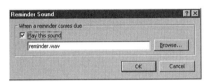

- **To show the appointment or event time as something other than Busy**—By default, the time that is allotted for the appointment or event is shown as Busy. You can also show it as Free, Tentative, or Out of the Office (see Figure 12.17). These settings are only useful if your schedule is viewed by others in your organization, so they can see if you'll be accessible during the meeting or willing to consider canceling the current appointment in favor of something else.

12

FIGURE 12.17

If you want to let people know the appointment isn't carved in stone, choose Tentative from the Show time as options.

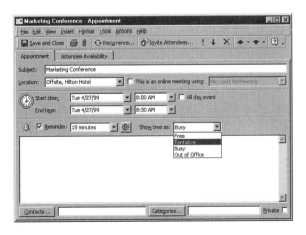

- **Mark the appointment as Private**—Again, if others will be viewing your schedule (by opening a copy of your calendar file through their computers), you might want to mark any appointments of a personal nature as private. To do so, click the Private checkbox in the lower-right corner of the Untitled Appointment dialog box (see Figure 12.18). Other users can see that the appointment exists, but they can't see any subject or description—just that you're busy at that time.

FIGURE 12.18

Maintain discretion when it comes to your personal commitments by turning on the Private option.

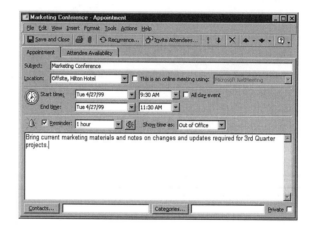

Creating Recurring Appointments

Many appointments and events happen only once. Some appointments happen many times, but not at regular intervals, making it impossible to set up appointments now for all future occurrences in your Outlook Calendar. If, however, your appointment is the first of a regular series of appointments, you can set it and all the recurrences now.

To create a recurring appointment, follow these steps:

1. In any view (Day, Week, Month), click the New button or press Ctrl+N. The Untitled Appointment dialog box opens.

2. Type a Subject for the appointment, such as Staff Meeting.

3. Select starting and ending dates and times (or adjust those that were chosen in Day view before opening this dialog box).

4. Click the Recurrence button. The Appointment Recurrence dialog box opens, as shown in Figure 12.19.

FIGURE 12.19

Choose the dates, times, and recurrence schedule for your series of appointments.

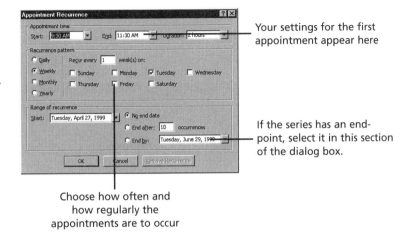

Your settings for the first appointment appear here

If the series has an end-point, select it in this section of the dialog box.

Choose how often and how regularly the appointments are to occur

5. Adjust the Start, End, and Duration settings as needed by clicking the list triangles for each box.

6. Set your Recurrence pattern by choosing Daily, Weekly, Monthly, or Yearly.

7. If your meetings happen every other day, week, or month, enter a 2 in the Recur every box.

8. Choose a day of the week for the recurrences. By default, the day of the week of the first occurrence is selected.

9. Set the Range of occurrences by choosing when the series will end. By default, No end date is selected.

10. When all settings are correct, click OK to return to the Untitled Appointment dialog box.

12

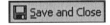

11. Review the Recurrence settings (see Figure 12.20) as they appear in the Appointment dialog box. If they are correct, click Save and Close.

FIGURE 12.20

A single sentence recaps your recurrence settings.

Read the description of your recurrence settings to make sure they're correct

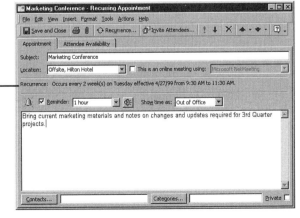

To make sure that you've created the correct recurrences for your appointments, switch to Month view and scroll through the months to see your new series of appointments. Figure 12.21 shows a biweekly Staff Meeting scheduled for Tuesdays at 9:30 a.m.

FIGURE 12.21

Create entries for a year of staff meetings with one simple procedure.

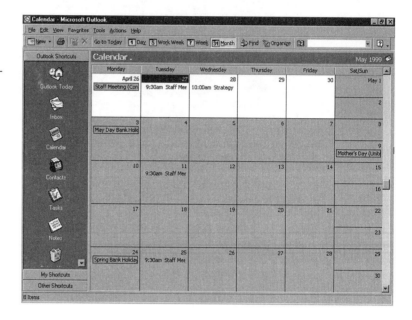

Editing Appointments and Events

After they are created, appointments and events are easy to edit—simply double-click them in the displayed Day, Week, or Month view. You can also use one of the following alternative methods to open an existing appointment for editing:

- Right-click the appointment and choose Open from the shortcut menu (see Figure 12.22).
- Choose File, Open, Selected Items.
- Click once on the appointment or event and press Ctrl+0.

Tip

If the appointment is one of a series of recurring appointments, you'll be asked if you want to open the entire series or just this particular occurrence.

FIGURE 12.22

*Shortcut menus give
you access to com-
mands that are related
to the selected item.
Choose Open to edit
the selected appoint-
ment or event.*

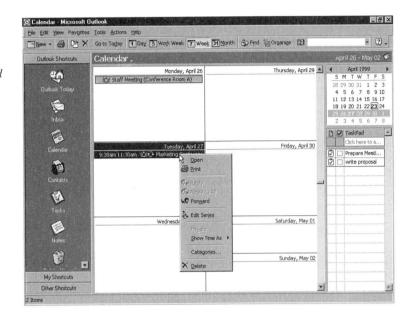

When the appointment is displayed, you can adjust anything about the meeting—its starting and ending dates and times, the subject, the location, or the description. When you've
completed your changes, click Save and Close, and the edited version of your appointment or event appears in your calendar.

Deleting Appointments and Events

It's almost too easy to delete an appointment. Luckily, using Edit, Undo or Ctrl+Z brings
an appointment back if you've deleted it in error. Choose one of the following methods
to delete an unwanted appointment or event (select the appointment first by clicking once
on it in any view).

- Press the Delete key on your keyboard.
- Click the Delete button on the toolbar.

Tip

If you attempt to delete an appointment that is one in a series of recurring
appointments, you are prompted to indicate whether you're deleting the
single occurrence or the entire series.

12

Edit, Undo saves your accidentally deleted appointment only if you catch the error immediately. If you realize that you didn't mean to delete an appointment only after you've performed any other action or after you've closed and then reopened Outlook, you can't bring the appointment back. *Always delete with care!*

Building and Maintaining a To-Do List

Nearly everyone's desk has a handwritten list of things to do, and the list contains everything from dentist appointments to staff meetings to remembering to pick up dry cleaning. These combined business and personal to-do items can be stored and displayed in Outlook, providing an onscreen reminder of the tasks that you need to perform.

To create a task in the Task List, you can choose one of the following methods:

- In the Calendar's Day, Work Week, or Week views, click in the TaskPad as indicated (see Figure 12.23). Type a short description of the task, and then press Enter.

FIGURE 12.23

Create a simple one-line description for your task in the TaskPad.

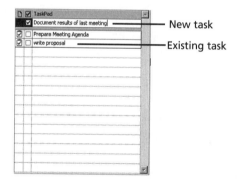

- Click the Tasks button on the Outlook Shortcuts panel. You can click in the Tasks window that opens (see Figure 12.24) and type a short description of the task. In this view you can also click to choose a due date for your task (when it is to be completed).

When a task is complete, you can mark it as such in either the TaskPad (seen through the Calendar) or the Tasks window by clicking the empty box next to the task. The box is checked and the text of the task is crossed out.

FIGURE 12.24

The Tasks window gives you access to the Due Date text box, in which you can type a date or click the triangle to select a date from a Navigator calendar.

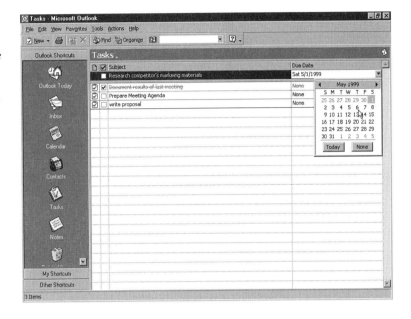

It's a good idea to leave completed tasks on the list for a short time, if only until you're sure your entire list is complete and all tasks have been properly performed. When you're ready to remove a completed task (or a task you decide not to perform at all) from your list, click once on the task and choose one of the following methods to delete it:

- Press Delete on your keyboard.
- Click the Delete button on the Outlook toolbar.
- Right-click the task and choose Delete from the shortcut menu.

After they are deleted, you can retrieve tasks by choosing Edit, Undo or pressing Ctrl+Z. This, of course, only works if you realize your deletion error immediately. If you delete a task and it's too late to Undo the deletion, simply recreate the task through the Calendar's TaskPad or through the Tasks window.

If your task requires additional explanation, or if you want to take advantage of task options such as recurring tasks (for example, recurring appointments) or assigning a priority to your tasks, double-click the task in the Task list or on the TaskPad. In the Task dialog box that opens (see Figure 12.25), you can establish specific settings or enter a more elaborate description of your task.

12

FIGURE 12.25

Set up a more complex to-do item in the Task dialog box.

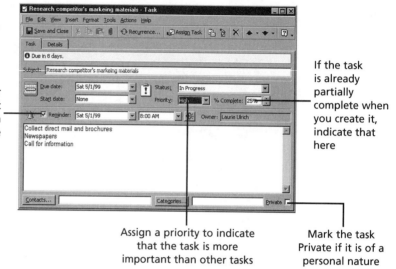

Turn on a reminder if your task must be performed by a certain time

Assign a priority to indicate that the task is more important than other tasks

If the task is already partially complete when you create it, indicate that here

Mark the task Private if it is of a personal nature

If your tasks are not completed at the end of the day on which they were created, they appear in the TaskPad until they are completed. If you set a due date for the task, the task appears in red in the TaskPad after the due date has passed.

Tip

You can assign your tasks to other Outlook users on your network. Click the Assign Task button in the Task dialog box and choose a user to whom to assign the task. You can view the task in your TaskPad and see when he or she has completed the assigned task.

Building a Contacts List

Outlook's Contacts list can be used to store name and address information about your personal and business associates. The names, addresses, phone numbers, and email contact information ties Outlook's Inbox, Calendar, and Tasks features together, providing a resource for email addresses and a list of people to invite to meetings or to whom you can assign tasks.

Building contacts is easy, although establishing a complete database of your contacts can be time consuming if you have a lot of them. The reward for doing so, however, is a central location for important data about customers, vendors, and other business resources, as well as friends and family.

To enter contact information, follow these steps:

1. On the Outlook Shortcuts panel, click Contacts. The Contacts window opens, as shown in Figure 12.26.

FIGURE 12.26

Double-click the main Contacts window to start your first Contact.

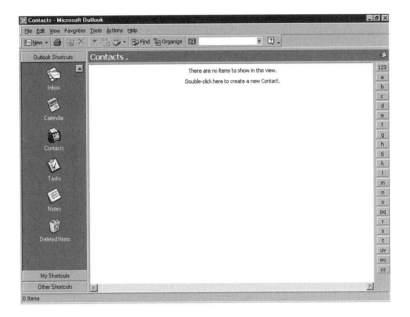

2. Click the New Contact button or press Ctrl+N.

3. In the New Contact dialog box (see Figure 12.27), enter the Full Name of your contact. Enter the first name first.

12

FIGURE 12.27

Enter the basic name, address, and phone information on the General tab.

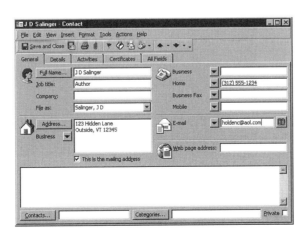

4. Click in each of the other boxes on the General tab for which you have and want to store information on this contact.

5. Click the Details tab if you want to enter additional information, such as the name of the contact's spouse and their birth date (see Figure 12.28).

FIGURE 12.28

Enter additional data on the Details tab.

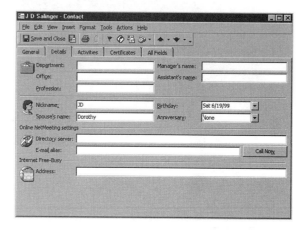

6. If you have another contact to enter, click Save, and then the New button. If this is your only entry at this time, click Save and Close.

Your contacts appear in alphabetical order (by last name) in the Contacts window, as shown in Figure 12.29.

FIGURE 12.29

Double-click any of the contacts to open it for editing.

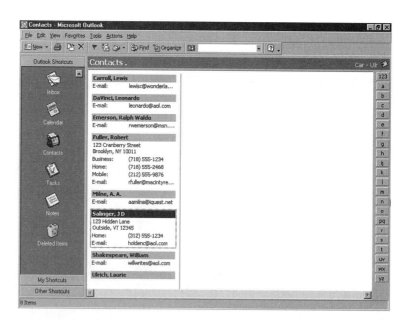

As the main window fills up, you can quickly view your contacts by clicking the alphabetical tabs on the right side of the window. In Figure 12.30, the G tab has been clicked, highlighting the first contact with a last name that starts with the letter G.

FIGURE 12.30

After you've entered all your contacts, click the lettered tabs to view them in alphabetical groups.

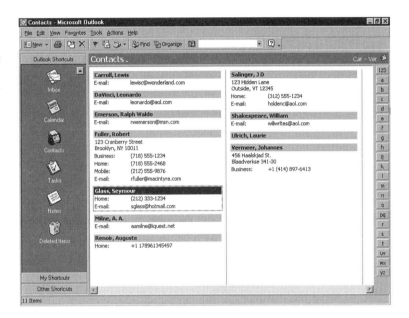

Editing Contact Information

Editing a contact requires opening the contact's record. To open this file, double-click the record's title bar (see Figure 12.31) in the Contacts window, or right-click the record and choose Open from the shortcut menu.

FIGURE 12.31

Double-click the blue bar bearing the contact name to open the contact for editing.

When the contact is open, you can edit any portion of the data on the contact, using a dialog box that is identical to the New Contact dialog box (shown earlier in Figures 12.27 and 12.28).

12

Searching for a Contact

If you have many contacts, finding a particular one can be difficult. Furthermore, you might forget a contact's last name, making it impossible to find the contact alphabetically. To search the text of all your contact records, click the Find button on the toolbar. The Contacts window changes to display a Find Items in Contacts pane (see Figure 12.32).

FIGURE 12.32

Search your contacts database for keywords or portions of words.

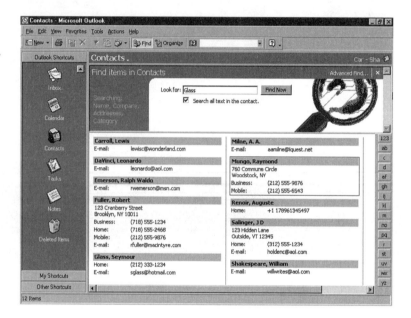

In the Look for box, type the text you want to use to find the missing contact. Outlook searches all the fields in all your contacts records for the text you've typed. Click the Find Now button to begin the search.

After it is found, the contact is displayed in the lower portion of the Contacts window. You can then view, edit, or delete the content of that contact's information.

Linking Contacts to Appointments, Events, and Tasks

As further incentive to enter all your business and personal contacts into Outlook, your contacts can be connected to other Outlook items, as shown in the following list:

- **Link a contact to an appointment**—If the appointment requires you to call or send a message to a particular person in your contacts list, click the Contacts button in the appointment dialog box (see Figure 12.33) and choose the contact that you want to link to the appointment.

FIGURE 12.33

Associate one or more of your contacts with a specific appointment.

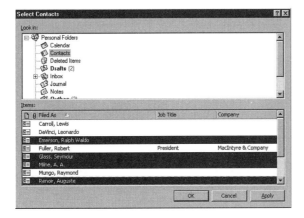

- **Quickly assign a task to a contact**—Drag the contact record from the Contacts window to the Tasks icon on the Outlook Shortcuts panel. An Untitled Task dialog box opens, in which you can describe the task and send a message to the assignee, as shown in Figure 12.34.

FIGURE 12.34

Simultaneously create and assign a task to anyone in your contacts list by dragging the contact record to the Tasks button.

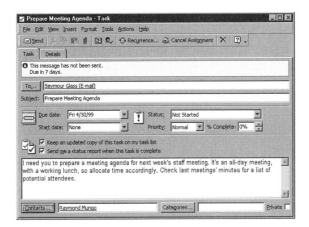

12

- **Create a meeting and invite a contact to it simultaneously**—From within the Contacts window, drag a contact to the Calendar icon on the Outlook Shortcuts panel; an Untitled Meeting window opens, addressed to the contact. All you need to do is enter the meeting specifics and click Send.

Inviting People to a Meeting

Many meetings are informally arranged—the people who need to be there receive a call, or someone stops at their desk to tell them about the meeting. If you have Outlook, however, you can invite people in your own office—or even people outside the office—by sending them an email message. Outlook's Calendar program enables you to schedule a meeting for yourself, select other attendees, view their availability (if they are connected to your network), and send them an email inviting them to the meeting, all within one procedure. To invite people to a meeting, follow these steps:

1. In an Untitled Appointment dialog box, set up the meeting (see Figure 12.35 for the basic settings for this sample meeting).

FIGURE 12.35

Enter whatever information you need to know about the meeting, plus any that might be useful to the attendees, into the Untitled Appointment window.

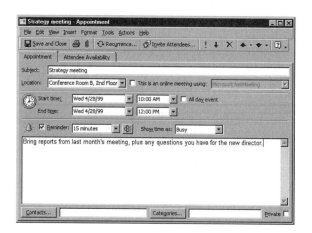

2. Click the Invite Attendees button.

3. Click the Attendee Availability tab in the dialog box.

4. Click to enter the name of the person you want to attend (see Figure 12.36). The name must be in your contacts list, and if you want to see the contact's availability, he or she must be on your network.

FIGURE 12.36

Type the person's first name, and Outlook checks your Contacts list and fills in their complete name for you.

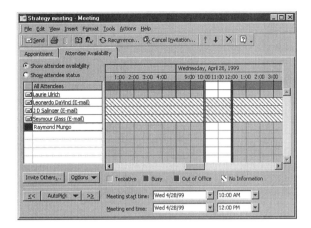

Color codes help you interpret the availability information of your attendees

If an attendee is not on your network, this pattern appears

5. Even if the attendees are not on your network, you can invite them to the meeting via email. Click the envelope button next to their name, and choose the Send meeting to this attendee option from the list (see Figure 12.37).

FIGURE 12.37

Send a message to invite this attendee to the meeting.

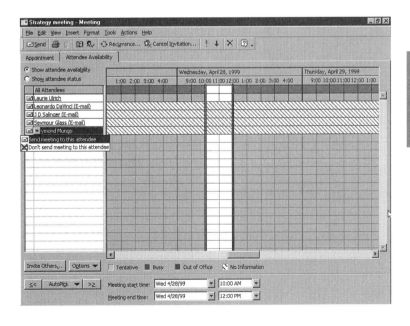

12

6. Repeat steps 3 and 4 for everyone you want to invite.

7. Click the Send button. Email messages that contain the date and times for the meeting are sent to everyone you invite.

The meeting now appears in your Calendar, with a picture in the box that indicates that others have been invited to the meeting (see Figure 12.38). As the attendees receive the email messages, they can respond to you, indicating their willingness to attend.

FIGURE 12.38

The picture that appears in your appointment box in Day, Week, or Month view reminds you that others have been invited to your meeting.

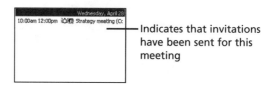

Indicates that invitations have been sent for this meeting

You can view your invitations in your Sent Items folder or your Outbox if you're working offline. Monitor your Inbox for responses from those people you've invited to your meeting and be sure to respond to their messages to confirm the meeting.

Tip

If your attendees are on your network, their acceptance of the meeting invitation results in the meeting being added to their calendar automatically.

Customizing the Outlook Calendar

Outlook's Calendar is designed to meet the needs of the average person—someone who works a typical day, works only from Monday to Friday, and schedules their time in half-hour increments. These settings work for most people, and they might work for you, too. If, however, you want to change one of these basic elements, Outlook gives you the Options dialog box so that you can establish settings that work the way you do. To access these settings, choose Tools, Options to open the Options dialog box. Within that box, click the Calendar Options button (see Figure 12.39).

FIGURE 12.39

Click the Calendar Options button in the Options dialog box to adjust the way you see your Calendar in daily, weekly, and monthly views.

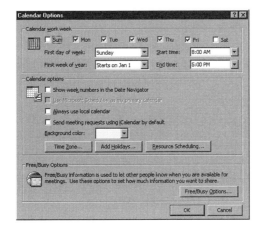

The Calendar Options dialog box enables you to change the following aspects of your Outlook Calendar:

- **Days of your work week**—Do you work Sundays? Add a checkmark. Make sure that there's a checkmark next to each day that you want to include in your work week.

- **Choose your starting and ending times**—People on a night shift will want to change the time that their workday starts and ends.

- **Choose a different color for the background in Day view**—If the bright yellow isn't right for you, click the list triangle and choose from a palette of other pastel colors (see Figure 12.40).

12

FIGURE 12.40

Studies show that people remember things better if they read them on a yellow background—but feel free to choose any other color in the palette.

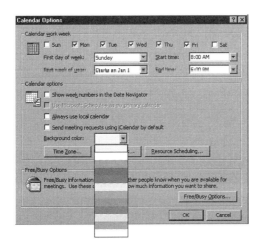

- **Add Holidays**—Click the Add Holidays button and choose the country you're in, or the country for which you want to see holidays (see Figure 12.41). The holidays appear in the day blocks in the Monthly view, and at the top of the window in Day view.

FIGURE 12.41

If your company has an office in the United Kingdom, it might be helpful to see their holidays as well as U.S. holidays in your Calendar.

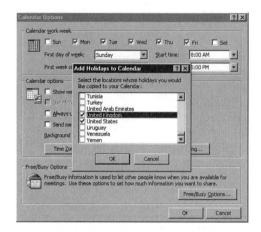

After you've adjusted the necessary settings, click OK to close the dialog box, and then click OK again to close the main Options dialog box. Your new settings are put into effect and, depending on your view, they are immediately visible onscreen.

Summary

Today covered the use of Outlook for maintaining a calendar of appointments and events, as well as a to-do list with tasks to be performed by yourself or others. In addition, use of Outlook's Contacts feature was covered, enabling you to store, edit, and use a list of personal and business contacts. Day 13, "Setting Up a Database," takes you to Microsoft Access, one of the major applications in the Office 2000 suite. You'll use Access to build and maintain a database and to create data entry forms for yourself and others to use in building your database records.

Q&A

Q Can I use Outlook even if I'm running Outlook on a standalone computer (not connected to a network)?

A Certainly. Although many of Outlook's features require connection to a group of other users on a local network, there are an equal number of features or variations on network-based features that work well even on a standalone installation.

Q Is there any limit on the number of contacts I can build into my database?

A No. You can enter an unlimited number of records into your Outlook database.

Workshop

The section that follows is a quick quiz about the day. If you have any problems answering any of the questions, see the section that follows the quiz for all the answers.

Quiz

1. List the four views through which you can read and edit your Outlook Calendar.

2. Describe two ways to open an existing appointment for editing.

3. True or false: As soon as you mark a Task as completed, it is removed from the TaskPad.

4. True or false: To create a series of identical appointments, you must use Edit, Copy, and Paste.

5. True or false: Deleted appointments go to the Deleted Items folder, where they can be retrieved if you deleted them in error.

Quiz Answers

1. You can view your Calendar in Day, Work Week (five days), Week (seven days), or Month view.

2. To edit an existing appointment, you can double-click the appointment as it is seen in any of your views, or you can right-click it and choose Open from the shortcut menu.

3. False. You must actively delete a completed task in order to remove it from the Tasks window or the TaskPad.

4. False. Although Edit, Copy, and Paste work to copy one appointment's settings to a new date (when you have two virtually identical appointments), Outlook gives you a specific tool to create a series of appointments. Use the Recurrence button in the Appointment dialog box to set the pattern and duration of the repeated appointments.

5. False. Deleted appointments do not go to the Deleted Items folder. Only if you press Ctrl+Z or choose Edit, Undo immediately after accidentally deleting an appointment can you get it back.

12

WEEK 2

DAY 13

Setting Up a Database

Microsoft Access is a database management program. This means that it is more than a tool for storing data: It is an application that enables you to store multiple databases and use them individually or in groups to create queries and reports. In addition, Access gives you a variety of ways to build and edit your data, including user-friendly data entry forms that you can create to meet your own needs or the needs of someone who is entering data for you. Today covers the creation of a database table, and discusses the skills that are required for customizing the way the table works and stores information. Specifically, you'll learn about the following topics:

- Naming, saving, and setting up a database table to store information
- Customizing database fields to maximize their effectiveness in storing specific data
- Building "user-friendly" forms for data entry
- Entering data into the database
- Editing and deleting records in the database

Creating a Database in Access

When you start the Access application from the Start menu's Programs list or by double-clicking a desktop icon, you are presented with a Microsoft Access dialog box (as shown in Figure 13.1) that asks you to choose how you want to start the process of building a database.

FIGURE 13.1

Start from scratch with a blank database.

Your choices are as follows:

- **Create a new Blank Access database**—This is your choice if you want to create something from scratch with little or no intervention from the application.

- **Use Access database wizards, pages, and projects**—This approach gives you help in the form of multiple dialog box wizards that ask you to define the type of database you're building, how it is to be used, and so forth. You will not pursue this path to start your database today, but you can research it on your own.

- **Open an existing file**—Today's project is based on the assumption that you have no existing data. However, Access provides an entire database management system—the Northwind Sample Database—that you need to look at on your own to see what Access is capable of beyond the basic database features that are covered today and on Day 14, "Making Use of Your Access Data."

To begin today's project, select Blank Access database and click OK. As soon as you do that, Access requires that you name your database. When you are naming it, remember that a database is a group of data tables, and not a single data list like you built in Excel on Day 8, "Building an Excel Database." The name needs to define the entire group of tables you'll be building. For example, if the database contains employee-related data in tables such as Staff, Insurance, Vacations, and Reviews (as does the database you'll create today), the entire database can be called "Employee Information." Type that name in the File name box, as shown in Figure 13.2, and click Create.

FIGURE 13.2

Name the database, keeping in mind the nature of the data that is to be stored in its tables.

After you name the database, the Employee Information: Database dialog box opens, as shown in Figure 13.3.

FIGURE 13.3

Choose a method to start building your first database table.

This dialog box proposes three ways in which you can build the first table in the database:

- **Create table in Design view**—Design view is the most straightforward view, and it's the one you'll use today. Using Design view, you see exactly how a table is created and you take on a much more hands-on role in the process.

- **Create table by using wizard**—Wizards help you, but they can also insulate you from the "nuts and bolts" of what's happening. Feel free to explore this approach for subsequent tables that you build on your own.

- **Create table by entering data**—This approach is fast, but it doesn't enable you to set up and customize your fields (the components of each record).

13

Double-click Create table in Design view; the Table1 window opens, as shown in Figure 13.4.

FIGURE 13.4

Use the blank design window to name and define the structure of your table by inserting fields.

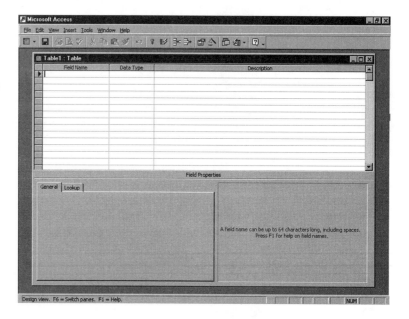

NEW TERM As you learned on Day 8, which discussed Excel databases, *fields* are the components of a database record. Each record is broken down into fields such as first name, last name, and address. The more fields you break your records into, the more you can do with your database—for example, sorting the records by a particular field or looking for certain records based on the content of their fields.

Building Data Tables

Design view gives you the capability to name and define the settings for each of your fields before you enter any data. Using this approach requires some forethought on your part: You must plan which fields you want to have in your database, what you want to call them, and how you want data to be entered into them. For example, if one of your fields contains numbers that must be entered in a specific way (such as a social security number, which must adhere to an *nnn-nn-nnnn* format), you need to think of that before you begin building your database.

Before you even begin typing in the Design View window, you need to make a written list of your field names, and notes pertaining to special requirements for any of those fields.

Be sure to break your records down into as many fields as possible. For example, don't create a single field called "Name"; break it into "First Name" and "Last Name" so that you can later sort by last name to put a list of people in alphabetical order, or so that you can search for a particular person by their first *or* last name.

Setting Up Database Fields

When you have a sense of what fields you need and any specific settings those fields might require, you can begin to build your database fields using the following steps:

1. Click in the first blank cell in the Field Name column and type Employee Number (the name of your first field).

2. On the toolbar, click the Primary Key button to indicate that each record in this field will contain unique data. A key icon appears next to the field, and the General tab is activated (see Figure 13.5).

Key icon indicates
Employee Number is
the Primary Key

Text is the default Data
Type (this can be changed)

FIGURE 13.5

Choose a field that contains unique data and make it the Primary Key.

The General tab
gives options for
customizing the way
the field works

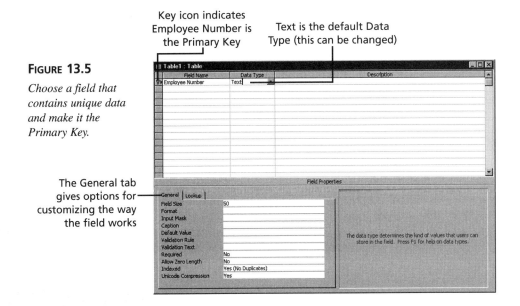

13

Note

> **NEW TERM** A *Primary Key* is a field that identifies the records in a database. The field must be one that contains unique data for each record, such as a social security or product number. If a database has no field that positively contains unique data, you can create a Primary Key by assigning a Record Number field, wherein each record is given a unique (consecutive) number.

3. The first field is now created. Continue building fields, as shown in Table 13.1. To move from cell to cell within Design view, press the Tab key or click in the desired cell with your mouse. To assign Data Types, click the list triangle in that cell, and choose the type from the list (see Figure 13.6).

FIGURE 13.6

Choose from nine basic field types for the Staff List data table fields.

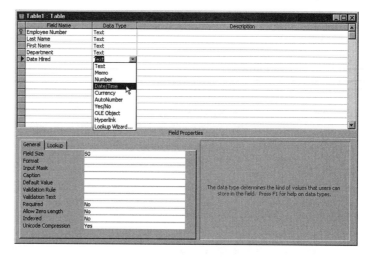

Tip

> If you want to add some information about the use or nature of a field, enter that text in the Description cell. To assist data entry personnel, the contents of the Description cell are displayed on the status bar in the data entry form for the table. You'll learn to create data entry forms later today.

TABLE 13.1   STAFF LIST FIELD NAMES AND DATA TYPES

Field Name	Data Type
Last Name	Text
First Name	Text
Department	Text
Date Hired	Date/Time
Current Salary	Currency
Insurance	Yes/No
Vacation Days	Number
Date of Last Review	Date/Time
Review Grade	Number

 Tip

When you're familiar with the available data types, you can select one by typing the first letter of the type. For example, to make a field a Date/Time field, click in the Data Type cell and type the letter D. This only works on new fields for which a data type has not been previously set—if you click on an existing field's data type and type a letter, that letter is added to the displayed data type name.

You now have a table with ten fields. For most simple database tables, the setup tasks you've performed to this point are adequate for creating a table and establishing a tool that can be used for data entry. To begin working with your table, choose File, Close, and then click Yes if you are prompted to save your changes. You can then open the database for data entry by double-clicking it by name in the main database window.

If, however, you want to take advantage of some powerful Access tools to control the nature and appearance of the data that is entered into your fields, before you close the Design view window for your table, explore the Field Properties section of the window. Using the General tab, you can establish an Input Mask and Validation Rules for any of the fields that you feel might require such controls. These controls are discussed in the following section.

Understanding Field Settings

Field settings (which can be found in the General tab while you're working in Design view) help you control the way your table is used. If someone other than yourself will be entering your data, it's a good idea to use these settings to apply certain controls to make

13

sure that the entries are correct. The following entry controls are available for a text field (some of these options do not appear, depending on the Data Type you have chosen for your field):

- **Field Size**—The default for text fields is 50 characters. You can enter a larger or smaller number, based on your knowledge of the possible entries for a given field. Be careful when reducing the number of characters—long last names or addresses, for example, might require more space than you anticipate, and you don't want to end up with a partial entry.

- **Format**—For Data Types such as Number and Date/Time, this option enables you to specify an exact appearance for the data that is entered into the field. Choose to have numbers appear as percentages, for example, or whether to display a four-digit year.

- **Input Mask**—Available only for Text and Date/Time fields, this feature provides an overlay or filter for the characters that are entered. The mask inserts spaces or symbols among the entered characters to provide proper formatting.

- **Caption**—If you're creating a Data Entry form, use this option to enter the instructive or descriptive text that accompanies the field.

- **Default Value**—Whatever text or numbers you type here appear in the field for all new records, potentially saving time during the data entry process. Depending on the other settings you choose, the user might or might not be able to edit this default entry.

- **Validation Rule**—If a field can only contain certain values, establish a rule that permits only those entries into the field. A Validation Rule prevents typos, improper terminology, or numeric values from being entered into an important field.

- **Validation Text**—This option enables you to dictate the error message that appears if the Validation Rule is broken during data entry.

- **Required**—This is a Yes or No option; choose Yes if the field cannot be left blank. Many fields that require entry also require a Validation Rule to make sure that what is entered is correct.

- **Allow Zero Length**—This is another Yes or No option; choose Yes to allow the field to be skipped.

- **Indexed**—This feature (when used) can speed up the sorting and searching of a table's data. There are three options—No, Yes (Duplicates OK), and Yes (No Duplicates). Yes (No Duplicates) means that the field must contain unique data for each record.

- **Unicode Compression**—This relates to the form in which Access data is stored. The default is No, and unless you are required by some external resource to use it, you want to leave it set to No.

> **Tip**
>
> If your field's Data Type is Number or Currency, you'll see a Decimals option added to the list in the General tab. You can click the option and select any number of decimal places, or you can leave the default Auto setting, which sets the decimal places to match whatever has been set in the Format property setting.

Using Input Masks to Control Data Entry

NEW TERM Some of the fields you created need further definition to ensure that the data that is entered into them is appropriate. One of the ways to control this is to apply an Input Mask. An *input mask* creates structure for the field, ensuring that the entered characters fall into a format such as *(nnn)nnn-nnnn* for a phone number or *nnn-nn-nnnn* for a social security number. The mask inserts the parentheses and dashes (and their automatic positioning) so that the data entry person need only type the string of numbers.

To apply an input mask to your Staff List table, follow these steps:

1. Click in the Employee Number field. In the General tab, click the Input Mask box to activate it. Click the ellipsis button (see Figure 13.7).

FIGURE 13.7

The ellipsis button indicates that there are options for this particular setting. Click it to open the list of options.

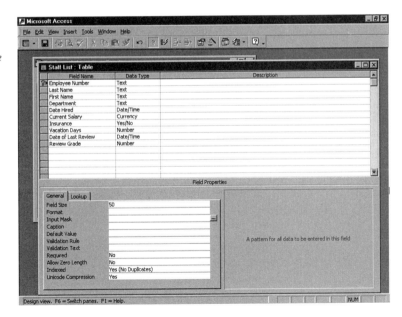

13

Tip

If you performed a Normal or Typical installation of Office 2000, the Input Mask Wizard might not have been installed. You'll be prompted to install it, which you can do by inserting your Office 2000 CD-ROM and following the instructions for adding programs.

2. You are prompted to save the table before applying an input mask. Click Yes to save, and give the table the name Staff List (see Figure 13.8).

FIGURE 13.8

You must name and save your table before invoking the input mask tool for the first time.

3. In the Input Mask Wizard dialog box (see Figure 13.9), choose the type of mask you need. In this case, choose Social Security Number.

FIGURE 13.9

Each of the masks has a specific structure. Choose the one that matches the data that is to be entered into the active field.

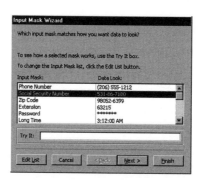

4. Click Next, and verify the format that is shown in the next dialog box (see Figure 13.10).

FIGURE 13.10

To make sure that the mask you've selected is correct, view the format; click in the Try it box and enter a string of characters to test the mask.

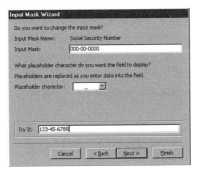

5. Click Next again, and choose how the data that is entered into this masked field is to be stored: with the mask-inserted dashes or without. Choosing to store the dashes can make the data appear more legible in table view, but other than that, there is no significant benefit to either selection.

6. Click Next, and then click Finish in the final wizard dialog box. The mask is applied and appears in the General tab, in the Employee Number field (see Figure 13.11).

FIGURE 13.11

An input mask controls the way data is entered into a field and forces a specific structure on the characters that are typed.

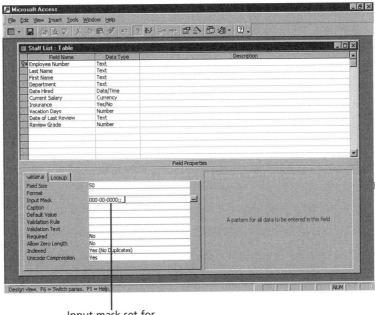

Input mask set for
Employee number field

Maintaining Consistency with Field Validation

Whenever a field must contain specific data, you want to use a Validation Rule to ensure that data that falls outside the list of acceptable entries isn't entered. Validation rules can be used for addresses, to make sure that only two-character state abbreviations are entered, or in the case of department names (as in your Staff List table). You can apply a Validation Rule to make sure that only a prescribed list of department names are accepted in the Department field.

Follow these steps to set up the rule:

1. Click in the Department field.

2. In the General tab, click the Validation Rule box. The Expression Builder dialog box opens, as shown in Figure 13.12.

FIGURE 13.12

The Expression Builder gives you the capability to create a list of acceptable entries, using Boolean expressions such as And, Or, and Not to indicate what data can be entered into the selected field.

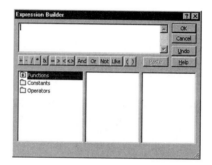

3. Type the first department name, Accounting.

4. Click the Or button. The word *Or* appears after the word *Accounting*, with spaces before and after it.

5. Type Administration, and click Or again.

6. Type Human Resources, and click Or.

7. Type Marketing, and click Or.

8. Type Sales. The list of acceptable Department names is complete.

9. Click OK to apply the Validation Rule and close the dialog box.

The General tab now shows the list of acceptable entries for the Department field (see Figure 13.13). This rule prevents users from entering misspelled names, abbreviations (such as *Acctg* or *Mktg*), or any other incorrect data. Controlling the entries that go into this field makes it easier to later create reports that list employees from specific departments; if the department names are not consistent, this is impossible.

Caution   Be careful to spell your Validation Rule entries correctly—you don't want your typos to become the rule!

FIGURE 13.13

Now that a Validation Rule is set, any attempt to enter data that is not on this list of entries results in an error message onscreen.

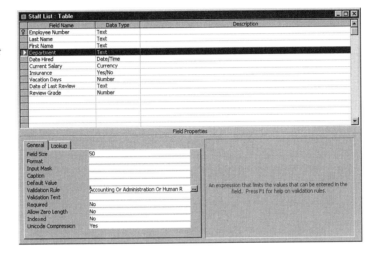

If you want to control the nature of the error message that appears if the user attempts to enter data that is not on the list of acceptable entries, click in the Validation Text box and type the error message you want to appear. Figure 13.14 shows the text you can enter for the Department field.

FIGURE 13.14

Create a simple error message to explain the rule to those persons entering data into the selected field.

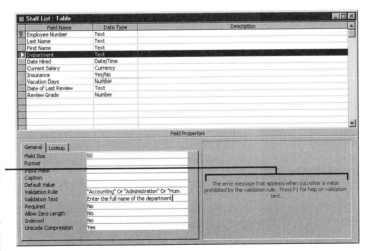

This text appears in an error message if any data other than the words in the prescribed list is entered into the Department field

13

| Although Access prompts you to save when you close your Design window (by clicking the Close button), you need to save periodically throughout the process of building your fields and setting them up. This prevents you from losing your work if the software or your computer shuts down unexpectedly.

Creating Additional Database Tables

To complete the Employee Information database, you need to create three more tables:

- Insurance
- Vacations
- Reviews

These three tables complete the Employee Information database, and they provide a foundation for the reports and queries you will create on Day 14.

To create the Insurance table, create the fields that are listed in Table 13.2.

TABLE 13.2 INSURANCE TABLE FIELDS

Field Name	Data Type	General tab settings
Employee Number	Text (make it the primary key)	Apply the social security number input mask
Insurance	Yes/No	This should be Required
Chosen Carrier	Text	Apply a Validation Rule that accepts only Blue Cross or HMO
Payroll Deduction	Currency	Apply a Validation Rule that accepts only entries of 5.00 or 10.00. Also, create Validation Text that says that HMO=$5.00 and BC=$10.00.
Policy Start Date	Date/Time	None

To create the Vacation table, create the fields that are listed in Table 13.3.

TABLE 13.3 VACATION TABLE FIELDS

Field Name	Data Type	General tab settings
Employee Number	Text (make this the primary key)	Apply the social security Input Mask
Vacation Days	Number	Required
Used in Current Year	Number	None

To create the Reviews table, create the fields that are listed in Table 13.4.

TABLE 13.4 REVIEWS TABLE FIELDS

Field Name	Data Type	General tab settings
Employee Number	Text (make this the primary key)	Apply the social security Input Mask
Date of Last Review	Date/Time	Required
Reviewed By	Text	Required
Attendance Grade	Number	Apply Validation Rule accepting only the numbers 1–5
Productivity Grade	Number	Apply Validation Rule accepting only the numbers 1–5
Socialization Grade	Number	Apply Validation Rule accepting only the numbers 1–5
Overall Grade	Number	Apply Validation Rule accepting only the numbers 1–5
Recommendations of Reviewer	Text	Set Allow Zero Length to No

Enter data (approximately ten records) into each table. There must be data in the tables in order for the reports and queries that you will create on Day 14 to have content.

Entering Your Data

After setting up your tables' fields, you can begin entering your data. First, close the Design window for the table by clicking the Close button in the upper-right corner of the window. The Database window remains open, as shown in Figure 13.15; your table is now listed in the main pane of the window.

13

FIGURE 13.15

Double-click your table to begin entering data.

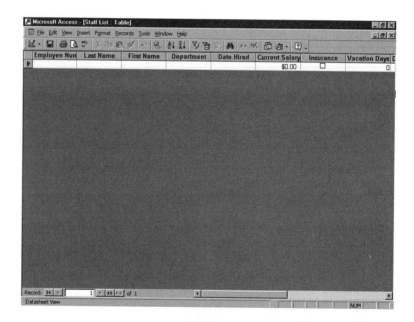

Click once on the table's name and then click the Open button or double-click the table. In either case, the table opens in Table view, as shown in Figure 13.16.

FIGURE 13.16

Looking very much like an Excel work-sheet, the table opens with your field names in the first row.

Begin entering your records, row by row, pressing Tab to move from left to right. Press Shift+Tab to move backward one field. Figure 13.17 shows the first record in the Staff List table.

FIGURE 13.17

Your data is entered, adhering to the Data Type, and any Input Masks or Validation Rules are applied to the fields.

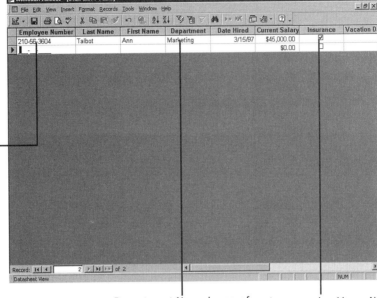

Employee number follows Input Mask structure

Department Name is one of the accepted entries, based on the Validation rule

Insurance is a Yes or No, based on Data Type

Tip

To place a checkmark (to say "Yes") in the Yes/No Insurance field, press the spacebar.

Tip

Don't worry about entering records in alphabetical or numerical order—the data can be sorted later. It's a waste of time to try to put the data in order for the purposes of data entry.

13

Creating Data Entry Forms

Table view is a very economical, simple format for the entry of your table data. It is, however, not very easy on the eyes, and for the purposes of entering many records in one sitting, it can be a very dull process with a high margin for error. Users might find it difficult to keep the right data in the right cell, and they might become confused when they look up from the paper—or whatever source they're using for the information that's being entered into the table—to the screen.

To make the process of data entry more enjoyable and less visually confusing, you might want to create a Data Entry Form. The form shows only one record onscreen at a time, making it less likely that you will enter data into the wrong record or field.

To create a Data Entry Form for the Staff List table, follow these steps:

1. With the Employee Information: Database window open, click once on the Forms button in the Objects panel (see Figure 13.18).

FIGURE 13.18

The Forms list gives you options for creating a new form, and in the future, it will list your existing data entry forms.

2. Double-click Create form by using wizard.
3. In the Form Wizard dialog box (see Figure 13.19), choose the table you want to use (you only have one at this point, but you can click the Tables/Queries list to choose an alternative table after you've built more).

FIGURE 13.19

Select the table on which the form is to be based. The fields from that table are then available for placement on the form.

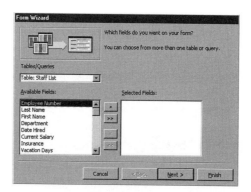

4. From the Available Fields list, click the first field you want to place on the form, and then click the right-pointing arrow to place that field in the Selected Fields list. Figure 13.20 shows the Employee Number field added to the Selected Fields list.

FIGURE 13.20

Click the double right-pointing arrows to add all your fields at once.

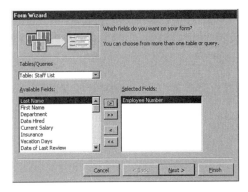

5. In the order in which you want them to appear on the form, continue adding fields, one at a time, to the Selected Fields list. Although you don't have to include all fields when creating a form, for this procedure you *will* use all your fields.

Tip

To insert all the records at once, in the order in which you want them to appear in the table, click the >> button. You can also remove any individual fields that you add through this method by selecting them in the Selected Fields list and clicking the < button.

6. Click Next to continue with the Form Wizard.

7. Choose the layout you prefer for the form. To see what each type (Columnar, Tabular, Datasheet, and Justified) looks like, click the option buttons next to each option and view the sample (see Figure 13.21).

FIGURE 13.21

Choose the overall layout for your form. Columnar and Tabular are the most "user-friendly" layouts.

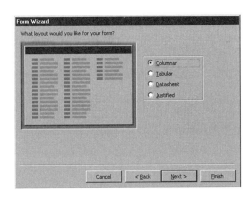

13

8. Click Next to proceed to the next step in the Form Wizard.

9. Choose a Style for the form. Sample each of the ten different styles by clicking once on the style's name (see Figure 13.22).

FIGURE 13.22

Styles give your form a professional look, and they make the workspace visually interesting. This is helpful when you (or someone else) will be spending a lot of time entering records.

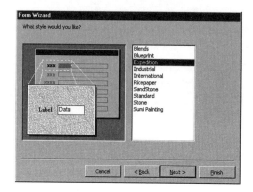

10. When you've selected a style you like, click Next to proceed.

11. In the last step in the Form Wizard, give your form a title. It's a good idea to name it something other than the table name so that you can easily tell them apart. In this procedure, use the name `Staff Data Entry` for the form (see Figure 13.23).

FIGURE 13.23

Indicate the purpose of your form when choosing its name.

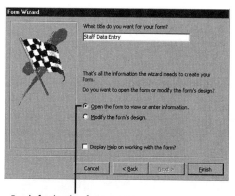

By default, the form opens
and allows data entry as
soon as you click Finish.

12. Click Finish to build the form based on the selections you made during the Form Wizard process.

The resulting form opens onscreen, ready to accept your entries (see Figure 13.24). To use it again later, you can select it from the Employee Information: Database window by clicking the Forms button and double-clicking the name "Staff Data Entry." When you're finished working with a form, simply close the Form window by clicking the Close button in the upper-right corner of the window.

FIGURE 13.24

Begin your entries with the first field (the cursor is already there), and press Tab to move from field to field.

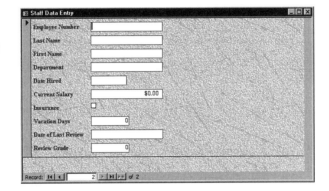

> **Tip**
>
> When choosing fields to include in the form, you can leave out any fields that might contain sensitive or confidential information. For example, in your Employee Information database, you might create a form without the Salary field so that you can keep that data confidential. Another form called "Salaries" can be created for use by someone who has access to that information.

Editing the Structure of an Existing Table

Although there is no need to alter the structure of your existing tables, it's important to know how to change the way your table is laid out—rearranging, adding, and removing fields—to meet the changing needs of your database. Your options are as follows:

- **Changing the order of the fields**—To change the order of your existing fields, switch to Datasheet view of your table. Click once on the name of the field that you want to reorder. Click again on that field name and drag to the left or right, releasing the mouse when you are pointing to the location at which you want to place the field. Figure 13.25 shows the First Name field being placed in front of the Last Name field in the Staff List table.

13

Small box accompanies your mouse pointer
while the field column is in transit

FIGURE 13.25

*Change the order of
your fields to facilitate
logical data entry.*

Dark vertical line
indicates place-
ment of field as
you drag your
mouse

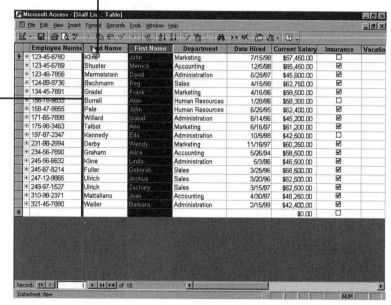

- **Inserting a new field**—To insert a new field (again, this is best done in Datasheet view), click once on the name of the field that is to follow the new field. Choose Insert, Column. Change the name of the new column to the desired field name (double-click the Field#) and begin entering data as needed. You can switch to Design view to make any changes to the new field's setup. Figure 13.26 shows a new field with the default name selected for replacement.

- **Deleting a Field**—To delete a field, click once on the field name in Datasheet view, and then choose Edit, Delete Column. You'll be asked to confirm your intention to delete the selected field. Click Yes.

Caution

When you are deleting fields, be very sure that you've selected the correct field and that you really want to get rid of the field and any data in it. Undo is not available after a field deletion, so you'll have to recreate the field and all its data if you delete the wrong field.

Editing Table Data

After your table records are entered, you no doubt need to edit them—misspellings, out-of-date information, and simple typos need to be corrected. In addition, you might need to delete records to keep the table data accurate and relevant.

To edit your table data, you can work in either Form view or Table view. For faster data editing, Table view is recommended—you can see many rows of records at one time, making it easier to find the record that needs to be edited (see Figure 13.27).

Selected default field name

FIGURE 13.26

Replace the default Field# name with any name you choose.

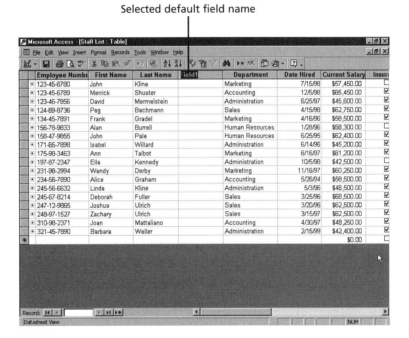

Form view requires that you scroll through all your records using the Record controls (see Figure 13.28). This process can increase the time it takes to edit and delete records; however, it also decreases the chance of deleting or editing the wrong record because only one record is visible at a time.

Deleting a record in Form view requires that you choose Edit, Delete Record. A prompt appears (see Figure 13.29), asking you to confirm your intention to delete the record. These extra steps can make it much more difficult to delete the wrong record; therefore, using Form view for editing is advisable if the person who is editing the table is likely to make mistakes or is not familiar with the data.

13

FIGURE **13.27**

Open your table in Table view to edit and delete records quickly.

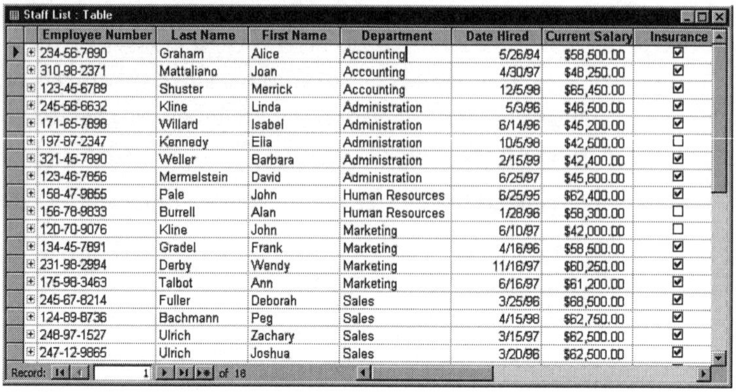

FIGURE **13.28**

Take a careful approach to data editing by editing in Form view.

Click this button to create a new record

Last record

Next record

Number of the currently displayed record

Previous record

First record

FIGURE **13.29**

You must confirm your deletion before Access will remove a record from your data table.

Deleting records in Table view is somewhat simpler, and this increases the margin for error—it might be too simple to remove the wrong record. To delete a record in Table view, click once on the gray button to the left of the record (see Figure 13.30) and press Delete.

FIGURE 13.30

Select an entire row by clicking next to the record you want to delete.

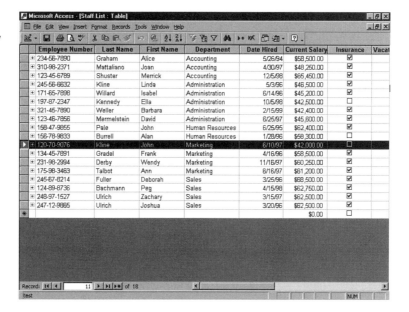

The record disappears and a prompt appears, asking you to confirm your intention to delete the record (the same prompt that is shown in Figure 13.29). Press Enter or click Yes to delete the record.

Tip

To delete several contiguous records at the same time, drag through the gray buttons to the left of the records. When they're all selected, press the Delete key. You'll be prompted to confirm your intention to delete the records—be sure you really want to delete them before clicking Yes because you cannot Undo a record deletion.

Caution

Many users become cavalier in their use of the Enter key and press it before reading prompts that appear onscreen. When you are deleting records, however, this can have unwanted results because the Yes button in the deletion confirmation prompt is the selected button—pressing Enter is the same as clicking Yes. Always read the prompts thoroughly before responding to them.

13

Summary

Today you learned how to build a database in Access. Because a database consists of multiple tables, you learned to name the main database and create the tables that make up the database, setting up fields for each table, customizing the way individual fields accept and store data, and entering the data into each table. On Day 14, you'll learn to use these tables, to sort and query the data within them, and to use the entire database to create informative reports.

Q&A

Q Is there a limit to the number of tables I can store in a single database?

A No. You can have an unlimited number of tables in a single database. Conversely, if you need only one table, a database need not have more than one table in it.

Q Why do all the tables in Day 13, "Setting Up a Database," have a common field (Employee Number)?

A If you want to have a truly relational database through which reports and queries that pull data from more than one table can be created, the tables must have a common field. A unique common field is best, and Employee Number is the best choice for this role in your Employee Information database.

Q Can I use Excel lists in my Access tables?

A Yes. If you already have data stored in Excel and you want to create a similar table in Access, you can copy the Excel list to the Clipboard, and then use Edit, Paste Append to place the field names and data from Excel into a blank Access table.

Workshop

The section that follows is a quick quiz about the day. If you have any problems answering any of the questions, see the section that follows the quiz for all the answers.

Quiz

1. How do you create a Primary Key for a table?
2. Explain the use of an Input Mask.
3. True or False: Each field that is created in Design view must have a description.
4. True or False: A data entry form enables you to enter, but not edit or delete, records.
5. Explain the use of a Validation Rule.

Quiz Answers

1. With the field that is to become the Primary Key selected, click the Primary Key button on the keyboard. A key icon appears next to the field.

2. An Input Mask creates structure for the field, controlling how the entered characters appear in the field and how they are stored. In the case of a social security number, using an Input Mask prevents you from entering too few or too many numbers, and it makes sure that they appear in the right format.

3. False. The Description area need only be filled in if you feel that users who will be entering or editing data in the table need further explanation as to the nature or purpose of a particular field. Use of this area is not required.

4. False. You can enter, edit, and delete records through a Data Entry form. The only difference between working in a form and working in Table view is that you can only see one record at a time in Form view.

5. A Validation Rule establishes a list of acceptable entries for a field, and if the user attempts to enter anything other than the words or numbers in that list, an error message results.

13

DAY **14**

Making Use of Your Access Data

The incentive to create an Access database is that Access enables you to both store and use your data, and the tables that make up the database can be used together to create reports. Although Excel provides a tool for storing lists of data, you can't do much with the lists—you can sort them and filter them (as you learned on Day 8, "Building an Excel Database"), but you can't create reports that draw related data from more than one list. The capability to use Access tables in a relational way—having tables related to one another through a common field—is the main reason users choose to store data in an Access database rather than an Excel worksheet. Today concentrates on these and other uses regarding your Access database. Specifically, you'll learn about the following topics:

- Displaying and printing table data in different sorted orders
- Querying the database for records that meet specific criteria

- Generating database reports that draw data from one or many tables in the database
- Using Access data in Excel, and vice versa, to save time and maintain consistency between files

Sorting Table Data

When data is sorted, all the records remain onscreen; they merely appear in a different order. This, as you recall from Day 8 and Day 12, "Managing Your Time with the Calendar," is why it doesn't matter in what order you enter your records—you can always sort them later. Sorting your records (in one or more of your database tables) enables you to view the list of records in an order that makes sense to you—for example, you can search by name if you're looking for someone in particular, or by date if the chronology of the data is important. You can sort on any field in your data, making it possible to view your records from many different perspectives.

To sort the Staff List table in last name order, follow these steps:

1. Open the Staff List table from within the Employee Information database list of Tables. The table appears in Figure 14. 1.

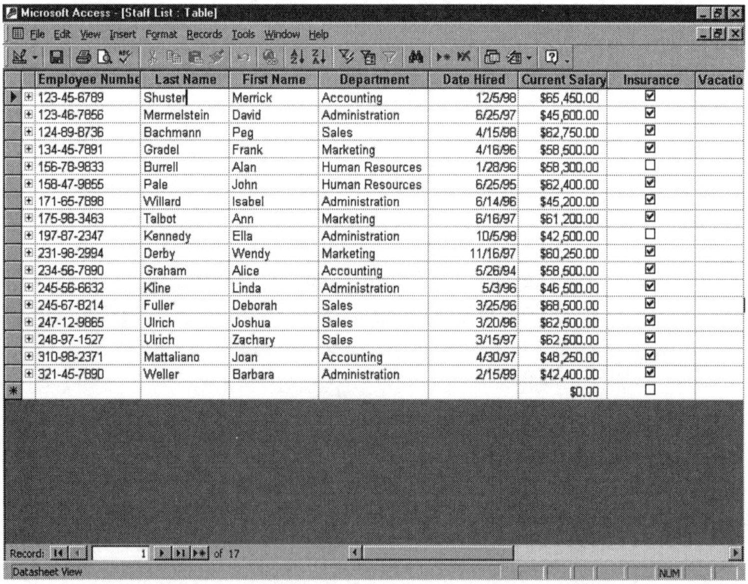

Employee Numbe	Last Name	First Name	Department	Date Hired	Current Salary	Insurance	Vacatio
123-45-6789	Shuster	Merrick	Accounting	12/5/98	$65,450.00	☑	
123-46-7856	Mermelstein	David	Administration	6/25/97	$45,600.00	☑	
124-89-8736	Bachmann	Peg	Sales	4/15/98	$62,750.00	☑	
134-45-7891	Gradel	Frank	Marketing	4/16/96	$58,500.00	☑	
156-78-9833	Burrell	Alan	Human Resources	1/28/96	$58,300.00	☐	
158-47-9855	Pale	John	Human Resources	6/25/95	$62,400.00	☑	
171-65-7898	Willard	Isabel	Administration	6/14/96	$45,200.00	☑	
175-98-3463	Talbot	Ann	Marketing	6/16/97	$61,200.00	☑	
197-87-2347	Kennedy	Ella	Administration	10/5/98	$42,500.00	☐	
231-98-2994	Derby	Wendy	Marketing	11/16/97	$60,250.00	☑	
234-56-7890	Graham	Alice	Accounting	5/26/94	$58,500.00	☑	
245-56-6632	Kline	Linda	Administration	5/3/96	$46,500.00	☑	
245-67-8214	Fuller	Deborah	Sales	3/25/96	$68,500.00	☑	
247-12-9865	Ulrich	Joshua	Sales	3/20/96	$62,500.00	☑	
248-97-1527	Ulrich	Zachary	Sales	3/15/97	$62,500.00	☑	
310-98-2371	Mattaliano	Joan	Accounting	4/30/97	$48,250.00	☑	
321-45-7890	Weller	Barbara	Administration	2/15/99	$42,400.00	☑	
					$0.00	☐	

FIGURE 14.1

The Staff List table contains a list of employees and their job-related information.

2. View the table, and click on any record in the Last Name field. Do not click on the field name itself.

3. Click the Sort Ascending button on the toolbar. The table data is sorted alphabeti-
    cally, from A to Z, by the entries in the Last name field.

After sorting on one field, you can sort additional fields, creating a multiple-level sort. In
the Staff List table, Last Name (the field on which you sorted in the preceding procedure) is a unique field. It isn't intended to be—it's just that there aren't too many duplicate last names in the pool of employees. If, however, you sort first on a field with a lot
of duplicate entries, your sort creates groups; for example, sorting by Department first
places the employees in groups by department, starting with Accounting. Subsequent
sorts by Salary or Date Hired leave the records in Department order but sort each of
those groups by salary or the hire date, creating sorted tiers within the data.

To perform a multiple-level sort, follow these steps:

1. In Table view, open the Staff List table from within the Employee Information
    database.

2. Choose Records, Filter, Advanced Filter/Sort. The Staff ListFilter1 window opens,
    as shown in Figure 14.2.

FIGURE 14.2

*The Filter window
enables you to look for
records that meet cer-
tain criteria, or to sort
your records on more
than one field.*

3. Click the Field box, and then choose the field on which you want to perform the
    first-level sort. In Figure 14.3, Department is selected.

FIGURE 14.3

*Choose the field for
your first-level sort.*

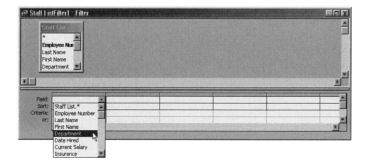

14

Tip You can also drag the field names from the Table box down to the field box to designate a field on which to sort.

4. In the Sort box, click the list and choose Ascending (see Figure 14.4).

FIGURE 14.4

Choose Ascending (A-Z) or Descending (Z-A) order for the sorted field.

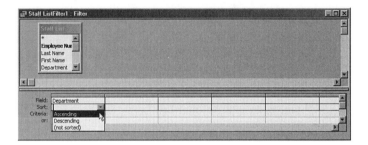

5. Click in the second Field box (see Figure 14.5) and choose Current Salary.

FIGURE 14.5

Working from left to right, choose additional fields on which to sort.

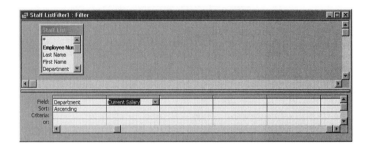

6. In the second Sort box, choose Ascending (see Figure 14.6).

FIGURE 14.6

Choose the order for your second-level sort.

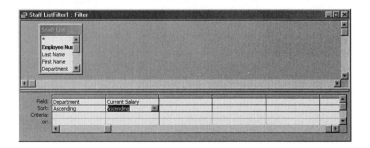

7. Choose Filter, Apply Filter/Sort, or click the Apply Filter button . The table is sorted into groups by Department; within those groups, the records are sorted in Salary
order. Figure 14.7 shows how the table looks after this two-level sort is performed.

A secondary sort by Salary puts the
Department groups in order.

FIGURE 14.7

*When you are sorting
on multiple fields, sort
on fields with many
duplicate records first;
use fields with fewer
duplicates in your sec-
ond, third, and fourth-
level sorts.*

Employee Numbe	Last Name	First Name	Department	Date Hired	Current Salary	Insuranc
810-96-2371	Mattaliano	Joan	Accounting	4/30/9	$48,250.00	☑
234-56-7890	Graham	Alice	Accounting	5/26/9	$58,500.00	☑
123-45-6789	Shuster	Merrick	Accounting	12/5/98	$65,450.00	☑
321-45-7890	Weller	Barbara	Administration	2/15/99	$42,400.00	☑
197-87-2347	Kennedy	Ella	Administration	10/5/98	$42,500.00	☐
171-65-7898	Willard	Isabel	Administration	6/14/96	$45,200.00	☑
123-46-7856	Mermelstein	David	Administration	6/25/97	$45,600.00	☑
245-56-6632	Kline	Linda	Administration	5/3/96	$46,500.00	☑
156-78-9833	Burrell	Alan	Human Resources	1/28/96	$58,300.00	☐
158-47-9855	Pale	John	Human Resources	6/25/95	$62,400.00	☑
123-45-6780	Kline	John	Marketing	7/15/98	$57,450.00	☐
134-45-7891	Gradel	Frank	Marketing	4/16/96	$58,500.00	☑
231-98-2994	Derby	Wendy	Marketing	11/16/97	$60,250.00	☑
175-98-3463	Talbot	Ann	Marketing	6/16/97	$61,200.00	☑
247-12-9865	Ulrich	Joshua	Sales	3/20/96	$62,500.00	☑
248-97-1527	Ulrich	Zachary	Sales	3/15/97	$62,500.00	☑
124-89-8736	Bachmann	Peg	Sales	4/15/98	$62,750.00	☑
245-67-8214	Fuller	Robert	Sales	3/25/96	$68,500.00	☐
					$0.00	

Record: 1 of 18

Sorting by Department creates groups.

Extracting Useful Data with a Query

Unlike a sort, which changes the displayed order of your records but leaves all the
records onscreen, a query displays only those records that meet the criteria that you set.
For example, to see only the employees in the Accounting department, you might query
the Department field for the word *Accounting*, which results in a query table that contains only those records for people in the Accounting department. You can also query
multiple fields from multiple tables. Access also enables you to save your queries so that
you can run them again as you update the content of your tables over time.

Note

 A *query* is a question you pose to the database by presenting
criteria and asking that only the records that meet the criteria
be displayed. In Access, the action of creating a query generates a query
table that contains the records that met the criteria that were presented.

14

This description of queries might sound a lot like the Excel AutoFilter feature you
learned about on Day 8; in theory, it is. Using queries in Access, however, gives you the
capability to query more than one table at a time, making it a much more powerful

feature. For example, using your Employee Information database, you can create a query that provides a list of people in the Sales department who earn more than $50,000, and who have Blue Cross insurance and an overall employee grade of 3 or better. Such a query would pull data from the Staff List, Insurance, and Review tables, combining the data into one query result.

For your first query, you'll query a single table. To query the Staff List table for all employees in the Sales department, follow these steps:

 1. Open the Employee Information database and click the Queries button in the Objects panel (see Figure 14.8). Two options for creating your query are presented.

FIGURE 14.8

You can create a query from scratch, or you can use a Wizard to help you.

2. Double-click Create query in Design view. The Show Table dialog box opens, as shown in Figure 14.9.

FIGURE 14.9

The Show Table dialog box displays a list of all the tables in your database.

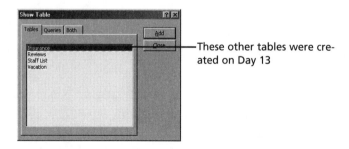

These other tables were created on Day 13

3. Choose the Staff List table and click Add. The Staff List table's fields appear in a box at the top of the Select Query window, as shown in Figure 14.10.

FIGURE 14.10

Choose the table from which your query is to extract data.

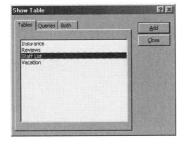

4. Click Close to remove the Show Table dialog box.

5. In the first Field box (see Figure 14.11), click to see the list of fields, and then choose Department.

FIGURE 14.11

You can also drag the field from the Staff List box down to the Field box on the Design worksheet.

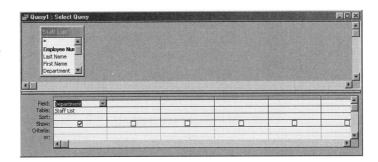

6. In the Criteria box, type `="Sales"`.

7. In the remaining columns, choose the other fields you want to see on the query's onscreen output. For this procedure, choose First Name and Last Name, as shown in Figure 14.12.

FIGURE 14.12

For fields that you want to show in the query table, but that are not being queried, simply select them by name and make sure that a checkmark appears in the Show box.

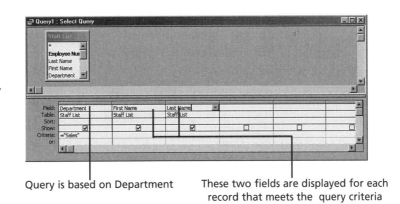

Query is based on Department

These two fields are displayed for each record that meets the query criteria

14

8. Click the Run button on the toolbar or choose Query, Run. The query is performed, and the records that meet your criteria are displayed, as shown in Figure 14.13.

FIGURE 14.13

A query quickly shows only those records that match your criteria settings.

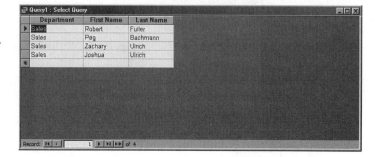

Tip

 You can sort the records in your query table the same way you sort the records in your data table. Click on any one of the records in the field on which you want to sort, and click the Sort Ascending or Sort Descending button.

A table that is based on a single query is no different in scope or power than an AutoFiltered Excel list. You started with a simple query, however, to help you get started. Now, the real power of an Access query can be demonstrated by performing a multiple-table query; follow these steps:

1. Open the Employee Information database, and click the Queries button in the Objects panel.

2. Double-click Create query in Design view. The Show Table dialog box opens.

3. Press the Ctrl key and click the Insurance, Reviews, and Staff List tables. All three are selected, at which time you can release the Ctrl key (see Figure 14.14).

FIGURE 14.14

Use the Ctrl key to select multiple tables in the Show Tables dialog box.

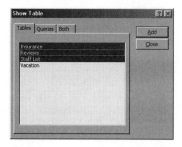

4. Click the Add button, and then click Close to close the Show Table dialog box. The three selected tables appear in boxes at the top of the Select Query window, as shown in Figure 14.15.

FIGURE **14.15**

Your query is built using fields from these three tables.

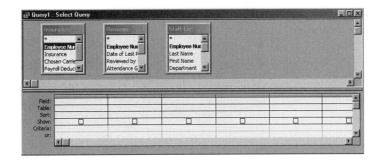

5. In the first column, choose First Name from the Staff List table. Set no Criteria, and make sure that there is a checkmark in the Show box.

6. In the second column, choose Last Name, again from the Staff List table. Set no Criteria, and make sure that there is a checkmark in the Show box.

7. In the third column, select the Department field in the Staff List table, and set the Criteria to ="Marketing".

8. In the fourth column, choose the Chosen Carrier field from the Insurance table, and set the Criteria to ="Blue Cross".

9. In the fifth column, choose Overall Grade from the Review table, and set the Criteria to >3. Figure 14.16 shows the entire five-column query setup.

FIGURE **14.16**

Five fields from three different tables are output through this query.

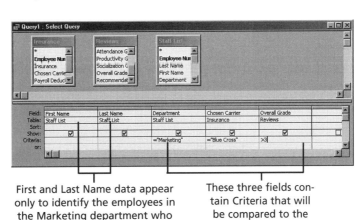

First and Last Name data appear only to identify the employees in the Marketing department who use Blue Cross and have a review grade higher than 3

These three fields contain Criteria that will be compared to the data in the tables

14

10. Click the Run button on the toolbar or choose Query, Run. The query is performed, and displays in a table (as shown in Figure 14.17).

FIGURE 14.17

A single employee meets the criteria you set.

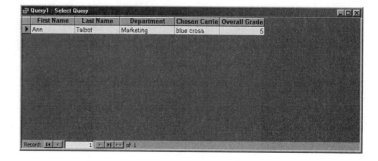

Saving and Using Queries

By saving a query, you make it possible to rerun it at any time in the future using new or edited data. If you don't save your queries, you must redesign them each time you need to extract certain records from one or more of your database tables.

Saving a query is simple. As soon as it's run, choose File, Save. The Save As dialog box opens (see Figure 14.18). Type a name for the Query and click OK. The query is saved to the Queries list in the open database.

FIGURE 14.18

Save the queries that you think you'll need again in the future.

When naming your Query, choose a name that explains the purpose of the query, such as "Insurance Use by Department."

When you're ready to use a saved query, click the Queries button in the Objects panel of the open database. Double-click the query you want to run, and its result appears onscreen in its own window.

Tip

Queries can also be printed—simply choose File, Print while the query results are onscreen. The records that meet your query criteria print out just as they appear onscreen.

Caution

If your previously saved query fails to run as expected (blank fields, incorrect data or fields displayed), it might be because you've edited the structure of your table since you created and saved the query. To redesign your query, click once on the query's name in the Queries list, and then click the Design button on the toolbar. You can then edit the tables, fields, and criteria for your query and resave it.

Selecting Records with Filters

Sometimes a query is overkill. Perhaps you simply want to see a list of people in a particular Department or with a specific Review Grade. You don't need to save the results, you just want to view (and maybe print) them, and then go back to work on something else. If you want to do a simple, transient filter (similar to AutoFilter in Excel) on your table data (in Table view), you can use the Filter buttons on the toolbar as described in the following list:

- **Filter by Selection** —Click on the cell in the table that contains the data for which you want to filter. Figure 14.19 shows all the employees in the Sales Department.

FIGURE 14.19

Click on any Sales cell in the Department field and click the Filter by Selection button. Only the records for the employees in the Sales department are displayed.

Employee Numbe	Last Name	First Name	Department	Date Hired	Current Salary	Insurance
245-67-8214	Fuller	Robert	Sales	3/25/96	$68,500.00	☑
124-89-8736	Bachmann	Peg	Sales	4/15/98	$62,750.00	☑
248-97-1527	Ulrich	Zachary	Sales	3/15/97	$62,500.00	☑
247-12-9865	Ulrich	Joshua	Sales	3/20/96	$62,500.00	☑
					$0.00	☐

Staff List : Table

Tip

To return to a view of your entire table of records, turn off the filter by clicking the Toggle Filter button .

14

• **Filter by Form** —This feature is very similar to AutoFilter in Excel (Day 8). Click the field list box and select the record content you want to use for your filter. Figure 14.20 shows the data for the Vacation Days field.

FIGURE 14.20

Turn your table into a Form for selecting specific records. You can filter on more than one to refine the list of displayed records.

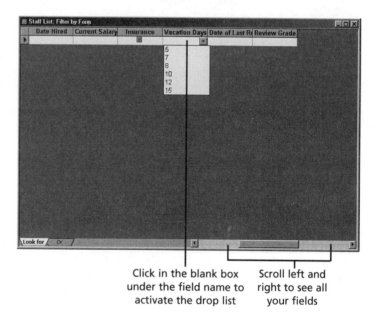

Click in the blank box
under the field name to
activate the drop list

Scroll left and
right to see all
your fields

 • **Apply Filter**—Click this button to show only the record that is currently selected. The button works like a toggle switch—click it again to show the entire list of records.

 Tip

You can use the selected cell to exclude data from your filter. Click on the table cell that contains the data you that don't want to see in your filter results—for example, click on a cell containing the word *Sales* in the Department field to exclude all Sales department employees—and then choose Records, Filter, Filter Excluding Selection.

 Note

Filters cannot be saved, and unless you print the list of records that results from the applied filter, you'll have no permanent record of the filter.

Building Database Reports

Reports are a lot like queries—you choose which tables you want to use and select the fields that you want to see in the final output from within those tables. If reports are so much like queries, why create a report? Because Access reports can be easily formatted to give your output (whether printed on paper or viewed onscreen) a professional, polished look. Figure 14.21 shows a report that was created with the Access Report Wizard, a tool that formats your selected data for you.

FIGURE 14.21

Your reports can be saved for repeated use and edited to accommodate your changing needs.

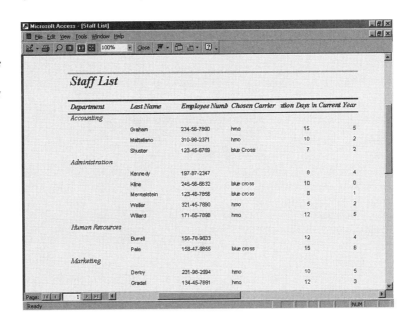

An Access *report* is a document that is built by drawing data from existing data and query tables; it is then formatted for a professional and visually pleasing appearance. When you create an Access report, you select which tables you want to use, which fields you want to use within those tables, and what style of report you want to see—everything from choosing a layout to giving the report a name so that you can run it again in the future.

Establishing Table Relationships

Before beginning the report creation process, it's important to make sure that you have created relationships between your tables. The fact that your Employee Information database tables all contain a common field (Employee Number) isn't enough. You must formally relate the tables by this common field so that the reports you create know to draw common data from common records (linked by that common field) and place it in the report. Without these established relationships, Access won't know that the John Smith in Staff List is the same as the John Smith in the Insurance table, even though their Employee Number is the same.

To create relationships between the tables you want to use in your report, follow these steps:

 1. With the Employee Information database open, choose Tools, Relationships, or click the Relationships button on the toolbar. The Relationships window opens.

 2. If not all your tables are showing, click the Show Table button to open the Show Table dialog box (see Figure 14.22).

FIGURE 14.22

Choose the tables for which you want to establish relationships. Small boxes with a list of the tables' fields are displayed in the Relationships window.

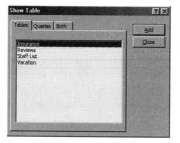

3. Double-click each table you want to display in the Relationships window. When all the tables you want are displayed, click Close to close the Show Table dialog box. Figure 14.23 shows the four tables from the Employee Information database.

FIGURE 14.23

For the Employee Information database, create a relationship between all four tables.

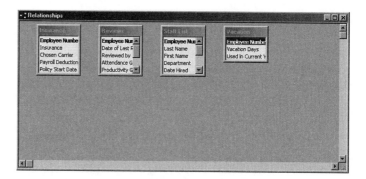

4. To connect each table, start with the leftmost table and drag the Employee Number field to the next table box, connecting to that table's Employee Number field. Figure 14.24 shows this connection in progress.

FIGURE 14.24

Drag the Staff List table's Employee Number field to the Insurance table's Employee Number field. A line connects the tables by this common field.

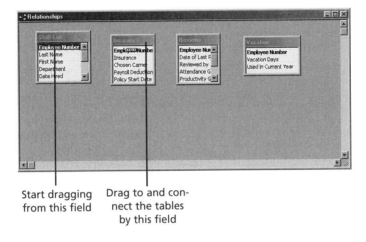

Start dragging   Drag to and con-
from this field   nect the tables
by this field

5. Confirm the connection between tables in the Edit Relationships dialog box (see Figure 14.25). Click Create.

FIGURE 14.25

Verify the table and field names, and then click Create to confirm the table relationship.

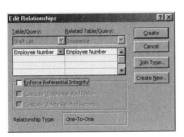

6. Link the remaining tables in the same way, creating a chain from one table to the next, linked by this common field (Employee Number). Lines form between each table, pointing to these connected fields (see Figure 14.26).

7. Click the Close button in the Relationships window and click Yes to save the Relationships layout.

Tip

You can resize the Table boxes in the Relationships window by dragging their edges. When your mouse turns to a two-headed arrow, drag outward to increase the size and to view more (or all) of the table's fields.

14

FIGURE 14.26

When all four tables are related, lines connect the tables.

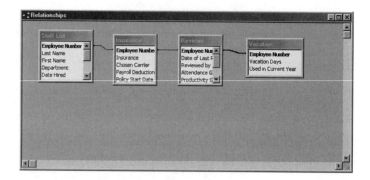

After these relationships are established, Access sees the tables as connected and pairs like data between tables in your report.

Using the Report Wizard

As soon as your tables are properly related, you can begin creating your report. The first step in that process is to select the tables from which data is to be drawn for the report itself. For your report, you'll draw data from the Staff List and Vacation tables to create a report that shows all your employees, the number of vacation days to which they are entitled, and the number of days they've taken so far this year.

To select the tables for your report, follow these steps:

1. In the Employee Information Database window, click once on the Reports button on the Objects panel.

2. Double-click Create report by using Wizard. The wizard takes you step by step through the report creation process, making it easier for you to understand the steps and do a report on your own later.

3. In the Report Wizard dialog box (see Figure 14.27), choose the first table from which you'll pull fields and data. Choose Table: Staff List from the Tables/Queries list.

4. From the list of Available Fields in Staff List, double-click Employee Number, Last Name, and Department. These fields are placed in the Selected Fields box.

5. Choose Table: Insurance, and select Chosen Carrier.

6. Choose Table: Vacation, and select Vacation Days.

7. Click Next to move to the next step in the Report Wizard, in which you can choose to group the report's fields in levels.

8. Double-click Department to group the report by department. The sample display shows the result (see Figure 14.28).

FIGURE 14.27

Select the tables and fields within each table that are to be used in your report.

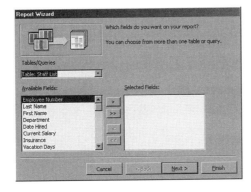

FIGURE 14.28

Group your records by a field that contains many duplicates. In the Employee Information database, Department is the best choice.

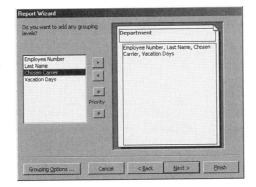

9. Click Next to proceed to the next step in the Wizard, in which you can choose to sort your records (see Figure 14.29). Choose to Sort them by Last Name, in A-Z order (the default).

FIGURE 14.29

Within the groups, choose a field that puts the records in a logical, useful order. Last Name puts them in alphabetical order.

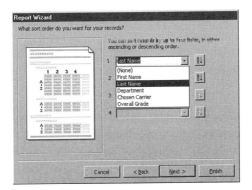

14

10. Click Next to proceed. Choose a Layout and Orientation for your report (see Figure 14.30).

FIGURE 14.30

If you have more than four or five fields to output, choose Landscape orientation.

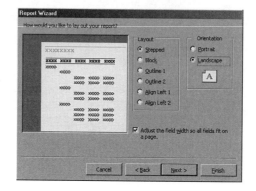

11. Click Next to select a Style for your report (see Figure 14.31).

FIGURE 14.31

Click on each style by name to see a preview of it in the Wizard dialog box.

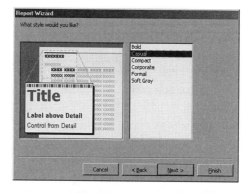

12. Click Next and then give your report a name. This saves the report to the Employee Information Database, enabling you to select and run it again in the future. Name this report `Staff Benefits`.

13. Click Finish to run the report with your current settings. The report that results from the procedure in this section appears in Figure 14.32.

After viewing the onscreen display of your report, you can choose File, Print to print the report as it is displayed. If you see layout or content problems either onscreen or after viewing the report on paper, you can delete and re-create the report.

FIGURE 14.32

Grouped by Department, each employee is listed along with their social security number, insurance carrier, and vacation status.

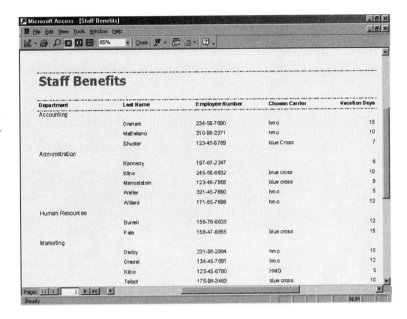

Tip

You can redesign your report, but for most reports, it's faster and easier to simply start over if you don't like the way the report looks or if you need to change the fields that are included.

Integrating Access and Excel

The tabular nature of an Excel worksheet makes it obviously compatible with Access. Access data can be copied to an Excel worksheet, and vice versa, enabling you to save time (by not reentering your work) and achieve consistency between applications that track or use the same information.

Access table data can be used to build an Excel worksheet, where Excel's calculation tools and charting capabilities can be put to effective use. Conversely, if you're already storing data in a list in an Excel worksheet, it can be reused to create or flesh out an Access table. Bringing your simple Excel list into an Access table makes it possible for you to use the data in a larger database, working with other related tables of data.

14

Using Access Tables in Excel

To take Access data and use it in Excel worksheet, you use the Clipboard to Copy and Paste. The rows of your Access tables can then be turned into rows in an Excel worksheet. Follow these steps:

1. Open the Access table that contains the data you want to add to an Excel worksheet.

2. Select the rows you want to copy, and then choose Edit, Copy. Figure 14.33 shows a series of table records selected.

FIGURE 14.33

Drag through the gray buttons to the left of the records you want to copy. If you want to select noncontiguous records, press and hold the Ctrl key as you click to select them.

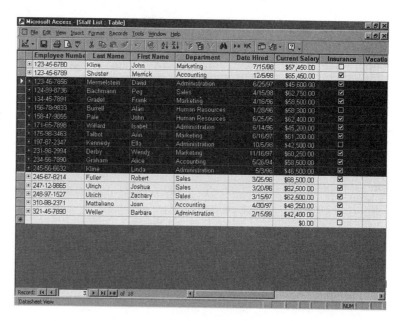

3. Switch to or open the Excel workbook into which you want to copy the data, and then click on the worksheet tab that is to contain the data copied from the Access table.

4. Click in the first cell in the range that you want to contain the data, and choose Edit, Paste. Figure 14.34 shows the copied Access data, which is now in an Excel worksheet.

Your Access table data is now part of your Excel worksheet and can be treated like any other worksheet content. You can place a row of field names above the first row of content so that the list can be sorted or filtered (the field names from Access do not come with the data), and cells can be used in typical Excel formulas and functions.

FIGURE 14.34

The records from your Access table become rows of Excel worksheet content.

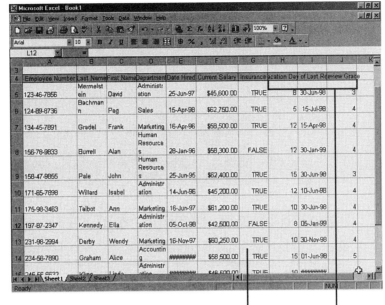

Some data formatting doesn't make the transition—here a Yes/No field is converted to True/False

Some columns need to be widened to show full field names and cell content

If you want to use an entire Access table as an Excel worksheet, click once on the table in the Database window and choose File, Export. Choose the Microsoft Excel .xls format (see Figure 14.35), and give the file a name (you can keep the existing name if it won't create confusion for you to have two files of the same name). To use this new worksheet, simply open Excel, and open the new worksheet that is to use the data—the fact that the data came from Access has no bearing on its appearance, use, or functioning in Excel.

Note

You can use your Access table in a Word document, where it will appear as a Word table. After pasting the table data into your Word document, the records can be used for a mail merge, or simply as a structured display for columns and rows of text or numbers. Complete coverage of every feature of Access, including its use with the other Office 2000 applications, can be found in *Special Edition Using Access 2000*.

14

FIGURE 14.35

*Export an entire
Access table as an
Excel worksheet.*

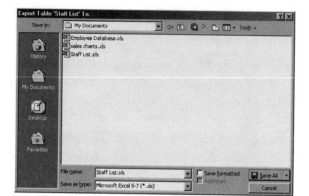

Building an Access Table from an Excel List Database

Many Microsoft Office users "get their feet wet" with databases by using Excel to maintain a simple list (covered on Day 8); then, as their skills improve and their need for more complex database management tools increases, they move to Access to build a true database management system. If you've already built a list in Excel, why not reuse it? It can easily serve as one of the tables in a large database, and reusing it saves you from having to reenter your records.

To use an existing Excel list database as an Access table, follow these steps:

1. In your Excel worksheet, select the entire collection of records. Click in the first cell (your first field name) and scroll to the last field in your last record. Press and hold the Shift key, and click in that last cell, selecting your entire database. Figure 14.36 shows a selected database in Excel.

2. Choose Edit, Copy. Your database is now on the Clipboard.

3. Open or switch to Access, and open a new, blank table in your database, in Datasheet (Table) view.

4. Choose Edit, Paste Append. The cells from your Excel worksheet appear in the Table (see Figure 14.37). Be sure to click Yes to indicate your intention to paste the records.

5. Note that your field names from the Excel worksheet appear as the first record in the new Access table. Double-click the Field1 button at the top of the column and type the correct field name, using the field name under the button in the first row of the table's records (see Figure 14.38).

FIGURE 14.36

Be sure to select every record, and the field names row, from within your Excel database worksheet.

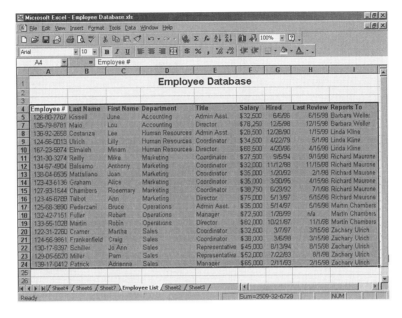

FIGURE 14.37

The records you copied from your Excel worksheet now become the records in an Access table.

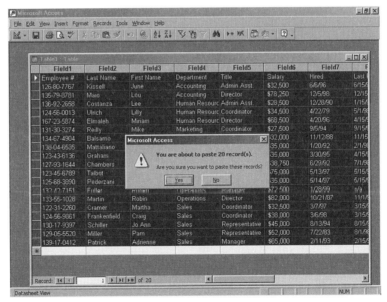

14

*Using the first
"record" for reference,
create your field names
at the top of each col-
umn. Then delete the
row that contains the
field names from the
Excel worksheet.*

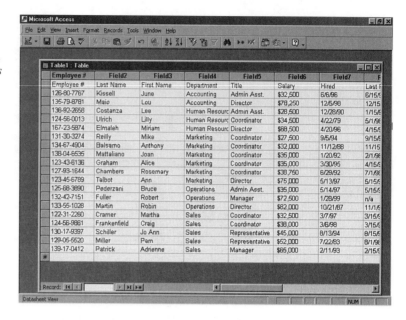

6. Repeat step 5 for each of the fields in your table.

7. Delete the first record (your field names from Excel).

8. Save the table in Access, giving it an appropriate name.

9. Edit the table as needed (and resave after your changes), or close it.

Your new Access table can be customized in Design view to change field settings (to
change field types or lengths, and to add input masks or validation rules), and resaved
with any changes.

Summary

Today you learned to utilize the Access database you created on Day 13, "Setting Up a
Database"—sorting your records, querying the database, and generating reports on the
data. In addition, you learned effective ways to use Access data in an Excel workbook,
and how to bring Excel worksheet content into an Access table. Tomorrow takes you to
PowerPoint, where you will create a slide presentation.

Q&A

Q Can I use a saved query in a report to take advantage of the Report Wizard's tools for layout and style?

A Yes. When selecting tables for the report, you'll see any saved queries in the list as well. Select the query you want to use and then choose which fields from that query you want to see in the report.

Q Can I rename my fields after I've entered records into my database? I might not spot the need for a new name until I've created a report and see that a current field name isn't appropriate.

A Yes. In Design view, select the current name and type a new one. In Table view, double-click the current field name (in the gray cell atop the column) and type a new field name.

Q Are there any drawbacks to renaming a field after you've entered records?

A Only if you've created any queries or reports that use that field. When these saved queries or reports are run, they'll be looking for the old field name. You might have to re-create or edit your queries or reports to use the new fieldname.

Workshop

The section that follows is a quick quiz about the day. If you have any problems answering any of the questions, see the section that follows the quiz for all the answers.

Quiz

1. Explain the difference between sorting your records and querying them.
2. Why must tables be related before you can use them in a report?
3. True or False: Like Excel's AutoFilter feature, the results of a query exist only as long as you display them.

Quiz Answers

1. Sorting records places all the table's records in order by any field you select. Querying a table results in the display of only those records that meet the criteria you set.
2. If your report draws data from more than one table, those tables must be related so that Access can see a connection between the tables and match like data between them.

14

3. False. Queries can be saved for future use. When a query is created, the original table is left intact, and a saved query (a separate object) can be run on that table's data at any time.

DAY 15

Developing a PowerPoint Presentation

PowerPoint is an appropriate name for Microsoft's presentation software because it enables you to make a point in a powerful way. Today you will learn how to use PowerPoint's tools to build a sales presentation—a series of slides that utilizes text, tables, and charts to express ideas and important information in an entertaining way that maintains the attention of the audience. Specifically, today covers the following topics:

- Selecting the approach and basic layout for your presentation
- Building the text backbone of your presentation
- Structuring text and numeric data with tables
- Visually expressing the hierarchy of your company and staff with an organization chart
- Converting numeric data to eye-catching column and pie charts

Starting a Presentation

After starting the PowerPoint application (from the Start menu or a desktop shortcut), you are presented with a dialog box that asks how you want to begin building your presentation (see Figure 15.1).

FIGURE 15.1

Choose how you'll approach your new PowerPoint presentation.

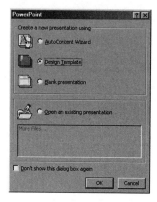

Your three choices for creating a new presentation are as follows:

- **AutoContent Wizard**—This wizard asks you a series of questions about your presentation—intended length, goals, and specifics such as your company name and the name of your presentation. The wizard then compiles this information into a presentation for you, with a number of slides that matches the presentation length you indicated. The slides contain instructional sample text (see an example in Figure 15.2) that you can replace with your own text. You can add and delete slides as needed, but this approach assumes that you have no idea how to begin. You won't use this approach today, but it's worth checking out on your own.

- **Design Template**—Like hiring a decorator to tell you what colors to use in your house and how to accessorize your living space with complementary pieces, PowerPoint's Design Templates make it easier to dive in and get started with the content of your presentation. If you start with a Design Template, you don't have to worry about designing a slide background or which fonts and colors to use (see Figure 15.3). This is the approach you'll take today.

- **Blank Presentation**—Some users prefer to work with a truly blank slate—no background, no colors, and the default font (Times New Roman) for all their slides (see Figure 15.4). If you use this approach, you'll have to apply a slide Design Template later, unless you want simple slides with no background content.

15

FIGURE 15.2

If you have no idea how to begin, try the AutoContent Wizard and let PowerPoint dictate the order and depth of coverage for your presentation topics.

Slide titles indicate what information is to be covered in each slide

Bullet points contain sample text that you replace with your own content

FIGURE 15.3

Design templates contain background graphics, complementary colors, and effective fonts.

Graphic borders and watermark images give your slides a visually dynamic look with little or no effort on your part

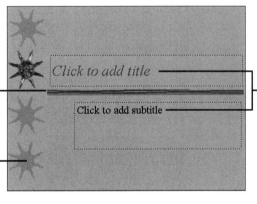

Fonts and colors are selected for you so you don't risk making choices that clash or detract from the overall look of your presentation

FIGURE 15.4

If you start with a Blank Presentation, you can build your presentation content and then go back and apply a Design Template later.

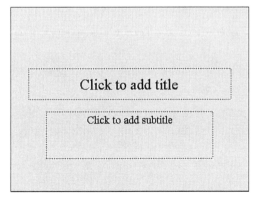

Note

Many organizations like to select a specific Design Template for all the presentations that are generated for their firm—it gives all their seminars and other events a similar look and feel, and it provides consistency. PowerPoint slides can be copied and pasted as graphics for use in reports in Word and worksheets in Excel, bringing the graphical content of a presentation (and the look of your Design Template) to your other Office 2000 application files.

Choosing a Design

After selecting Design Template from the opening PowerPoint dialog box, the New Presentation dialog box opens, as shown in Figure 15.5. The Design Template tab is automatically in front, and a series of templates is displayed.

Click the Details button to see the name and size of the template file, plus the date of the last modification.

FIGURE 15.5

Preview the templates by clicking once on the template name. The template then appears in the Preview box.

Click the template name

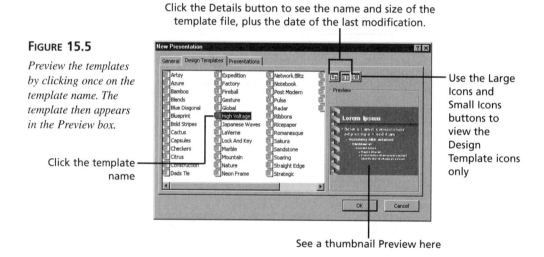

Use the Large Icons and Small Icons buttons to view the Design Template icons only

See a thumbnail Preview here

When making your selection from this large group of Design Templates, keep the following two concepts in mind:

- **Potential output for your presentation**—If you're printing your slides on a black and white printer, don't choose a template with a complex or dark background. Stick to templates with a light or white background and graphical content on the borders of the slide only. If you're running the presentation onscreen or via an

15

overhead projection device (which projects your monitor's display onto a wall or screen), choose any template you want.

- **Overall tone**—Is your presentation on a sober topic such as the stock market or insurance? If it is, don't choose a light-hearted or festive template. Stick to a serious, conservative look. Conversely, if your presentation celebrates sky-rocketing sales or an exciting new product, choose a template with bright colors and eye-catching graphics.

 Caution

Keep your potential presentation content in mind. If you know your slides will contain a lot of their own graphical content—charts and clip art—don't pick a template with a busy background. You don't want your template content to compete visually with the information on your slides.

For today's presentation, you'll be using the Nature template (see Figure 15.6). You can choose any template you want, although you need to be prepared to switch templates (you'll learn how to do that later) if you find that the one you've chosen doesn't work with the text and charts you add as today's project continues.

FIGURE 15.6

The Nature template has an interesting graphical border and a light background— great for both onscreen and transparency slide shows.

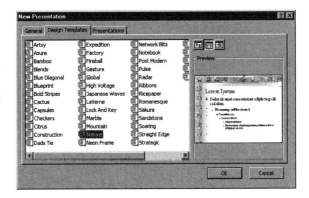

Note

NEW TERM PowerPoint slides can be printed on sheets of clear plastic, also called *transparencies*. These sheets are then placed on a traditional overhead projector to show the slides on a wall or screen. You'll learn more about creating a slideshow and your output choices (including transparencies) on Day 16, "Creating a Multimedia Presentation."

Note

NEW TERM
You can create an *onscreen presentation* in PowerPoint, which means that your PowerPoint slides can be projected through your monitor onto a wall or screen. This enables you to include the color and animation that can be applied to the slides in the presentation. There are a variety of devices that you can connect to your monitor to project your slides for an audience (you'll find out more about giving a slide presentation on Day 16).

Selecting a Slide Layout

After you choose the Design Template for your presentation, your next task is to select the layout for your first slide in the New Slide dialog box (see Figure 15.7).

FIGURE 15.7

By default, PowerPoint selects the Title Slide layout for your first slide.

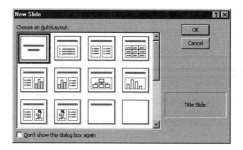

You can choose any layout for your first slide, although PowerPoint's default (Title Slide) is your best choice. The first slide in a presentation typically shows the presentation name (for example, "Earth's Garden Sales Meeting") and a subtitle, which is often the date or location of the meeting (for example, "The Philadelphian Hotel, July 8, 1999"). Double-click the slide layout of your choice or accept the default by clicking OK.

Your first slide appears in Normal view (see Figure 15.8), awaiting the entry of your title and subtitle.

Follow the instructions contained in the first slide's sample text. You'll end up with a slide that looks similar to the one in Figure 15.9.

FIGURE 15.8

The graphical content from your template might appear in a slightly different configuration on a Title Slide.

The Outline panel accompanies your Slide in Normal view

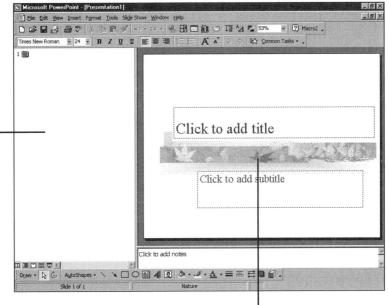

Nature border is beneath the title instead of around the edge of the slide, as it appeared in the Preview

FIGURE 15.9

Enter your slide title, the location, and the date of the presentation in the appropriate text boxes.

Text typed on the slide also appears on the Outline panel

Slide title in format dictated by template's settings

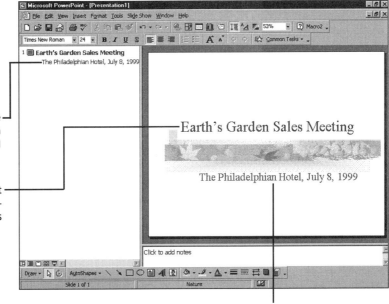

Subtitle text

15

Planning Your Content

Earlier today you learned about the AutoContent Wizard—a tool that creates a series of slides with sample instructional content on them to help you build your presentation. Although you aren't using that approach today, it is a good idea to map out what you'll cover and in what order you'll cover it. You want to start the presentation building process with a plan, normally in the form of an outline. You can build that outline in Word or by simply writing your list of topics on paper. In either case, planning what you're going to say, the points you want to make, and how you're going to support them (through additional text, charts, and graphics) is an important first step.

Your outline needn't be formal or formatted in any special way in order for it to be useful in planning your presentation. If, however, you want to create a Word outline that you can use for both planning and actually creating your presentation, use Word's Heading 1 and 2 styles in your outline to rank the text. Text that is intended to be slide titles needs to be formatted in Heading 1 style, and bulleted text needs to use Heading 2, as shown in Figure 15.10.

FIGURE 15.10

Build a quick and simple Word outline to map out your slide titles and the major points on each slide. You can edit and add text later.

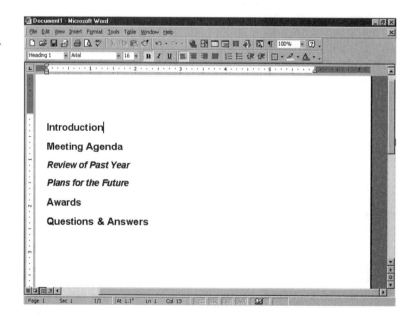

After you've created the outline, choose File, Send To, Microsoft PowerPoint from within Word. A PowerPoint presentation is automatically generated for you, and appears in PowerPoint on the Outline panel (see Figure 15.11).

FIGURE 15.11

Whereas most presentations start in Slide View, a presentation that is created from an external outline (from Word, in this case) starts in Outline View.

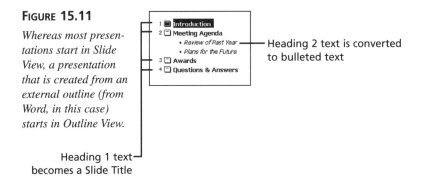

Heading 2 text is converted to bulleted text

Heading 1 text becomes a Slide Title

15

Building a Presentation in the Outline Panel

PowerPoint's Outline view is a great tool for building a presentation from scratch. Whether you started with a Word outline and used Send To to bring it into PowerPoint or you merely started with notes jotted on paper, your text is the backbone of any presentation. Slide titles tell the audience what major topics are covered in the presentation, and bulleted text supports these topics in short, informative sentences.

To use Outline view to build the basic structure of today's sales presentation, follow these steps:

1. Using the Outline panel on the left side of the screen in Normal view, click at the end of the subtitle text in Slide 1.

2. Press Enter. The cursor moves down to create a second line of subtitle text on Slide 1.

 3. Click the Promote button, or press Shift+Tab to create Slide 2 (see Figure 15.12).

4. Type `Today's Topics` and press Enter.

 5. Slide 3 is created. Press Tab or click the Demote button to create the bulleted text for Slide 2.

6. Type the following lines, pressing Enter after each one:

   - `Getting Acquainted`
   - `Quarterly Performance`
   - `New Products`
   - `Visions of the Future`

FIGURE **15.12**

Create a new slide by promoting subtitles or bulleted text.

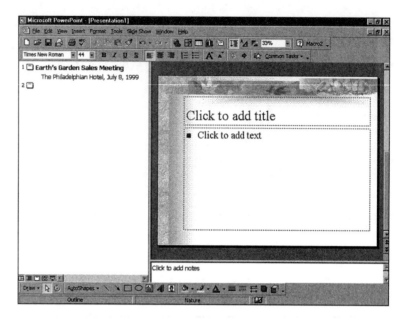

7. Press Enter to create a fifth line for Slide 2, and then click the Promote button to turn that bullet into Slide 3.

8. Type Getting to Know Us, and then press Enter to create Slide 4.

9. Type Sales Performance Awards, and then press Enter to create Slide 5.

10. Type New and Improved Products, and then press Enter to create Slide 6.

11. Type On the Earth's Horizon... as the title for Slide 6.

The Outline panel now appears with six slides (see Figure 15.13).

FIGURE **15.13**

Create a series of slides quickly and easily in the Outline panel.

Slide content built through the Outline panel

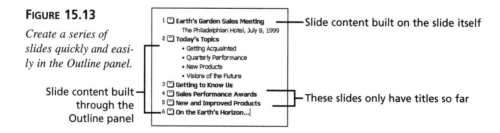

After building the basic structure of your presentation by creating slides with titles, you can go through your slides and flesh them out with subtitles, bulleted text, and miscella-

15

neous text boxes as needed. You can do this through the Outline panel or by working directly on the slides in Normal or Slide view.

 Note Only text that is part of the slide's layout (titles, subtitles, bulleted lists) can be entered in the Outline panel; text boxes, which are not part of a slide's layout, must be created on the slide itself, in Normal or Slide view.

Creating Presentation Content

Your presentation's content needs to be informative, accurate, and interesting to look at. It should not be detailed, verbose, or complex—your accompanying narrative can be all three of these things, but the slides themselves need to be spare in terms of text, and not crowded with too many charts, graphics, or other distractions. When choosing what to say and how to say it, keep the following points in mind:

- **Keep bullet points to a minimum**—Try not to have more than five bullet points on any one slide. If a given topic requires a lot of points, break it into two separate slides with a repeated title. If your audience sees a slide come up with volumes of text on it, they'll quickly lose interest.

- **Avoid complete sentences**—When typing your bullet points on a slide, say things such as "Sales up third consecutive year" as opposed to "Sales are up again for the third year in a row." Short, punchy phrases are easier to read and simpler to interpret.

- **Whenever possible, express numeric data with charts, and general concepts with clip art**—People like pictures, and they prefer images to text. Break up your text-heavy slides with graphic images as much as possible. You'll learn to insert and manipulate clip art images on Day 16.

- **Keep everything simple**—Don't put more than one chart or more than two clip art images or photographs on any one slide. It's better to have a greater number of simple slides than a few slides that are crowded with content.

 Caution Although the use of charts and graphic images can improve audience attentiveness, keep the tone of your presentation in mind. If your topic is a serious one, avoid using brightly-colored pie charts (use muted and dark colors instead), and skip the cartoon clip art images in favor of business-like images that evoke the sober feeling of your topic. Keep all graphic items to a conservative minimum to avoid a circus-like atmosphere in your presentation.

Entering Bulleted Text

Nearly every slide in your presentation will have text on it, and it will usually be in the form of bulleted text. Bulleted text lists the major points that are discussed while a slide is onscreen. These points can be numbered, or they can appear as separate paragraphs with no bullets or numbers preceding them. To change from bullets to numbers, select the list and click the Numbering button. To eliminate bullets or numbers from a list, click the button again (either Bullet or Numbering) to turn them off. Figure 15.14 shows a combination of bulleted, numbered, and paragraph text on a slide.

FIGURE 15.14

Select specific lines of text and apply bullets or numbering, or turn them off to create simple paragraphs.

A distinct paragraph with no bullets or numbers preceding it

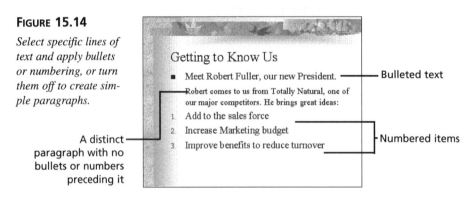

When you build a slide in the Outline panel, the first text that is typed below the title is bulleted by default. Figure 15.15 shows a slide and a blank bullet point that is awaiting text.

As you type your bulleted list, you get a new bullet each time you press Enter at the end of a line. Bullets can be hierarchical, as shown in Figure 15.16.

Tip

If you want to promote a sub-bullet back to full or main bullet status, click on the text and press Shift+Tab.

To complete the bulleted lists for today's presentation, type the text that is shown in Figure 15.17, which displays the text content for slides 4, 5, and 6. (Previous figures have shown the text you need to add to slides 2 and 3.)

After you start to build your presentation, be sure to save it. For this project, name the presentation Earth's Garden Sales Meeting. You'll reuse this presentation on Day 16, so don't delete it after today's project is completed.

FIGURE 15.15

Cover your basic topics with a simple bulleted list.

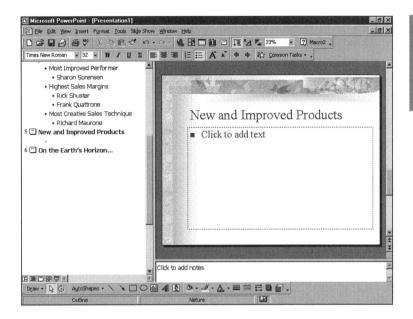

FIGURE 15.16

Create sub-bullets below your main bullet points by pressing Tab to demote the bullet.

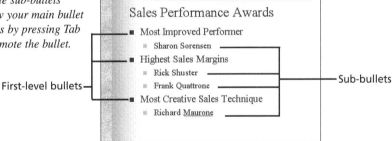

First-level bullets

Sub-bullets

15

 Caution

Due to its highly graphical nature, PowerPoint is more likely to "crash" or become unstable than are Word and Excel. To protect your work, be sure to save early and often while building your presentation.

FIGURE 15.17

Flesh out this sales presentation by entering bulleted text in the Outline panel or directly on the slides themselves.

Formatting Slide Text

Although the Design Template you chose for the presentation dictates the size, font, and color of your text, you might want to change it. PowerPoint offers a Formatting toolbar for making quick and easy changes to the appearance of your text. You'll recognize most of the buttons from Word's Formatting toolbar.

To format text using any of these buttons, follow these steps:

1. On the slide in Normal view, select the text you want to reformat. If you want to reformat an entire text object (such as a title, a list of bullet points, or a text box), click the object's border so that the entire object is selected.

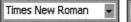
2. Click the Formatting button you want to use. Only Font and Size require a selection from a drop-down list—all the other buttons have an immediate effect.

3. Click away from the formatted text object to view your results.

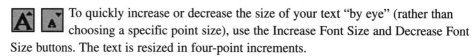 To quickly increase or decrease the size of your text "by eye" (rather than choosing a specific point size), use the Increase Font Size and Decrease Font Size buttons. The text is resized in four-point increments.

To format a single word, click inside the word (between any two letters) and apply the formats you want.

> **Note**
>
> In addition to formatting your text, you can format your bullets. Select the bulleted text object to format all the bullets in the object, or select one or more lines of the text in the object to format just the selected lines; then choose Format, Bullets and Numbering. Select a different bullet, color, or size from within the Bullets and Numbering dialog box, and click OK to apply the changes.

15

Creating Text Boxes

If your slide needs text that isn't a title and isn't bulleted text, you can create a text box. Text boxes can be placed anywhere on a slide, and can be moved and resized to accommodate other objects on the slide such as existing text, charts, or graphic images.

To create a text box, follow these steps:

1. Make sure that the Drawing toolbar is displayed by right-clicking on any displayed toolbar and choosing Drawing from the list (see Figure 15.18).

FIGURE 15.18

The Drawing toolbar is displayed by default in your PowerPoint application window, but if it's missing you can easily redisplay it.

2. On the Drawing toolbar, click the Text Box button. Your mouse pointer turns into an upside down T, as shown in Figure 15.19.

3. Click on the slide itself—you can't use the Outline panel—in which you want the text box to appear; then drag to draw a rectangle the size that you want your text object to be. Note that when you begin to drag, the upside down T turns to a crosshair. When you release the mouse, a small box (the width of the box you just drew) forms around a blinking cursor (see Figure 15.20).

FIGURE 15.19

Similar to a standard text "I-beam," the text box pointer helps you position your text box.

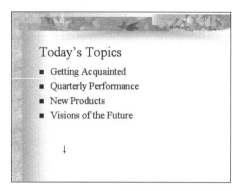

FIGURE 15.20

Click to place the cursor in the location at which you want your text box to appear after the text has been typed inside it.

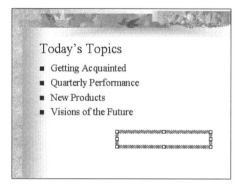

4. Type your text. The text wraps within the box you drew, and the box lengthens to accommodate additional text. While you are typing, do not press Enter unless you want to create separate paragraphs within the text box.

5. When you finish typing, click the border of the text box to select the entire box and all the text inside it.

6. Using the handles (the small white boxes that appear in Figure 15.21), resize the text box to fit among the surrounding slide elements. When your mouse pointer turns to a two-headed arrow, drag from the handle (outward to increase size, inward to decrease size) until the text box is sized appropriately. You can repeat this process on as many different handles as necessary to achieve the desired dimensions for the text box.

Your text box can be moved (point to its border and your mouse turns to a four-headed arrow) and resized as needed. To delete a text box, simply click on it to select it, and then click its border. Press the Delete key, and the text box disappears.

FIGURE 15.21

As you resize the text box, the text wraps to fit inside its newly-sized container.

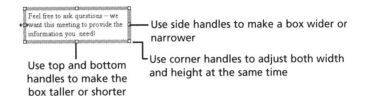

Use side handles to make a box wider or narrower

Use top and bottom handles to make the box taller or shorter

Use corner handles to adjust both width and height at the same time

Figure 15.22 shows a text box on Slide 2.

FIGURE 15.22

Add this text box to Slide 2. The additional text provides extra information without taking up a lot of space on the slide.

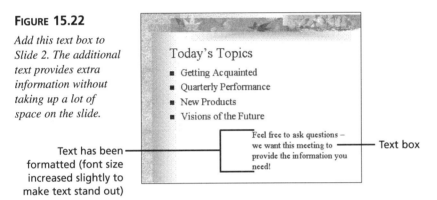

Text box

Text has been formatted (font size increased slightly to make text stand out)

Adding and Deleting Slides

Assume that this sales presentation requires more slides than you created on the Outline panel, and that it requires specific slide layouts for these additional slides. You'll often discover the need for additional slides in the process of building a presentation, or you'll want to change the layout of your existing slides to accommodate content you hadn't planned on when you started the process.

To add a slide and select a special layout for it, follow these steps:

1. Using the Outline panel, click once on the slide before which you want to add the new slide. In this presentation, click on Slide 6.

2. Click the New Slide button or choose Insert, New Slide. The New Slide dialog box opens, as shown in Figure 15.23.

3. Double-click the Organization Chart layout. The new slide is added, and an organization chart object appears on the slide (see Figure 15.24).

FIGURE 15.23

For each slide you add, you must select a layout.

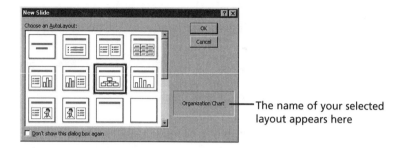

The name of your selected layout appears here

FIGURE 15.24

The slide's layout determines what object boxes appear on the slide. An Organization Chart layout gives you an Organization Chart object.

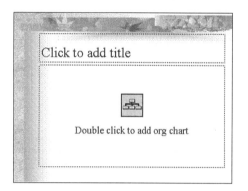

4. Click in the Title box, or next to the slide icon on the Outline panel, and type Our Dedicated Staff.

Add another slide before what is now Slide 7, choosing the Chart layout. Give this new slide the title Changing Palates in the US. This slide will eventually contain a column chart.

Changing Slide Layout

If one of your slides is currently set to a layout that doesn't include an object that you need (such as a chart or table object), you can change the layout.

To change the slide layout of an existing slide (Slide 5, in this case), follow these steps:

1. Click once on the Slide 5 icon on the Outline panel, or click anywhere on the slide itself in Normal or Slide view.

2. Delete the bulleted text box (which contains text that you typed) by clicking its border and pressing Delete.

3. Choose Format, Slide Layout. The Slide Layout dialog box opens.

4. Double-click the slide layout you want (Table), or click the desired layout once and click Apply.

15

The displayed slide changes to reflect the new layout. In this case, a table object is added, as shown in Figure 15.25.

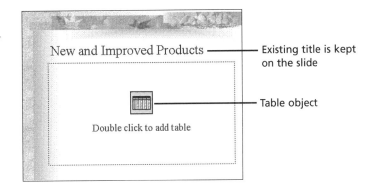

New and Improved Products —————— Existing title is kept on the slide

————— Table object

Double click to add table

Caution

If your slide has existing bulleted or other text, a change in layout does not remove this text—the new layout's object appears on top of the existing content. For this reason, be sure to delete any content that doesn't fit the new layout before applying the layout to the slide. To remove the bulleted text box, click its border and press Delete.

Tip

Like most actions, the change of a slide's layout can be undone. If you realize that you've applied the wrong layout or that you didn't need to make the change in the first place, choose Edit, Undo.

Working with Tables

Tables give structure to slide content by providing a grid of cells into which short text strings (words, phrases), paragraphs, and numeric data can be typed. On Day 4, "Building a Complex Document," you used table tools to build a table in Word—today you'll use those same tools to create a table on Slide 5.

To fill in the table object that you placed on Slide 5, follow these steps:

1. Double-click the table object on Slide 5. The Insert Table dialog box opens (see Figure 15.26), into which you can enter the dimensions of the table.

FIGURE 15.26

Enter the number of columns and rows you want in your table.

2. Type 3 in the columns box and 3 in the rows box. Press Enter or click OK to create the table and close the dialog box.

3. To enter text into the table's cells, click in the first cell and type. To move to the next cell, press Tab or click in the cell in which you want to type. Figure 15.27 shows the completed table that will appear on Slide 5.

FIGURE 15.27

Format a PowerPoint table just as you format a table in Word. Both the cell content and cell dimensions can be changed and reformatted.

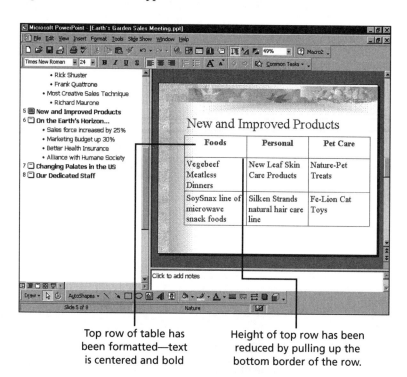

Top row of table has been formatted—text is centered and bold

Height of top row has been reduced by pulling up the bottom border of the row.

4. To reposition the table, click on its border (between handles) and, when your mouse turns to a four-headed arrow, click and drag to move the table. Figure 15.28 shows Slide 5, with the table in transit.

FIGURE 15.28

PowerPoint tables can be moved and resized like a graphic—drag it by its border to move it, drag the handles to resize it.

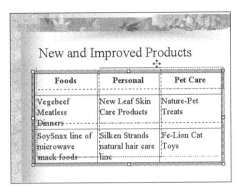

Creating an Organization Chart

Slide 8 in your presentation will contain an organization chart. An organization chart is a series of boxes that are connected by lines to show the hierarchy of the company (or any type of organization). You can create organization charts that show departmental hierarchies, with department names instead of people listed in the boxes, or that show the actual structure of your company's staff, with people's names and titles in each box. You will create the latter type of organization chart on Slide 8.

To build an organization chart, follow these steps:

1. Be sure that the slide that will contain the chart is set to the Organization Chart layout. If it isn't, change it by choosing Format, Layout, and then double-clicking the Organization Chart layout.

2. In the properly formatted slide, double-click the Organization Chart object. The Microsoft Organization Chart Object window opens, as shown in Figure 15.29. Maximize this window.

3. To fill in the top box, simply begin typing (the name area is already selected). Type the name `Robert Fuller` and press Enter.

4. Type this person's title, which is `President`.

5. Click on the first box (on the left) in the lower tier of boxes, and type the name `Rosemary Chambers`.

6. Press Enter, and then type her title, `Marketing Director`.

7. Click in the next box and type `Tom Talbot`; give him the title `Sales Director`.

8. Click in the last box and type `Lillie Ulrich`; give her the title `Accounting Director`.

FIGURE 15.29

Microsoft Organization Chart is a program that runs within PowerPoint for the sole purpose of creating organization charts for PowerPoint slides.

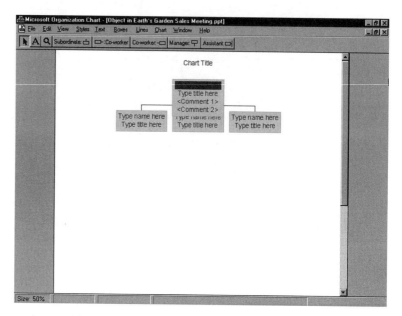

For most organizations, four boxes aren't enough. You probably need to add another second-tier box and some subordinates for the directors. To add new boxes, follow these steps:

1. Click the Subordinate button and then click on Robert Fuller's box to indicate that the subordinate will be his. A box appears at the end of the three second-tier boxes (see Figure 15.30).

2. Click the Subordinate button again, and then click on Rosemary Chamber's box. A subordinate box appears below her (see Figure 15.31).

3. Repeat step 2 for each of the other Directors, and enter names and titles (as in the Organization chart shown in Figure 15.32).

Last, you'll add an assistant to the President. Click the Assistant button, and then click on Robert Fuller's box. The Assistant's name is June Kissell and her title is Executive Assistant.

You can add as many subordinates as you want, and you probably want to add extras for some of the directors and give some of the third-tier employees their own subordinates. Using the skills you've learned thus far, create the completed organization chart shown in Figure 15.33.

15

FIGURE 15.30

Choose which type of employee you want to add, and then click the existing box to which the new box relates.

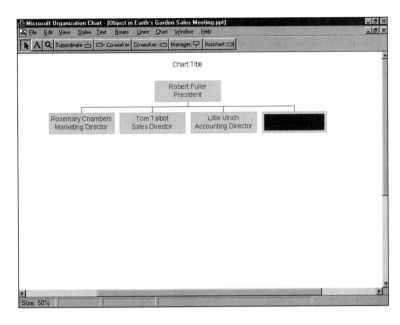

FIGURE 15.31

Add as many subordinates as you want by clicking the Subordinate button and then clicking the box for their superior.

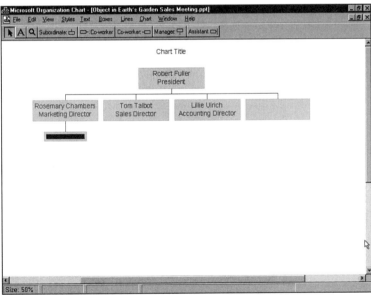

FIGURE 15.32

*Create a third tier of
employees who report
to the directors.*

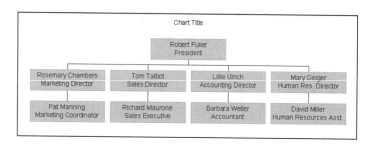

FIGURE 15.33

*Each box that is added
causes the surrounding
boxes to move, and
lines form to join the
new box to the entire
chart.*

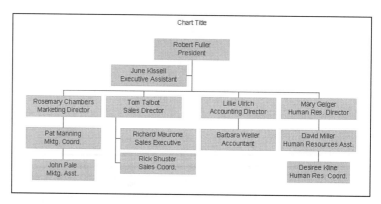

Select a group of subordinates and apply a vertical style (from the Styles
menu). This has been applied to the Sales subordinates in Figure 15.33.

You can format the color of the boxes, text, and lines on your chart, and you
can apply different fonts and line styles. Simply click on the part of the chart
you want to reformat and make the appropriate selection from the Text,
Boxes, or Lines menus.

Boxes can be deleted if people leave your organization, or they can be
moved if the reporting structure changes. To delete a box, click once on it
and press Delete. To move a box, drag it from its current position to its new
one by dragging the employee's box to the box that belongs to his or her
new superior. When the mouse pointer reflects the type of relationship (co-
worker or subordinate) you want to establish, release the mouse.

If you delete a person with subordinates, the first of their subordinates replaces them in the hierarchy. If this person wasn't promoted to management in real life, you'll have to edit the organization chart to reflect the new structure in that department.

15

To save your chart and return to the presentation, choose File, Exit and Return. You'll be prompted to update the object (see Figure 15.34); click Yes to have your organization chart appear in the active slide.

FIGURE 15.34

If you don't choose to update the chart, the work you've done in the Organization Chart window is not reflected in the presentation.

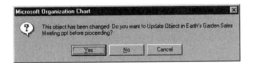

After your chart has been updated to the slide, you can edit it at any time by double-clicking it—the Microsoft Organization Chart window reopens, and you can edit the chart as needed. When you're finished editing, be sure to choose File, Exit and Return and then choose Yes to update the chart with your latest changes.

When you are creating an organization chart that will be viewed onscreen through some projection device, remember that legibility is an issue. If you have more than ten or 12 boxes in your chart on a single slide, the text will be so small that many people in the audience won't be able to read it. It's better to create separate charts for each department (each on its own slide) than to try to cram every person in your organization onto one chart.

Adding Charts to Illustrate Numeric Data

It's not advisable to fill your slides with numbers for the same reason that it's not a good idea to generate slides that are filled with text: When a slide appears onscreen, an abundance of text or numbers can quickly put your audience to sleep. The problem of too much text is easily solved by breaking text-heavy topics into multiple slides, and placing clip art or photographs on the slides to create visual interest. When it comes to numbers, however, the best way to share them with your audience is by converting them to charts—a picture that represents potentially boring numeric data goes a long way in maintaining audience attention and giving your presentation an overall professional and visually polished appearance.

In your sales presentation today, instead of a list of sales numbers for a series of products, you will create a column chart. After you create that chart, you will take a portion of the same data and create a pie chart.

To build the column chart, follow these steps:

1. Go to Normal or Slide view of Slide 7, and double-click the chart object. A Datasheet appears, and the toolbar changes to offer charting tools (see Figure 15.35).

FIGURE 15.35

The Datasheet contains the data that is plotted on the chart.

Each number is a data point

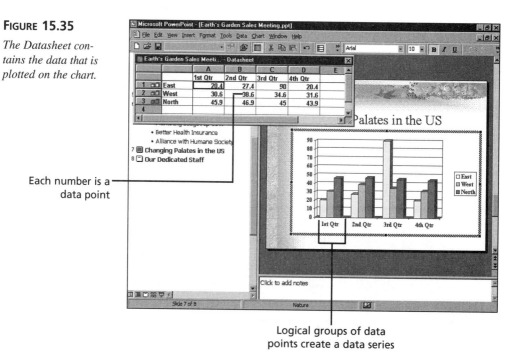

Logical groups of data points create a data series

2. Note that the Datasheet contains sample data, which is also represented on a chart on the slide. This sample data must be removed and replaced with your data. Click the first gray button in the upper-left corner of the Datasheet (indicated in Figure 15.36). When all the cells in the Datasheet turn black, press the Delete key.

FIGURE 15.36

Select the entire Datasheet so that you can remove the sample data quickly.

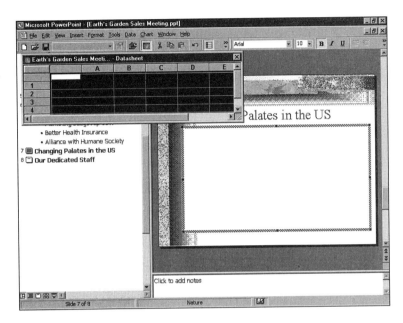

15

3. Enter your data in the Datasheet, as shown in Figure 15.37. Be sure to enter the data in the exact locations that are shown in the figure.

FIGURE 15.37

Enter your own data into the Datasheet and watch your chart form on the slide.

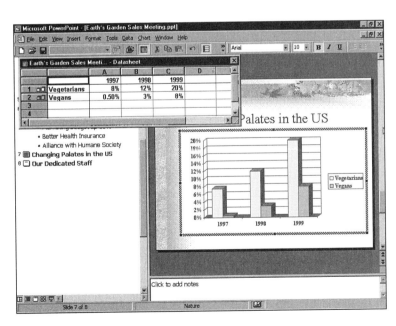

4. As you make your entries, the chart is built on the slide. When your entries are complete, click on the slide, outside of the chart—this brings back the normal PowerPoint toolbars, and the Datasheet disappears. Figure 15.38 shows the finished chart.

FIGURE 15.38

Your numeric data is now an interesting picture that your audience will enjoy viewing and discussing.

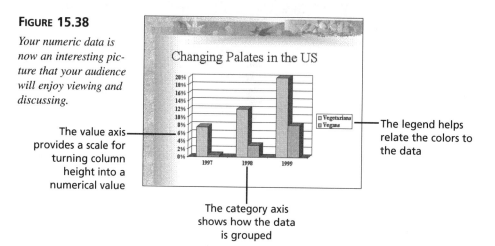

The value axis provides a scale for turning column height into a numerical value

The legend helps relate the colors to the data

The category axis shows how the data is grouped

After it is created, your chart can be edited (by changing the content of the Datasheet), formatted (to change the appearance of the chart's elements), and moved or resized (to accommodate other objects on the slide).

Editing Chart Data

You might need to change the text and numbers in your Datasheet to reflect updates or to fix mistakes that were made when the data was originally entered. If your presentation will be used more than once, you probably need to enter new data to make sure that your charts are accurate and relevant as time goes by. In any case, to edit chart data, follow these steps:

1. To activate the chart and its charting tools and Datasheet, double-click the chart on Slide 7. The Datasheet reappears, and the toolbar changes to offer charting tools. If your chart is already active, there is no need to double-click—choose View, Datasheet to redisplay the Datasheet for editing.

2. Edit the Datasheet by clicking in the cells that need to be changed and typing new content. If you need to add a column or row, resize the Datasheet by dragging the corner (as shown in Figure 15.39).

15

FIGURE 15.39

Resize your Datasheet to add more columns or rows of data to your chart.

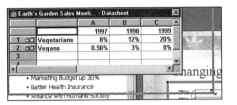

Tip

Widen your Datasheet columns by dragging the seam on the right side of the column letters. This works just as it does in an Excel worksheet.

3. As you make your edits, you'll see the chart change. Edit the Datasheet to match the data shown in Figure 15.40, and then click on the slide, outside of the chart, to reactivate the normal PowerPoint tools and close the Datasheet.

FIGURE 15.40

The Datasheet and the chart are linked, so changes that are made to the Datasheet are immediately reflected on the chart.

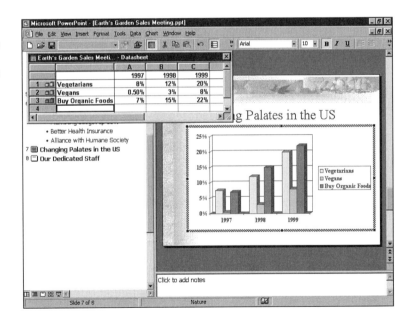

If you double-click your chart and can't see the Datasheet, click the View Datasheet button on the toolbar. This button toggles the Datasheet on and off as needed.

Formatting Chart Appearance

The colors of your columns and the fonts used in your chart's axis labels and legend are dictated by the template you choose for your presentation. There might be times that you want to adjust these settings: Perhaps you don't like a particular color, or maybe two of the contiguous columns (or bars or pie slices) are too similar and you want to choose a different color for one of them.

You can adjust the appearance of virtually any chart element, for whatever reason. In the following procedure, you will change the color of the columns in one of the data series and move the legend to a different location on the chart.

First, to change the color of a data series, follow these steps:

1. Click once on any bar in the series you want to recolor. Handles appear on all the columns in the series, as shown in Figure 15.41.

FIGURE 15.41

To select an entire data series, click on just one of the columns in that series.

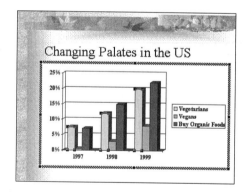

2. Choose Format, Selected Data Series. The Format Data Series dialog box opens, as shown in Figure 15.42.

3. Choose a different color in the Area section of the Patterns tab. Click OK to apply the color to your chart and close the dialog box.

 Tip
You can also use the Fill Color button on the Drawing toolbar to recolor the selected data series. If the Drawing toolbar isn't showing, choose View, Toolbars, Drawing to display it.

FIGURE 15.42

The charting menus and tools are context-sensitive, meaning that the tools and commands that are offered are appropriate for the chart element that is selected at the time.

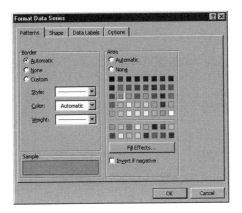

To change the location of your legend, follow these steps:

1. Click once on the legend. Handles appear on its perimeter, as shown in Figure 15.43.

FIGURE 15.43

Select the legend before you attempt to move it.

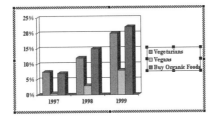

2. Choose Format, Selected Legend. The Format Legend dialog box opens.

3. Click the Placement tab, and then choose Bottom (see Figure 15.44).

FIGURE 15.44

Choose the location for your legend. PowerPoint automatically moves and resizes the legend accordingly.

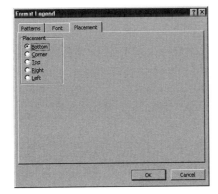

4. Click OK to apply the change and close the dialog box. Figure 15.45 shows the legend in its new location on the chart.

FIGURE 15.45

Although you can drag the legend to a new spot manually, using the Format Legend dialog box results in the legend being moved and resized automatically to fit its new location.

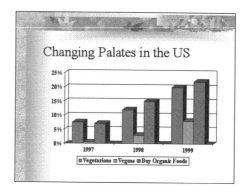

As you have probably discovered throughout these two procedures, you can reformat any chart element can by clicking on it to select it, and then choosing Format, Selected *Element* where *Element* is the name of the selected portion of the chart. A dialog box opens, offering options that are appropriate for the selected chart element.

Adding Chart Titles

Although your slide's title probably makes it clear what data is shown in your chart, adding chart titles can help the audience to better understand the content and intended message of your chart. To add chart titles, choose Chart, Chart Options while the chart is active; on the Titles tab (see Figure 15.46), type a title for the entire chart and add titles for the category and value axes as needed.

Creating a Pie Chart

In this procedure, you will reuse a portion of the data from the column chart's datasheet and create a pie chart that shows the sales of one particular product over three years. Pie charts can only show one data series at a time, whereas column charts can show as many data series as needed.

FIGURE 15.46

Add axis titles to explain the nature of your chart's data.

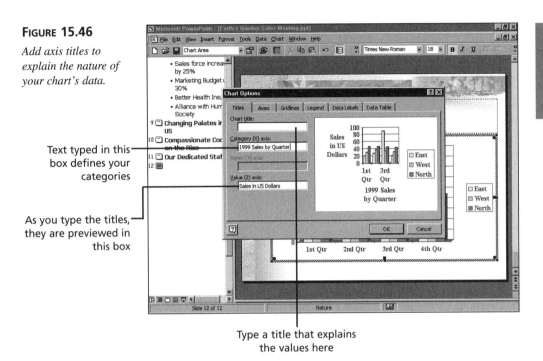

Text typed in this box defines your categories

As you type the titles, they are previewed in this box

Type a title that explains the values here

To reuse the chart data and create a pie chart on Slide 8, follow these steps:

1. Double-click the column chart on Slide 7. The Datasheet appears.

2. In the Datasheet, select all the data.

3. Choose Edit, Copy. The data is now on the Clipboard.

4. Create a new Slide 8 by inserting a new slide between 7 ("Changing Palates in the US") and the current Slide 8 ("Our Dedicated Staff"). Choose the Chart layout for this new slide.

5. Give the new Slide 8 the title Compassionate Cooking on the Rise.

6. In the new Slide 8, double-click the chart object to open the Datasheet and charting toolbar.

7. Delete the sample data from the Datasheet.

8. Click in the first cell of the now blank Datasheet, and then choose Edit, Paste to paste the copied data from the Slide 7 Datasheet.

9. Select columns A and B by dragging through the control buttons at the top of the columns (see Figure 15.47).

FIGURE 15.47

Select the portions of the data that you want to exclude from your chart.

Earth's Garden Sales Meeti... - Datasheet				
	A	B	C	D
	1997	1998	1999	
1 Vegetarians	8%	12%	20%	
2 Vegans	0.50%	3%	8%	
3 Buy Organic Foods	7%	15%	22%	
4				

10. Choose Data, Exclude Row/Col. The column chart now has only one data series displayed (1999 for all three items in the legend).

11. To change from the default column chart to a pie chart, choose Chart, Chart type. In the Chart Type dialog box (see Figure 15.48), choose Pie from the list of types, and then select the second pie in the top row of subtypes.

FIGURE 15.48

Choose a Pie chart, and select the 3D pie with all the slices together.

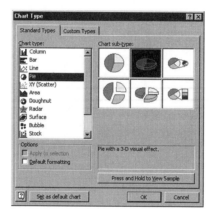

12. Click OK to change types and create a chart based on the Datasheet. The resulting chart is a solid-color pie.

13. Choose Data, Series in Columns. The pie now has three different colored slices.

14. Choose Chart, Chart Options, and click the Data Labels tab (see Figure 15.49).

15. Select the Show label and percent option. This displays the year and calculates the percentage of the whole for each pie slice.

16. Click the Legend tab and remove the checkmark from the Show legend box. With labels and percentages applied, there is no need for a legend.

17. Click OK to apply these two changes. Figure 15.50 shows the finished chart.

You can edit and reformat your pie chart just as you did the column chart. Reactivate the chart by double-clicking it, and then edit the datasheet or change the color of pie slices as necessary.

15

FIGURE 15.49

Choose to display the Palate category and the percentage of the total that each slice represents.

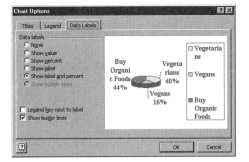

FIGURE 15.50

With no legend, there is more room for the pie. Displaying the labels and percentages makes the chart much easier to interpret.

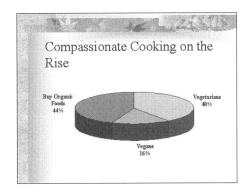

> **Tip**
>
> If you want to draw attention to one particular slice in the pie, explode it. Click twice on that slice (don't double-click), and when handles appear around just that slice, drag it slightly away from the center of the pie. Complete coverage of this effect can be found in Day 9, "Creating and Using Charts," which covers the use of charts in Excel. The slice-exploding procedure is the same in both Excel and PowerPoint.

Summary

Today you learned to build a basic PowerPoint presentation—selecting a Design Template to create a cohesive look for the presentation, building slides and slide titles, and entering text content on each slide. In addition, you learned to create a table to organize text, and you learned to add an organization chart, a column chart, and a pie chart to your slides. Day 16 will complete your coverage of PowerPoint by adding clip art and drawings to the presentation (you'll continue using the presentation you created today). By setting up animations, sound, and other interesting visual effects, you will create a multimedia slideshow.

Q&A

Q Can I create my own template?

A Yes. Any presentation you create, be it with text and charts or with just basic formatting applied (that is, fonts and colors), can be saved as a template for future use. Choose File, Save As, and choose Design Template (*.pot) from the list. After you name the template and click Save, the template is available—along with the installed Design Templates—for your future presentations.

Q What can I do to keep my PowerPoint presentation files' sizes as small as possible? I transfer presentations via email and diskette, and I can't always assume that the recipient can unzip compressed files.

A Reduce the amount of graphical content. Choose a Design Template with very little decoration and a white background; or, better yet, start with a blank presentation and add minor decorations of your own, and only to certain slides. As you'll learn on Day 16, graphics, video, sound, and animation effects also add to file size. Keep these to a minimum if you need to create small presentation files.

Q Why does PowerPoint crash more often than Word or Excel?

A If your computer doesn't have a lot of RAM, PowerPoint might crash frequently. If you can't increase your RAM, try to avoid having more than one additional application open while you're using PowerPoint, and save often so that you don't lose work if the software still crashes.

Workshop

The section that follows is a quick quiz about the day. If you have any problems answering any of the questions, see the section that follows the quiz for all the answers.

Quiz

1. Describe the tools that are available to you in Normal view for building a presentation.

2. How do you promote a paragraph of bulleted text to a slide?

3. True or False: After you've assigned a layout to a particular slide, you cannot change it. If you need a different slide layout, you must delete the slide and create a new one with the proper layout.

4. What, if any, limitations are there to the use of pie charts?

5. Explain what is meant by the term *data series*.

6. In an organization chart, how many tiers of boxes can you have on a chart?

15

Quiz Answers

1. In Normal view, you have the active slide itself, into which you can type text, insert charts, clip art, or text boxes, and you have the Outline panel, through which you can create all your slides and give them titles, subtitles, and bulleted text points.

2. While working in the Outline panel, you can promote text that is currently a first-level bullet to a slide by pressing Shift+Tab or by clicking the Promote button. Second- and subsequent-level bullets can also be promoted to higher level bullets, and ultimately to slides.

3. False. Any slide, even one with content, can have a new layout applied to it. Choose Format, Slide Layout, and select a new layout for the slide. Any existing content has to be moved or deleted to accommodate any elements that come with the new layout, however.

4. A pie chart is limited to displaying only one data series at a time. For example, if your data consists of sales numbers for several products over a three-year period, the pie chart can only show a single year for all products or one product over three years. If you need to plot more than one data series, consider a column, bar, or line chart.

5. A data series is any logical grouping of data points. Sales by product for a single year is a data series; sales of a single product over several years is another.

6. You can have an unlimited number of tiers or levels of employees in your organization chart. Keep in mind, however, that the more boxes you have on your chart, the smaller each box and its text becomes. For legibility when the slides are projected on a wall or screen, keep the number of boxes per chart to no more than 12. If the chart will be printed on paper, make 25 or fewer boxes your target.

DAY **16**

Creating a Multimedia Presentation

Day 15, "Developing a PowerPoint Presentation," showed you how to build a basic PowerPoint presentation with most of the visual tools that help to make your slides informative, effective, and interesting to look at. Today takes this a step further, addressing the use of graphic images, drawing tools, and the application of sound and animation to create a dynamic slideshow. Specifically, today covers the following topics:

- Adding graphic images—for example, clip art and photographs—to your slides to maximize your message
- Using PowerPoint's drawing tools to create your own shapes and lines
- Choosing effective animation and sound effects for your slideshow
- Automating your slideshow with preset timings and recorded narration
- Distributing your slideshow—even to people who don't have PowerPoint—with the PowerPoint Viewer

Inserting and Working with Graphics

Just as a chart can turn potentially boring numeric data into an interesting graphic image, the use of graphics—that is, clip art, photographs, and scanned drawings—can enhance your presentation by replacing an excess of text. Even if you can't find a graphic image that conveys your message to the extent that you can eliminate some of your text, you'll find that clip art, cartoons, photographs, and other graphic items can help maintain audience attention. Just having pictures on your slides can keep people interested.

 Caution

> Like most things in life, graphics must be used in moderation. As effective as having a few pictures throughout your presentation can be, too many of them can be distracting. Don't confuse or crowd your text with the overuse of clip art, photos, or drawings; a busy slide looks unprofessional, and the message gets lost in the shuffle.

Adding Clip Art Images

Office 2000 comes with an extensive collection of clip art, and you'll find additional images on the CD that comes with this book. Furthermore, you can find collections of clip art at local office supply stores, and there are thousands of free images available at various Web sites on the Internet. Why so much clip art? Because it's effective, it can be fun, and it breaks up the monotony of text-heavy documents such as reports, spreadsheets, and PowerPoint presentations (which are the focus of this particular project).

Consider these potential uses for clip art on your PowerPoint slides:

- **To accompany a chart**—Are sales up? Include an image of piles of cash, or perhaps a picture of some item that can be awarded to the sales rep with the highest sales. Images of money, luxury products, or other coveted items help convey the message that high sales are everyone's goal.

- **To replace excess text**—Rather than writing three paragraphs to explain that your new health insurance carrier is much more accommodating, include a picture of a smiling doctor and patient on a slide that lists (succinctly) the new, more lenient policies of your new provider.

- **Remind them who you are**—Make sure that your logo is featured prominently on important slides. Your logo—or at least your company name—needs to appear on the first and last slides in a presentation. You can even add your logo to every slide by adding it to your presentations Master (more on how to do that later).

After you've decided where to use a piece of clip art, you have to add it to your slide. To insert clip art into your presentation, follow these steps:

1. Move to the slide that will contain the clip art image. In this case, switch to Slide 6.

2. Click the Insert Clip Art button on the Drawing toolbar, or choose Insert, Picture, Clip Art. The Insert ClipArt dialog box opens, as shown in Figure 16.1.

16

FIGURE 16.1

If you opted to install all the clip art when you installed Office 2000, you'll have more than 50 categories to choose from.

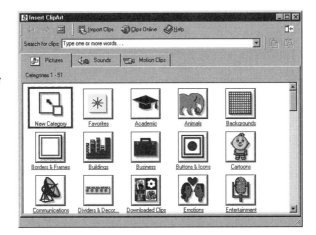

3. On the Pictures tab, choose an image Category. The images in that category are then displayed, as shown in Figure 16.2. For this procedure, choose the Animals category.

Click here to go back to the categories and choose something else

FIGURE 16.2

Click the Back button to go back to the Categories tab if none of the images in the current category meet your needs.

4. When you've selected your image, right-click it and choose Insert from the short-cut menu (see Figure 16.3).

FIGURE **16.3**

You can also drag the image out of the Insert ClipArt dialog box and onto your slide if the slide is visible while the dialog box is open.

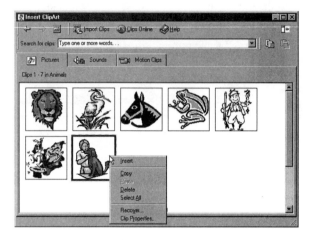

Caution

Another method for inserting a clip art image is to click it once and choose the first symbol on the resulting menu. This method is unreliable, however, in that you can insert clip art unintentionally—if you click on the image and move your mouse slightly, you might inadvertently select the Insert Clip Art symbol from the menu and add an unwanted image to your slide.

5. Close the Insert ClipArt dialog box by clicking the Close button in the upper-right corner.

Moving and Resizing Clip Art

The inserted clip art appears in the middle of your slide, where it is probably obscuring text or some other slide content. The Picture toolbar also appears, but typically, you won't need it for clip art images. To move the clip art to a more appropriate location on the slide, point anywhere in the image itself and drag it to a new spot. Figure 16.4 shows the selected image being moved to the lower-right side of the slide.

Your clip art might also require resizing. In this case, you want to make it a little bigger. To change the size of your clip art image, use the handles (shown in Figure 16.5) to change the width or height of the image.

Figure 16.6 shows Slide 6 with the clip art moved and resized to fit the slide.

FIGURE 16.4

Move your clip art to a spot where it enhances the overall composition of the slide, balancing the title text and any other graphic content.

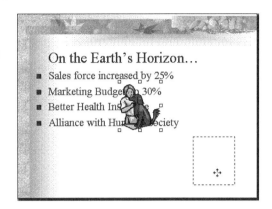

16

FIGURE 16.5

Change the size of your clip art image by dragging the handles outward to increase size, or inward to make it smaller.

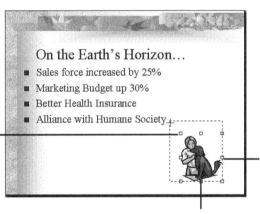

Maintain the current width/height ratio by dragging from a corner handle

Use the side handles to make the image wider or narrower

Make your image taller or shorter by dragging the top or bottom handles

FIGURE 16.6

The last bullet item's message is enhanced by the use of this particular image.

Inserting a Graphic File

Some presentations require the use of photographs—pictures of your staff, the factory you opened recently, a product that you carry—and there isn't any clip art that will do. In other cases, drawings or other artwork (done by hand and then scanned) are needed. For the Earth's Garden presentation, you'll be adding a photograph to Slide 5.

To insert a graphic file, follow these steps:

1. With the slide that will contain the graphic file onscreen in Normal or Slide view (Slide 5 in this case), choose Insert, Picture, From File.

2. The Insert Picture dialog box opens, as shown in Figure 16.7. Note that the My Pictures folder is the default location in which to look for images—if you store yours elsewhere, navigate to the folder or drive on which the image you need is stored.

FIGURE 16.7

PowerPoint starts in the My Pictures folder, but you can look anywhere for the picture you want to insert.

3. To select a particular image, click once on the image and check the preview on the right side of the dialog box. When you're sure you're looking at the file you want, double-click the filename or click Insert.

The image appears in the middle of the active slide, as shown in Figure 16.8. In most cases, this requires that you move the image to somewhere else on the slide, and perhaps that you resize the image as well. The same techniques that are employed for moving and resizing clip art also apply to pictures—drag the image to move it, drag the handles to resize it.

After you've changed the placement and size of the image, it should complement the slide's composition—don't place it too close to any other slide elements or to the edge of the slide.

FIGURE 16.8

The Picture toolbar appears when you insert a picture into your slide. Use its tools to adjust the color, brightness, and contrast of the picture, as well as to cut away unnecessary content.

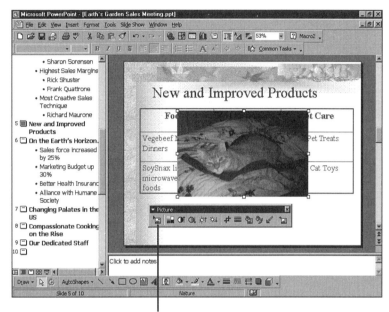

Click the Format Picture icon to access a dialog box in which the picture size and position can be adjusted.

 If there are any parts of a photograph that you don't want, use the Crop tool. With the Crop tool activated, drag from the handle closest to the spot you want to cut away. Drag toward the center of the image until the dashed line appears where you want the new edge of the image to be. You might have to crop from more than one side or from a corner to cut away everything you want to get rid of. Figure 16.9 shows the image in place, moved, resized, and with portions of the picture cropped away.

Note

The cropped portions of the picture aren't deleted, they're merely removed from view. You can always bring the cropped portions back by using the Crop tool and dragging the handles outward. The original file remains intact no matter what you do to it on the slide.

Figure 16.9

To avoid excessive shrinking of an image to make it fit on the slide, cut away unwanted content.

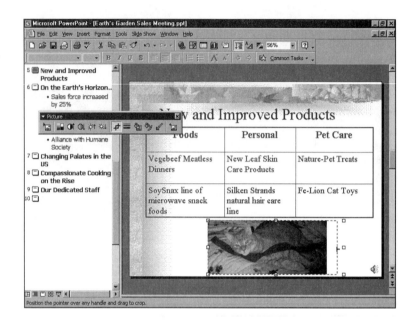

Using PowerPoint's Drawing Tools

PowerPoint's drawing tools are not for creating elaborate or complex drawings. Their simplicity works to your advantage, however, because they don't require you to be an artist or especially coordinated in your use of the mouse in order to make effective use of them.

Before you begin using the Drawing toolbar tools, it's a good idea to identify each one and learn more about their use. Table 16.1 lists the Drawing tools.

TABLE 16.1 THE DRAWING TOOLBAR

Button Name	Button function
Draw ▾ Draw	Click this button to displaya menu of commands that enable youto manipulate the placement of andrelationship between your drawn objects.
▷ Select Objects	Use this arrow tool to click ondrawn objects. Using this tool tells Excel that you're dealing with your drawn objects and not the work sheet's cell content.

Button Name	Button function
Free Rotate	Click this tool and then the object you want to rotate, and drag the object's handles in the direction in which you want to spin the object.
AutoShapes ▼ AutoShapes	Click this button to display a list of AutoShape categories, such as Basic Shapes and Flowchart. From these categories, choose shapes from a palette of drawing tools.
Line	Use this tool to draw straight lines of any length. You can later forma the lines to varying lengths and styles, as well as add arrowheads to make the line point to something.
Arrow	If you know your line will be an arrow, draw one using this tool. You can later select arrowheads for one or both ends of the line.
Rectangle	This tool enables you to draw simple rectangles and squares.
Oval	Draw elliptical shapes and true circles with this tool.
Text Box	When you need a text object that can be placed on top of your cells and placed anywhere on the worksheet, use this tool to create the box and type the text.
Insert WordArt	Create artistic text headlines and banners with this tool. The WordArt program, with its own toolbars and menus, opens to give you the capability to create text objects with a wide variety of color, shape, and fill options.
Insert Clip Art	Click this button to view and insert objects from a categorized list of clip art images that were installed with Office 2000.
Fill Color	Choose from a palette of solid colors to fill your drawn shape.
Line Color	Click this button to display a palette of colors that you can use to color your line, arrow, or the outline of a shape.
Font Color	Apply a color to text box text or to text within your work sheet cells.
Line Style	Choose from various line weights and styles for double and triple lines.

16

continues

TABLE 16.1 CONTINUED

Button Name	Button function
▦ Dash Style	If you want your line to be dashed, dotted, or a combination thereof, click this button and select a style from the palette.
⇄ Arrow Style	Turn a simple line into an arrow, or change the arrowheads on your existing arrow line. Choose from ten different styles.
▦ Shadow	Choose from 20 different shadow settings, each with a different light source and angle. Applying a shadow gives your object depth, and it can be applied to shapes or lines.
◪ 3D	Apply up to 20 different 3D effects to your shapes. Unlike a shadow, which merely repeats the object in a flat 2D state behind the original, 3 settings add sides and depth to your object, and shade the sides for a true 3D effect.

Slides 7 and 8 will be enhanced in this section as you add a shape to Slide 8 and an arrow to Slide 7. Feel free to experiment with other shapes and lines on the other slides in the presentation, remembering to place them so that they don't compete with other slide elements, and so that they contribute to the effectiveness of the slide's message.

Drawing Shapes and Lines

Drawing closed geometric shapes (AutoShapes) is very simple. Select the shape you want to draw by clicking the Rectangle or Oval button or by choosing the shape from an AutoShapes palette, and then click and drag on the slide to draw the shape. Figure 16.10 shows the AutoShapes menu and the Stars and Banners palette.

FIGURE 16.10

Choose from more than 200 different AutoShapes, from the six different shape palettes on the AutoShapes menu.

When drawing your shape, drag away from your starting point in a diagonal direction. The distance from your starting point and the angle at which you drag determine the dimensions of your shape. Figure 16.11 shows a star drawn on Slide 8.

FIGURE 16.11

This star will soon contain text, doubling its effectiveness on the slide.

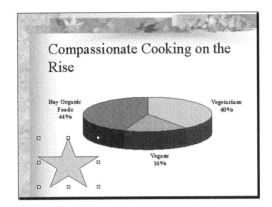

16

> **Tip**
>
> **NEW TERM** You can control the vertical and horizontal ratio (also known as the *aspect ratio*) by pressing the Shift key as you drag to draw a shape. Rectangles are drawn as perfect squares, Ovals as circles; other AutoShapes are drawn with an equal height and width. Be sure to release the mouse before you release the Shift key when you're finished drawing the shape or the ratio is lost.

Drawing lines is equally simple. Select the Line or Arrow tool from the Drawing toolbar, and then click and drag away from your starting point. The lines (for Lines or Arrows) remain straight even though they might appear jagged onscreen if the line isn't drawn at an exact 90-degree angle.

Figure 16.12 shows an arrow drawn on Slide 7.

FIGURE 16.12

Use lines and arrows to emphasize or draw attention to important information.

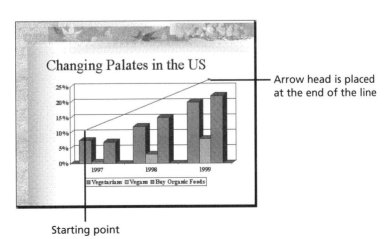

You can adjust the thickness of your selected line by clicking the Line Style button and choosing a thickness from the palette (see Figure 16.13).

FIGURE 16.13

If the line must be seen from a great distance (during the slideshow), make it thick enough to stand out.

 Note

When you thicken the line on an arrow, the arrow head also becomes larger.

 Tip

You don't have to stick with the default arrow head—you can use the Arrow Style button and choose to have heads on both ends of the arrow line, or you can select a circle or diamond tip for the line.

Manipulating Drawn Objects

Depending on where you drew your shape or line and how well you controlled the mouse, the placement and size of your shape might be just what you wanted. In most cases, however, the placement and size of the shape need to be adjusted.

Resizing shapes and lines employs the same techniques that are used to resize clip art or other graphics—drag the item to move it, and use its handles to resize it. Figure 16.14 shows the star on Slide 8 as it is being resized.

FIGURE 16.14

Keep the composition of your entire slide in mind as you resize your shape—don't make it overwhelmingly large or so small that it isn't noticed.

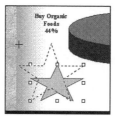

Resizing a line is very simple—drag the handles at either end of the line to lengthen or shorten the line. You can also drag the handles (one at a time) to change the direction in which a line or arrow points. Figure 16.15 shows the arrow on Slide 7 being redirected and lengthened at the same time.

FIGURE 16.15

Change the length and direction of your arrow line at the same time by dragging a handle.

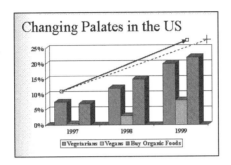

16

Adding Text to AutoShapes

Your AutoShapes can perform two tasks: add graphical interest to your slides and provide information. To make your AutoShapes informative, add text. By typing when an AutoShape is selected, you insert text into the shape, thus turning it into a text box. By default, the text is centered both horizontally and vertically within the shape, and the font is dictated by the Design Template you're using for the presentation.

Figure 16.16 shows text in the star on Slide 8.

FIGURE 16.16

Fill your AutoShapes with text, but not too much. Stick to single words and short phrases

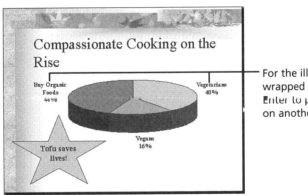

For the illusion of wrapped text, press Enter to place a word on another line

Note

If you must type more than a short string of text into your shape, choose Format, AutoShape while the shape is selected; on the Text Box tab, use the Word wrap text in AutoShape or Resize AutoShape to fit text options. You can apply these options before or after you've typed the text into the shape.

 Tip

Format the text in the shape by selecting the entire shape and using the Formatting toolbar's text formatting tools.

Changing the Appearance of Shapes and Lines

The Design Template you're using for your presentation dictates the default fill color for the shapes you draw (lines and arrows are always black by default). You can change the color of these items, as well as their style, by using the Drawing toolbar's buttons for formatting shapes and lines.

To apply a new fill or outline color, or to use the other Drawing toolbar style buttons, follow these steps:

1. Select the shape or line you want to change.
2. Click the Fill Color, Line Color, Line Style, Dash Style, or Arrow Style buttons on the toolbar. Each one displays a palette of choices for you to apply to the selected object. Figure 16.17 shows the Fill Color palette.

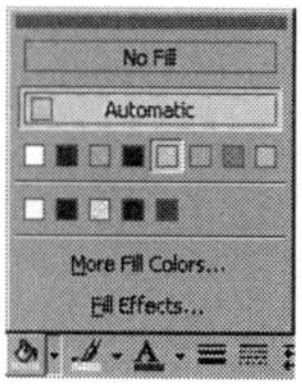

FIGURE 16.17

Choose a color to fill the selected object. The Fill Effects option opens a dialog box, through which you can apply gradient, patterned, and picture fills.

3. Make your selection from the palette. The object changes accordingly, and you can apply another effect; or you can deselect the item by clicking on an empty spot on the slide.

16

Tip

Do drawn objects overlap? Objects are stacked in the order in which they were drawn. If you want to change their stacking order, choose Draw, Order, and choose the direction in which you want to move the selected item in the stack—to the front, the back, or one layer at a time (Bring Forward or Bring Backward).

Note

The Shadow and 3D buttons on the toolbar work better with shapes than with lines and arrows. Applying a shadow or 3D effect gives your slide visual depth, and when the slide is displayed onscreen or projected onto a screen or wall, this effect can give a much more interesting and "high-tech" look to your presentation.

Tip

If your slide contains several drawn objects, you might want to group them so that their relative placement cannot be accidentally changed. Select the group of items by clicking on each one with the Shift key depressed, and then choose Draw, Group. After they are grouped, the items move as a group if you drag any one of the items. Furthermore, any formatting that is applied to one item in the group is automatically applied to them all.

Preparing a Slideshow

The purpose of creating PowerPoint slides is to create a slideshow. The slideshow can be output to transparencies (sheets of plastic), 35mm slides, or paper. These manual slideshows don't allow for any animation, nor do they enable you to incorporate sound into your show unless recorded sound such as music or a speech is played in the room during the show. If you don't have a projection panel (a device that projects your monitor's display onto a wall or screen), these might be your only options for running a show.

If, however, you have a projection panel or a large monitor that can be attached to your computer, you can run an animated slideshow. Furthermore, if you have a sound card and speakers on your computer, you can integrate sounds into your presentation, set to play at specific times during the show. PowerPoint was designed for this type of multimedia slideshow, combining the visual (charts, graphics, animation, video) effects with sound. A multimedia presentation is much more effective than a static show (transparencies, 35mm slides) because it involves more of the viewers' senses and enables you to do more things to keep their attention.

Applying Slide Transitions

The first and easiest way to add movement and sound to your presentation is to apply slide transitions. A slide transition is the animated effect that occurs as the slide appears onscreen. Slide transitions are applied to your slides in Slide Sorter view, as shown in Figure 16.18.

Click this list to see your transition choices

FIGURE 16.18

Slide Sorter view offers a birds-eye view of your entire presentation, as well as tools for selecting and applying transition effects to your slides.

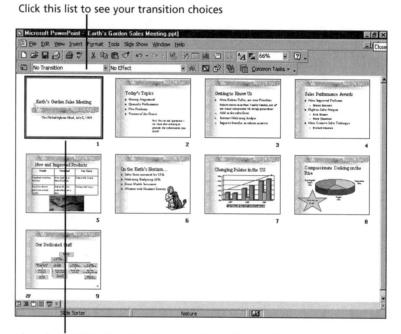

The selected slide (to which the transition will apply) has a dark border

You can apply a transition to all your slides at once by pressing Ctrl+A to select all your slides, or to smaller groups of slides by pressing Shift and clicking on each slide you want to select. Some people try to apply a different transition to each slide, but that's not advisable—the variety of transitions becomes distracting to the audience.

After selecting the slides to which you want to apply a transition, follow these steps:

1. Click the Slide Transitions Effects button to see a list of the available transitions. There are 40 different transitions (see Figure 16.19).

2. Make your selection from the list, and note that a symbol appears beneath the selected slides, indicating that a transition has been set (see Figure 16.20).

FIGURE 16.19

Choose an interesting visual effect from the list of transitions.

FIGURE 16.20

It's easy to forget which slides have transitions set. The symbol beneath the slide helps you remember, and if you select the slide, the selected transition is displayed on the toolbar.

Indicates that a transition has been set for this slide.

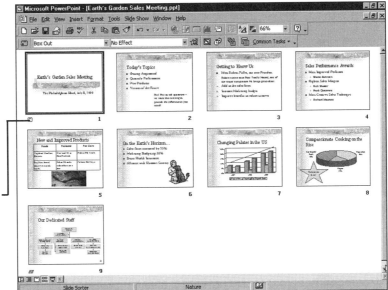

3. Continue to select slides and apply transitions from this list until you have applied transition effects to all your slides.

> **Tip**
>
> When choosing which transition effect to apply, remember that you can evoke a certain feeling in your audience by virtue of the transition you choose. Transitions that have motion going up or to the right evoke a positive feeling. Transitions that move to the left or down on the slide evoke negativity.

 To have greater control over your transition effects as they are applied to your slides, you can also use the Slide Transition button. This button opens the Slide Transition dialog box (shown in Figure 16.21), through which you can preview the transition effects, choose the speed at which they occur, and choose a sound to accompany them.

FIGURE 16.21

Watch the bull terrier turn into a key as your transition effect is previewed.

Note

The Advance option in the Slide Transition dialog box gives you the capability to choose what triggers the transition—a mouse click is the default, but you can choose to have the slide appear Automatically after a certain number of seconds. Don't use this latter option, however, unless you are willing to relinquish control over the pace of your presentation and risk the slides progressing before you're finished discussing them—timings are best used when the slideshow is self-running, with no human presenter.

After making your choices in the Slide Transition dialog box, you can click Apply to apply the selection to the selected slides, or you can choose Apply to All to apply the selection to every slide in your presentation, regardless of which slides are selected at the time.

Using either the Slide Transition Effect list or the Slide Transition dialog box, apply transitions to every slide in the presentation.

Tip

It can be very effective to apply a single transition to the entire presentation and then go back through your slides and choose specific slides that will have a different transition effect, based on their content. For example, you might apply Dissolve or Fade through Black to a slide that follows a discussion of old procedures or last year's data.

Animating Bulleted Text

Your animation options are not limited to the transitions that occur as new slides appear onscreen. You can also animate your bulleted text so that the bullet points (and their sub-bullets) appear one at a time. This has two benefits—it adds more motion to your slides, and it enables you to control what topic your audience is reading and thinking about as you give your presentation.

NEW TERM If you have five bullet points on a slide and they all come up at once, each person in the audience will be reading the entire list as you begin speaking about the first item. In addition, if any item on the list is of personal interest to a given audience member, he or she might be dwelling on that topic as you discuss other things. Applying Preset Animations (also known as *bullet builds*) to your slide text can keep people from seeing or thinking about a topic until you're ready to discuss it.

To apply Preset Animations (bullet builds) to your slides, follow these steps:

1. Select the first slide that contains bulleted text (even if you've turned bullets off or applied numbers to the list of paragraphs or lines, the text is still considered "bulleted").

2. Click the Preset Animations list (see Figure 16.22), and choose the way in which you want the bullet points to appear on screen. Fly from Left is a popular choice because the text moves to the right, which has a subliminally positive effect.

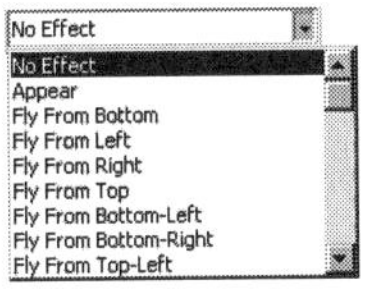

FIGURE 16.22

Choose from many different build options in the Preset Animations list.

3. Continue to select slides that contain bulleted text, and apply Preset Animations to each one. A preview of the effect you've chosen appears on the slide, and a symbol appears beneath the slides to which you've applied a build (see Figure 16.23).

Tip

Think about the nature of your bulleted text. If the bullet points list names or information in a prioritized order, you might consider Fly from Top or Fly from Bottom to cause the bullet points to stack onscreen as you click your mouse, to bring each line onscreen one at a time.

Customizing Animation and Sounds

The slide transitions and bullet builds you apply work based on certain defaults, such as the speed at which they occur or, in the case of bullet builds, how much text builds on each mouse click. You can adjust these settings using the Custom Animation dialog box, which is accessed through the Animation Effects toolbar.

FIGURE 16.23

Symbols indicate the slides to which you've applied effects. In a large presentation, this is very helpful.

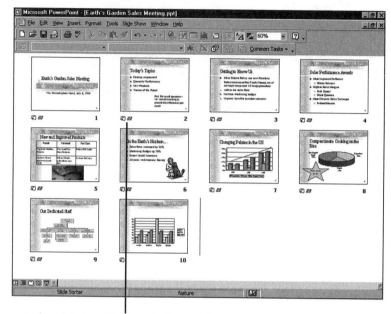

Both a slide transition and bullet build set

To access this toolbar and the controls for customizing each slide's animations and sound, follow these steps:

1. Switch to Normal or Slide view for the first slide you want to customize.

 2. Click the Animation Effects button on the Formatting toolbar to display the Animation Effects toolbar (see Figure 16.24).

FIGURE 16.24

When you're ready to animate the elements on your slide, activate the Animation Effects toolbar.

3. Click the first element on the slide that you want to animate, or for which you want to customize the existing animation settings.

Tip

To make selecting the individual items that are to be animated on the slide easier, you might want to switch to Slide view or increase the Zoom percentage in Normal view so that you're working with a larger view of the slide.

16

 4. Choose an animation effect: Drive In, Flying, Camera, or any of the other animation effects that are available while the slide element is selected.

 5. To choose the timing for this effect and the sound that is to accompany it, click the Custom Animation button. The Custom Animation dialog box opens, as shown in Figure 16.25.

FIGURE 16.25

Access more options for when and how to animate the selected element. You can also choose from a variety of sounds to accompany the animation effect.

The item you're currently animating is checked here

Default sound associated with the selected animation effect

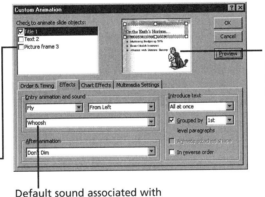

Click Preview to see the effect you've chosen demonstrated in this sample box

6. Using the four tabs in this dialog box, customize the following aspects of your slide's animation and sound:

- **Order & Timing**—Choose when this particular element is to appear onscreen. In the case of slide titles, it needs to be the first thing to appear. You can also select what triggers the animation or sound—a mouse click or a certain number of elapsed seconds.

- **Effects**—Choose which sound is to accompany the animation, or choose a different animation than the one you've already set. In the case of text, you can also choose how much text is animated—will the slide title, for example, appear one word at a time, or will the entire title appear all at once?

Tip

The Effects tab offers you the capability to dim bullet points as new points are displayed. This gives you further control over the attention of your audience, keeping them from dwelling on a previous bullet point after you've gone on.

- **Chart Effects**—If the element you're animating is a chart, you can animate its appearance on the slide, and even choose to have individual boxes, bars, or pie slices appear one at a time by choosing by Elements in Series from the Introduce chart elements list. The Chart Effects tab also enables you to choose a sound to accompany your chart animations.

- **Multimedia Settings**—If your slide has sound or video objects on it, you can use this tab to choose when and how they'll play while the slide is onscreen.

Note

To insert a sound (.WAV file) or a video clip (.AVI or .MPEG file), you can choose Insert, Object, and click the Create from file option. Browse to the drive or folder that contains the sound or video clip you want to use, and click OK. After it is inserted, the object appears as an icon on the slide; you can double-click that icon during the slideshow when you want it to play, or you can use the Multimedia Settings tab to customize and automate its use in the slideshow.

7. After making your selections on one or more of the Custom Animation tabs, click OK to put your selections into effect and close the dialog box.

Note

 As you make your selections in the Custom Animation dialog box, you'll see a preview of the effects in the slide sample in the dialog box. After you've applied them and closed the dialog box, you can click the Slide Show view button to run the selected slide. Press Esc when all the slide's elements have appeared onscreen and you've checked all your effects to make sure they're what you want.

Testing and Running Your Slideshow

When all your transitions, builds, and customizations have been set, you're ready to run your slideshow. Of course, you don't want to wait until your audience is in their seats to run it for the first time; you want to test it many times—preferably running some of these test shows in the room where the show will be given in order to test visibility and acoustics—and make any adjustments to the show before you do your final show for an audience.

It's easiest to run your slideshow if you start in Slide Sorter view. This makes it possible for you to choose the starting slide or choose to Hide (skip) one or more of the slides in the presentation when the show is run.

To test your slideshow, follow these steps:

1. In Slide Sorter view, click once on the slide that is to be the first slide in the show. For your presentation, the first slide is Slide 1.

2. Click the Slideshow button or choose Slide Show, View Show. The shortcut key is F5.

3. The first slide appears onscreen, including any transitions, builds, and animation effects you applied. If you chose to have your animations occur automatically, the timings that you set apply. If you left the default setting (On mouse click) in place, you'll have to click the mouse for each animated element to appear in the order you specified.

4. At the end of the first slide (when all its elements have appeared), click your mouse to move to the next slide.

5. Continue clicking through your slides, checking to see that the slide elements appear in the order you want, and that the transitions, animations, and sounds are working properly. After the last slide, PowerPoint returns automatically to Slide Sorter view.

Tip

> To jump out of the show and return to Slide Sorter view (or whatever view you were in when you started the show), press Esc. In addition, if you started the show from Slide or Normal view, the slide that was showing when the show was ended prematurely is displayed in that view.

16

Automating Your Slideshow

Throughout the animation customization process, you have the opportunity to automate your slideshow—you can choose how many seconds are to elapse between animated elements, or you can opt to have the elements appear only when you click your mouse. You can achieve a greater degree of automation through two other methods:

- **Rehearse slide timings**—In Slide Sorter view, click the Rehearse Timings button and run your show. PowerPoint records the amount of time each slide is onscreen, as well as the amount of time between animated elements. Go through your entire show, running it at the pace at which you want it to go when it runs on its own. At the end, click Yes in response to the prompt that asks if you want to record and use the timings you've rehearsed. Figure 16.26 shows a slide onscreen with the Rehearse Timings timer running.

Timer bar controls for pausing, going back to the previous slide, and repeating the current slide or element

FIGURE 16.26

Don't go too fast as you move through your show. If you go too fast, the audience might not have time to read each slide and absorb all the information.

Time for the last element activated on current slide

Total time for the show so far

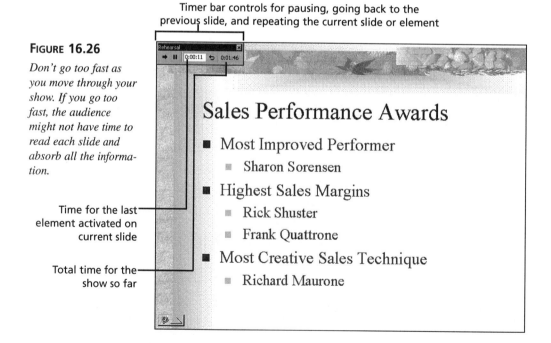

- **Record a macro**—Before running your show, choose Tools, Macro, Record New Macro. Give your macro a name, and click OK to begin recording. Start your show, and use your mouse to move through the slides and their elements. At the end of the show, allow PowerPoint to return to Sorter view (or press Esc to end it on a particular slide), and then click the Stop button (see Figure 16.27). You can then run the show by invoking the macro (click Tools, Macro, and then choose the macro from the list).

FIGURE 16.27

Creating a macro builds a program that contains each of the tasks you perform while the macro is recording.

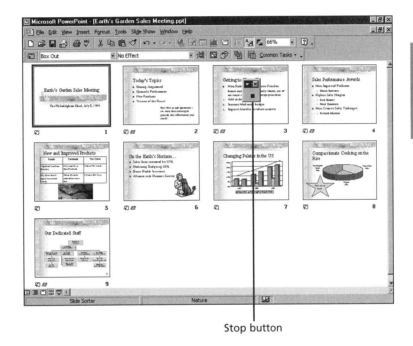

Stop button

By far, the Rehearse Timings approach is easiest. You can rehearse your timings repeatedly, saving the new set of timings each time.

 Caution

> When recording your timings for a show that will be given with a live speaker, be sure to allow enough time for the speaker to discuss the slide's content, and allow for delays—someone in the audience coughing, questions—so that the slides don't progress before the speaker is ready.

Recording a Narration

If your presentation will be self-running—with timings set for each slide—you might want to completely remove the human element by recording a narration to accompany the slideshow. This is especially helpful for people who have stage fright; or, if you don't like the sound of your own voice, you can have someone with a great voice record your narration for you!

16

Note

> You must have a sound card and speakers on your computer, as well as a microphone, in order to record a narration.

To record a narration for your slideshow, you'll need notes if you'll be doing the narration, or a complete script if you're asking someone who is unfamiliar with the content to provide their voice for the narration. Also, make sure that your microphone and speakers are on and functioning properly before you begin recording. After you've prepared these tools, you can begin:

1. In Slide Sorter view, click once on the first slide in the show.

2. Choose Slide Show, Record Narration. The Record Narration dialog box opens, as shown in Figure 16.28.

FIGURE 16.28

The current settings for your recording equipment are displayed in the Record Narration dialog box.

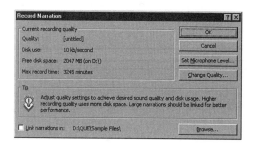

3. Click OK to begin recording. The slideshow begins onscreen, and you can begin speaking.

4. Click your mouse to move through the slides' elements, moving at a pace that matches your narration—as long as you're discussing a certain element, that element needs to be onscreen.

5. When your show and narration are complete, press Esc; or, if you're ending with the actual last slide, allow the show to end naturally. After the last slide, a prompt appears (see Figure 16.29). Click Yes to save the slide timings, along with your narration.

Now that your narration has been recorded and saved, it plays as soon as you start your show. Notice that a small speaker icon appears in the lower right corner of each slide (switch to Normal or Slide view to see it). This indicates that narration has been recorded (see Figure 16.30).

FIGURE 16.29

The timings that are set during your narration override any slide timings you set or rehearsed previously.

FIGURE 16.30

You can drag the narration icon to any position on the slide if its default location interferes with any of your slide's visual elements.

Narration sound icon

Caution

If you make a mistake during the recording of your narration, or if you later change the order or content of your slides (thus making the current narration inappropriate), you must rerecord the entire narration. Save the recording process until your slides are completed and you're certain things won't change. When you record it, work from notes and keep outside distractions and noise to a minimum.

Saving Your Presentation as a Show

If your monitor is attached to an overhead projection device or a larger monitor for displaying your presentation to a group in a large room, it might be a good idea to save your presentation as a show (as opposed to the normal presentation format). What does saving your presentation as a show do for you? It saves you from having to open PowerPoint, open the presentation, and start the slideshow. When a presentation is saved as a show, all you have to do is open the file (from within the Windows Explorer, My Computer, or from a desktop icon that represents the show file), and the show begins.

To save your presentation as a show, follow these steps:

1. Run your slideshow to make sure that everything works as required—animations, sounds, the order of slides—and record your slide timings, if needed. All these details are saved as part of the show file.

2. With your presentation open and displayed (in any view) onscreen, choose File, Save As. The Save As dialog box opens.

3. In the Save as type list, select PowerPoint Show (.pps). The list of file types is shown in Figure 16.31.

FIGURE 16.31

Choose the PowerPoint Show format from the list of file types in the Save As dialog box.

4. Give the file a name (if you want it to have a different name than the presentation file), and click Save.

> If you're running the slideshow from the computer on which you're saving the show, choose to save it to the Desktop instead of to the folder where the presentation file is saved. As a result, you'll only have to double-click the show icon on the desktop to start your slideshow.

Using the PowerPoint Viewer

The PowerPoint Viewer is a program that enables people who don't have PowerPoint on their computers to run a PowerPoint slideshow. This makes it easy for you to send a sales presentation on disk to a client who might or might not have PowerPoint, or to run your show at a location where you don't have control over what software is on the computer (such as a seminar held at a conference center). If you're using a laptop to run the slideshow, you can save hard disk space by loading just your presentation and the PowerPoint Viewer program—no need to have the entire PowerPoint program installed.

The PowerPoint Viewer (Ppview32.exe) is on your Office 2000 CD-ROM, or it might have been installed on your computer when Office was set up. If it's on your computer, it will be in the Program Files\Msoffice\Office\Xlators folder.

If you don't find the Viewer program in that folder on your hard drive, check the CD-ROM in the Pfiles\MSOffice\Office\Xlators folder.

After you locate the program, you can copy it to the computer that will be used to run the slideshow, or you can use the Pack and Go Wizard to place the Viewer program and your presentation on a disk that you give to your client or that you take with you to run a slideshow on any Windows 95 or 98 computer.

To use the Pack and Go Wizard, follow these steps:

1. Open the presentation you want to place on disk with the PowerPoint Viewer.

2. Choose File, Pack and Go. The Pack and Go Wizard starts, as shown in Figure 16.32.

FIGURE 16.32

Use the Pack and Go Wizard to place your presentation and any linked files on a disk with the PowerPoint Viewer program.

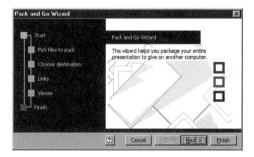

3. Follow the Wizard's prompts—selecting the presentations to pack, choosing the drive on which to place the files and Viewer program, and directing the Wizard to the location of the Viewer program.

4. After choosing to include the Viewer (the fifth step in the Wizard), click Finish. The Viewer program and the selected presentations are packed onto the disk.

Note

If these two files exceed the size of a single high density disk, you'll be prompted to insert a second disk.

Tip

Can't find the file on your computer and you've lost your Office 2000 CD-ROM? Try the PowerPoint Web site at www.microsoft.com/powerPoint.

When you (or your client) want to run the presentation, merely open the file on the disk; the PowerPoint Viewer starts, running your slideshow onscreen.

Caution

It's a good idea to enclose instructions if you send the disk to a client or to someone who might not be familiar with computers in general or PowerPoint in particular. If there are no timings set for your show, the recipient needs to know that he or she must click to move through the slides and slide elements, and how to end the show.

Summary

Today you learned how to turn the presentation that you created on Day 15 into a multimedia slideshow—adding clip art, photographs, and drawn objects to the presentation and then creating movement and integrating sound. The animations and automation techniques you learned will enable you to turn a simple series of static slides into a slideshow that grabs and keeps the attention of your audience.

Q&A

Q Do the additions of graphics and the use of animation and sound increase the size of the presentation file?

A Yes. For example, the presentation you created on Day 15 should have been approximately 250KB. After the addition of the graphical slide elements, animation, sound, and automation (timings and narration), the size of the file exceeds 1MB.

Q Are there any drawbacks to adding animation and sound to a presentation?

A Only if you add too many of them. Use them only where they are effective, and try not to animate more than two items per slide. Sound also needs to be used sparingly, unless your audience is particularly animated themselves or you expect to have trouble keeping everyone's attention.

Q You only used sounds and clip art that comes with Office 2000. Can I use *any* sound files and graphic files with PowerPoint?

A Yes. If you find other .WAV files on the Internet or from other sources, feel free to use them. You can Browse to the folder or drive on which you're storing the files from within the Custom Animation dialog box. As far as clip art and graphics are concerned, you can insert virtually any graphic file, assuming that the format is one of the many formats represented on the Files of type list in the Insert Picture dialog box.

16

Workshop

The section that follows is a quick quiz about the day. If you have any problems answering any of the questions, see the section that follows the quiz for all the answers.

Quiz

1. Describe at least two ways to insert clip art onto a slide.

2. When drawing AutoShapes, how do you keep the width and height equal?

3. True or False: After you crop an image (clip art, graphic, photograph), the portions you cut away are deleted.

4. True or False: If you don't apply a slide transition for your slide, it won't come up during the presentation.

5. Describe the benefits of applying Preset Animations (bullet builds) to bulleted text.

6. True or False: You can only run a PowerPoint presentation on a computer that has PowerPoint running on it.

Quiz Answers

1. You can insert a clip art image in any one of the following ways:
   - Click the Insert ClipArt button on the Drawing toolbar
   - Choose Insert, Picture, ClipArt
   - Choose one of the Slide Layouts with a clip art element, and double-click that object on the slide in Slide or Normal view.

2. To maintain equal height and width while drawing an AutoShape, press and hold the Shift key while drawing the shape. Be sure to release the mouse before the key when you're finished drawing the shape.

3. False. The complete graphic file remains on the slide—the cropping procedure merely masks portions of it so that they don't show onscreen.

4. False. A slide without a transition applied to it appears during the slideshow—it just won't come up with any interesting animated effect. To keep a slide from appearing in the show, right-click it in Sorter view and choose Hide from the short-cut menu.

5. Building your bulleted text one paragraph or line at a time controls the attention of your audience. Rather than having them reading the entire slide while you talk about the first point, you show them only the point you're discussing. You can also dim previous points to discourage anyone from dwelling on a topic you've already discussed.

6. False. With the PowerPoint Viewer, a program that is found on the Office 2000 CD-ROM (or on your computer if the program was installed with Office 2000), you can pack the Viewer and your presentation on a disk to run on any computer that is running Windows 95/98, even if PowerPoint is not installed.

WEEK 3

DAY 17

Creating a Report with Office

The first 16 days that you've spent learning Office 2000 have prepared you for today's project. What you've learned about Word, Excel, Access, and PowerPoint will now be put to use as you create a document that brings content from all four applications into one file. By the end of today, you'll know how to tie text, data, and graphic images together to create a professional-looking, dynamic document, complete with links to the source data so that the document remains up-to-date as your data is edited over time. Specifically, you'll be performing the following tasks:

- Using Word's Outline view to create the backbone of the report
- Bringing in Excel and Access data and linking it to the report
- Using an Excel chart and a PowerPoint slide in the report to create consistency with presentations
- Adding graphic images to the report
- Using WordArt to create a title logo
- Working with document setup and printing options to create a two-sided, bindable document

Getting Started with an Outline

The first step in any large project is to map out what tasks need to be performed. In the case of a large document, that process includes creating an outline of what topics are to be covered in the document, and in what order they'll be covered. Although this sounds like extra work, if you do it right, the outline can become the backbone of the document—the topic headings and subheadings in the outline can and will become the headings and subheadings throughout the document.

Word will be used to create the document, and the document will contain text typed in Word, Excel data and charts, Access data, and a PowerPoint slide. The Excel and Access data will come from files you'll find on the CD that accompanies this book, and the report will be for the company for which you created a presentation on Days 15, "Developing a PowerPoint Presentation," and 16, "Creating a Multimedia Presentation," Earth's Garden. In addition, clip art will be used to give the document a graphical look. The outline will provide the spine to which all these components are attached.

Working in Word's Outline View

When building an outline in Word, it's best to use Outline view. You can work in Normal or Print Layout view and use tabs to manually assign the rank of items in the outline, but Outline view provides a much more effective environment for the task, as shown in Figure 17.1.

Outline view gives you the tools you'll need to set up the topical sections of your report, and it makes it easy for you to change the order and hierarchy of your topics. Figure 17.2 shows the outline you want to create to begin the report.

 To create this outline, switch to Outline view in a new, blank document (go to View, Outline or click the Outline View button), and follow these steps:

1. Type the first heading, Sales Goals, and press Enter.

2. Press Tab to demote the next line, which will be a subheading. Type Increase Sales through Education. Press Enter. You can also use the Demote button to reduce the rank of the line before or after typing the text.

3. Type Motivate Sales Force through Improved Compensation. Press Enter.

4. Type Develop Informative and Environmentally-Friendly Packaging. Press Enter.

5. Press Shift+Tab to promote the new line to a first-level heading. Type Educational Opportunities. You can also use the Promote button to raise the rank of the new line before or after typing the text.

Use the Promote
and Demote buttons
to move items up
and down in rank

Click the
numbers to
assign rank
to selected
text

FIGURE 17.1

Type your heading text and assign it a rank— level 1 being the highest, level 7 the lowest.

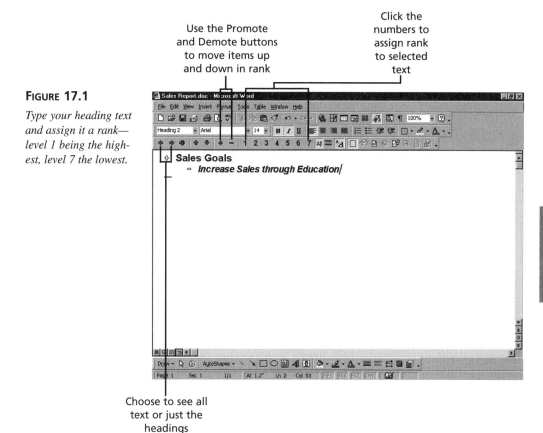

Choose to see all
text or just the
headings

6. Press Enter and then Tab. Type Advertising.

7. Press Enter and type Alliances with Schools.

8. Press Enter and then Tab. Type Elementary and Grade School Education.

9. Press Enter. Type High School and University Education.

10. Press Enter and then Shift+Tab to promote the new line. Type Direct Contact with Consumers.

11. Press Enter and then Tab. Type Alliance with Supermarkets and Small Groceries.

12. Press Enter and type Seminars at Bookstores and through Alternative Healthcare Locations.

13. Press Enter and then Shift+Tab twice to promote the new line to a first-level heading.

14. Type Sales Motivation. Press Enter, and then Tab.

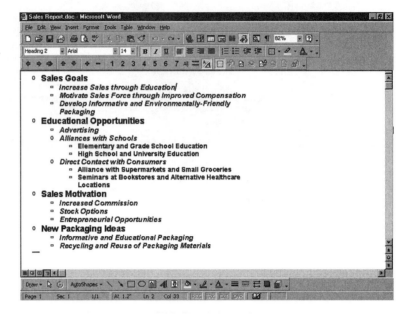

FIGURE 17.2

Type the list and then rank the topics as indicated.

15. Type Increased Commission, and then press Enter.

16. Type Stock Options. Press Enter.

17. Type Entrepreneurial Opportunities. Press Enter.

18. Press Shift+Tab twice to promote the new line to first-level rank.

19. Type New Packaging Ideas. Press Enter and then Tab.

20. Type Informative and Educational Packaging. Press Enter.

21. Type Recycling and Reuse of Packaging Materials.

22. Save the file as Sales Report. Don't type the file extension (.doc)—let Word apply it for you.

The outline is complete. Each topic you typed is, by virtue of its rank, a heading in the document.

When you switch back to Normal or Print Layout view (by clicking View, Normal or View, Print Layout) to begin entering text under each heading, you'll notice that the Heading 1 style is applied to the first-level topics, the Heading 2 style is applied to the second-level topics, and Heading 3 is applied to the third-level topics. Figure 17.3 shows the outline in Print Layout view.

Tip You can quickly change views by using the Print Layout View | or Normal View buttons in the lower-left corner of the Word widow.

FIGURE 17.3

Level numbers in Outline view match Heading style numbers in Normal or Print Layout view.

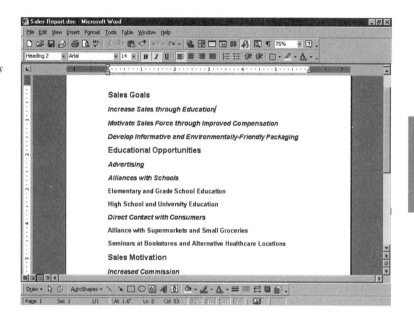

17

Tip Normal ▼ You can switch back to Outline view at any time to change the rank of topics or to add new ones. You can also promote and demote headings by applying higher- or lower-ranked styles from the Style button on the Formatting toolbar.

Building the Basic Report Document

After building your outline, you can begin to flesh out the text of your document. You can type that text directly under each heading, or you can insert text from existing documents via the Clipboard or by using the Insert, File command. In either case, you'll end up with the informative and descriptive paragraphs that make up the foundation of your report. You can also add information in the form of tables from Excel and Access and charts from Excel.

Note

> Don't forget to number your pages and put any important information—
> such as the date and the title of the report—in a header or footer. The use
> of headers and footers was covered on Day 5, "Improving Document
> Function."

To copy existing text from another document, follow these steps:

1. Open the document that contains the text you want to reuse in your report.

2. Using your mouse or keyboard, select the portions of the text that you want to
   reuse, as shown in Figure 17.4.

FIGURE 17.4

*Use text selections
from any documents
(Word- or other appli-
cation-based) and copy
them to the Clipboard
for pasting into your
report.*

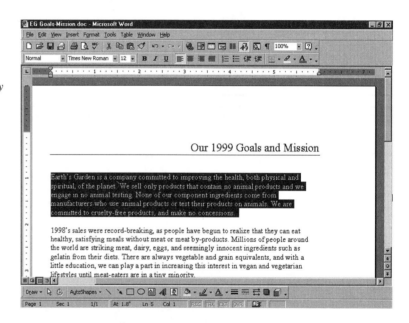

 3. Choose Edit, Copy, or click the Copy button on the Standard toolbar.

4. Switch to or open the Sales Report document, and click to position your cursor
   where the copied text is to be pasted.

 5. Choose Edit, Paste, or click the Paste button. The text is pasted into the Sales
   Report document, and you can begin formatting it as needed.

> **Tip**
>
> To position your cursor between headings in the Sales Report document, click at the end of the heading that is to precede your pasted content and press Enter. A blank line appears beneath the heading, and the style for that line is set to Normal. This is a function of the Heading styles.

If you need to insert an entire existing document rather than just a portion of one, follow these steps:

1. Position your cursor at the point in the Sales Report document where you want to insert the file.

2. Choose Insert, File. The Insert File dialog box opens, as shown in Figure 17.5.

FIGURE 17.5

Select the file that you want to insert in its entirety.

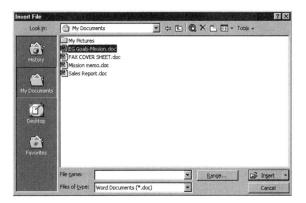

17

3. Navigate to the folder that contains the file you want to insert (if it's not in the default My Documents folder), and select the file.

4. Click Insert or double-click the file. The text of the inserted file appears in the Sales Report document.

This technique can also be used to insert files other than Word documents. For example, if you have a word processing document created in WordPerfect or Lotus WordPro, you can save that document as a text file (.txt) in its native application, and then choose that format from the Files of type list in the Insert File dialog box. You might lose some formatting by saving your original file as a text file, but the text content is saved, and inserting the file in this way saves you the trouble of retyping the content of the non-Word file.

> **Tip**
>
> If the document you want to use contains a lot of formatting or graphic content that you don't want to lose, save it in Rich Text (.rtf) format. This needs to be done from within the application that was used to create the file.

> **Note**
>
> Throughout today's project, you'll see figures that show text added to various sections of the report—you can type this text into your report to make it match the report in the book (also available on the CD-ROM).

Inserting Content from Other Office Applications

For most Word users, the only other applications on their computer are the remaining programs in the Office 2000 suite. Office 2000's interoperability makes it easy to take content from one application and use it in another, be it in the form of copied sections or an entire file.

You can insert content from Excel, Access, PowerPoint, or Publisher into your Word document, and your Word content can go the other way—use it in an Excel worksheet, an Access data table, a PowerPoint slide, or a Publisher file. For this report, however, the content will flow into Word from these other applications.

Using existing data from Excel and Access does two things—it saves you the trouble of retyping information into the document, and it assures accuracy and consistency between files. Bringing content from PowerPoint (you won't be using any Publisher content in this project) assures you that the look of your PowerPoint presentations is maintained in your Word-generated reports. This is a valuable step in creating a cohesive set of marketing or educational materials, such as your Sales Report.

Adding Excel Worksheet Content

Your report will contain numbers: sales figures, projections, and compensation data. These numbers already exist in the Excel workbook called Report Data, which can be found on the CD that accompanies this book. In the real world, the data might be in several different Excel workbooks, but for the sake of simplicity, you've got all the data you need in one workbook.

Although you can insert entire worksheets into the Sales Report document, this project requires that only pieces of these worksheets be added to the document. For this reason, you want use the Clipboard to copy and paste sections of these worksheets into the appropriate spots in the Sales Report document.

When Excel data is copied into a Word document, it changes from a spreadsheet to a table. A table's structure is similar to a spreadsheet, so this is a compatible format for the Excel data. After it is pasted, the table can be moved, reformatted, and edited as needed.

Positioning Pasted Tables

To paste a portion of an Excel worksheet into the Sales Report document, follow these steps:

1. Open the Excel workbook (Report Data.xls), and click the Compensation worksheet tab.

2. Select the range of cells from B2 to E22, and then choose Edit, Copy. You can also click the Copy button or press Ctrl+C. Figure 17.6 shows the selected Excel content.

FIGURE 17.6

Select the portion of the worksheet that you want to reuse in the Sales Report.

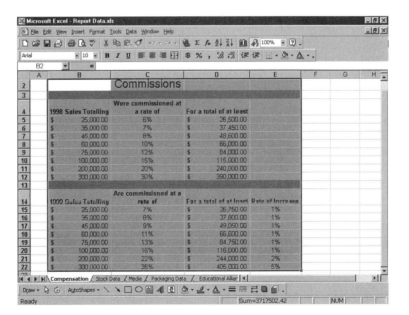

3. Switch back to the Sales Report document and position your cursor under the Increased Commission section of the document. Figure 17.7 shows this location.

FIGURE 17.7

Before pasting, make sure that your cursor is in the right spot within the document.

Cursor indicates the future loca-tion of pasted content

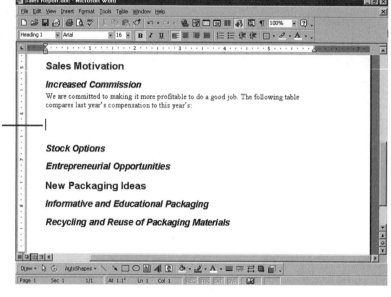

 4. Choose Edit, Paste, or click the Paste button. The worksheet content appears as a table in the Word document, as shown in Figure 17.8.

FIGURE 17.8

Excel worksheet content becomes a Word table.

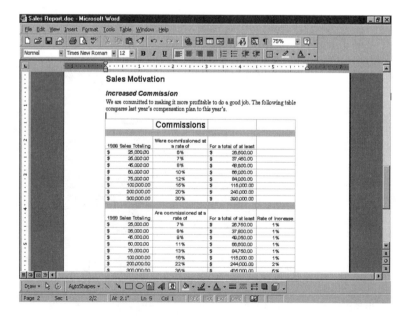

There are other portions of the Report Data workbook that can be pasted into the Sales Report document. Use the steps in the preceding procedure to paste the following parts of the workbook:

- Copy cells A1 through E15 from the Stock Data tab to the Stock Options section of the Sales Report document.
- Copy cells A1 through D18 from the Media tab of the Report Data workbook to the Advertising section of the Sales Report document.

Tip

After pasting these portions of the workbook, be sure to save the document to reflect these additions.

17

After the tables are pasted, they can be moved. You can click and drag a table into any position, even alongside text. Figure 17.9 shows the Stock Analysis table with paragraph text wrapped around it. On Day 4, "Building a Complex Document," you learned to adjust the text wrapping settings for a table in a Word document. The fact that this table was created from Excel content has no bearing on the formatting that can be applied to it.

FIGURE 17.9

Use Word's table-formatting tools to adjust the placement and appearance of the table that you created by pasting Excel content.

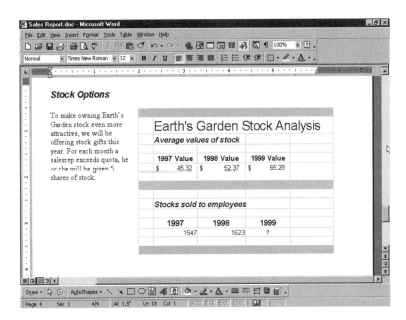

Nesting a Table

When you have two sections of Excel content that are separate within their source workbook but need to be placed together in a Word document, you can paste one set of data first, and then paste the second set inside it. The data that is pasted first creates one table, and the second set of data becomes a table nested within the first table.

To demonstrate this technique, you need data in the Educational Alliances tab in the Report Data workbook. After you've opened that workbook, follow these steps:

1. On the Educational Alliances tab, select the range of cells from A1 to G20, as shown in Figure 17.10. This includes two blank rows at the bottom of this section of the worksheet.

FIGURE 17.10

Select the cells from the worksheet that you want to use in the Sales Report document.

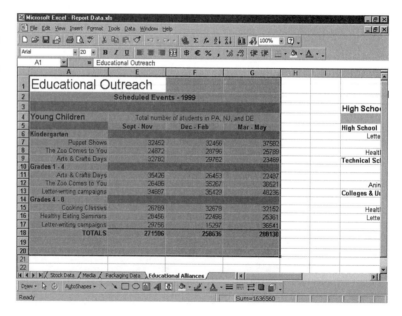

2. Copy this range to the Clipboard (use Edit, Copy, or click the Copy button).

3. Switch to the Sales Report document, and click to position your cursor beneath the Alliances with Schools heading.

4. Choose Edit, Paste, or click the Paste button. The data from the worksheet appears as a table (see Figure 17.11).

FIGURE 17.11

The columnar structure of the cell range is maintained when it is pasted into the Word document, where it appears in the form of a table.

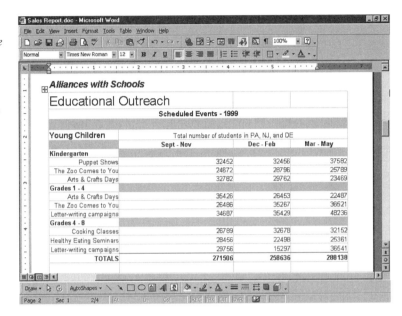

5. Select the blank cells at the bottom of the table, and choose Table, Merge Cells. This creates a cell that is wide enough for the next table to be nested in it.

6. Switch back to the Educational Alliances worksheet, and select the range of cells that begins with J3 and ends with M17 (see Figure 17.12).

FIGURE 17.12

Because the two portions of the worksheet are not contiguous, you must copy and paste them individually.

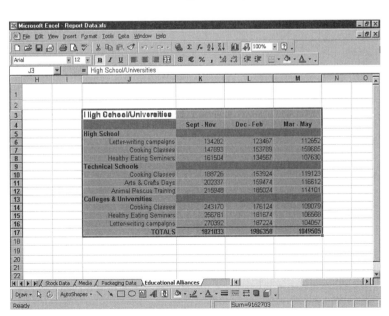

7. Copy this second range to the Clipboard (the Clipboard toolbar might appear).

8. Switch back to the Sales Report document; click inside the table you just pasted, in the large blank merged cell at the bottom of the first pasted table.

 9. Choose Edit, Paste, or click the Paste button to paste the last item that was placed on the Clipboard. The data from the second range of cells appears as a table nested within the first table, as shown in Figure 17.13.

FIGURE 17.13

Nest related data in an existing table, rather than creating a separate table from the pasted content.

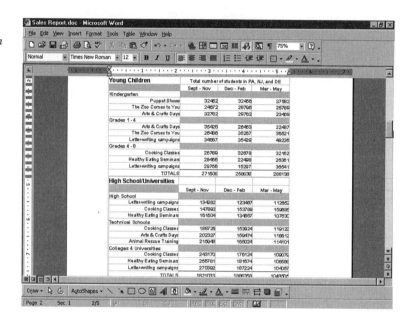

The entire table (including its nested portion) can be moved and reformatted as usual.

 Note Why nest these tables? For two reasons: First, you can't copy noncontiguous ranges of cells from an Excel worksheet, so the data can't be pasted in one step; second, by nesting the data, you create one table instead of two separate tables (having two distinct tables implies that the data within them is unrelated).

Linking an Excel Chart

Nothing turns a simple document into a report the way a chart does. Charts, as you learned in Day 9, "Creating and Using Charts," turn numeric data into pictures that are easily understood and interpreted. They also create visual interest in a way that rows and columns of numbers can't.

If you've already created your Excel chart, you can use it in your Word document. If you haven't created the chart yet but you have Excel data that can be turned into a chart, you can create the chart and then copy it into the Word document. The process of copying the chart into a document is simple; just follow these steps:

1. Open the Report Data workbook and click the Packaging Impact tab. This tab contains a chart.

2. Click once on the chart to select it. Handles appear around the perimeter of the chart, as shown in Figure 17.14.

FIGURE 17.14

Make sure that the entire chart (not just a portion of it) is selected.

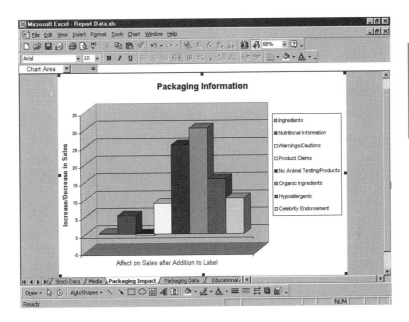

3. Copy the selected chart to the Clipboard using Edit, Copy, or by clicking the Copy button.

4. Switch back to the Sales Report document, and click to position your cursor in the New Packaging Ideas section, just under the heading Informative and Educational Packaging.

5. Choose Edit, Paste Special. The Paste Special dialog box opens, as shown in Figure 17.15.

6. Click the Paste link option, and then click OK to paste a Microsoft Excel Chart Object. The chart appears in the document and, by virtue of the link, can be updated whenever changes are made to the data (and thus the chart) in the Excel workbook.

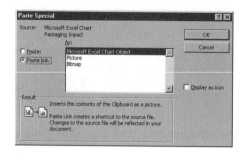

FIGURE 17.15

Choosing Paste Special gives you the option to link the copied content to the document, creating a connection between the worksheet and the report.

Updating Linked Content

While both the Sales Report document and the Report Data workbook are open (just after you paste the chart as a linked object), any changes that are made to the Excel data that created the chart update both the Excel chart and its copy in the Sales Report document. Use the following steps to demonstrate this:

1. Switch to the Report Data workbook and click the Packaging Data tab.
2. Change the content of cell B8 to 45.25. Press Enter.
3. Switch to the Packaging Effects tab and note that the chart has changed—there is now one bar in the chart that is considerably taller than all the other bars.
4. Switch to the Sales Report document. Scroll to look at the chart that is pasted in the New Packaging Ideas section. Note that the corresponding bar in this chart has also been changed to reflect the edited data (see Figure 17.16).

FIGURE 17.16

The linked data updates the chart in both Excel and Word.

This bar has changed to reflect the new data

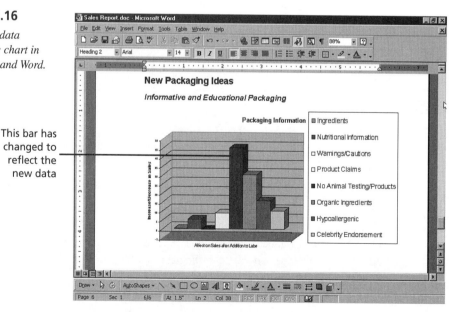

After you close either or both of the files, the link between them remains. When you open the Sales Report document again, a prompt appears, indicating that the document contains linked data; you are asked if you want to update it. If you choose Yes, any changes that are made in the interim to the Excel packaging data are updated in the chart in the Word document. If you choose No, the chart remains intact; the link is not severed if you answer No.

> **Tip**
>
> To maintain the link that is established between these two files, you cannot delete or rename either file (Report Data or Sales Report). If you do rename or delete either file, you sever the link.

17

To break the link between Report Data and Sales Report, choose Edit, Links from within the Sales Report document to open the Links dialog box; then select the link (see Figure 17.17). Click Break Link, and then click OK to close the dialog box. The link is severed, and even though the data remains in both locations, it is not updated (nor are you prompted to update it) in the document if any edits are performed on the Excel data.

FIGURE 17.17

Sever the ties between the source (worksheet) and target (report) by clicking Break Link.

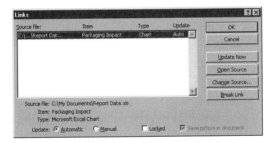

Using Access Data in a Word Report

Access table data is as easily added to a Word document as Excel worksheet content—the tabular structure of the Access table makes it compatible with Word tables; therefore, it is simple to add valuable content to the Sales Report from an Access database.

For this procedure, you can use the Access database entitled Employee Information.mdb, which is found on the CD that accompanies this book. You'll be copying records from one of the tables within this database for use in the Sales Report document; follow these steps:

1. Open the Employee Information database in Access. The Database window opens, as shown in Figure 17.18.

FIGURE 17.18

The Access database consists of tables, queries, and reports. You'll use table data for the Sales Report.

2. Double-click Staff List to open that table. The table contains 18 records (see Figure 17.19).

FIGURE 17.19

Choose only those records that relate to your Sales Report. In this case, choose the employees in the Sales department.

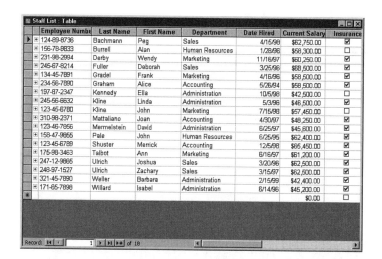

3. Sort the records by department. Click in any record in the Department field for that record, and then click the Sort Ascending button. This places the list in order by department so you can copy just the records for employees in the Sales department.

4. Select the last four records that are shown onscreen (see Figure 17.20)—the four employees in the Sales department.

FIGURE 17.20

Sorting the records by department makes it easier to select just those employees in the Sales department.

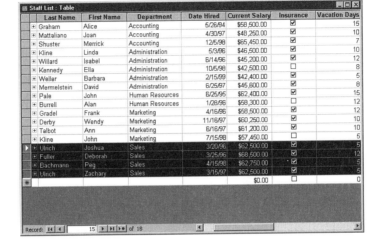

5. Choose

 Edit, Copy, or click the Copy button.

6. Switch to the Sales Report document, and click to position your cursor beneath the Entrepreneurial Opportunities heading, as shown in Figure 17.21.

FIGURE 17.21

Insert the names here to show the people who are directly affected by this portion of the report.

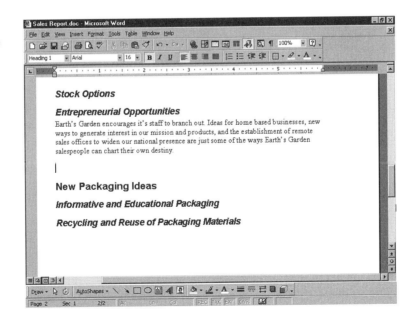

17

7. Choose Edit, Paste, or click the Paste button. The field names and the records for
       the employees in the Sales department are pasted into the document, as shown in
       Figure 17.22.

FIGURE 17.22

*Pasted Access data
appears in your Word
document, along with
a shaded row of field
names to help identify
the data.*

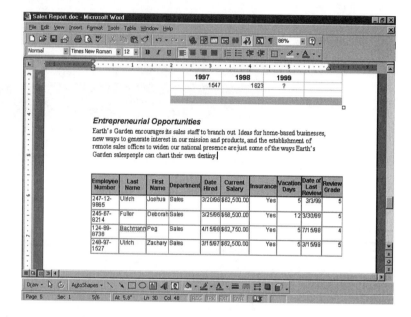

After it is pasted, this data can be edited and the table can be reformatted. The shaded
row of field names can be removed if necessary, and the column widths can be adjusted.
Figure 17.23 shows the Access data in the Sales Report document after some minor
reformatting to make it fit more neatly into the report.

Using PowerPoint Slides in a Report

If your company has a presentation format that all its slideshows follow (for example, a
specific Design Template or general rules of thumb for building a presentation), they
probably care about having a consistent look in published documents—reports on paper
or presentations that are run onscreen. Consistency in marketing materials is important
whether you're marketing to your internal customers (staff) or the outside world.

Using an existing PowerPoint slide in your report serves two purposes—it saves you the
trouble of retyping the content of the slide, and it shares the look of the presentation with
the report. When you are using PowerPoint slides in any other Office 2000 file, you can
use the Clipboard to quickly copy one or more slides from a presentation.

Columns that contain confidential information (Review Grade, Salary) have been deleted from the pasted table

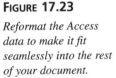

FIGURE 17.23

Reformat the Access data to make it fit seamlessly into the rest of your document.

Headings are now italic, but not bold

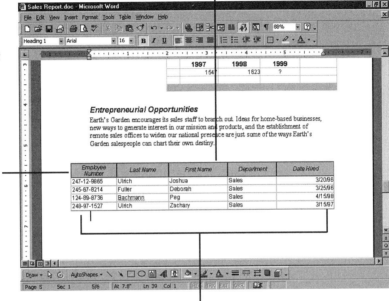

Column widths adjusted to spread out remaining columns

To share a PowerPoint slide with the Sales Report document, follow these steps:

1. Open the PowerPoint presentation that contains the slide you want to use. In this case, it is the Earth's Garden Sales Meeting presentation you created on Days 15 and 16. If you no longer have access to that file on your own computer, you can find it on the CD-ROM that accompanies this book.

2. Switch to Slide Sorter view, and click once on Slide 7 (Changing Palates in the US), as shown in Figure 17.24.

3. Choose Edit, Copy, or press Ctrl+C. You can also click the Copy button.

4. Switch back to the Sales Report document, and click to place your cursor under the New Packaging Ideas heading.

5. Choose Edit, Paste, or press Ctrl+V. You can also click the Paste button. The slide appears in the document, as shown in Figure 17.25.

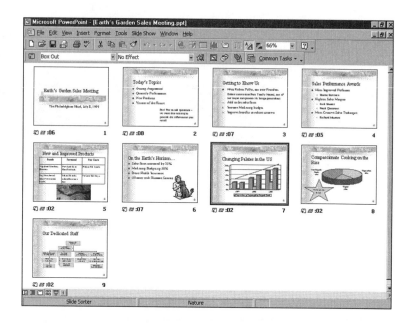

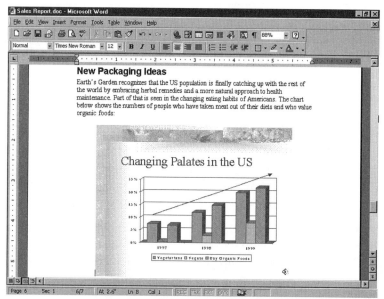

To format the pasted graphic, click once on it and choose Format, Object. The Format
Object dialog box opens, as shown in Figure 17.26. From within this box, you can adjust
the way text wraps around the object on the Layout tab, or you can use the Size tab to
change the image size.

> **Tip**
>
> To open the Format Object dialog box, you can also right-click the graphic and choose Format Object from the shortcut menu.

FIGURE 17.26

The Picture tab in the Format Object dialog box gives you the capability to crop the slide image or adjust the brightness and contrast.

17

After making your changes, click OK. The image changes to reflect your adjustments.

> **Tip**
>
> If you prefer to use the Picture toolbar to tinker with the slide image, right-click any of the displayed toolbars and choose Picture from the list. With the slide image selected, begin using the Picture toolbar tools to adjust the color, brightness, and contrast of the image, or to crop away unnecessary content.

Inserting Clip Art and Graphic Images

Using clip art and graphic images such as scanned photographs or drawings can add visual interest to your report's pages, as well as increase the amount and variety of information that is imparted by the report. Just as converting numeric data to a chart can make boring financial information more interesting, using clip art or other graphics can effectively drive home a message or set the tone of the document.

> **Caution**
>
> If you work for a very staid or conservative company, you might want to avoid using clip art or drawings in your presentation—they might be considered too informal or too much fun, given the tone of the reports you're likely to create in that setting. Stick to scanned photographs if you need graphic content at all.

Inserting clip art in a Word document is much the same as inserting it into a PowerPoint presentation; review that portion of Day 16 as needed, and then follow these simple steps:

1. Click to position your cursor in the Sales Report document in which you want to place the clip art image. For this report, place your cursor below the first main heading in the report (Sales Goals).

2. Click the Insert Clip Art button on the Drawing toolbar (if displayed), or choose Insert, Picture, ClipArt. The Insert ClipArt dialog box opens, as shown in Figure 17.27.

FIGURE 17.27

Select a category from which to select a clip art image for the report.

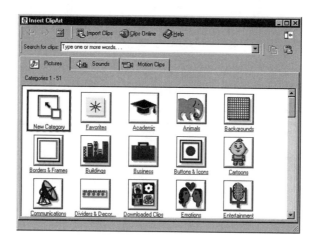

3. Click once on the Plants category (you might have to scroll down to find it), and view the images that are available (see Figure 17.28).

FIGURE 17.28

The Trees image works nicely in your Earth's Garden Sales Report.

The selected image has a thick border around it to indicate selection

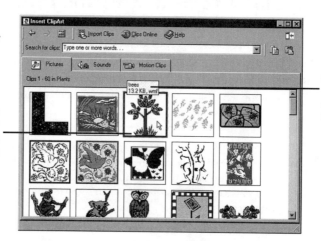

Name and size of the image appear in a ScreenTip

4. Right-click the Trees image and choose Insert from the shortcut menu. Click the Close button in the upper-right corner of the Insert ClipArt dialog box to close it and return to the document.

The clip art appears in the document, where it can be moved, resized, or reformatted with the Picture toolbar. Figure 17.29 shows the Trees clip art in the Sales Report, with text wrapping around it.

From the Layout tab in the
Format Picture dialog box, Tight
wrapping was selected

FIGURE 17.29

*The clip art image can
stand on its own with
text above or below it,
or you can flow any
existing text around the
image.*

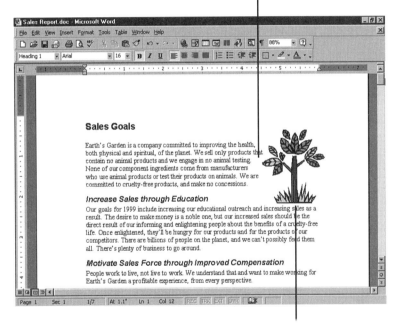

17

The image was dragged to
the right side of the page

> **Tip**
>
> Right-click on any object in your document, and the resulting shortcut menu offers a Format command (Format Object or Format Picture, for example). Selecting this command opens a Format dialog box from which you can adjust any settings that are available for the given object.

Creating a Cover Page

Unlike a letter that you put in an envelope and mail, a report needs a cover page. The cover page tells the reader what to expect inside, just as the cover of this book told you what to expect on its pages.

Many users create a cover page as a separate document and bind it with the report later. For this project, you'll create a cover page as the first page of the Sales Report document. Assuming that your page numbering is set to not show a number on the first page of the document, the cover page is not numbered.

To create a cover page, follow these steps:

1. Press Ctrl+Home to go to the top (beginning) of the Sales Report document.
2. Press Ctrl+Enter. A blank page is added at the beginning of the document. Press Ctrl+Home again to go to that page.
3. Type `Earth's Garden Sales Report` and press Enter.
4. Type the date and press Enter.
5. Select these two lines of text, as shown in Figure 17.30.

FIGURE 17.30

Select your report's title before adjusting the placement of the text on the cover page.

6. Choose File, Page Setup. The Page Setup dialog box opens, as shown in Figure 17.31. Click the Layout tab.

Choose how the
text is to be aligned
from top to bottom
on the page

Select the portion of
the document to
which these settings
are to apply

FIGURE 17.31

Adjust the vertical alignment so that your title is placed in the vertical center of the page.

17

7. Change the Vertical alignment setting to Center.

8. In the Apply to list, choose Selected text.

9. Click OK to apply this change and close the dialog box.

 10. With the text still selected, press Ctrl+E or click the Center alignment button on the Formatting toolbar. This centers the cover page text horizontally.

The text is centered from top to bottom and from left to right on the cover page, as shown in Figure 17.32.

FIGURE 17.32

The title is placed at the literal center of your page, measured from top to bottom as well as from left to right.

Whole Page zoom
is chosen to show
the entire page

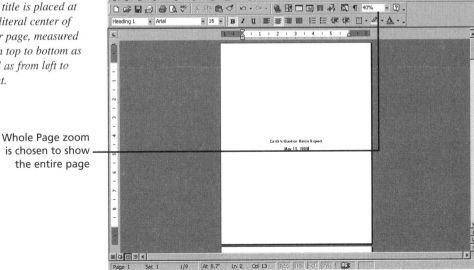

> You might end up with an extra blank page after your cover page, depend-
> ing on your mouse technique for selecting the cover page text. If you do,
> click at the top of that extra blank page and press Delete. This brings the
> text of the report back onto page two.

Designing a Title with WordArt

Imagine that Earth's Garden doesn't have a formal logo, or that they are considering
changing the one they have. They want an interesting logo of their name for the Sales
Report. This next procedure uses WordArt, an Office 2000 utility that is accessed through
the Drawing toolbar.

To create a WordArt logo of the company name, follow these steps:

1. On the cover page, select the words *Earth's Garden*; press Ctrl+X or click the Cut
   button to Cut the words to the Clipboard.

2. Click the WordArt button on the Drawing toolbar. You can also choose Insert,
   Picture, WordArt.

> If the Drawing toolbar isn't displayed, choose View, Toolbars, and select
> Drawing from the list.

3. Select a WordArt style from the WordArt Gallery, as shown in Figure 17.33; then
   click OK.

FIGURE 17.33

*The WordArt Gallery
offers 30 different
artistic text options.*

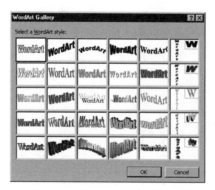

4. In the resulting Edit WordArt Text dialog box, press Ctrl+V to insert the words that you cut to the Clipboard in step 1. Figure 17.34 shows this text in the dialog box.

If desired, change the font of the text

Apply a larger or smaller font size if needed

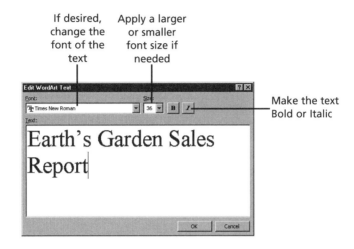

Make the text Bold or Italic

5. Click OK to place the text in the style you chose on the cover page (see Figure 17.35). The WordArt toolbar appears to accompany the graphic.

17

The WordArt text is placed in the vertical and horizontal center of the page, and therefore might need to be moved so that it appears above the date. You might want to resize it. Like any other graphic object, a WordArt object can be moved or resized. If you want to change to a different style, use the WordArt toolbar's WordArt Gallery button. The Gallery reopens, and whatever style you select is applied to the selected text object on the cover page.

Using Page Setup to Prepare for Binding the Document

After building the document text, bringing in content from other Office 2000 applications, and polishing the report with graphics and a cover page, you're ready to print. Actually, you're ready to prepare to print: For such a long document, you have to consider your binding options and set up the document to allow for placing the report in a folder or other type of jacket.

To adjust the document's settings for this purpose, follow these steps:

1. In the Sales Report document, choose File, Page Setup, and click the Margins tab (see Figure 17.36).

FIGURE 17.36

Set up margins to accommodate a document that is printed on both sides of the paper, creating facing pages.

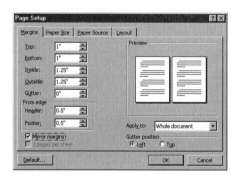

2. Click the Mirror margins option. The Preview changes to show two pages side by side (see Figure 17.37).

3. Click OK.

Your document is now set up so that you can print on both sides of the paper. Odd-numbered pages have a larger left margin, and even-numbered pages have a larger right margin. This increased margin allows for binding that doesn't cut through or obscure text on the inside of facing pages.

FIGURE **17.37**

Note that the Left and Right margins now display as Inside and Outside because Mirror margins is turned on.

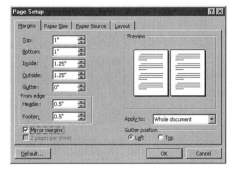

Printing a Two-Sided Document

To complete the task of printing your Sales Report, you must now go to the Print dialog box. Choose File, Print; the Print dialog box opens (see Figure 17.38).

FIGURE **17.38**

All the potential adjustments to your printer settings and all the printing options for this particular document are available through the Print dialog box.

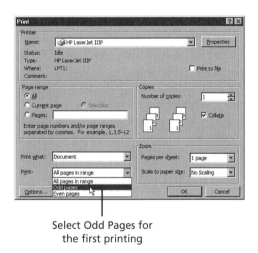

Select Odd Pages for
the first printing

> **Tip**
>
> Most toolbar buttons perform the same task as their menu counterparts; not so in the case of the Print button. If you click this button, a print job is immediately sent to your default printer—no dialog box opens, and one copy of every page of your document prints out.

On Day 3, "Enhancing a Basic Word Document," you learned your way around the Print dialog box. The only setting you need to adjust here (other than the number of copies you want and the printer to which you want to send the job) is the Print setting in the lower-left corner of the dialog box. Display this list box, and choose Odd pages. Make sure that your paper is in the printer's tray, and that the printer is on and ready, and click OK. The odd-numbered pages print out, starting with the cover page.

 Caution   The necessity of doing a Print Preview of your document is never more essential than when you're dealing with a long document. Choose to view multiple pages of the document in the Print Preview window. You might see the need to insert some page breaks throughout the document to create a more pleasing flow of information and to get rid of breaks within tables. Close the Print Preview and go back to your document, where you can make these changes before you print.

After printing the odd-numbered pages, take those pages and put them back in the printer tray, upside down. Your printer's settings for whether the top of the page goes in first or last determines your exact procedure here. After putting the pages in the printer, reopen the Print dialog box. In the Print list, select Even pages, and click OK. Your odd pages go back through the printer and the even pages' content prints on their reverse, giving you a two-sided document that is ready for binding.

Tip   If you need to make a lot of copies of this document, don't waste your laser toner or inkjet cartridges. Print one clean master copy (try using a bright white or glossy paper to get a crisp output) and take the master to a printing store to have the copies made and bound. If your office has a good copier that makes consistently crisp, clear copies (that don't look photocopied), you can use it to make the copies.

Summary

Today represented the culmination of your skills in using Word, Excel, Access, and PowerPoint. By creating a report in Word that used data and content from existing files that were created in these other applications, you learned to use your skills with the individual applications together. In addition, the cross-application features—the Clipboard, insertion of clip art and pictures, tools for manipulating objects—were fully utilized, showing you how much you really have learned.

Q&A

Q Can I distribute the report via email instead of sending printed copies to everyone who needs to see the report?

A Yes. You can send the report document as an attachment to an email message through Outlook or any other email package you use. When sending a report with links in it, however, be aware that the recipient sees the same prompt regarding the updating of links in the document that you see, and probably can't update them because the source documents might not be available to them. Either Break Links before sending the report, or put the source documents on a public drive on your network and reestablish the links so that their copy of the report can be updated when they open it.

17

Workshop

The section that follows is a quick quiz about the day. If you have any problems answering any of the questions, see the section that follows the quiz for all the answers.

Quiz

1. How do you create an outline in Word?

2. True or False: When you paste Excel worksheet content into a Word document, it appears as a fully-functioning worksheet.

3. True or False: If an Excel chart is pasted and linked to a Word document, the chart is updated every time the document is opened.

4. Describe the differences between pasted Access table data and pasted Excel worksheet content in a Word document.

5. Describe the procedure for copying a PowerPoint slide to a Word document.

6. Are there any differences between the procedures for inserting clip art and graphics in Word and in the other Office 2000 applications?

Quiz Answers

1. In a blank document, switch to Outline view (View, Outline) and begin typing the outline. Tab demotes subjects, Shift+Tab promotes them.

2. False. Excel content becomes a table when it is pasted into a Word document.

3. False. You have the choice to update linked content each time you open a document containing links, but you can decline the option, leaving the content intact.

4. The primary difference is the automatic inclusion of the field names from the Access table. When Excel data is pasted, only the copied cells are pasted and converted to a table. When Access data is pasted, a row of field names accompanies the pasted records.

5. The simplest method starts in Slide Sorter view in the presentation. Select the slide you want to copy, and copy it to the Clipboard. Switch back to Word and paste it into the document.

6. No. The procedures are the same in Word, Excel, and PowerPoint. The Insert ClipArt button is on the Drawing toolbar in any of these applications, and the Insert, Picture commands work the same way, too.

DAY 18

Designing a Web Page with FrontPage

Gone are the days when knowledge of HTML (hypertext markup language) was required to create a Web page. Businesses large and small—as well as individuals—are creating their own Web sites, and the need for a tool that doesn't require programming skills is obvious. Microsoft originally met that need by enabling Office users to save Word files as HTML, converting text and graphics to Web page content. Now, with the inclusion of FrontPage in the Office 2000 suite, Microsoft not only provides the right tool for the job, it puts it in every user's hands. Today you'll design and create a Web page, including heading and body text, graphics, and links to other Web pages. Specifically, you'll learn the following skills:

- Designing the overall look of a Web page, choosing from different formats
- Adding tables and frames to give the page structure and functionality
- Creating text content
- Inserting graphic images, including animated graphic files

- Turning text and graphics into links to Web sites and files
- Manipulating the appearance of graphic images through PhotoDraw

Web Page Design Basics

The best way to choose the right page for your purposes is to look at other people's pages—surf the Web and look at the Web sites of your competitors and peers. Make note of the things you like and don't like, and design your page accordingly. In lieu of or in addition to doing this sort of online research, FrontPage offers you a wide variety of Web page templates—pick the one that's closest to the type of page you want to create, and use it as the foundation for your own unique Web page.

 Note

> NEW TERM   FrontPage draws a distinction between a Web *page* and a *Web*. A Web page is but one page in a total Web site, and a Web is the entire site. Most users design a multipage Web site one page at a time, but FrontPage also gives you Web templates that start you out with multiple pages that you fill in with your own content. Today takes the one-page-at-a-time approach, and you'll start by building a single page.

When you first open the FrontPage program (from the Start menu's Programs list or by double-clicking a desktop icon), you are given a blank Web page, as shown in Figure 18.1.

 Tip

> The first time you use FrontPage, you are prompted to choose whether to make FrontPage your default Web page editor. The choice is up to you—if you choose Yes, the next time you double-click an HTML document in My Computer or the Explorer, FrontPage is opened with that file displayed. Choosing No makes no changes to the default file-format associations, and Internet Explorer is the default program for opening HTML files.

This page enables you to literally start from scratch—there is no layout to work within, no text to guide you, no hints on composition. To create a Web page with some assistance (by starting with a template), follow these steps:

1. Close the current blank page by choosing File, Close.
2. Choose File, New, Page to access the available templates. Figure 18.2 shows the New dialog box.

Standard toolbar contains
buttons for previewing, printing, saving, and inserting
tables, pictures, and hyperlinks

Formatting toolbar
helps you change
the way text looks
on the page

FIGURE 18.1

*If the design you have
in mind is completely
unique, you might
want to start with a
blank page, in Page
view.*

FIGURE **18.1**

*If the design you have
in mind is completely
unique, you might
want to start with a
blank page, in Page
view.*

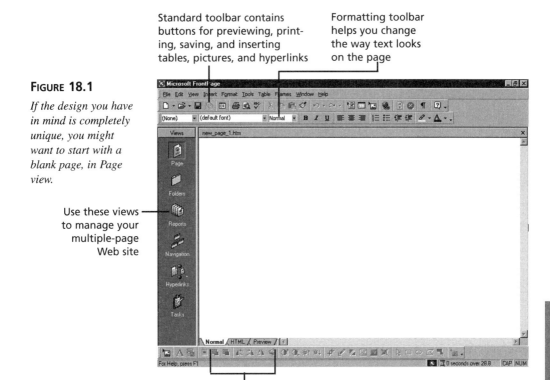

Use these views
to manage your
multiple-page
Web site

18

Choose between these three
views when designing your page

FIGURE **18.2**

*Click once on the tem-
plate icons on the
General and Frames
Pages tabs to Preview
your page layout
options.*

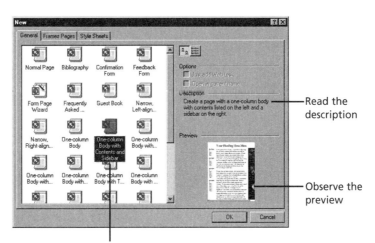

Read the
description

Observe the
preview

Click an icon (the template
you'll use for today's project)

3. Double-click the One Column Body with Contents and Sidebar template.

After selecting the template, the Web page opens onscreen, as shown in Figure 18.3. Replace the instructional text and paragraph text with your own content.

Replace heading with your own

FIGURE 18.3

Layout and overall composition decisions are made for you—all you have to do is insert your own text and pictures.

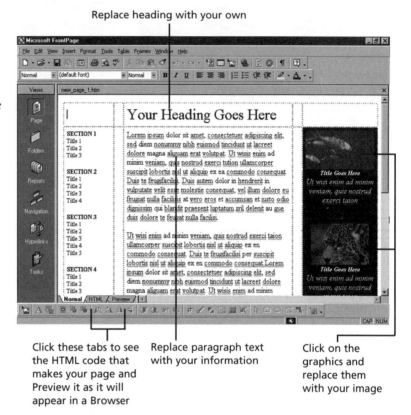

Click these tabs to see the HTML code that makes your page and Preview it as it will appear in a Browser

Replace paragraph text with your information

Click on the graphics and replace them with your image

As you develop your page, work in Normal view. If you know any HTML, you can click that tab to see the HTML programming code that supports your page layout and content. Figure 18.4 shows the HTML view of the page, with sample content still in place.

Tags are instructions that indicate the appearance and purpose of the text between them

*Even if you don't know
anything about HTML,
you can learn a little
about it merely by
viewing your page in
HTML view.*

Opening tag
Closing tag

Tags that indicate
font sizes and
spacing between
page elements

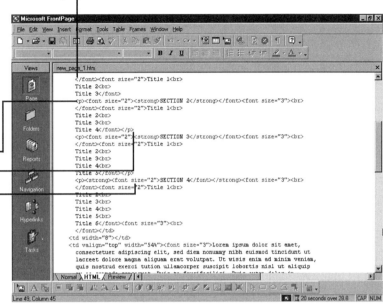

Note

| **NEW TERM** | *HTML* is the abbreviation for *Hypertext Markup Language*, the
programming language that is used for creating Web pages. |

The language enables programmers to create a Web page with a series of
commands and explicit codes that indicate where text and graphic content
are to be placed, and how they will look onscreen. Most Web page design
programs enable you to design your page graphically, typing text and inserting graphics; then, when you save the file, your page content is converted
to HTML for use on the Web.

If you want to see your page the way it will look to people who are viewing it through
their browser (Internet Explorer, Netscape, and so on), click the Preview tab. Figure 18.5
shows the Preview of the Web page with its sample content.

FIGURE 18.5

In a browser, the table cell borders are invisible, and spelling errors are not flagged.

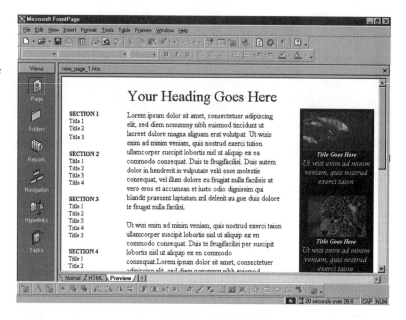

As you work on your site, it's a good idea to switch to Preview view periodically, especially if you're making any changes to the layout of the template. By making these periodic checks, you can see how the content you're adding and changes you're making will look to the people who view your site on the Web.

Note

Keep the monitor resolution (number of pixels used to display the screen) of your audience in mind when designing your Web page. Although the most common setting is 800x600, some people with older monitors might be using 640x480, in which case much of your content might not fit on their screen without their having to scroll all around to see it. To test your design in the three available resolutions (640x480, 800x600, and 1024x768), choose File, Preview in Browser, and then select the Window size you want. This setting applies to your Preview tab view, and enables you to make sure you're not excluding two thirds of the browsing audience by designing with only one resolution in mind. Test your design in all three window sizes before posting your page to the Web.

Note

NEW TERM Your monitor's display is made up of thousands of *pixels*, or small dots. An 800x600 setting for your monitor means that the screen image is made up of 480,000 pixels. The more pixels you have, the clearer and crisper your screen display is.

Inserting Heading and Body Text

The first step in building the page is to replace the sample text with your own. Starting with the heading (shown selected in Normal view in Figure 18.6), insert your own company name or Web page title.

FIGURE 18.6

Select the sample text with your mouse and then type the replacement text. The sample text is deleted, and your text appears simultaneously.

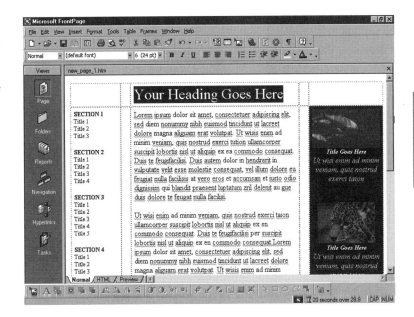

It's a good idea to have your content prepared before you begin widespread replacement of the sample text—don't just begin typing in a stream-of-conscious manner. If you have text prepared in an existing Word document, you can copy it from that document and paste it directly to your Web page.

Figure 18.7 shows the heading, paragraph, and section text replaced with "real" content. Use this figure to guide you as you make your own replacements.

Heading replaced

FIGURE 18.7

You don't need to use as much text as there was in the sample—if you don't need four sections on the left, delete the ones you don't need.

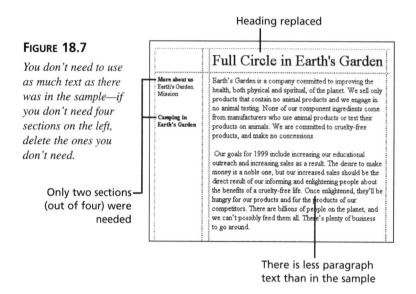

Only two sections (out of four) were needed

There is less paragraph text than in the sample

The images on the right side of the page are replaced next, along with the caption text.

 Caution

Avoid creating a scattered or confusing Web page! It's a good idea to move through your page in a linear way, making replacements from top to bottom and left to right. Move through your content in the order that people who view it on the Web will read it. This helps ensure that your information is presented in the most logical and useful order. It's also a good idea to have someone else proofread and troubleshoot your page before you post it to the Web, just to get an objective reaction to your content and layout.

Inserting Clip Art and Photographs

As with a PowerPoint presentation, a Web page is made more interesting and effective by the use of graphics. Nothing causes someone to skip over your page faster than a screenful of text and nothing else to look at. If you want people to linger at your site, reading all your content, following all your links, and coming back to the main page for more, you have to keep the page visually interesting. The easiest and most effective way to do that is with graphic content.

There are some drawbacks, however, to using graphics on your Web page, so consider the following issues before adding any images to your page:

- **Graphics can slow the loading of your page**—A page with a lot of pictures loads much more slowly than a text-only page. This is even more of a problem if the graphic files you add to your site are large. Although it's usually worth the wait (and users are accustomed to having to wait a few seconds for images to compose), don't make people wait too long—they'll click the Stop button in their browser and go elsewhere.

Tip

It's a good idea to keep graphic file sizes at 100K or less. Anything larger takes too long to load. How do you tell how big the file is? Go to the Windows Explorer or My Computer, make sure that your view is set to show file details (View, Details), open the folder or drive on which the graphic file is stored, and check its size.

- **Animated graphics can be interesting, but too many of them make your site look silly**—Keep this in mind especially if your site pertains to a serious topic—you don't want to use too many "cute" graphics or graphics that move.

Tip

There are some animated GIFs on the CD-ROM that accompanies this book, and you can find more on the Web. Try www.barrysclipart.com for lots of images, most of which are free.

18

- **Be careful about copyrights**—Don't be cavalier in the selection and use of photographs and drawings. Clip art images (the ones that come with Office and any you buy on CD) are free to use, but if you use someone's copyrighted work, you must either pay them for the right to use it or give them credit at the site for their work. This can be as simple as listing a copyright symbol (©) under a picture. Don't skip this step—you can be sued by the artist if you fail to acknowledge their rights to the images.

The template you started with today has a series of three graphics on the right side of the page. Each graphic is accompanied by a caption in italics. These images (and later, the captions) are replaced by your own—clip art from the Office 2000 clip art selection or from other sources, or scanned photographs and drawings. The images that you'll use today can be found in the Office 2000 clip art image gallery.

Using Static Graphic Images

Static images are images that don't move, and you'll find these on many Web sites. Using clip art, drawings, and photographs to represent information on a Web site makes it more interesting to look at.

Tip

The use of graphic images also saves space on each page; rather than putting several paragraphs of text on the page to describe something, use a picture that also serves as a hyperlink to another page where the descriptive text is found.

Note

NEW TERM A *hyperlink* is text or a graphic that points to another file or Web page. You can turn anything on your Web page—a single word, a phrase or sentence, a picture—into a hyperlink. You'll find out how to do this later today.

To replace the sample pictures on the right side of the Web page, follow these steps:

1. Click on the first image you want to replace. Figure 18.8 shows the top image selected.

2. Choose Insert, Picture, Clip Art. This opens the Clip Art Gallery dialog box, as shown in Figure 18.9.

3. Choose the Plants category by clicking the Plants icon once. From the group of Plants clip art images, right-click Sunshine, which is the second image from the left in the top row, and choose Insert from the shortcut menu. If you don't have this image (shown selected in Figure 18.10), choose another, similar image.

4. The Sunshine image appears at the top, on the right side of the Web page. The image is larger than the one it replaced, and therefore must be resized. Figure 18.11 shows the image reduced in size.

FIGURE 18.8

FrontPage replaces the selected image with your chosen clip art file.

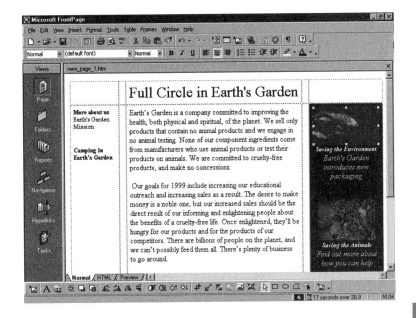

FIGURE 18.9

Choose your clip art category from the many that are offered in the Clip Art Gallery dialog box.

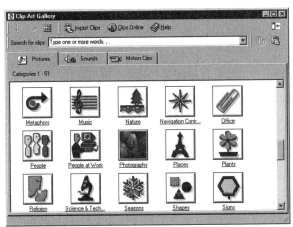

5. Don't forget to edit the sample text under the image. Figure 18.12 shows that the replacement text has been reformatted as well.

FIGURE 18.10

Office 2000 comes with hundreds of clip art images if you do a full install or pull them from the Office 2000 CD, so you should have no trouble finding the right image for your Web page.

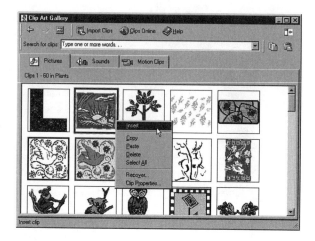

FIGURE 18.11

Resize the image from a corner handle to retain the current width/height ratio.

FIGURE 18.12

When you change the images, don't forget to provide descriptive or instructional text nearby to tell people what the picture represents.

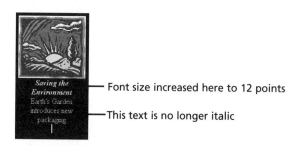

Font size increased here to 12 points

This text is no longer italic

Note

When you resize an image in FrontPage, you'll see the image change as you drag the handles. Also, the surrounding objects move to accommodate the new dimensions of the image. This differs from what you've experienced with the other Office applications—in Word, PowerPoint, and Excel, the image doesn't change to its new size until you release the mouse.

The second and third images can also be replaced by clip art or scanned photos or drawings. Choose images from the Office clip art collection or from others that you have on your computer. Figure 18.13 shows the new images and their corresponding captions.

FIGURE 18.13

Finish replacing the graphic images and supplying appropriate captions.

 Note   You can also use the drawing tools (visible at the bottom of your screen when you are in FrontPage's Normal view) to create your own shapes and lines. Tools you'll recognize from your use of the Drawing toolbar in Word and PowerPoint also appear on this toolbar, enabling you to flip, rotate, and change the stacking order of items you draw.

18

Using Animated GIFs

Although using too many animated graphics can create a circus-like atmosphere on your Web page, one or two images that move can add visual interest. If your Web site pertains to a light-hearted or entertaining subject, you can use more of them.

To insert an animated graphic on the Web page, follow these steps:

1. Click to position your cursor where you want the image to be placed. Figure 18.14 shows the cursor blinking on the right side of the Web page, below the last line of text.

 2. Choose Insert, Picture, From File, or click the Insert Picture From File button on the Standard toolbar. The Picture dialog box opens with the Select File dialog box on top, as shown in Figure 18.15.

FIGURE 18.14

To save yourself the time and effort of moving the file after insertion, position your cursor at the desired location first.

Cursor positioned
here

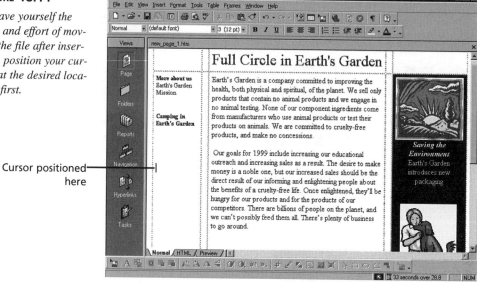

FIGURE 18.15

The Picture dialog box shows you the contents of the C:\My Documents\My Webs folder.

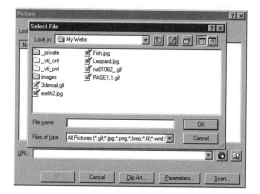

3. Place the CD-ROM that came with this book in your CD-ROM drive and navigate to the CD-ROM drive from within the Select File dialog box.

4. Double-click the 3Demail.gif file.

The animation won't appear until you switch to Preview. Click that tab to see the animated effect. Figure 18.16 shows the animated graphic in place on the Web page.

FIGURE 18.16

This animated graphic will later become a link that sends an email message.

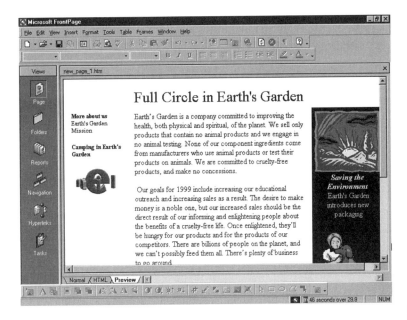

Connecting to Web sites and Files with Hyperlinks

As was stated previously, anything—a single word, a sentence, a graphic—can be a hyperlink. Essentially, whatever you have selected at the time that you click the Hyperlink button becomes a link that points to a Web site on the Web or a file on your intranet.

18

> **Note**
>
> **NEW TERM** An *intranet* is a closed version of the Internet, normally run by a company on their local area network. Departments and individual employees can create and maintain their own intranet Web pages, and information that is useful to people on the job can be viewed and retrieved from these pages.

Creating Text and Graphic Hyperlinks

Before creating a hyperlink, it's a good idea to know the exact name and location of the file or Web site to which the hyperlink will point. If the hyperlink will point to a Web site, be sure you know the exact URL; if it will point to a file, be sure you know the entire and correct path and filename.

Note

NEW TERM A *URL* (*Uniform Resource Locator*) is the address of a Web site. For example, www.samspublishing.com is the URL for this book's publisher. The www indicates that it's a site on the World Wide Web; samspublishing is the domain name (normally the organization's name); and .com is the extension that indicates that the site is a commercial site for a commercial organization. Other extensions include .org (for nonprofit organizations), .edu (for schools), and .gov (for government sites).

Tip

When you are creating a hyperlink that points to a file, make sure that the file is located on a drive to which all readers have access. If the file is on your local drive or points to a file on CD-ROM or floppy disk, other Internet or intranet users can't access it.

After you know where the hyperlink will point, you can create the hyperlink. Follow these steps:

1. Select the text or graphic object that is to become a hyperlink. Avoid using large selections of text, restricting your selection to single words or short phrases within a sentence. In this case, select the first section heading from the left side of the screen, as shown in Figure 18.17.

FIGURE 18.17

This text will point to a Web page.

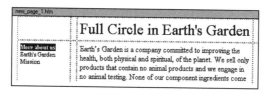

2. Choose Insert, Hyperlink, or click the Hyperlink button on the Standard toolbar. The Create Hyperlink dialog box opens, as shown in Figure 18.18.

3. In the URL box, type the following address (be sure to place it after the existing http:// content):

   www.limehat.com/earthsgarden

4. Click OK to create the hyperlink and close the dialog box.

Switch to Preview and point to the section heading; notice that your mouse pointer turns to a pointing hand, as shown in Figure 18.19. If your computer is currently connected to the Internet, you can click the link and go to the site to which the hyperlink points.

FIGURE 18.18

Your hyperlink can point to any URL or file you select.

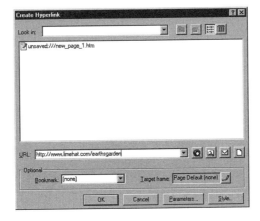

FIGURE 18.19

You know you're pointing to a hyperlink if your mouse pointer turns into a pointing hand.

By default, Hyperlink text turns blue and is underlined

18

To create a graphic hyperlink, you can follow the steps from the preceding procedure, except that you start by selecting a graphic instead of text. To turn one of your page's graphics into a hyperlink that links to and starts the Earth's Garden Sales Meeting presentation, follow these steps:

1. In Normal view, select the graphic at the top of the panel on the right side of the Web page (see Figure 18.20).

FIGURE 18.20

Your graphics can serve two purposes—decoration and function—when you turn them into hyperlinks.

2. Choose Insert, Hyperlink, or click the Insert Hyperlink button on the toolbar.

 3. In the Create Hyperlink dialog box (see Figure 18.21), click the Make a hyperlink to a file on your computer button.

FIGURE 18.21

Indicate your intention to create a hyperlink that points to a file rather than a Web page.

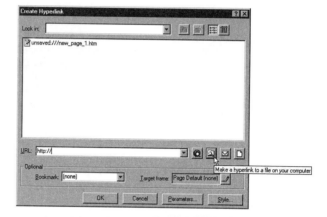

4. The Select File dialog box opens and defaults to the My Webs folder, which was created when FrontPage was installed (see Figure 18.22). Navigate to the Earth's Garden Sales Meeting.ppt file on your local drive (the file was created on Days 15, "Developing a PowerPoint Presentation," and 16, "Creating a Multimedia Presentation"). If you don't have the file, you can copy it from the CD-ROM that accompanies this book.

FIGURE 18.22

Navigate to the folder that contains the presentation and double-click it to create the hyperlink and close the open dialog boxes.

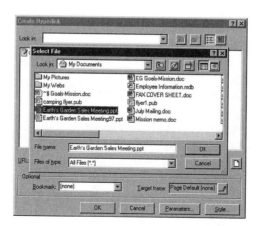

After you select the presentation file, the Select File and Create Hyperlink dialog boxes both close, and your graphic turns into a hyperlink. Switch to Preview and test the link—the presentation starts, and the slide timings go into effect, running the slideshow on your screen. To end the show before the last slide, click the Normal tab.

Tip

When you test your page in a Web browser, you can click the Stop or Back buttons to end the slideshow to which your hyperlink points.

Creating an Email Hyperlink

So far, you've created two hyperlinks—one points to a Web site on the Internet, the other to a file on your local drive. Now, you'll create a link that sends an email message, which is a common item found on Web sites. By providing such a hyperlink, you make it possible for people who visit your site to contact you.

To create an email hyperlink, follow these steps:

1. In Normal view, click once on the animated GIF that was added to the bottom of the Web page.

2. Click the Insert Hyperlink button to open the Create Hyperlink dialog box.

3. Click the Make a hyperlink that sends Email button. The Create E-mail Hyperlink dialog box opens, as shown in Figure 18.23.

18

FIGURE 18.23

Turn any text or graphic into an email link that addresses a message to the email address that you specify.

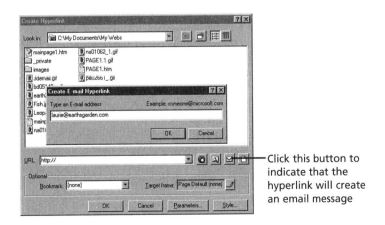

Click this button to indicate that the hyperlink will create an email message

4. Type the exact email address to which messages are to be sent, and click OK.

5. Click OK to close the Create Hyperlink dialog box.

Switch to Preview and test your link—if your computer is configured for Internet access, a New Message window opens, addressed to the email address you indicated when you created the email hyperlink. Figure 18.24 shows the email hyperlink graphic and the resulting New Message window.

FIGURE 18.24

A great tool for soliciting questions and feedback from visitors to your site, an email link makes it easy for people to send you messages.

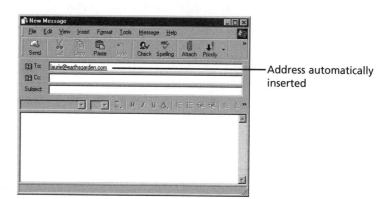

Address automatically inserted

Creating and Enhancing Graphic Images with PhotoDraw

What if you don't like any of the clip art images that come with Office 2000, and you've surfed the Web for clip art and graphic images and can't find anything you like? Maybe you need an interesting design to serve as a button that the reader clicks to activate another page on your Web site.... Prior to Office 2000, if you needed to create any original artwork, you had to use a third-party program or go to an application such as Adobe Photoshop or CorelDRAW. The Office 2000 Premium Edition, however, includes PhotoDraw, an exciting new tool for enhancing graphic images and creating original artwork.

Today you'll create your own original artwork in PhotoDraw and use it on the Web page you're designing in FrontPage. To begin, follow these steps:

1. With your FrontPage Web page in progress, save it (name it `MainPage1`) and open PhotoDraw by selecting it from the Start menu's Programs list.

2. In the Microsoft PhotoDraw dialog box (see Figure 18.25), choose Blank Picture, and then click OK.

FIGURE 18.25

To create your own unique image, choose the Blank Picture option.

3. In the New dialog box, leave Default Picture selected, and click OK. This gives you a blank worksheet on which to draw your image.

4. The PhotoDraw workspace is displayed, as shown in Figure 18.26. Many of the drawing tools that you see on the PhotoDraw toolbar will look familiar.

18

FIGURE 18.26

The PhotoDraw work-space gives you room to draw and edit, and tools with which to create exciting visual effects.

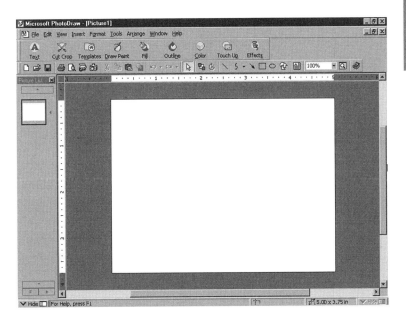

5. Click the Ellipse tool and, using the Shift key to draw a perfect circle, drag to draw the shape. Figure 18.27 shows the resulting circle. The color and thickness of the line are the results of PhotoDraw's default settings.

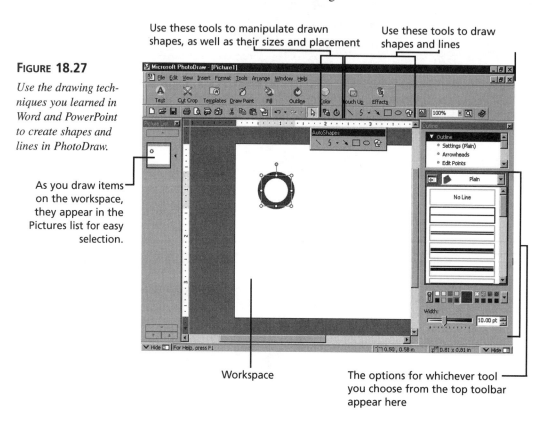

Use these tools to manipulate drawn shapes, as well as their sizes and placement

Use these tools to draw shapes and lines

FIGURE 18.27

Use the drawing techniques you learned in Word and PowerPoint to create shapes and lines in PhotoDraw.

As you draw items on the workspace, they appear in the Pictures list for easy selection.

Workspace

The options for whichever tool you choose from the top toolbar appear here

6. Using the Outline panel that appears on the right side of the screen (see Figure 18.28), change the color of the circle to green and adjust the width of the outline to 5.00 points.

7. The resulting circle isn't terribly exciting, so you need to apply more interesting effects. Click the Effects button and choose 3-D. The Outline panel changes to a 3D panel, as shown in Figure 18.29. Click to select and apply one of the 3D images to your circle.

8. Click and drag the green rotate handle (see Figure 18.30). Drag to the right until the circle is standing on its side.

FIGURE **18.28**

The Outline panel contains options for changing the appearance of your drawn or scanned objects.

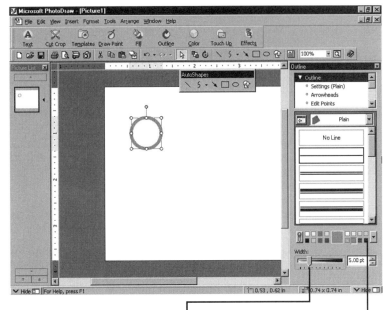

Drag to increase or decrease the width of the line or the outline of the selected shape

Choose a color from the color palette

18

FIGURE **18.29**

3D tools and options appear in this panel when you choose 3D from the Effects list.

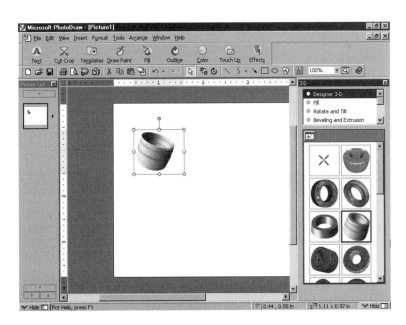

FIGURE 18.30

Rotate the object by eye until it reaches the desired angle.

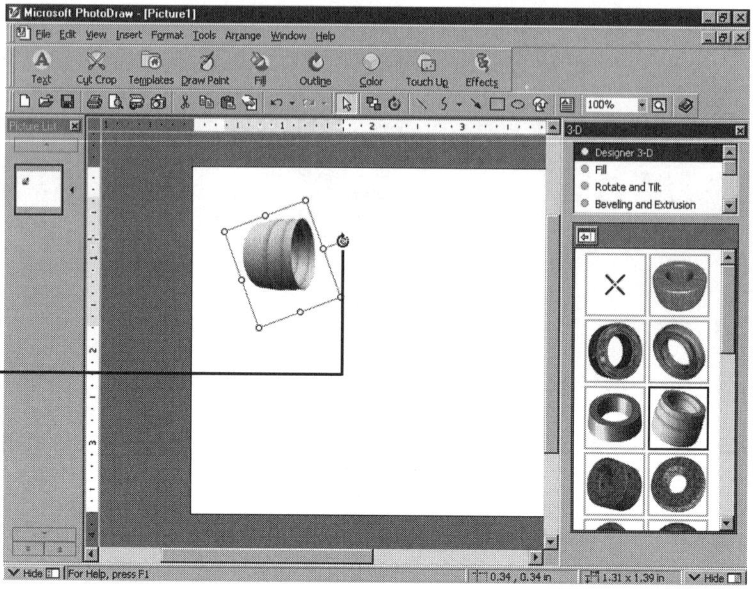

Drag from this handle to rotate the selected object

9. With the circle selected, choose Edit, Copy.

10. Switch back to FrontPage, and click in the empty cell to the left of the heading text (see Figure 18.31).

FIGURE 18.31

Position your cursor where you want the new shape to appear.

Cursor is positioned here to indicate placement of image on the Clipboard

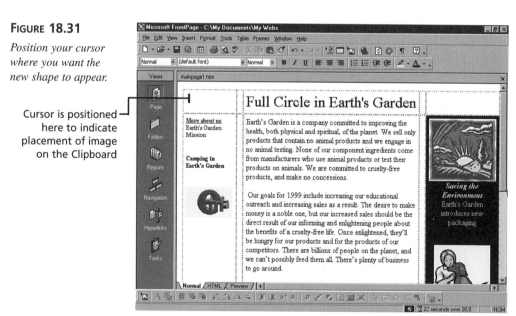

11. Choose Edit, Paste to insert the circle image you drew in PhotoDraw. The image appears (see Figure 18.32), and can be resized as needed.

FIGURE 18.32

The shape you created and enhanced in PhotoDraw can be used as a hyperlink, or merely as a decorative logo next to the heading.

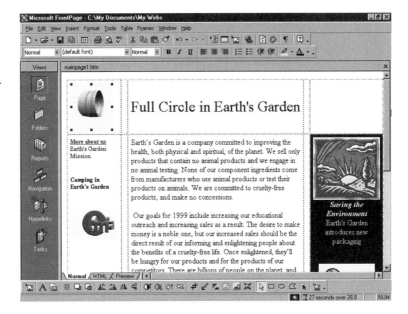

18

Note

If you want to use this particular shape again, you can save it. From within PhotoDraw, choose File, Save for Use In. Select On the Web, and click Next to begin working with the Save for Use in Wizard. This wizard asks you questions about how the graphic is to look and work in its potential Web surroundings. The file is saved as a GIF (by default) with a name that you specify.

Previewing Your Web Page with a Browser

After you complete the first phase of Web page design, it's a good idea to preview it in a real browser, not just the Preview view in FrontPage. You can use Internet Explorer or Netscape to preview your Web page, or you can even open it in a product such as America Online, if that is the browser you use most often. It's a good idea to preview your Web page in two or more different browsers before you post it to your Web server—this enables you to see how the page will look to people using a variety of browsers to view your page.

To open your Web page in a browser, follow these steps:

1. Make sure that your Web page is saved.

2. Open the browser of your choice. You don't need to be online—you're going to be previewing a file that's on your computer, not the Web.

3. In the browser, choose File, Open. In the Microsoft Internet Explorer dialog box (see Figure 18.33), locate and select the Web page.

FIGURE 18.33

Indicate the path and filename of the Web page you want to preview.

4. Click OK in the Open dialog box to open the selected file.

5. Your Web page opens in the browser window. Maximize the window to see the entire page, and test your links—if your links point to Web sites, of course, you must be connected to the Internet in order to test them.

Figure 18.34 shows the Web page that you created today, previewed in Internet Explorer 5 (which comes with Office 2000).

Posting Your Web Page to a Web Server

Before you can post your Web page to a server, you must have, or have access to, a Web server. If you're creating a Web page for your company or organization, they will either have a server or they will have purchased space on one for use in storing their Web site. Access to that site will be by password only, and you will need FTP (File Transfer Protocol) software in order to upload your Web page from your local drive to the remote server. If the server is in your same physical location, and your computer is connected to it via cable, you can copy the Web page file to the server, into the appropriate folder.

> WS_FTP Pro is contained on the CD-ROM that accompanies this book. Install it by double-clicking the executable (WS_FTP.exe) on the CD-ROM—the software installs in its own folder and creates its own desktop icon for you.

FIGURE **18.34**

See your page as the world will see it on the Internet by previewing it in at least one popular browser.

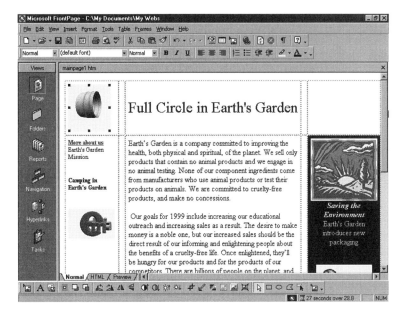

Small businesses and home users can take advantage of server space through their ISP (Internet service provider) or an online community such as America Online. Through the ISP, you can rent space on their Web server and create your own Web site. In some cases, you can email your Web page to the ISP, who can take care of posting it for you.

Summary

Today you learned how to use Microsoft FrontPage, Office 2000's Web page design and creation program. Starting with a Web page template, you replaced sample text and graphics with your own, and inserted additional graphic images to enhance the page. Both text and graphics were turned into hyperlinks, linking the Web page to an existing Internet Web site, a file on your local drive, and to email. In addition, you learned to use PhotoDraw, one of the new programs in the Office 2000 suite, to draw and enhance a shape for use on the Web page.

Q&A

Q **Today I created a single Web page. How do I create a Web site with multiple pages?**

A By creating a series of independent pages, each one linked to the others via text and graphic hyperlinks, you can create an entire Web site. All the pages must be on the Web server, in the folders specified when you build your interpage links.

Q **Is there any limit to the number of pages I can have in a Web site?**

A No, other than the amount of server space you have. If you're purchasing space, you might need to purchase more if you create a lot of pages with large graphic files on them.

Q **Can I add sound to my Web page?**

A Yes. Although the use of sounds on a Web site is generally considered unprofessional, if yours is a business that is normally associated with fun or entertainment, you can add music to your site. To add music (or any other type of sound) that plays when the site is opened (also known as a background sound), right-click the page (in Normal view) and choose Page Properties from the shortcut menu. On the General tab's Background Sound section, click the Browse button to open the folder that contains the sound file you want to use, and double-click to select it. In the Page Properties box, leave the Forever option checked so that the sound plays the entire time the page is onscreen, or remove the checkmark and enter the number of times the sound is to play consecutively. Click OK to exit the dialog box after your choices have been made.

Workshop

The section that follows is a quick quiz about the day. If you have any problems answering any of the questions, see the section that follows the quiz for all the answers.

Quiz

1. What does HTML stand for, and what is it?
2. Describe the purpose of the Preview tab in Page view.
3. True or False: To replace the sample graphics on the Web page, you must delete them and then insert a new graphic.
4. Describe the benefit of using graphics as hyperlinks.
5. Why is the amount of graphic content on your Web page important?

Quiz Answers

1. HTML stands for Hypertext Markup Language, and it is the programming language for Web pages. Hypertext code tells the computer what to display (text and graphics), as well as how and where to display it.

2. The Preview tab shows you how your Web-page-in-progress will look when it is viewed through a Web browser. Even after using the Preview tab, you need to open your page in Internet Explorer or Netscape to check it in a true browser environment before posting the Web page.

3. False. If the sample image is selected when you insert the new image, the deletion and replacement are simultaneous, and no separate deletion need take place.

4. Using graphics as hyperlinks adds visual interest to your site, and saves you the space taken up by potentially boring text. As the old saying goes, "A picture is worth a thousand words."

5. Having too many graphic images can detract from the professional appearance of your Web site, and using many or large graphic files can cause your page to load very slowly online.

18

DAY **19**

Distributing Data Through a Web Page

Building on the Web page created on Day 18, "Designing a Web Page with FrontPage," today focuses on the use of Web pages for the storage and distribution of business data. Whether your Web site is on the Internet or your company's intranet, you can use Office 2000 to generate the Web page itself and store Excel worksheet data, Access table data, and PowerPoint presentations and their inherent information. After it is stored, this information can be easily retrieved for manipulation on a user's local drive. These concepts are covered today; specifically, you will learn the following skills:

- Adding an Excel worksheet and Access table data to an existing Web page
- Working with data on the Web site
- Publishing a PowerPoint presentation to the Web and running it from a Web site
- Copying Web data to your local drive for manipulation in Excel or Access

Using Excel and Access Data on a Web Page

In addition to the Web's marketing and sales potential, many organizations use their Web sites to disseminate business data. Sharing important information with employees and customers alike enables people to make faster and more effective business decisions. In addition, the use of a central location for important information makes it easier to keep information up-to-date and to eliminate the error prone "grapevine" that many companies have relied on in the past.

Your Excel worksheet and Access table data are great resources unto themselves, and are easily shared with customers and co-workers via the Web. Adding Excel and Access content to a Web page is simple, as is using that data after it's posted to the Web page.

Inserting Worksheet Content

You can add an entire workbook, a single worksheet, or a section of a worksheet to your Web site. Today you will add a section of a worksheet to a Web page. For this procedure, start with the Web page you created on Day 18. If you don't have this on your local drive, you can copy it from the CD-ROM that accompanies this book—the file is called mainpage1.htm.

Before adding Excel worksheet content to the Web page, you must create a page for it and link that page to the mainpage1.htm document. To do so, follow these steps:

1. Open mainpage1.htm through FrontPage and view it in Pages view, on the Normal tab, as shown in Figure 19.1.

 2. Create a new page by clicking the New button. This starts a new page with the blank Normal page template.

 3. Save the new page as datapage1.htm by choosing File, Save, or by clicking the Save button.

4. Using the Window menu, switch back to mainpage1.htm.

5. On the page you created on Day 18, select the words *increasing our educational outreach* in the second paragraph in the center column of the page. The selected text is shown in Figure 19.2.

6. Click the Hyperlink button; in the Create Hyperlink dialog box, double-click the datapage1.htm document in the My Webs folder.

The hyperlink is created, and you can see that the text has turned blue and is underlined, as shown in Figure 19.3. You can switch to Preview to test the hyperlink.

FIGURE 19.1

Open the main page you created on Day 18, and then build a new page to which this page will connect via hyperlink.

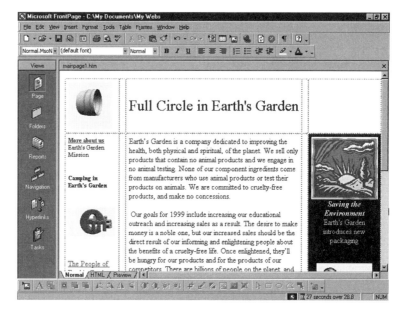

FIGURE 19.2

The selected text becomes a hyperlink that points to the data-page1.htm document, which holds pertinent Excel worksheet data.

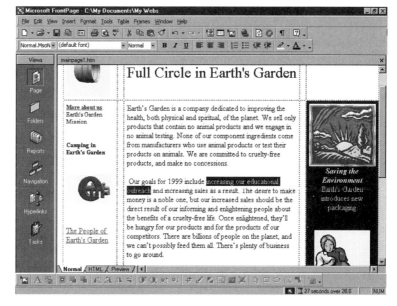

19

FIGURE **19.3**

*Hyperlink text is blue
and underlined. Click
the link in Preview to
see that it points to the
as yet blank page, dat-
apage1.htm.*

> Our goals for 1999 include increasing our educational
> outreach and increasing sales as a result. The desire to make
> money is a noble one, but our increased sales should be the
> direct result of our informing and enlightening people about
> the benefits of a cruelty-free life. Once enlightened, they'll
> be hungry for our products and for the products of our
> competitors. There are billions of people on the planet, and
> we can't possibly feed them all. There's plenty of business

Now that the page that will hold the Excel data is created and linked to the main page,
you can insert the Excel worksheet data onto the page. Follow these steps:

1. Switch to the datapage1.htm document. Your cursor is blinking, awaiting your
   entries onto the page, as shown in Figure 19.4.

FIGURE **19.4**

*You can type text or
insert graphic content
onto this now blank
page in preparation for
the Excel data that is
to be added.*

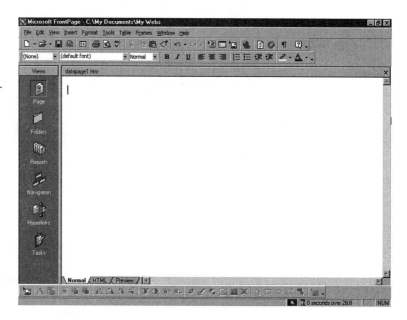

2. Open the Report Data.xls file, which is found in the Sample Files folder on the
   CD-ROM that accompanies this book. After it is open, save it to your My
   Documents folder to avoid accessing it from the CD during this procedure.

3. In the Report Data.xls file, click the Educational Alliances tab. Select cells
   A1–G18, as shown in Figure 19.5.

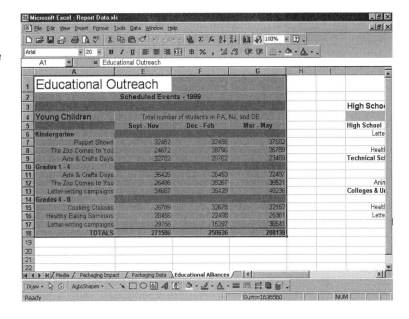

4. Choose File, Save as Web Page. In the Save As dialog box (see Figure 19.6), click the Selection option (the range of cells is displayed next to it).

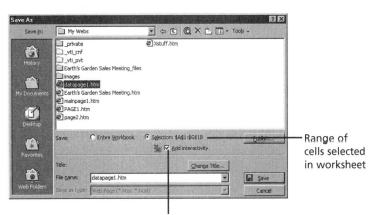

Range of cells selected in worksheet

Turn on the Add interactivity option

19

5. Click to place a checkmark the Add interactivity checkbox. This option, which is available only if Selection is selected, enables people who are viewing the data through a browser to utilize Excel's tools on the Web page to manipulate the data.

6. Open the My Webs folder and double-click the datapage1.htm file. A prompt appears, replacing the Save As dialog box (see Figure 19.7). Click the Add to File button to add the selected worksheet data to the existing page rather than replace the page entirely.

FIGURE 19.7

Choose Add to File to insert the selected portion of the worksheet into the existing Web page.

7. Switch back to FrontPage and close the datapage1.htm file without saving it (click the No button when you are prompted).

8. Reopen the datapage1.htm file (File, Recent Files, datapage1.htm). The data from the Excel worksheet is displayed, as shown in Figure 19.8.

A small group of Excel tools is available for use in editing, summing, sorting, and filtering the data

FIGURE 19.8

After you reopen the Web page, the added Excel worksheet data appears.

Drag the handles to reposition the data

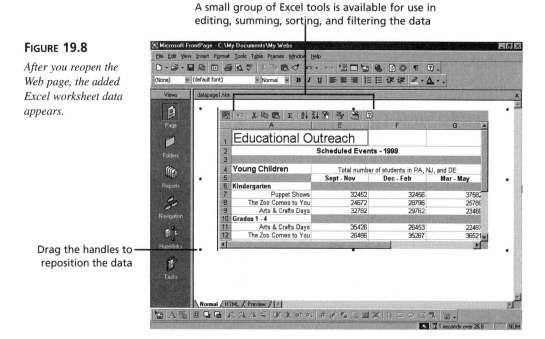

Switch to Preview or choose File, Preview in Browser to see exactly how the Excel content will appear on the Web. Note that Excel tools, as well as column letters and row

numbers, appear around your data. You can select and interact with the cells within the data, as shown in Figure 19.9.

FIGURE 19.9

Select cells on the Web page (either previewed offline or after you've posted it to the Web) and copy them to a local worksheet.

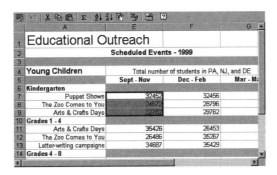

| **Note** | If you prefer to start from within the application that contains the data you'll be using on your Web page, you can skip the process of creating the blank Web page first. From within Excel, choose File, Save As Web Page. Choose to save the Entire Workbook or just the active Sheet, and then give the Web page a name. You can then go to your home page and create a hyperlink to this new page. Remember that unless you only save a selection as a Web page, the Add Interactivity option won't be available, limiting your use of the data on the Web page. |

| **Caution** | You might consider adding some explanatory or warning text just below your data, informing Web page visitors that the changes they make to the data that is displayed are transient. Some people might be concerned about making changes, afraid that they're changing the actual data, whereas others might be disappointed that their changes don't have a permanent effect. |

19

Inserting an Access Table

Access table data is as easily inserted as Excel worksheet content, and the process is nearly identical. Either work with the Employee Information.mdb file you created on Day 13, "Setting Up a Database," or copy the file from the CD-ROM that accompanies this book (you'll find it in the Sample Files folder). If you copy the file from the CD-ROM, copy it to your local My Documents folder so that you can follow this procedure as it is written.

Before accessing this data, however, you need to create a Web page to hold it. Follow these steps to build a third Web page in FrontPage:

1. In FrontPage, click the New button to create a blank Web page. Save the new blank page as datapage2.htm.

2. Assuming that the mainpage1.htm file is still open, switch to it and click above the email graphic, as shown in Figure 19.10. If necessary, click on a blank line above the graphic and press Enter to move the email graphic down slightly.

FIGURE 19.10

Position your cursor to create a text hyperlink that will point to the new page that contains Access data.

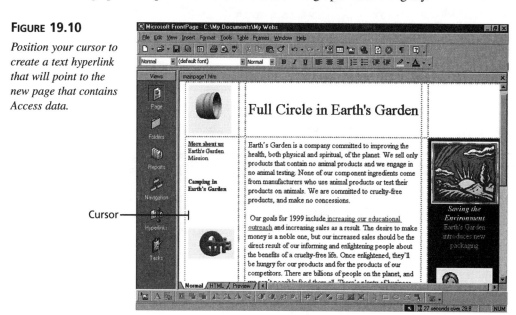

3. Type the words The People of Earth's Garden, and then select the text, as shown in Figure 19.11.

FIGURE 19.11

Type the text that will become your hyper-link.

4. Click the Hyperlink button and, in the Create Hyperlink dialog box, double-click the datapage2.htm file.

The hyperlink to the new page is created, and you can test it in Preview. Figure 19.12 shows the new hyperlink text.

FIGURE 19.12

Test your link from within Preview mode. Be sure that it points to the new page.

The next step is to add Access data to the new page. To accomplish this task, you need to open Access and then open the Employee Information.mdb file and follow these steps:

1. In the Employee Information.mdb file (see Figure 19.13), right-click the Staff List table icon.

FIGURE 19.13

You'll use portions of the Staff List data on the Web page.

 2. Choose Copy from the shortcut menu, and then click the Paste button on the toolba. The Paste Table As dialog box opens, as shown in Figure 19.14.

FIGURE 19.14

Create a copy of the Staff List table so that you can edit the table for use on the Web page without affecting the data in the original table.

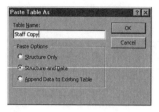

3. Type Staff Copy in the Table Name box. Be sure that in the Paste Options section of the dialog box, Structure and Data is selected; click OK.

4. Double-click the Staff Copy icon to open the copy of Staff List. Now rearrange and delete some of the fields to make the table's data appropriate for the Web page.

5. Click the First Name button at the top of that column in the table. Drag the column to the left until your mouse pointer is between Employee Number and Last Name. Release the mouse, and see that the First Name field now precedes the Last Name field, as shown in Figure 19.15.

FIGURE 19.15

To place your employee names in the more friendly first-name-first order, rearrange your fields.

Employee Numbe	First Name	Last Name	Department	Date Hired	Current Salary	Insurance
123-45-6780	John	Kline	Marketing	7/15/98	$57,450.00	☐
123-45-6789	Merrick	Shuster	Accounting	12/5/98	$65,450.00	☑
123-46-7856	David	Mermelstein	Administration	6/25/97	$45,600.00	☑
124-89-8736	Peg	Bachmann	Sales	4/15/98	$62,750.00	☑
134-45-7891	Frank	Gradel	Marketing	4/16/96	$58,500.00	☑
156-78-9833	Alan	Burrell	Human Resources	1/28/96	$58,300.00	☐
158-47-9855	John	Pale	Human Resources	6/25/95	$62,400.00	☑
171-65-7898	Isabel	Willard	Administration	6/14/96	$45,200.00	☑
175-98-3463	Ann	Talbot	Marketing	6/16/97	$61,200.00	☑
197-87-2347	Ella	Kennedy	Administration	10/5/98	$42,500.00	☐
231-98-2994	Wendy	Derby	Marketing	11/16/97	$60,250.00	☑
234-56-7890	Alice	Graham	Accounting	5/26/94	$58,500.00	☑
245-56-6632	Linda	Kline	Administration	5/3/96	$46,500.00	☑
245-67-8214	Deborah	Fuller	Sales	3/25/96	$68,500.00	☑
247-12-9865	Joshua	Ulrich	Sales	3/20/96	$62,500.00	☑
248-97-1527	Zachary	Ulrich	Sales	3/15/97	$62,500.00	☑
310-98-2371	Joan	Mattaliano	Accounting	4/30/97	$48,250.00	☑
321-45-7890	Barbara	Weller	Administration	2/15/99	$42,400.00	☑
					$0.00	☐

Record: 1 of 19

6. Delete the following fields one at a time by clicking on their field name and choosing Edit, Delete Column. You can also right-click the column and choose Delete Column from the shortcut menu. You'll be prompted each time to confirm your intention to delete (click Yes):

   - Employee Number (you'll see an additional prompt when you delete this field, asking if you intend to delete the primary key—click Yes)

- Date Hired
- Current Salary
- Insurance
- Vacation Days
- Date of Last Review
- Review Grade

 7. The remaining three fields can now be sorted alphabetically so that they appear in Last Name order when they are added to the Web page. Click on any of the employees' last names, and click the Sort Ascending button.

 8. Select all 18 records by dragging through the Record Selector buttons. Choose Edit, Copy, or click the Copy button. Figure 19.16 shows all 18 sorted records selected.

FIGURE 19.16

Select the records that you want to appear on your Web page—in this case, you'll use all of them.

9. After sorting and copying the 18 records, switch back to FrontPage and display the blank datapage2.htm Web page.

 10. Choose Edit, Paste, or click the Paste button. The records appear as a table on the Web page. Figure 19.17 shows the Access data on datapage2.htm in Preview mode.

You can use the FrontPage Table menu and other formatting tools to change the placement and dimensions of the table as needed—these tools work much like the table tools you encountered in Word. You can also add descriptive text above or below the table, as well as graphic content for added visual impact. Figure 19.18 shows the page with added content, including an icon that links back to the home page (mainpage1.htm). See if you can insert a graphic on your copy of this page and create a hyperlink back to the mainpage1.htm document.

19

FIGURE 19.17

Your Access data appears on the Web page, including the field names.

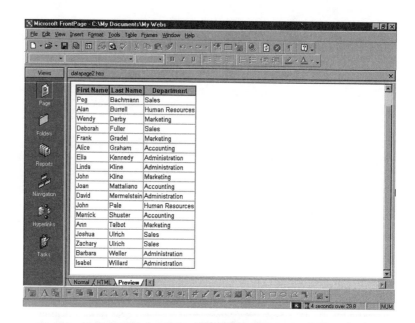

FIGURE 19.18

Complete your Web page with some text, graphics, and a hyperlink to take the visitor back to your home page.

A single table cell with text and graphic is added above the data table

This graphic links back to the home page

Table is centered (through Table Properties dialog box)

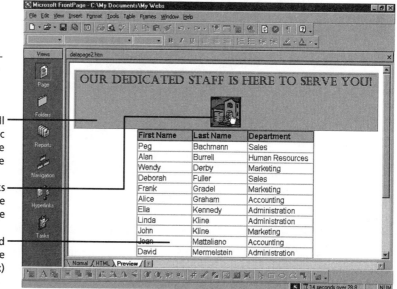

Note

> The Export command in the Access File menu can be used to export selected records as HTML (you see .htm as an option in the Save As dialog box that opens when you choose the Export command). This isn't a recommended technique, however, for adding data tables to Web pages—the field names don't appear with the data, and the visual formatting of the content isn't as visually pleasing as the results you get by pasting the records directly onto the Web page.

Working with Web Data

The data you place on your Web pages can become a resource for your customers to find out more about your company, and for your employees to find information they need to do their jobs. Many companies maintain Web sites full of information to which their employees or customers need access. Before the popularity of the Web, companies had to store information on a mainframe or other central computer, and employees had to search for and comb through open files to find the data they needed. Customers were generally unable to tap into the company's computer, relying on requests for information or marketing materials that might not contain the data they needed. By utilizing the Internet, an organization can market itself and distribute important data at the same time, using a vehicle (a Web browser) to which both their employees and their customers have access.

Web page data can simply be viewed by looking at the Web pages through a browser, or it can literally be used—copied to the visitor's computer and manipulated in their own software. If, for example, a customer needs to see a complete product list, he or she can look at it on your company's Web page, and then copy it to his or her computer. After it is copied, the data can be printed or played with—the user can enter costs and prices and create a report or purchase order from the data.

In addition, as was demonstrated when the Excel data was added to a Web page, you can use the Add interactivity option to make Excel tools (a limited set of the most commonly used tools) available right on the Web page. Figure 19.19 shows the Excel content that is added to datapage1.htm, with changes made to the data, as well as a group of numbers totaled with AutoSum. These changes appear only on the user's screen, and disappear when the page is refreshed through the browser.

Today you will be doing some cost analysis on the Educational Outreach data on the datapage1.htm Web page. After copying the data to a new blank worksheet, cost information is added and calculations are created to determine the cost of the educational programs. This level of manipulation requires copying the content to a new worksheet (on a local installation of Excel) because the interactivity tools that are available with the data on the

19

Web page don't allow additional columns to be added, nor do the changes that are made last beyond the time that the Web page is displayed.

FIGURE 19.19

Play with the Excel content on the Web page, making transient changes to the cells' content and creating simple formulas.

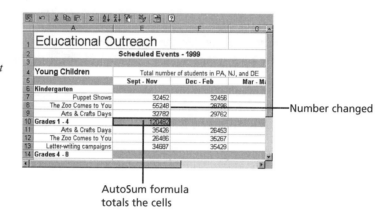

Number changed

AutoSum formula
totals the cells

To copy content from the Web page to a local copy of Excel, follow these steps:

1. Through your browser (to simulate a visitor viewing your page on the Web), open mainpage1.htm; click the link that opens datapage1.htm, as shown in Figure 19.20.

FIGURE 19.20

Click the hyperlink text in the second paragraph to open the page that contains educational outreach data.

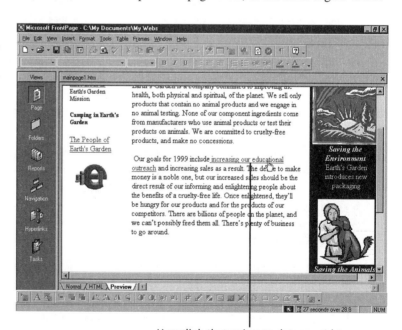

Hyperlink that points to datapage1.htm

2. When you are in the datapage1.htm document, click and drag through the cells on the Web page. Figure 19.21 shows the cells selected.

FIGURE 19.21

Select the content that you want to use on your local computer.

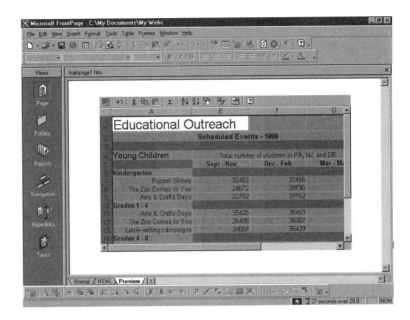

FIGURE 19.21

Select the content that you want to use on your local computer.

3. Choose Edit, Copy, or click the Copy button along the top of the data.

4. Switch back to or open Excel and start a new blank workbook.

5. Click in a cell on Sheet1, and choose Edit, Paste, or click the Paste button.

6. The column widths might need to be adjusted in the pasted content—widen them as needed for legibility, as shown in Figure 19.22.

7. Enter your costs per student, as shown in Figure 19.23.

8. Create calculations that multiply the number of students by the cost per student for a total cost per event. Figure 19.24 shows the formula for the cost of a year of Puppet Shows in cell J9.

9. Save the workbook as Educational Costs.xls.

After it is created, this workbook can become its own Web page, accessible from the datapage1.htm page. Save this new page as a Web page (File, Save as Web Page) and create a hyperlink from the datapage1.htm Web page to your new cost data page. Be sure to test the new page and hyperlink through your browser.

19

Drag the column border to widen these three columns

FIGURE 19.22

The pasted content is a bit tight—widening these columns makes it easier to work with the data.

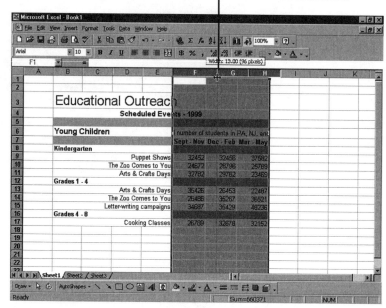

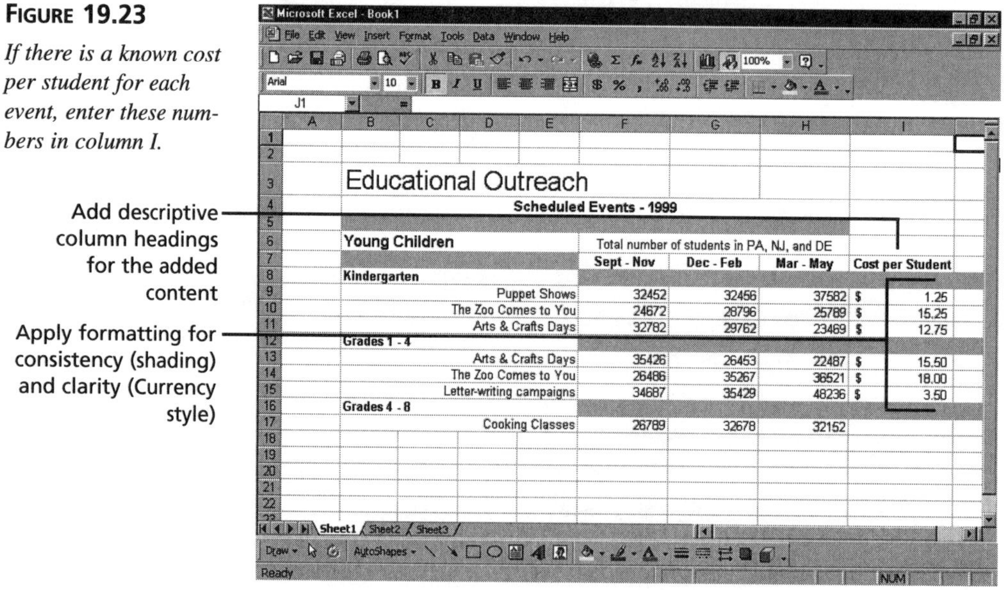

FIGURE 19.23

If there is a known cost per student for each event, enter these numbers in column I.

Add descriptive column headings for the added content

Apply formatting for consistency (shading) and clarity (Currency style)

FIGURE 19.24

Calculate the total number of students for the year, and multiply that by the cost per student.

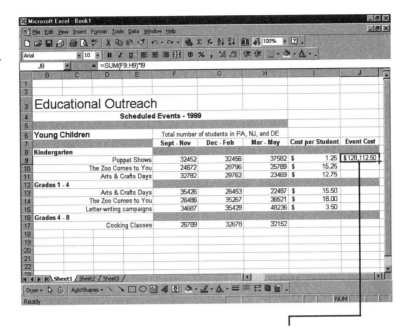

After creating the formula once, paste it down the entire column of events

Publishing Your Web Page with PowerPoint

A PowerPoint presentation can become an online event—users can click a hyperlink that points to the presentation (stored on a Web page) and view the presentation slide-by-slide.

How is this useful? Instead of mailing your presentation (with the PowerPoint Viewer program) on disk to prospective customers or sending your salespeople around to client sites to run the show, you can place your show on your Web site. Through email or an inexpensive mass mailing (which is cheaper because no disk needs to be mailed, reducing the weight of the mailing), you can contact your existing and prospective customers and direct them to your Web site.

Tip

If you choose to send an email message, you can insert a hyperlink into that message to take them directly to your site. Most email programs give you the capability to do this—in Outlook, if you type a correctly-constructed Web address, such as www.limehat.com, into the text of your message, that URL text automatically turns into a hyperlink that points to that site. If the email recipient reads their mail while they are online, they can click the link within the message and go to the Web site.

19

Today you will publish the Earth's Garden Sales Meeting.ppt presentation to a Web page; if you don't have the file you created on Days 15, "Developing a PowerPoint Presentation," and 16, "Creating a Multimedia Presentation," you can obtain a copy of the file on the CD-ROM that accompanies this book. You'll find the file in the Sample Files folder on the CD, and you can copy it to your My Documents folder before beginning the following steps:

1. Open the Earth's Garden Sales Meeting.ppt file from your My Documents folder. You might find it on your File menu's most recently used file list.

2. Choose File, Save as Web Page. The Save As dialog box opens, and the Save as Type list box is already set to Web Page (*.htm, *.html) for you, as shown in Figure 19.25.

FIGURE 19.25

When you publish your presentation as a Web page, it is saved as an HTML file, and the .htm extension is automatically added to the filename.

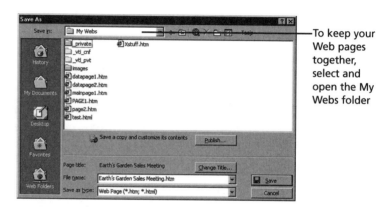

To keep your Web pages together, select and open the My Webs folder

3. Click the Publish button to open the Publish as Web Page dialog box, shown in Figure 19.26.

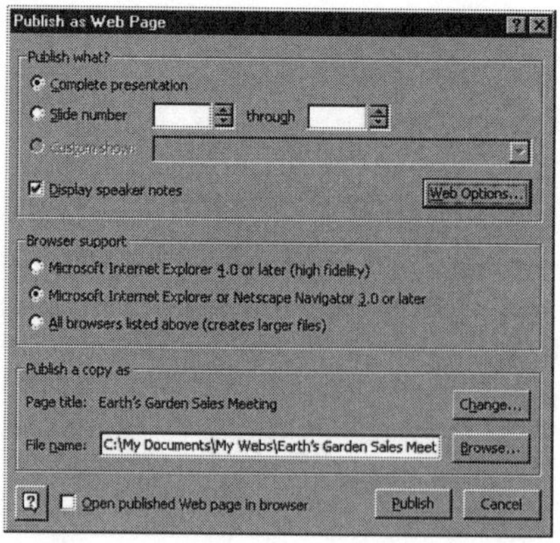

FIGURE 19.26

Choose which slides to include and where to store the published Web page.

Tip

In addition to an .htm version of your presentation file, a folder containing all your slide elements —graphics, sounds, and so forth—is created and given the same name as the file.

4. Leave the Complete presentation option selected in the Publish what? section. Remove the Display speaker notes checkmark.

5. In the Browser support section, choose Microsoft Internet Explorer or Netscape Navigator so that users of either browser can view your presentation.

6. Click the Web Options button to open the Web Options dialog box, as shown in Figure 19.27. To include the animations you added to your presentation on Day 16, click the Show slide animation while browsing option.

FIGURE 19.27

The General tab's options enable you to control how your presentation will look and work in a Web browser.

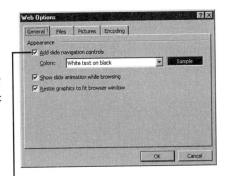

This option creates a list of slides (by title) along the right side of the browser window

7. Click OK in the Web Options dialog box to return to the Publish As Web Page dialog box.

8. Click Publish to create the HTM version of the presentation and publish it to a Web page.

Test your Web presentation in a Web browser (either Internet Explorer or Netscape Navigator). It's a good idea to test it in both to make sure it works well for all your visitors, no matter which of browser they use to visit your site. Figure 19.28 shows the presentation in Internet Explorer.

FIGURE 19.28

The Web presentation opens, with a panel that lists each slide by title, and with the slides themselves displayed in full.

Click the slide name on the left panel to display the slide on the right

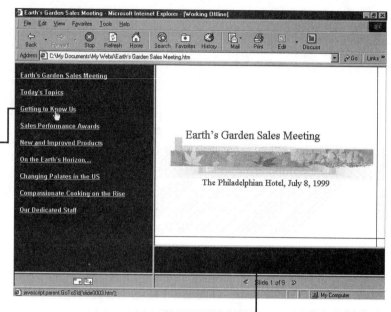

Any speaker's notes made during the creation of the presentation appear here

Tip

Because people who aren't familiar with PowerPoint might browse your presentation, consider adding instructive text to the slides from within PowerPoint, before publishing as a Web page, telling the user to click the mouse to move the presentation along. This can take the form of a small text box in the corner of the slide, or you can use the Speaker's Notes area of the slide (these notes appear in the browser).

After creating the presentation page, you can create a link to it from within the main-page1.htm document you created on Day 18. Choose any of the text or graphics on that home page and create a hyperlink that points to the Earth's Garden Sales Meeting.htm file.

Note

Obviously, not all the content in the Earth's Garden Sales Meeting presentation is appropriate for a Web presentation—the solicitation of questions from the audience, for example, is useless in an online presentation. You'll want to tweak your slides to get rid of any content that only works in a live presentation before you publish the presentation.

Tip What if you only want to place a single slide on a Web page? In Slide Sorter view, select an individual slide and copy it to the Clipboard. Then, on your Web page (open in FrontPage, in Normal mode), paste the slide onto the page. The slide becomes a graphic image that you can resize as needed to fit it among the other slide elements.

Summary

Today you learned how to use Office 2000 content on the Web—Excel worksheets and Access table data—and how to publish a PowerPoint presentation to the Web. In addition, you learned to copy content from the Web to your local installation of Office to make use of the business data that can be stored on a Web site. Tomorrow uses yet another Office 2000 application to market your business and distribute information—you'll be using Publisher to create a promotional flyer.

Q&A

Q Can I use content from Word on a Web page as well?

A Of course. Many users copy text content from a Word document to their Web pages as they develop them in FrontPage, and you can also build a Web page from within Word, converting your document's text and graphics to an .htm file that can be posted to the Web.

Q Are there any special considerations when creating a Web page for an intranet?

A Other than content, no. The pages function the same way on an intranet as on the Internet. Obviously, intranet pages contain information you probably don't publish to the Internet—information about your company, products, and employees that isn't intended for worldwide distribution.

Q One of my hyperlinks has stopped working—when I click it, it says the page can't be found. What went wrong and what can I do to fix this?

 A If you rename or delete a file to which a hyperlink points, be it a file stored on your local or network drive or an actual Web page, the hyperlink won't work anymore. To reestablish the link, re-create the hyperlink—select the text or graphic, click the Hyperlink button, and choose the file/page to which the selected item is to point.

 19

Workshop

The section that follows is a quick quiz about the day. If you have any problems answering any of the questions, see the section that follows the quiz for all the answers.

Quiz

1. True or False: You can publish an entire workbook to the Web.

2. Describe the procedure for taking content from a Web page and reusing it in a workbook on your local copy of Excel.

3. Can an Excel worksheet be turned into a Web page (as opposed to placing Excel content on an existing page)?

4. True or false: To put a PowerPoint slide on the Web, you can simply copy and paste it to a Web page.

5. If your Excel content appears on a Web page with accompanying Excel tools, do the changes you make (editing cell content, creating formulas, sorting or filtering the data) permanently change the data on the Web page?

Quiz Answers

1. True. When you choose File, Save as Web Page from within Excel, one of your options is to save the entire open workbook or just part of it (the active sheet or a range of selected cells). If you choose to save the entire workbook as a Web page, only the cells that contain content on each sheet in the book are displayed on the Web page—unused sheets do not create blank sections on the page.

2. With the Web page displayed in your browser, drag through the table cells that you want to reuse and choose Edit, Copy. Return to your Excel workbook and paste the content to a worksheet. At that point, you can use the data as you use any other worksheet content.

3. Yes. You can save a workbook or worksheet, or a portion thereof, as a new Web page. Choose File, Save as Web Page and, after selecting how much of the workbook to save as a Web page, give the file a name. The page you create can then be posted to the Web or to your company's intranet.

4. True, although the slide simply appears as a graphic, and not as a presentation or slide. To copy an individual slide, select the slide in Slide Sorter view, copy it to the Clipboard, and then paste it to a spot on the Web page on which you want to use it. It can then be resized as needed.

5. No. The changes that the person browsing the data chooses to make are transient— they appear only while the page is displayed for that one user. If the user clicks the Back and then Forward buttons (to return to the page) or the Refresh/Reload button, the changes disappear and the pristine version of the data is displayed.

19

DAY 20

Creating a Flyer with Publisher

Microsoft Publisher isn't a new product, but its inclusion in the Office suite of programs *is* new. Microsoft's desire for Office 2000 to be a well-rounded suite, providing a tool for every major business task, is behind the decision to include Publisher in the suite. What can Publisher do for you? You can use it to create any sort of business or personal publication, from a newsletter to a greeting card—and many other items in between. Publisher makes creating a polished, professional-looking publication easy—publication layouts are already there for you, complete with sample text and graphics that you replace with your own content. Although you can build a publication "from scratch," you don't need to—even veteran desktop publishers will welcome the speed and simplicity that are offered by Publisher. Today focuses on the creation of a flyer, one of the most commonly used business publications. Specifically, you'll learn the following skills:

- Starting the Publisher program and selecting a publication type
- Setting up the flyer through the Publisher Wizard

- Replacing the sample text with your own and formatting it as needed
- Replacing sample graphics and moving or resizing them to meet your layout needs
- Customizing the publication with additional drawn shapes and lines
- Printing your flyer

Getting Started with Publisher

Publisher 2000 starts out assuming that you're going to want a lot of help. You can ignore the help when it becomes too intrusive and accept it when it's helpful. When you start the program by choosing it from the Start menu's Programs list or by double-clicking a desktop icon, you are presented with the Microsoft Publisher Catalog, as shown in Figure 20.1. The Publications by Wizard tab is in front, and it offers a list of Wizards that help coach you through the process of building up to 25 different types of publications.

FIGURE 20.1

Whether you want to create a brochure or a paper airplane, you'll find the Wizard to help you.

A diamond indicates that no sample list is available

Click the triangles to see sample layout categories

Wizard list

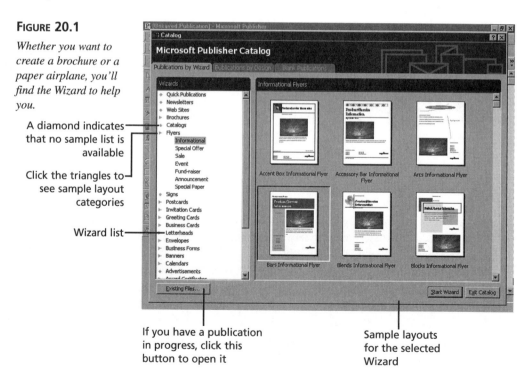

If you have a publication in progress, click this button to open it

Sample layouts for the selected Wizard

Note

The Publications by Design tab offers very specific publications, such as invitations, restaurant menus, and calendars, that you can choose and then customize on your own by replacing sample content. The Blank Publications tab gives you just that—a series of blank documents for everything from a postcard to a banner, with no design or sample content to start with. The Blank Publications tab is for users who literally want to start from scratch and have time to create their own design.

Choosing a Flyer Layout

To use the Wizards, simply click on a publication type, and then double-click the layout on the right that you like best. For today's project, choose the Bars Informational Flyer (second row, on the left). The document opens onscreen; a prompt might appear (see Figure 20.2), asking you for your personal or company data—name, address, and so forth—so that the document can be loaded with these specifics without any further work on your part.

FIGURE 20.2

Fill in as much or as little of the requested information as you want.

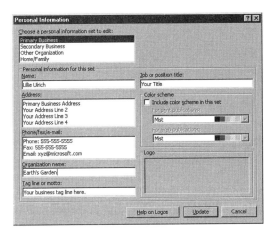

20

Tip

If you don't want to use the Wizard, click the Cancel button. This same prompt appears the next time you open a new publication, so you have another chance to enter the data even if you choose not to this time.

Working with the Publisher Wizard

After you've selected a sample layout and are faced with the document (see Figure 20.3), you can begin replacing the sample content with your own content. As soon as you click on any part of the sample document, however, a Wizard dialog bubble appears, as shown in Figure 20.3.

FIGURE 20.3

If you attempt to do anything on your own, the Wizard responds by redirecting you to the Wizard panel on the left.

Wizard panel ——————

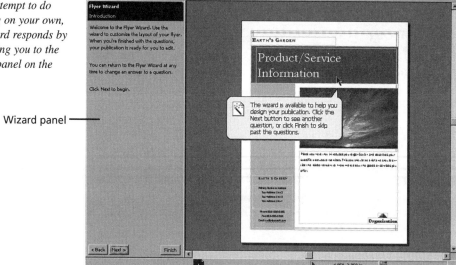

On the Wizard panel (also known as a *pane*), click Next to go through the process of building your flyer step-by-step. Figure 20.4 shows the Color Scheme step in the Publisher Wizard, in which you choose the colors for your flyer. Each scheme consists of a group of complementary colors, and as you click them, you see them previewed on the sample flyer. When you've found a scheme you like, leave it selected and click Next.

In the next step of the Wizard, you can indicate your need for a graphic. Most layouts already include them, so the default (see Figure 20.5) is Yes. Click Next.

NEW TERM The Wizard's next question is whether you want Tear-Offs (see Figure 20.6) and, if so, which ones. *Tear-Offs* are order forms, coupons, things that are torn or cut from the main document. None is the default; for this project, leave None selected. Click Next to proceed.

FIGURE 20.4

Choose a color scheme for your flyer. It's a good idea to choose colors that match your organization's existing publications.

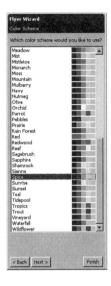

FIGURE 20.5

Even a very conservative publication can use a graphic—accept the default (Yes) to allow a photo, clip art, or a chart to be pasted from PowerPoint or Excel.

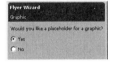

FIGURE 20.6

If your flyer announces a seminar for which people need to register, you might want a Response form tear-off. You don't need one for this flyer.

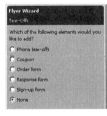

20

Next, the Wizard wants to know if your flyer will be mailed (see Figure 20.7). By asking if you want a placeholder for the recipient's address, the Wizard is actually asking if you'll be folding the flyer into thirds and putting a label on it. In this case, leave No selected and click Next.

FIGURE 20.7

The flyer you create today will not be mailed, so you don't need to leave a space for the recipient's address.

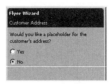

This brings you to the end of the Wizard. After choosing which information from the original Wizard dialog box you want to insert into the document, if any, click Finish. You can also click Back to go back through earlier steps if you want to change your mind about any of the selections you made. After you click Finish, the Wizard panel changes, offering a list of its steps in case you want to go back to one of them, and reiterates its Introduction text. Figure 20.8 shows the flyer that was created by your responses to the Wizard's various questions.

FIGURE 20.8

After completing the Wizard, you can roll up your sleeves and start working on the publication yourself.

Click the items in this list to reactivate steps in the Wizard

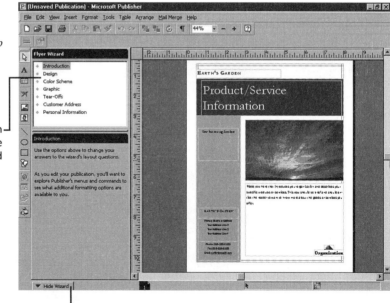

Click the Hide button to remove the Wizard panel from the screen.

Tip

If you want more room to work on your flyer and you won't be needing the Wizard, click the Hide Wizard button at the bottom of the Wizard panel on the left. When it is hidden, you can redisplay it by clicking the Show Wizard button.

Your next task is to make the flyer your own, replacing the sample text and graphics with your own images. The following sections take you through this process.

Adding Text to the Flyer

The text that appears on your flyer—besides the text that was inserted through your responses to the first Wizard dialog box—is instructional. Figure 20.9 shows a closer zoom on the publication, showing the sample text.

FIGURE 20.9

Although you might not need all of them, the sample text boxes show you where to put specific information.

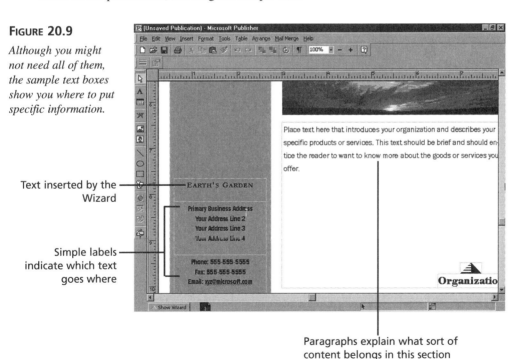

Text inserted by the Wizard

Simple labels indicate which text goes where

Paragraphs explain what sort of content belongs in this section

20

Tip Use the Zoom Out and Zoom In buttons to adjust your visual distance from the flyer's content. If you want to zoom in on a particular object, select it before clicking the Zoom In button.

 Tip To quickly zoom in to 100%, press the F9 key. If you press F9 again, you zoom out to 38% (or another small percentage, depending on your monitor's settings).

The first text you need to replace is the flyer's title. The sample Product/Service Information text must be replaced with the title for this flyer, `Camping in Earth's Garden`. In Figure 20.10, the Promotion Title text box is selected, and can be replaced with the title you want on your flyer.

FIGURE 20.10

Select the sample text and replace it with your own.

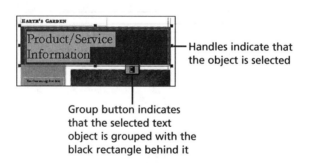

Handles indicate that the object is selected

Group button indicates that the selected text object is grouped with the black rectangle behind it

Whatever text you type to replace the sample text is formatted the same as the sample text was—these settings are part of the layout's template (like a PowerPoint presentation template). You can change them if you want to, and you'll learn how to do so later. Figure 20.11 shows the new title for the flyer-in-progress.

Now you can go through the remaining text boxes and remove them (click on them and press Ctrl+Shift+X) or select their text content and replace it with your own. Figure 20.12 shows the flyer after the sample text has been replaced with relevant text. To make your flyer match this one, replace the text in your text boxes with the text you see in the figure.

FIGURE 20.11

Your flyer begins to take shape quickly as you enter your own text.

FIGURE 20.12

Remove the text objects you don't need and replace the remaining text with content that is relevant to your flyer's topic.

Text replaced in these text boxes

Organization Graphic object from original layout removed from this spot

> **Tip**
>
> **A** You can add new text objects by clicking the Text Frame tool , which is located on the left side of the window. Click and drag a text box, and then type text inside it.

20

Before you continue to work on your flyer, save it—in fact, you've probably seen a prompt appear by now, reminding you to save your work. This prompt comes up periodically as you work on your flyer, and after you've saved your file (given it a name), clicking Yes in response to the prompt updates the saved file. Saving your flyer for the first time can be performed like a first-time save in any Office 2000 application: Simply choose File, Save, or click the Save button. Give your file a name (in this case, `Camping Flyer` might be a good choice), and choose a folder in which to save it. Click Save to create the file and close the dialog box.

> **Tip**
>
> If you're in the process of experimenting with a photo or some formatting effect in your publication, go ahead and click No in response to the prompt that reminds you to save your work. As soon as your experiment is over and your file is in a condition that you want to preserve, save the file.

Formatting Flyer Text

As was stated previously, the text you type to replace the sample text is automatically formatted to match the sample text. Font formats are part of the sample flyer you started with, and for the most part, you need to keep the settings that are in place. Choosing complementary and effective fonts is a tricky business if you're not familiar with desktop publishing or graphic design. Following are some things to keep in mind if you decide to reformat the text on your flyer:

- **Don't use too many different fonts**—No publication needs more than three fonts, and two is preferable. If you have more than three, they all tend to cancel each other out visually.

- **Pay attention to font types**—There are three main font types—serif (with flourishes on the letters, such as Times New Roman), sanserif (with no flourishes, such as Arial), and artistic (such as Old English Text). Don't use more than one of each in any publication. Figure 20.13 shows part of the list of available fonts and identifies samples of the three font types.

FIGURE 20.13

Choose fonts that complement, rather than compete with, each other. One fancy font and one simple font is a good combination.

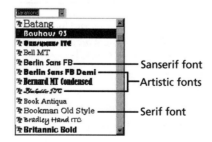

- **Think about the overall tone or feeling of your publication**—If your flyer pertains to a serious or conservative topic, choose conservative fonts. Don't use very ornate or casual fonts unless they match the tone of your topic.

If you must reformat your text, follow these steps:

1. Select the text object; in this case, select the title. Handles appear around it and the text is selected, as shown in Figure 20.14.

FIGURE 20.14

If you feel the need to make your mark by reformatting text, the title is a good choice— a font that's different from your other text makes the title look more like a logo.

2. Click and drag through the text within the object to select it.

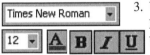

3. Using the Formatting toolbar, change the Font, Font Size, or Font Color. You can apply styles such as Bold, Italic, or Underline as well.

4. When the text appears as you want it, click on an empty spot on the flyer to deselect the text. Figure 20.15 shows your reformatted title.

Tip

A large selection of fonts is available for installation with Office 2000, and the number that were installed on your computer depends on the installation you performed.

20

Moving Text Boxes

Although the flyer layout you selected needn't be changed, you can move things around a bit to customize the look of the publication. After an object is selected, you'll notice that your mouse pointer turns into a truck with the word *Move* on it when you point any-where on the object itself(see Figure 20.16).

Figure 20.15

Choose a font that doesn't clash with sur-rounding text, and don't make it too big or small for the overall composition.

A **bold** artistic font (*Castellar*) was select-ed to stand out against the remaining flyer text

Figure 20.16

Move mode is indicat-ed by a mouse pointer that looks like a mov-ing van.

For this portion of today, you'll experiment with moving the title text object. Drag the title down on the flyer so that it overlaps the top half of the sunset photo. You'll notice after you move it that the text is much smaller, and appears just above the edge of the photo (see Figure 20.17).

Figure 20.17

The photo object forces text to wrap around it.

When this happens, you can do one of three things:

- Adjust the size or placement of the photo object so that there is room for the text to be read alongside it.

- Place the photo object behind the text so that the text completely overlaps it. To place the photo object behind the text (changing its stacking order), select the photo object and choose Arrange, Send to Back, or click the Send to Back button. The text now overlaps the photo, as shown in Figure 20.18.

FIGURE 20.18

Create overlapping objects by changing their stacking order.

Now the shaded rectangle on the left is pushing the title text aside

Stacking order is determined by the order in which objects were created. The first objects are on the bottom, and as objects are added, they are higher in the stack. This stacking order applies even if the items don't overlap or touch, but only becomes an issue if they do.

- Format the photo object's *frame properties* so that the text flows around the actual content of the photo, rather than the frame. To take this approach, follow these steps:

  1. Click on the picture object you want to reformat. When handles appear around it, choose Format, Picture Frame Properties, or click the Picture Frame Properties button on the Formatting toolbar.

  2. In the Picture Frame Properties dialog box (shown in Figure 20.19), choose the Wrap text around setting that you prefer. Picture only is a good choice if the graphic is a photograph or if your picture takes up most of the frame (the thin line surrounding the image).

20

FIGURE 20.19

*When text and graph-
ics overlap or are
placed very close
together, you must
adjust the way text
wraps around the
graphic.*

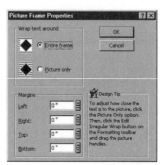

3. Adjust the Margins to dictate how close to the image the text is to wrap. You can adjust one or more of the margins by clicking the spinner arrows next to each margin setting, or by typing a number in the boxes.

4. When your settings are complete, click OK. Figure 20.20 shows what happens when the sample photo's wrap settings are adjusted.

FIGURE 20.20

*The title reappears
after the picture frame
properties are
changed.*

After experimenting with this process, move the title back to its original position, approximately a half-inch above the photograph. It returns to its original font size. You can also click the Undo button until the title returns to its original position.

Inserting Graphic Images

Just as sample text must be replaced by your own content, sample graphic images also need to be replaced. The flyer layout that was chosen for this project contains a large photograph of a sunset; you can replace the sunset photograph with any scanned photo you have, or you can use the picture shown later in Figure 20.23, which can be found on the CD-ROM that accompanies this book.

To replace the sample picture with one of your own, follow these steps:

1. Click on the sample photograph to select it. Like any selected object, handles appear on its perimeter (see Figure 20.21).

FIGURE 20.21

Select the sample photograph before locating its replacement. The picture you choose then takes the sample's place automatically.

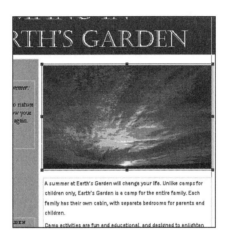

2. Choose Insert, Picture, From File. The Insert Picture dialog box opens (see Figure 20.22).

FIGURE 20.22

By default, Publisher looks in the My Pictures folder for picture files.

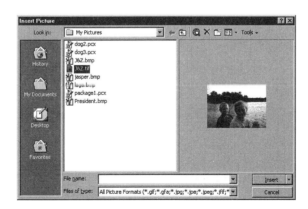

20

3. Navigate to the folder or drive that contains the picture you want to use, and double-click it. Figure 20.23 shows the replacement photograph in place, in need of adjustments in terms of size and exact position.

FIGURE 20.23

Chances are that the photo you want to use won't be the same exact size as the sample it replaces; be prepared to make minor adjustments.

Dashed border indicates edges of picture, not frame

Moving and Manipulating Graphics

When you are adjusting the size and placement of objects in Publisher, it's important to watch your mouse pointer. Depending on its appearance, you can either move or resize the selected object to which you're pointing. Figure 20.24 shows an object in resize mode.

FIGURE 20.24

If your mouse turns to a two-headed arrow and you see the word resize *below it, you can drag the borders of the image to resize it.*

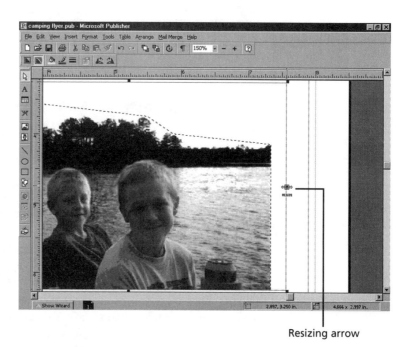

Resizing arrow

When you are resizing an object, the handle you use determines your results. Dragging from a left or right side handle adjusts the object's width, the top and bottom handles adjust height, and corner handles can be used to adjust both width and height simultaneously.

If you want to move an object, point anywhere but the object's visible frame border. Your mouse pointer turns into a picture of a truck with the word *move* on it. Drag to reposition the item, as shown in Figure 20.25.

FIGURE 20.25

Intended to look like a moving van, the truck mouse pointer indicates that the selected object is in Move mode.

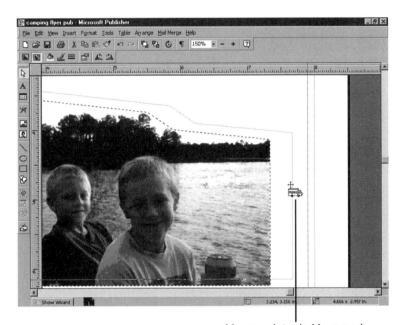

Mouse pointer in Move mode

 Caution
Earlier today, you moved the title to overlap a picture, and the text was adversely affected. Resizing a graphic so that it now touches or overlaps a text box has the same result, requiring reformatting of the picture's frame properties if the two objects are to effectively coexist.

20

Adding Shapes and Lines

The flyer layout you chose contains a couple of geometric shapes: a black box that has been placed behind the title, and a brightly-colored, long box behind the text boxes on the left side of the flyer. These are examples of how shapes can be used to enhance a publication; rather than drawing miscellaneous shapes and lines, you want to create objects that enhance the overall composition of the flyer and that draw the readers' eyes to important information.

Drawing Shapes

To draw shapes on your flyer, follow these steps:

 1. Click the Oval or Rectangle, or choose one of the Custom Shapes on the Objects toolbar on the left side of the Publisher window. Figure 20.26 shows the palette of Custom Shapes.

FIGURE 20.26

*Choose from 36 differ-
ent Custom Shapes.*

2. Move your mouse onto the surface of the flyer. Your mouse pointer now looks like a thin cross, as shown in Figure 20.27.

FIGURE 20.27

*A cross pointer indi-
cates that you're about
to draw a shape—an
oval, a rectangle, or
one of the Custom
Shapes.*

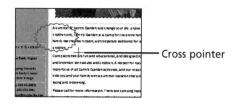 ———— Cross pointer

3. Click and drag diagonally to draw a shape. The farther from your starting point you drag, the larger the shape is. Release the mouse when the shape reaches the desired size. Figure 20.28 shows a new shape added to the flyer.

 Tip

To draw a shape of equal height and width, press and hold the Shift key while you are drawing.

FIGURE 20.28

Simple geometric shapes are best for business publications. Save fun images such as stars and lightning bolts for your personal creations.

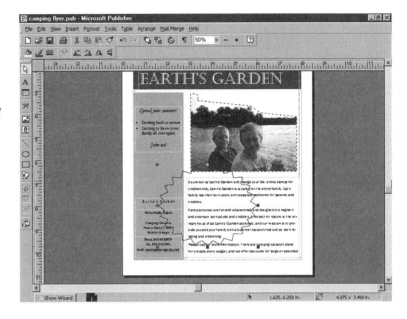

Working with Filled Shapes

 After the shape is drawn, you can move or resize it just as you might any other object (text box or picture box). In addition, you can give the shape a fill. To apply a fill, select the object and click the Fill Color button on the Formatting toolbar; then choose a color from the palette.

 By default, shapes are empty, enabling you to place them anywhere—even on top of existing objects. If a shape has no fill, the objects it overlaps are not affected—text is not moved or obscured. If you give the shape a fill, however, any text that the object overlaps is forced to wrap around the shape—this might or might not have a desirable effect. Figure 20.29 shows a shape added to the flyer, with the paragraph text wrapping to its right side.

20

> **Tip**
>
> To remove the outline of a drawn shape, click the Line Color button on the Formatting toolbar and choose the same color as the fill color.

FIGURE 20.29

If the shape's effect on surrounding text is undesirable, you might need to move or resize the shape so that it doesn't touch the text.

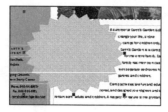

Helping Shapes and Text Work Together

What if you want the shape to be the size it is, and you also want it to stay in its current location? If you want to leave the shape where it is but don't want it to affect the text nearby, put it behind the text. With the shape selected, choose Arrange, Send to Back or Send Backward. This puts it behind the next item in the flyer's stacking order, but on top of the existing vertical rectangle (on the left side of the flyer). Figure 20.30 shows the shape sent backward so that it is behind the text.

FIGURE 20.30

The text box has a white fill, so now the text is obscuring the shape.

By sending the new shape to the back, you put it behind the text and the rectangle

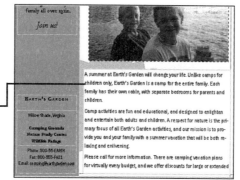

If you want the color of your shape to show through, change the fill color of the text box by following these steps:

1. Select the text box.

 2. Click the Fill Color button on the Formatting toolbar. Choose No Fill from the palette (see Figure 20.31).

3. Click on an empty spot to deselect the text box and view your results (see Figure 20.32).

FIGURE 20.31

No Fill makes the text box (not the text) transparent so that the shape behind it is seen through the text.

FIGURE 20.32

The shape now draws attention to and complements the text, rather than competing with it.

Tip

| 45% ▼ |

To "step back" and view your overall composition, choose View, Zoom, Whole Page. You can also choose Whole Page from the Zoom tool or press the F9 key twice (once to zoom to 100%, once to zoom out to a whole page view).

Drawing and Working with Lines

The Line tool on the Objects toolbar enables you to draw straight lines at any angle on your flyer. To use the tool, select it, and then click and drag on the flyer to draw a line. The farther from your starting point you drag the mouse, the longer the line becomes, as shown in Figure 20.33.

After drawing the line, you might want to make it thicker so that it stands out, or you might want to change its color. To make these changes, select the line and choose Format, Line and Border Style, More Styles. You can also double-click the drawn line. In either case, the Line dialog box opens (see Figure 20.34), through which you can change the line thickness, apply arrowheads to one or both ends of the line, change the line's color, or turn it into a dashed line (great for indicating that part of the flyer can be cut or torn away).

20

FIGURE 20.33

*Draw a line to sepa-
rate the sections of the
flyer.*

Starting point

FIGURE 20.34

*Customize the appear-
ance of your selected
line or border.*

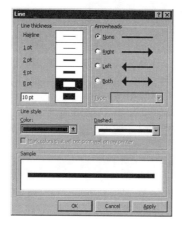

Tip

Each object on your flyer is in a frame, which normally doesn't show unless
the object is selected. To turn that frame into a visible and printable border,
open the Line dialog box while the object is selected and make the line
thicker.

Grouping Objects in the Publication

After you've painstakingly worked to position shapes, text, and pictures on the flyer so
that they contribute to an effective overall composition, you need to protect their placement by grouping them. Grouped objects cannot be moved individually, thus protecting,
for example, the position of the shape behind and relative to the text (see Figure 20.35).

To group two or more objects, follow these steps:

1. Click to select one of the items that is to be grouped. Handles appear around the
   object, as shown in Figure 20.36.

FIGURE 20.35

Don't allow an accidental nudge to move the shape away from its current position behind the text. Group the text and the shape so that they move as a unit.

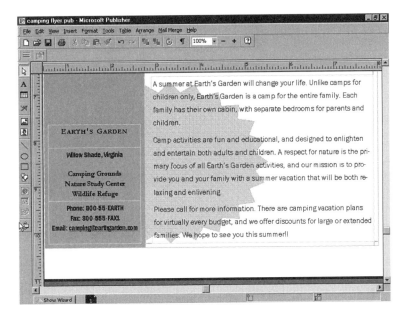

FIGURE 20.36

Select the shape behind the text by clicking on a portion of the shape that isn't touching any other object.

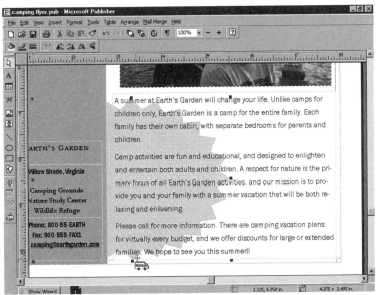

2. Press and hold the Shift key, and click the second item to be grouped (the text box). Handles appear around the second item, and the handles around both grouped items turn gray (see Figure 20.37).

FIGURE 20.37

Gray handles indicate that more than one object is selected.

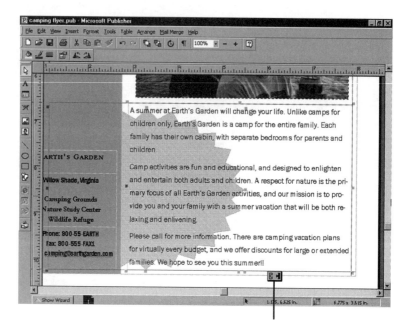

Click the Group Objects button on the flyer to group the selected objects

3. Choose Arrange, Group Objects. You can also click the Group Objects button that appears onscreen whenever multiple objects are selected.

When items are grouped, they cannot be moved individually. You can continue to format them individually—change the font of the text or the fill color of the shape—but you can't change their relative positions.

Tip

When the items are grouped, you can ungroup them by selecting the group (just click any one of the items in the group) and choosing Arrange, Ungroup Objects. You can also click the Ungroup Objects button on the flyer, which is displayed whenever a set of grouped objects is selected.

Printing the Flyer

In order to distribute your flyer, you need to print it. You can distribute it electronically (send it as an email attachment or put it on your Web site), but the flyer that you created today needs to be printed out so that it can be distributed by hand to customers and included in mailings. Before printing your flyer, however, you need to consider the following questions:

- **Is your printer capable of generating the quality you need?**—First of all, if your flyer is to be in color, you need a color printer. Second, if the flyer contains photographs or detailed graphical images, does your color printer achieve the appropriate level of detail and clarity?
- **How many copies do you need?**—If you need more than ten or 20 copies, consider making color photocopies or having it printed commercially rather than wasting your toner or ink cartridges.

If you only need a few copies and your printer is capable of the quality printing you need, go ahead and use it. Choose File, Print, and enter the number of copies you need; then click OK—the Print dialog box in Publisher is virtually identical to the Print dialog boxes in the other Office 2000 applications.

If, however, you need a lot of copies or your printer doesn't give the crisp images you want, take it to a commercial printer—they can make color photocopies from your original or reproduce your image on their high-resolution color printers.

> **Tip**
>
> If you decide to make color photocopies, make sure that your original is as crisp and clean as possible. Consider purchasing glossy bright white paper, sold especially for this purpose. You can buy small quantities (20 or 50 sheets) at most office supply and stationary stores.

Using Pack and Go to Transport Your Publication

If you've decided to have a commercial printer create your flyer, you can do one of two things:

- Save the file as a Publisher file (.pub) and hope that the printing company has Publisher on their computers and can therefore support that file format.
- Use Publisher's Pack and Go. This option invokes a Wizard that helps you to save your publication so that a printer can use it to print your flyers.

The first of these two options requires no special skills that you don't already have—simply choose File, Save As (you should have already been saving your flyer as you've been working, however), and save it to the A: drive.

20

The second option, Pack and Go, requires the use of the Pack and Go Wizard. To use this option, follow these steps:

1. With the publication that you want to use open, choose File, Pack and Go, Take to a Commercial Printing Service.

2. The Pack and Go Wizard opens, as shown in Figure 20.38. Click Next to begin the Pack and Go process.

FIGURE 20.38

Pack and Go prepares your file for printing by a commercial printing company.

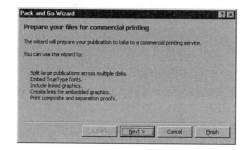

3. Choose where you want to save your file. To locate a folder on your hard drive or network, click the Browse button and choose a folder. You can also click the Save in list box and choose the A: drive.

4. After choosing a location in which to save your file, click Next.

5. The next step in the Wizard assumes that you want to embed your fonts, include linked graphics, and create links for embedded graphics (see Figure 20.39). None of these apply to today's flyer, but it's safe to leave them selected. Click Next.

FIGURE 20.39

Including fonts and linked or embedded graphics ensures that everything you see onscreen is part of the packed version of the file.

6. Click Finish to pack the publication. Publisher creates a file called packed01.puz, as well as an unpack.exe file that the printing service can use to unpack the packed file.

Don't turn off the option to Embed TrueType fonts. If you've used a font that your printing company doesn't have on their computer, you risk their software (or a member of their staff) making a font substitution. By embedding the fonts you've used in the Pack and Go file, you are assured that your fonts will be used in the commercially printed publication.

Summary

Today you used Publisher to create a flyer. While you were learning a new Office 2000 application that you can use on your own to create brochures, newsletters, and many other types of business publications, you also utilized skills you've learned in previous days—drawing shapes and lines, resizing objects, and reformatting text. You were able to use these skills effortlessly today because Publisher's tools are very similar to the Drawing and Formatting toolbars you've used in Word, Excel, and PowerPoint. Day 21, "Marketing with a Mass Mailing," will again require that you utilize skills and concepts you've learned before—you'll be generating a mass mailing that merges data from Access and a form letter built in Word.

Q&A

Q I see that Publisher can be used to create Web pages. Is there any benefit to using Publisher instead of FrontPage?

A FrontPage is not included in the Small Business Edition of Office 2000, so if that's the edition you have, Publisher is your best bet for building a Web page. If, however, you purchased the Premium edition of Office, you have both products, and can choose between FrontPage (a more powerful and sophisticated tool designed purely for creating Web pages) and Publisher, which is a user-friendly tool for creating a variety of publications, one of which happens to be Web pages.

Q If I see a tool that is the same as one I've seen in another Office 2000 application, can I assume that it works the same way in Publisher?

A Yes. For example, many of the Drawing toolbar's buttons, such as Free Rotate and Insert Clip Art, appear in the Publisher window. You can expect them to operate in the same way they do in Word, Excel, or PowerPoint. There are some exceptions, however. You'll see, for example, a tool that looks like the Insert Table tool, which is called the Table Frame Tool in Publisher. Although it creates a table in your publication, it doesn't work just like the tool you use in Word. Don't be afraid to experiment, though—Publisher is a very friendly program.

20

Workshop

The section that follows is a quick quiz about the day. If you have any problems answering any of the questions, see the section that follows the quiz for all the answers.

Quiz

1. You've just moved your text object to a new spot in the publication, and the text disappeared. Why?

2. The border you see around your text box when it's selected doesn't print, and you want it to. What do you do?

3. You've drawn a shape and it's obscuring a text box or other object on the page. How do you place the new shape behind these objects?

4. True or False: It makes your publication more interesting if you use a lot of different fonts and clip art images.

5. How do you make two or more objects move and resize as a unit?

Quiz Answers

1. Surrounding objects are either overlapping the text because they were created later in the design process or because the objects' wrap settings aren't allowing room for the text. In the former case, choose Arrange, Send to Back. In the latter, select the graphic object and choose Format, Picture Frame Properties and choose the Picture only wrap option.

2. Sometimes text boxes have a frame when they are selected, but that frame doesn't print. To give the object a visible and printable frame, double-click the object and choose a thickness other than None. You can also apply a color and choose on which sides of the object to place the borders.

3. Select the object that belongs behind the others and choose Arrange, Send to Back. You can also choose the object that belongs on top and choose Arrange, Bring to Front.

4. False. Too many fonts (more than two or three per publication) create a circus-like atmosphere, and the fonts become more distracting than interesting. Too many clip art images have the same effect—use one or two per page, at most.

5. Select the items using the Shift key to gather them, and then click the Group button that appears on the page; or choose Arrange, Group Objects.

DAY 21

Marketing with a Mass Mailing

On Day 17, "Creating a Report with Office," you combined your skills using Word, Excel, Access, and PowerPoint to create a report. Today will further test your use of multiple Office applications as you create a form letter and merge it with an existing database and then build a database of your own for a separate mailing. Specifically, today encompasses the following tasks:

- Choosing an Access table as the data source for your mailing
- Building a form letter in Word that makes use of the data
- Sorting the database for a bulk mailing
- Querying the database so that only specific records are merged with the letter
- Building a Word database from scratch for a small mailing
- Creating mailing labels in Word for any mass mailing

Understanding Mail Merge Concepts

 The term *mail merge* is fairly self-explanatory—something is being mailed (a document), and something is being merged (the document and a database). More specifically, you're merging a letter or a mailing label with a database of names and addresses, resulting in a series of letters or labels that can be mailed to the people listed in the database.

A mail merge session typically begins when you select an existing database—a list of names and addresses stored in an Excel worksheet or in an Access table. Perhaps the list is maintained on an ongoing basis, or maybe you're creating it purely for the purposes of this particular mailing. In any case, the database exists prior to beginning the mail merge process.

You can, of course, build a database in Word, within the mail merge process itself. That will be covered later today, as part of the preparation to create a sheet of mailing labels. For now, however, you'll be working with an existing database and generating form letters for selected people in that list.

> **Note**
>
> Although form letters and mailing labels are the most common output of a mail merge, you can also merge data with a document to create envelopes—which is only advisable if your printer has an envelope feeder—or a catalog. The catalog can be set up so that product information that is stored in a database can be merged with a Word document that contains the page numbers and other general text. You can then insert pictures of the product and print and mail the catalog to customers.

To begin the mail merge process, follow these steps:

1. Open a new blank Word document. You can also open an existing document that contains the text that you'll be using for a form letter.
2. Choose Tools, Mail Merge. The Mail Merge Helper dialog box opens, as shown in Figure 21.1.
3. Click the Create button in the first section of the dialog box. Choose Form Letters.
4. A prompt appears (see Figure 21.2), asking if you want to use the Active Window or a New Main Document. Choose Active Window.

At this point, the mail merge process has begun, and you've established what sort of document you'll be creating. The next step is to select the database with which you'll merge the document.

FIGURE 21.1

The Mail Merge Helper dialog box breaks the mail merge process down into three main sections— the document, the data, and the merging of these two components.

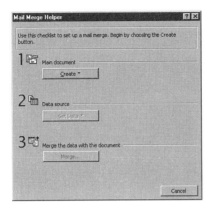

FIGURE 21.2

Choose to use the blank document with which you started by clicking the Active Window button.

Selecting a Database for the Mail Merge

Although the name of the feature you're using is *mail* merge, the form letters that you create needn't be mailed. You can, for example, create a memo to your staff, with data from your employee database inserted into the text of the memo. For this portion of today's project, you will use the Staff List table from the Employee Information database you created on Day 13, "Setting up a Database" (if you don't have it, you can access it on the CD-ROM that accompanies this book). This database will be merged with a memo to the staff of the Earth's Garden company, regarding new vacation policies.

To continue the mail merge process that was started in the preceding section and select a database, follow these steps:

1. In the open Mail Merge Helper dialog box, click the Get Data button. From the four choices that are offered (see Figure 21.3), choose Open Data Source.

2. In the Open Data Source dialog box (see Figure 21.4), change the Files of type option to MS Access Databases (*.mdb).

3. Navigate to the folder that contains your database. In this case, use either your copy of Employee Information.mdb or the copy that is on the CD-ROM that came with this book. Double-click the file when you locate it.

21

FIGURE 21.3

Choose to use an existing database (worksheet or table) as the data source for your merge.

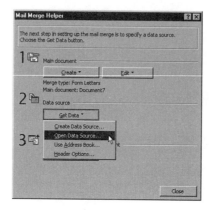

FIGURE 21.4

By default, Word looks for documents (.doc), but you can redirect the dialog box to display Access databases instead.

4. A Microsoft Access dialog box opens, showing a list of the tables in the selected database. Double-click Staff List, as shown in Figure 21.5.

FIGURE 21.5

Choose the specific table from which Word is to draw data for the merge.

5. A prompt appears, telling you that your main document (the blank document with which you started) contains no merge fields. Click the Edit Main Document button, as shown in Figure 21.6.

FIGURE 21.6

Word detects that there are no fields in your document that link it to the selected database, and suggests that you edit the document to include them.

Tip

You can also use your Outlook Contacts list as a database from which to draw addresses for your mailing. Choose Address Book from the Get Data list in the Mail Merge Helper dialog box.

You are now looking at a blank document, and a new toolbar appears on the screen, as shown in Figure 21.7. The next step in the mail merge process is to begin building your form letter (a memo, in this case).

FIGURE 21.7

The Mail Merge toolbar appears automatically when you begin to edit your document.

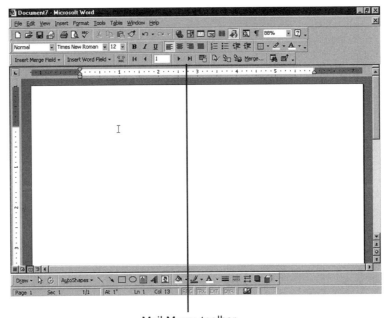

Mail Merge toolbar

21

Note

NEW TERM A *merge field* is a connection to your database that is inserted into your form letter. By placing a merge field in the text of your document, you are telling Word to access the selected database, pull data from a particular field, and insert it into a specific spot in the document. For example, if your salutation is "Dear <<First_Name>>" (where <<First_Name>> is the merge field), Word grabs the data from the First_Name field in the selected database and inserts it after the word *Dear*. The resulting salutation is "Dear John," for example, instead of the impersonal "Dear Customer".

Building a Form Letter

Everyone has received form letters, most of which are addressed to Current Resident or Valued Customer. Some form letters, however, have your name on them so that the salutation refers to you directly, either by title and last name (for example, Mr. Smith) or by your first name. The inclusion of this personal information, although not masking the fact that it's a form letter, makes the letter seem personal—you're more likely to read it than you might be if it were addressed to Occupant. The letter might also include reference to your address or some other personal information, more of the data that is on file about you in someone's database.

When typing your form letter, you can type the body and insert the merge fields as you go, or you can type the letter without the merge fields and then insert them as a second step. For this project, you'll take the latter approach; begin by typing the brief memo seen in Figure 21.8.

Note

Just like any document, you can insert graphics—clip art, pictures, drawn shapes and lines—to give the letter some visual impact. If you're creating a catalog, you'll want to insert pictures of your products. In either case, use the Insert, Picture command and select the image of your choice. If you format the picture so that text wraps around it, your merge fields (and later, your merged data) flow right along with the other paragraph text.

FIGURE 21.8

The memo will later contain fields that indicate where to place names and other information from the database.

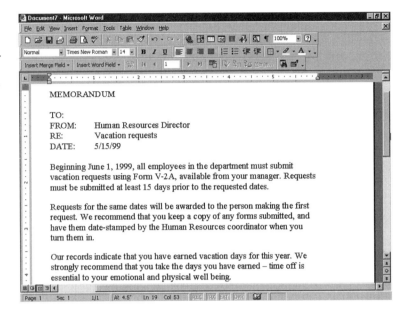

Inserting Merge Fields

After you've typed the main text of the document, you can begin to insert merge fields from the Staff List table. The placement of these fields is important—selecting the wrong fields or putting any of them in the wrong place can result in a letter that doesn't make sense or that includes incorrect information.

To insert the merge fields into your memo, follow these steps:

1. Click to the right of the colon after the word *To* to position your cursor. Press the Tab key twice to line the cursor up with the text below, and then click the Insert Merge Field button; a list of the fields in the Staff List table appears, as shown in Figure 21.9. Choose First_Name.

FIGURE 21.9

The fields from the database you selected in the Open Data Source dialog box appear in the list of merge fields.

21

2. Press the spacebar after the inserted merge field, and then click the Insert Merge Field button again. This time, choose Last_Name.

3. Click within the memo's first paragraph, between the words *the* and *department* in the first sentence, to position your cursor.

4. Click the Insert Merge Field button and choose Department. Figure 21.10 shows the memo with three merge fields inserted.

FIGURE 21.10

The name of the memo recipient and their department name are inserted into the memo text.

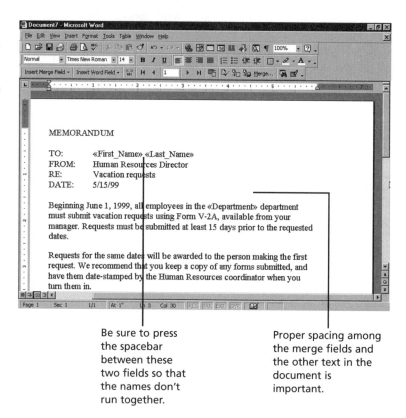

Be sure to press the spacebar between these two fields so that the names don't run together.

Proper spacing among the merge fields and the other text in the document is important.

5. Click between the words *have earned* and *vacation days* in the third paragraph.

6. Click the Insert Merge Field button and choose Vacation_Days.

Figure 21.11 shows the completed memo, including all three merge fields. Compare it to your own document to make sure that you have the same text and fields, and that the fields are inserted in the proper locations.

First_Name field   Last_Name field

FIGURE 21.11

Assuming you've selected the correct merge fields and your database is up-to-date, you're now ready to merge your document and data.

Department field —

Vacation_Days field —

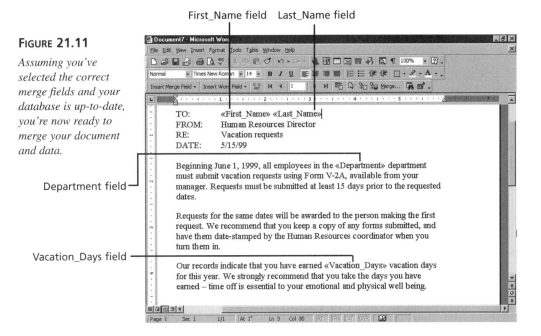

TO: «First_Name» «Last_Name»
FROM: Human Resources Director
RE: Vacation requests
DATE: 5/15/99

Beginning June 1, 1999, all employees in the «Department» department must submit vacation requests using Form V-2A, available from your manager. Requests must be submitted at least 15 days prior to the requested dates.

Requests for the same dates will be awarded to the person making the first request. We recommend that you keep a copy of any forms submitted, and have them date-stamped by the Human Resources coordinator when you turn them in.

Our records indicate that you have earned «Vacation_Days» vacation days for this year. We strongly recommend that you take the days you have earned – time off is essential to your emotional and physical well being.

Caution

If your database contains fields that hold confidential information, be careful not to select and insert them into the letter by mistake. In this project, for example, accidentally including Salary field data would be a major error.

Tip

Nearly every new mail merge user tries to type the merge fields in manually—typing two less than symbols, the field name, and two greater than symbols (<<*field_name*>>). This doesn't work. You can only insert merqe fields by selecting them from the Insert Merge Field list.

Sorting and Querying the Database

Before merging your records, you might want to change the order in which the records are merged (for example, putting them in Zip_Code order for a bulk mailing or in Department order to simplify internal distribution). You might also want to make sure that only certain records are merged with the letter. To access these options, reopen the

21

Mail Merge Helper dialog box by clicking the Mail Merge button; then click the Query Options button in the Mail Merge Helper dialog box.

The Query Options dialog box (see Figure 21.12) contains two tabs: Filter Records and Sort Records. You can use the tabs individually (to Filter or to Sort), or you can use them in tandem (to Filter for particular records and then sort just those records).

FIGURE 21.12

Choose to merge only certain records, or specify the order in which your records are to be merged.

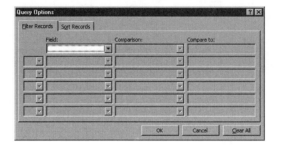

To filter your records, follow these steps:

1. Click the Field list box and select the field you want to filter from the list. In this case, select Vacation_Days.

2. Click the Comparison list box, and choose Greater than.

3. In the Compare to field, type a zero (0). This filter ensures that the memo doesn't go to people who have no vacation days.

You can, of course, filter on more than one field. Just like using AutoFilter in Excel or Query in Access, the more fields you filter on, the fewer records will meet the filter criteria.

Next, to sort the records so that the merged documents print out in a certain order, click the Sort Records tab and follow these steps:

1. Click the Sort by box in the Query Options dialog box, and choose Department from the list, as shown in Figure 21.13.

2. Click the first Then by box and choose Last Name.

3. Click OK. The records are now sorted so that the memos can be easily distributed to each department, and then handed out in alphabetical order within that department.

After setting your Query options, note that the Mail Merge Helper dialog box shows that Query Options have been set (see Figure 21.14).

FIGURE 21.13

You can sort your records by up to three fields.

FIGURE 21.14

Did you forget? Before performing the merge, check to see if your Query Options have been set.

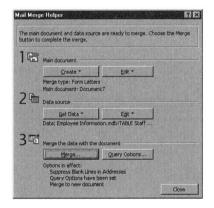

Note

In the Mail Merge Helper dialog box, the default Suppress Blank Lines in Addresses option doesn't apply directly to this particular form letter because there are no addresses included; however, the function is still relevant. This means that if there is no data in a field for a particular record in the database, Word won't leave a blank line or spaced gap between text or merge fields in the merged document. For example, if the Department field is accidentally left blank in one record, that person's memo does not have a big blank space where the name of their department should appear.

Tip

If you want to see blanks where data is missing (to help you check for database accuracy and completeness), click the Merge button in the Mail Merge Helper dialog box and click to turn on the Print blank lines when data fields are empty option.

21

Tip

If you want to edit your database before continuing with the mail merge process, click the Edit button in the Data Source section of the Mail Merge Helper dialog box.

Merging Your Letter with the Data

 After selecting your database, building your form letter, inserting your merge fields, and setting any necessary Query Options, you are ready to merge the Staff List table and the memo.

To merge the document and the data, follow these steps:

1. If the Mail Merge Helper dialog box isn't already open, click the Mail Merge Helper button to open it.

2. Click the Merge button to open the Merge dialog box, as shown in Figure 21.15.

FIGURE 21.15

Set the options for the output and content of your merged documents.

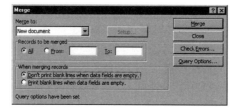

3. If you need to adjust the Query Options, click that button to reopen that dialog box and reset your sorting or filtering options. Otherwise, click the Merge button to perform the merge.

Because the default Merge to New Document setting was unchanged, the merged documents appear in a new document onscreen. One memo is generated (each on its own page) for each record in the Staff List table. Figure 21.16 shows one page of the new document.

 Caution

Although you can choose to merge to the printer directly rather than to a New document, it's not a good idea. If you've made any mistakes in the body of the letter or in your choice or placement of merge fields, you'll waste a lot of paper only to find out that you need to edit the document and merge again. Merge to a New document, proofread the merged pages, and then choose to print them if they're OK.

FIGURE 21.16

In the case of this project, the new merged document has 18 pages—one for each record in the database.

Full name inserted

Department name appears in first paragraph

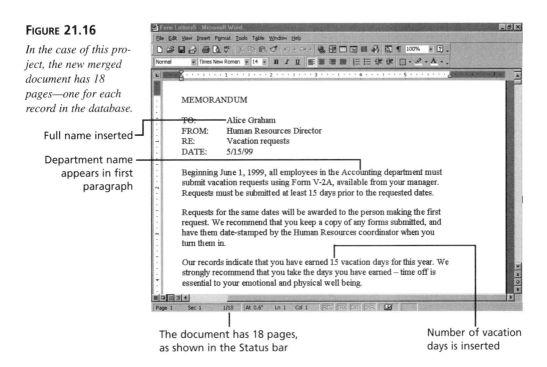

The document has 18 pages, as shown in the Status bar

Number of vacation days is inserted

After proofing each page of the new document, choose File, Print to print the memos. You can also click the Print button [018] to initiate the print job if you don't need to select a particular printer or choose the number of copies you want to print. You can save the new document for reprints, and you can save your merge document for future merges of the same form letter and database.

To save the merge document, choose it from the Window menu (in Figure 21.17, it appears as Document7; the number you see might vary), and then choose File, Save. Give the file a name, and click Save.

By saving this document, you save not only the form letter and merge fields, but also the Query Options and the selection of the Staff List table. To rerun the merge on a future date, simply reopen the document and click the Mail Merge Helper button (the Mail Merge toolbar appears whenever the document is open), and merge to create a new document.

FIGURE 21.17

Switch back to the merge document to remerge or to save it for future merges.

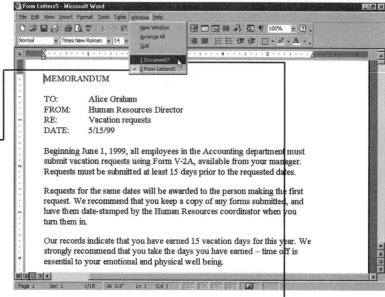

Form letter with merge fields

New document created by the merge

Building a Mailing Database in Word

What if you don't have a database created and filled with records before you go to do your mail merge? You can stop and create one quickly in Excel, or, if you don't realize that you don't have a database until you've already started the mail merge process, you can build one from within the Mail Merge Helper dialog box.

 Word gives you the capability to create tables, in a Word document, that contain any data you want to store. For the second portion of today's project, you'll build a small name and address list for the purpose of generating mailing labels. Use Word to build and store the database by following these steps:

1. Start a new blank document by pressing Ctrl+N or by clicking the New button on the toolbar. This mail merge is unrelated to the one you just created, so don't have any of those documents open.

2. Choose Tools, Mail Merge to open the Mail Merge Helper dialog box.

3. In the Mail Merge Helper dialog box, click the Create button and choose Mailing Labels (see Figure 21.18). When you are prompted, select Active Window to use your new blank document for the mailing labels.

FIGURE 21.18

Instead of a form letter, choose to generate mailing labels from your database.

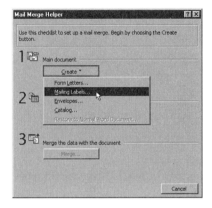

4. Click the Get Data button and choose Create Data Source. The Create Data Source dialog box opens, as shown in Figure 21.19.

FIGURE 21.19

A comprehensive list of name and address fields is already established for you, simplifying the database creation process.

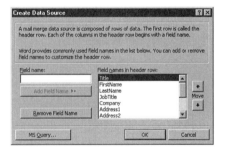

5. Word provides a list of fields for a typical name and address database: Title (Mr., Mrs., Ms.), FirstName, LastName, and so on. You can remove any of the existing fields by clicking to select them in the Field names in header row list box and clicking the Remove Field Name button. Remove the following fields:
   - Job Title
   - Company
   - Country
   - HomePhone
   - WorkPhone

6. Add a new field by clicking in the Field name box; then type CustNumber and click the Add Field Name button, as shown in Figure 21.20.

21

FIGURE 21.20

Add new fields to the database, making sure that you use no spaces in their names.

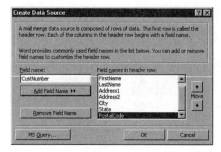

7. The new field is at the bottom of the list. You need it to be the first field. With the CustNumber field selected, click the Move up arrow until the CustNumber field is at the top of the list (see Figure 21.21).

FIGURE 21.21

Move any selected field up or down in the list until the fields appear in an order that's appropriate for your data entry purposes.

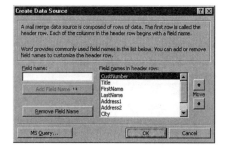

Tip

If you click the Move up arrow one time too many, the field goes back to the bottom. To bring it back to the top in one step, click the Move down arrow, and the field immediately goes back to the top of the list.

8. Click OK to close the dialog box. The Save As dialog box opens automatically.

9. Give your database a name. Type `July Mailing` in the File name box, and click Save.

10. A prompt appears, indicating that there are no records in the database. Click Edit Data Source to open the Data Form dialog box, as shown in Figure 21.22.

FIGURE 21.22

If Word detects that you have no records to merge with your labels, you are prompted to create them.

The fields appear in the order you specified in the Create Data Source dialog box

Use these buttons to move backward and forward through the records you've entered

11. Begin entering your records, pressing Tab between each field. At the end of the record, press Enter to begin entering the next record. Do not click OK until you have finished entering all the records.

12. Using the data in Table 21.1, enter the ten records. When you finish, you can scroll through them to check for typos, and then click OK.

 As soon as you click OK, you are returned to the blank document. Click the Mail Merge Helper button to reopen the Mail Merge Helper dialog box.

21

TABLE 21.1—DATA FOR MAILING LABELS

Cust Number	Title	First Name	LastName	Address1	Address2	City	State	Postal Code
MI276	Ms.	Betty	Miller	225 S. Chancellor St.		Newtown	PA	18940
TA335	Mr.	Tom	Talbot	3 Sunnyside		South Port	UK	CA 193 52
WI386	Mrs.	Isabel	Willard	321 Papermill Rd.		Huntingdon Valley	PA	19006
LA672	Mr.	Harry	Lambert	555 Lawnton Road		Willow Grove	PA	19044
AD289	Mr.	Dale	Adcock	3900 Philmont Ave.	Suite 3C	Huntingdon Valley	PA	19006
KI297	Mrs.	Violet	Kissell	125 Clementine St.		Jenkintown	PA	19047
CO875	Ms.	Lee	Costanza	1166 Hughes St.		Trenton	NJ	08123
CL987	Ms.	Sarah	Clarke	357 Elm Street.		Schenectady	NY	12345
CH765	Mr.	Martin	Chambers	5 Greenbank Ln.		Cumbria	UK	M5 567
MO432	Ms.	Julia	Mottram	22 Brides Lane	Apt. 5A	Philadelphia	PA	19115

Generating Mailing Labels

 If this were another form letter, you might simply begin typing the body of the letter and begin inserting merge fields. Instead, you need to perform an interim step wherein you choose the size and layout of your labels. This is done by clicking the Setup button in the Mail Merge Helper dialog box. The Label Options dialog box opens, as shown in Figure 21.23.

The default Tray is determined by your printer's setup through Windows.

FIGURE 21.23

Choose the Label manufacturer (Avery standard is the default) and select the product number for the labels you're using.

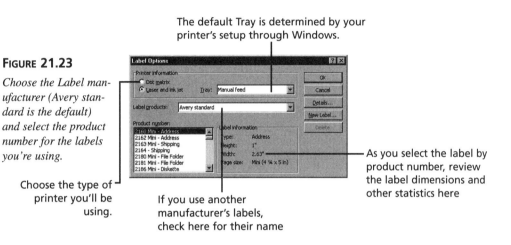

Choose the type of printer you'll be using.

If you use another manufacturer's labels, check here for their name

As you select the label by product number, review the label dimensions and other statistics here

> **Tip**
>
> If you don't see your label under any manufacturer's list, click the New Label button. You must give the label a name for future use, and then provide the dimensions and layout of your labels. The information you'll need to set up this new label is probably on the label's packaging.

After choosing your label, click OK. The Create Labels dialog box opens (see Figure 21.24). This dialog box replaces the blank document in terms of typing any text onto the label and inserting merge fields.

To build the content of your labels, follow these steps:

1. With your cursor blinking in the Sample label box, click the Insert Merge Field button. Choose Title, and then press the spacebar to prepare for the next field.

2. Click the Insert Merge Field button and choose FirstName. Press the spacebar again.

3. Choose LastName from the merge field list, and press Enter.

21

FIGURE 21.24

Use the Create Labels dialog box to set up your merge fields and type any extraneous text, such as Dated Materials *or* Personal and Confidential.

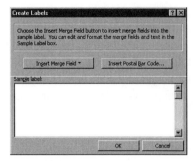

4. Choose Address1 from the merge field list, and press Enter.

5. Choose Address2 from the merge field list, and press Enter.

6. Choose City from the merge field list, and then type a comma followed by a space.

7. Choose State, press the spacebar, and then choose PostalCode from the merge field list. Press the Enter key.

8. Click the Insert Merge Field button one last time, and then choose CustNumber.

9. Press the Enter key, and type DATED MATERIAL, DO NOT DELAY. Figure 21.25 shows the completed label setup.

FIGURE 21.25

Although the address appears left- and top-aligned, the label text and data are centered both horizontally and vertically when merged.

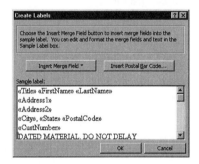

10. Click OK. The Create Labels dialog box closes, and you are returned to the Mail Merge Helper dialog box.

Tip

If you want Word to create a bar code based on the address that is merged with each label, click the Insert Postal Bar Code button.

When your labels are in the printer tray (or fed into the printer in the case of a dot matrix printer), click the Merge button in the Mail Merge Helper dialog box. The Merge dialog box opens. In this case you have no Query Options to set, nor do you want to change the default settings for where to Merge or for printing blank lines if data is missing. Click the Merge button; a sheet of labels appears onscreen in the form of a Word table, its cells matching the dimensions of the label product you selected. Figure 21.26 shows the labels you created in this portion of today's project.

FIGURE 21.26

If you spot errors on some of your labels, you can edit them directly onscreen or you can close the document without saving, repeat the label setup process, and remerge.

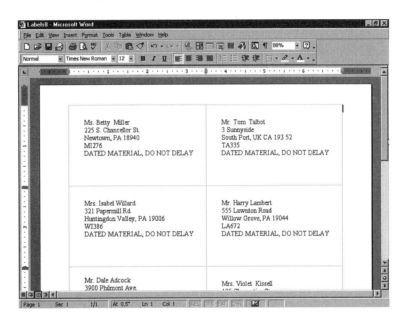

Note

Note that the addresses that didn't utilize the Address2 field (only two of the records used it) do not have a blank line below Address1 on the label. This is due to the default setting, which doesn't insert blank lines when data is missing.

Caution

If your print job doesn't use the entire sheet of labels, be careful if you attempt to use the sheet with the remaining labels for a future print job. Although Word's Envelopes and Labels feature enables you to print to specific labels on a partially-used sheet, this can jam your printer because the labels peel off inside.

21

If this is a group of people to whom you'll be mailing again, save the document. Be sure to save your Word table database by closing the merge document and choosing Yes to save the attached data source (see Figure 21.27).

FIGURE 21.27

When you close the merge document (label layout with merge fields), you can choose to save the database, which enables you to edit the table contents and reuse the addresses for a future mailing.

Summary

Today you learned how to use an Access table and a Word document together to create a form letter. In addition, you learned to create a mailing list in Word and use it to generate mailing labels. This is the last project in your 21 days; hopefully you felt at home in the Office 2000 environment and were able to navigate easily through dialog boxes you've seen before as well as through those that closely resemble others you've seen. The database concepts you learned in Excel (on Day 8, "Building an Excel Database") and in Access (on Days 13 and 14, "Making Use of Your Access Data") were used today, as were the Word skills you acquired on Day 4, "Building a Complex Document." The similarities and compatibility between Office applications pays off when you need to use files and features from two or more applications, and it has been the goal of this book to make you confident and comfortable enough with Office 2000 to perform a complex task such as a mail merge.

Q&A

Q Is there any benefit to using a Word table to store names and addresses for a mailing?

A The fact that you can create a Word table database from within the Mail Merge Helper dialog box is purely a convenience for users who don't have an established electronic database in Access, Excel, or any other Windows-based database product. If your database is large or will be used often, it's better to store it in Excel or Access than to build it for the long run in Word.

Q Can I record a macro of a mail merge so that I can skip the steps next time?

A Yes; if the next time you run the merge you want to use the same data and letter, and you have no additional Query Options, you can record yourself performing the mail merge (from the first step to the very last).

Workshop

The section that follows is a quick quiz about the day. If you have any problems answering any of the questions, see the section that follows the quiz for all the answers.

Quiz

1. Explain the term *merge field* in the context of a form letter.

2. When you select the data source for your mail merge, how do you access your Excel worksheet or Access tables?

3. True or False: You can either sort or filter your database records before the merge—you can't do both.

4. Explain the benefits of merging to a new document rather than directly to the printer.

5. What do you do if you don't find your label product number listed in the Label Options dialog box?

Quiz Answers

1. A merge field is a reference to a database field. When the letter and the associated database are merged, data from that field is inserted into the letter wherever the merge field occurs.

2. In the Open Data Source dialog box, change the Files of type selection to either MS Access Databases (.mdb) or MS Excel Worksheets (.xls). The files of that type in the selected folder then display.

3. False. You can both sort and filter your database records so that only certain records are merged with the letter or labels, and so that those records that are merged appear in a specific order.

4. Choosing to keep the default setting that merges to a new document saves you from potentially wasting paper if you have a typo in your form letter or if you have accidentally chosen the wrong fields to merge.

5. In the Label Options dialog box, click the New Label button and give the label a name and the dimensions of your sheet of labels—the margins, size of each label, and configuration of labels on the sheet.

21

APPENDIX A

Customizing Microsoft Word

Changing Word's Default Settings

Throughout the Office 2000 suite of programs, each application's default settings are created to give you the best and most generally appropriate foundation with which to start working on a new file. These defaults save you setup time for the vast majority of your files, so you can count on things working the same way every time.

There are times, however, when these defaults don't suit the way you work; in such cases, you must change one or more of these defaults to save you the trouble of changing settings each time you work with one of the Office 2000 programs. If you find yourself making changes each time you use one of the programs, it might be time to consider modifying one or more of the defaults; in this appendix, you'll learn to change the most commonly-changed default settings for Word 2000. Appendix B, "Customizing Excel," will show you how to make similar changes for Excel 2000.

Choosing Where Files Will be Saved

By default, files are saved to the My Documents folder on your local drive. If your files are saved elsewhere without your intervention, perhaps the default has already been adjusted—if you're using the computer at work, the person who set up your computer might have already selected an alternative default location for your saved files.

In any case, to change your default folder for new files, follow these steps:

1. Choose Tools, Options.

2. In the Options dialog box, click the File Locations tab (see Figure A.1).

FIGURE A.1

The list of file types that can be saved to alternative locations appears in the File Locations tab of the Options dialog box.

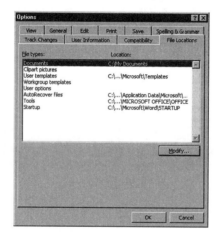

3. The Documents item is selected in the File Types list. Click the Modify button to change the default folder (the current default is listed on the right side of the dialog box).

4. The Modify Location dialog box gives you a standard navigation dialog box—much like an Open or Save As dialog box (see Figure A.2)—in which you can select a particular folder as your new default location. After making your selection, click OK.

5. Back in the Options dialog box, click OK to save your changes.

From this point on, when you save a document for the first time, the Save As dialog box goes to the folder you selected as your default. You can set and reset this default as many times as you want.

FIGURE A.2

Navigate to the folder (perhaps on a different drive?) to which you want your files saved by default.

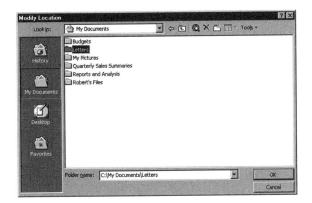

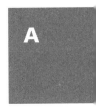

Customizing AutoRecover and Backup Settings

As you work, Word saves AutoRecover information about your document every ten minutes. It does this by default, without any interaction from you. AutoRecover information is used by Word to retrieve your document if your power is lost or the system crashes before you've had a chance to save your document formally (or if you've made changes to your saved file but have not updated the file to reflect the changes). When power is restored or your computer is rebooted, Word tells you if there is any recoverable version of the files you were working on when the system shut down. You can use these recovered versions to pick up and keep working.

You can change the AutoRecover setting to save more often, or you can have it save less often if you find that the AutoRecover process slows your computer down (it might if you don't have a lot of memory in your computer).

To adjust your AutoRecover settings, follow these steps:

1. Choose Tools, Options, and then click the Save tab.
2. As shown in Figure A.3, the setting for AutoRecover info is every ten minutes. Double-click the 10 and type the number of minutes you prefer.
3. Click OK to save your new settings and close the dialog box.
4. Back in the Options dialog box, click OK.

A backup copy of your documents can also be created by default, if you turn that particular setting on—it's off by default. A backup copy saves the original version of your file (or the version after the last save) each time you update the file as you're working. This makes it possible to go back to a previous version if you regret saving your latest changes or if your system shuts down unexpectedly before you've had a chance to save your latest changes. As long as you've saved at some point in your recent session, you'll have some form of the file to go back to.

FIGURE A.3

It's not a good idea to extend the AutoRecover interval to more than 15 minutes—to do so risks your losing valuable time and effort in the event of a power failure or system crash.

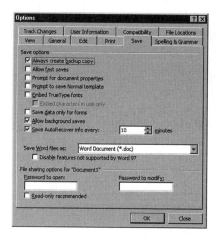

To turn on the setting to create backup copies of your documents, follow these steps:

1. Choose Tools, Options, and then click the Save tab.
2. Place a checkmark next to Always create backup copy (first item in the list on the tab).
3. Click OK to save your settings and close the dialog box.

When the backup version is created, the filename you've chosen is used, along with a .WBK extension. Both the .DOC and .WBK versions are saved in the same folder. To open a backup copy, simply look for your filename with a .WBK extension (you might have to change the Files of type setting in the Open dialog box to All Files in order to see anything aside from the .DOC versions of your files).

 Caution

If you turn on the setting to create backup copies, the Allow fast saves option is turned off automatically. It isn't possible to make backup copies unless a full and complete save has been performed, and a fast save doesn't perform a full save.

Selecting a Default Font

When you start a new document in Word, the font is Times New Roman, and the font size is 10 points. This is based on traditional business letter requirements. Many users, however, find that 10-point text is too small, and some users prefer a different font.

To change the default font for your new documents (those based on the Blank Document template), follow these steps:

1. In your current document, choose Format, Font.

2. Change the font or size to what you want to use for your new blank documents. Be sure that the font and size you select are appropriate for the vast majority of your documents.

3. Click the Default button (see Figure A.4).

FIGURE A.4

Keep the needs of your typical document in mind when selecting a default font or font size.

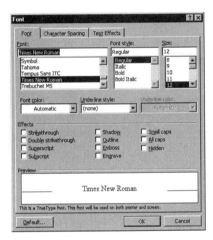

4. A prompt appears, asking if you intend to change the default to what you've selected (see Figure A.5). Click Yes to change the default.

FIGURE A.5

Click Yes to change your default font. Click No if you want to leave the default at its current setting.

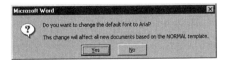

5. Click OK to close the Font dialog box.

From this point on, every new, blank document will start with the font and size you have set as your new default. You can reset the default as needed in the future.

Customizing Office Proofing Tools

Word's spelling and grammar checking tools are set to meet average standards for business letters. *Average* is a relative term, however, and you might want to adjust these settings to better suit your needs.

Changing Your Spell Check Defaults

To adjust your spell check settings, choose Tools, Options, and then click the Spelling and Grammar tab. The Spelling section of the dialog box (see Figure A.6) gives you a series of check boxes—click in them to turn them off or on to meet your spell check needs:

FIGURE A.6

Although the spelling defaults meet most people's needs, you might need to tweak them a bit to make them more effective for your documents.

- **Check spelling as you type**—When it is turned on, this setting results in the red underlines that appear when you type a word that's not in Word's dictionary. If the red lines bother you, turn this option off.

- **Hide spelling errors in this document**—If you generally want spelling checked as you type, but not in this particular document, turn this option on.

- **Always suggest corrections**—This is on by default, and is best left on. Why not let Word suggest alternative spellings for you?

- **Suggest from main dictionary only**—This is another setting that is best left in its default position—off. If you've added words to the custom dictionary (by clicking Add when doing a spell check), you'll be ignoring those words if you turn this option on.

- **Ignore words in UPPERCASE**—This is a good option to turn off if you type a lot of product names, abbreviations, or acronyms.

- **Ignore words with numbers**—If you type things such as GIZZMOB35A, leave this option on.

- **Ignore Internet and file addresses**—If this option is off, every time you type a Web address, Word turns it into a real hyperlink—the color of the text changes, and it is underlined.

If you want to start a new dictionary and set it as the default in which your new words (added by clicking Add during spell check) are stored, click the Dictionaries button. In the Custom Dictionaries dialog box (see Figure A.7), click New to create a new dictionary. After creating a new dictionary, you can specify it as the default by clicking in the option box next to its name in the Custom Dictionaries dialog box. Be sure to remove the check mark next to CUSTOM.DIC if you no longer want to use that dictionary.

FIGURE A.7

Choose to create a new dictionary to store all your unique words, terms, and spellings.

Changing Word's Grammar Settings

The Grammar section of the Spelling and Grammar tab offers four options:

- **Check grammar as you type**—This one is on by default, and results in the green underlines that appear whenever Word finds what it deems to be a grammatical error. If you're tired of the green underlines, turn this option off.

- **Hide grammatical errors in this document**—If you want Word to check your grammar as you type, but not in the current document, turn this option on.

- **Check grammar with spelling**—If you leave this option on, choosing Tools, Spelling and Grammar results in a check of your grammar as well as your spelling.

- **Show readability statistics**—Set to Off by default, this option displays a variety of ratings at the end of your grammar checking session. If you're interested in knowing what grade-level reader will be comfortable with your document, turn this option on.

To adjust the standards by which your grammar is checked, you can change the writing style setting. Click the Writing style list box (set to Standard by default) and choose Casual, Formal, Technical, or Custom instead.

To make more specific changes to the way Word checks your grammar, click the Settings button. The Grammar Settings dialog box opens (see Figure A.8), and you can use the Require, Grammar, and Style sections to turn on and off the settings you want (scroll through the list to see all your options). Click OK when your changes are complete.

FIGURE A.8

Customize the grammar checking defaults by turning settings on and off to meet the needs of your writing style.

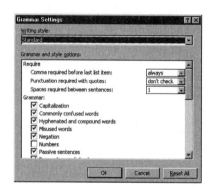

APPENDIX B

Customizing Excel

Customizing Excel's Save Options

By default, Excel saves your work to the My Documents folder on your local drive when you issue a Save command by pressing Ctrl+S; when you choose File, Save; or when you click the Save button on the Standard toolbar. You can adjust the default location for your new files and set up Excel to save your workbooks automatically by adjusting some important defaults.

Selecting a Default Folder

To choose another folder (or even a different drive) as the default location for your workbooks, follow these steps:

1. Choose Tools, Options, and click the General tab if it isn't already selected. Figure B.1 shows the Options dialog box.

FIGURE B.1

The General tab contains options for changing several of your Excel defaults.

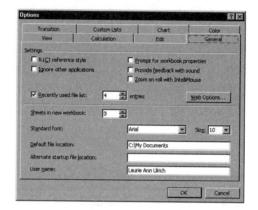

2. In the Default file location box, type a new path (drive letter and folder name) into which you want your files to be saved by default.

3. Click OK to put your setting change into effect and close the dialog box.

After making this change, you can see that the folder you've selected is the automatic location that is displayed in the Save As dialog box when you save a new workbook. You can reset this default as needed in the future.

Choosing How Often To AutoSave Your Work

AutoSave is a feature that isn't automatically installed when you do a typical Office 2000 installation. Rather, it is an add-in that you can install later if you're interested in using the feature.

How do you know if this add-in was installed? Check the Tools menu. If AutoSave is not one of the commands, you need to install it from the Office 2000 CD-ROM. If the command appears on the Tools menu, you can skip to the AutoSave procedures that appear later in this section.

To install the AutoSave add-in, follow these instructions:

1. Insert your Office 2000 CD-ROM, Disk 1. After AutoRun starts, the Microsoft
    Office 2000 Maintenance Mode dialog box opens as shown in Figure B.2.

FIGURE B.2

*The Microsoft Office
2000 Maintenance
Mode is opened when
you insert the Office
2000 CD-ROM.*

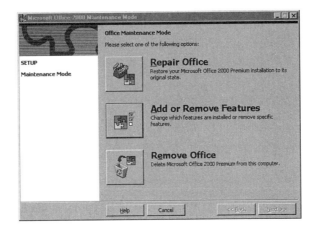

2. Click the Add or Remove Features button. The Update Features dialog box opens,
    displaying a list of feature categories (see Figure B.3).

FIGURE B.3

*You can customize
your Office installation
by adding and remov-
ing programs using
your Office 2000
CD-ROM.*

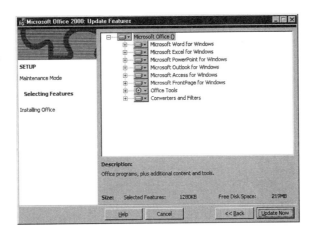

3. Click the plus sign (+) next to Microsoft Excel for Windows. A list descends; one of the items is Add-ins, as shown in Figure B.4.

FIGURE B.4

Expand the list of categories to display the Add-ins listing.

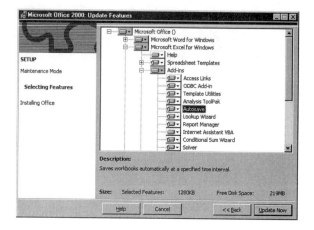

4. Click the plus sign next to Add-ins, and click the word AutoSave.

5. Click the Update Now button. The Update process begins, and AutoSave is installed on your computer.

After installation is complete, restart your computer before attempting to use the AutoSave feature; in fact, AutoSave doesn't appear in the Tools menu until you restart the computer.

> If, after restart, you still don't see AutoSave in the Tools menu, choose Add-Ins from the Tools menu, and place a checkmark next to AutoSave. You might be told that AutoSave wasn't completely installed; you are then asked if you want to install it. Follow the process as though you're installing it again (all that Office does is reconfigure itself to run AutoSave). When the process ends, open the Tools menu—you see AutoSave in the list.

After AutoSave is installed and you've restarted your computer, you can use AutoSave by following these steps:

1. Choose Tools, AutoSave.

2. The AutoSave dialog box opens (see Figure B.5). Enter the interval at which you want AutoSave to be performed. The default is every ten minutes.

FIGURE B.5

If you intend to rely on AutoSave to keep your work safe, don't make the intervals any longer than 15 minutes. If you increase them beyond that, you risk losing important work and valuable time.

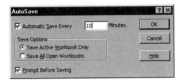

B

3. Change your Save Options as needed (Save Active Workbook Only or Save All Open Workbooks) and click OK to close the dialog box and put your AutoSave settings into efffect.

Tip

Leave the Prompt Before Saving option *on*. Otherwise, you'll risk updating workbooks that you might not want to update. Although AutoSave is automatic, you can bypass it by clicking No when the AutoSave prompt appears.

Selecting a Default Worksheet Font

For most users, Arial in ten points is a perfectly acceptable font and size for worksheet content. It's highly legible onscreen and in print, and it's bland enough that it doesn't clash with other fonts that might be applied to titles and column headings. If, however, you find that you really must have all your worksheet content in another font or another font size, you can adjust the default font to meet your needs.

To change the default worksheet font, follow these steps:

1. Choose Tools, Options, and click the General tab (see Figure B.6)

2. Choose a different Standard font as needed.

3. Click the Size list box to select a smaller or larger font size.

4. Click OK to put your new settings into effect and close the dialog box.

FIGURE B.6

*Choose a different
default font and font
size on the General tab
in the Options dialog
box.*

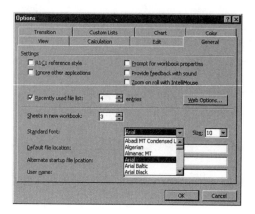

After you make this change, all new workbooks that are based on the Blank Workbook
template use your new font and size as the default. When making this sort of change,
make sure that the font or size you select works for the vast majority of your workbooks.
You'll know right away if the font or size you chose isn't appropriate for most of your
work—you'll find yourself resetting your fonts in each worksheet, and you'll end up
resetting the default to Arial ten points to avoid the extra effort.

Setting Workbook Display Options

By default, your Excel application window contains the onscreen features that you need
to get your work done: Formula bar, Status bar, column and row control buttons, and
scroll bars for moving around the worksheet. Although these defaults meet most users'
needs, you might find that you want to turn some of them off, or turn others on; Excel
makes this easy to do.

To adjust the display of your Excel application window, follow these steps:

1. Choose Tools, Options, and click the View tab (see Figure B.7).

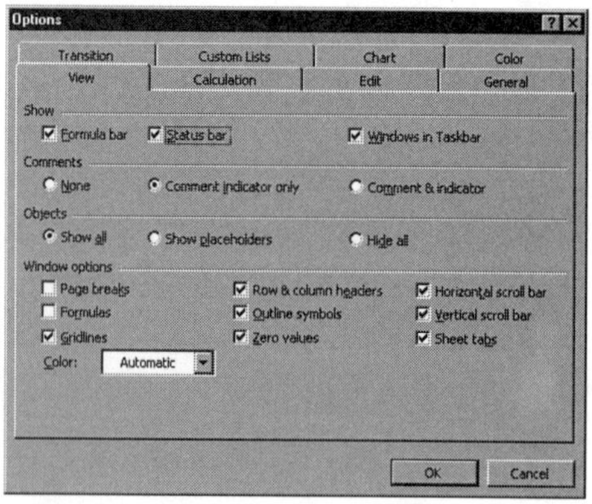

FIGURE B.7

*Look at the View tab to
change the onscreen
features in your Excel
workspace.*

2. In the Show, Comments, Objects, and Window options sections of the dialog box, remove checkmarks for items that you don't want to see and add checkmarks for items that you want to add to the default workspace.

3. When you've made all the changes you need, click OK to put them into effect and close the dialog box.

B

Tip

Changes that are made in the Show, Comments, and Objects sections apply to the current workbook *and* to all future workbooks. Changes in the Window options section apply only to the current workbook; the default settings are restored for new workbooks that you open thereafter.

Caution

Unlike most changes that you can make to your workbook or worksheet, changes made using the Options dialog box cannot be reversed through the use of Undo. If you want to revert to previous settings, you must choose Tools, Options; then, on the tab on which you made changes, set your options back to their previous settings.

APPENDIX C

Working with Small Business Tools

Office 2000 includes a group of tools that are designed to help small businesses get more out of the Office suite of applications. The tools are included in all the editions of Office 2000, and they're not just useful for small businesses—large businesses, home offices, and individual users can all find something useful in one or more of the following Small Business Tools components:

- The Small Business Financial Manager
- The Business Planner
- The Direct Mail Planner
- The Small Business Customer Manager

To access these components, click the Start button and choose Programs. From the Programs list, select Microsoft Office Small Business Tools, and then view the submenu and make your selection.

The Small Business Financial Manager

This small business tool adds a Financial Manager menu to your Excel menu bar, as shown in Figure C.1, although you can access it from the Programs list in the Start menu as well. The Financial manager menu offers a series of Wizards to help you create reports, and charts, and tools to assist you in making business decisions based on your worksheet data.

FIGURE C.1

If this menu doesn't show in your Excel window, choose Tools, Add-Ins, and click the Small Business Financial Manager checkbox.

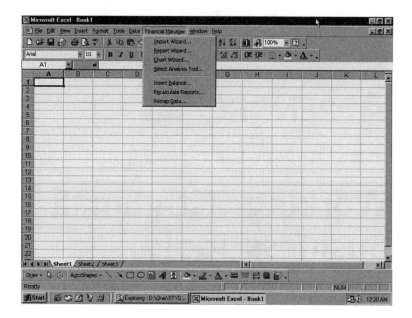

Using the Import Wizard

The Import Wizard enables you to build a new database that's based on the data you've built using your accounting software. When you select Import Wizard from the Financial Manager menu, the wizard begins, as shown in Figure C.2.

The New Database Wizard helps you to extract data from accounting software such as QuickBooks or Microsoft Money. An Access database is created, but a knowledge of Access is not required in order to use the database.

After entering information about yourself (your name and an optional password of your choosing), the Financial Manager searches your computer for accounting files. After they are found, you can choose which data to import, and your database is created. Figure C.3 shows an accounting database that lists accounting categories.

FIGURE C.2

Build a database for use in creating reports and using your work-sheets as true analysis tools.

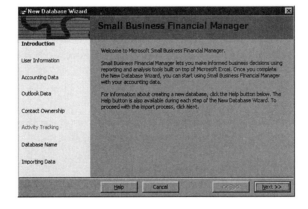

FIGURE C.3

Collate pertinent accounting information into one database.

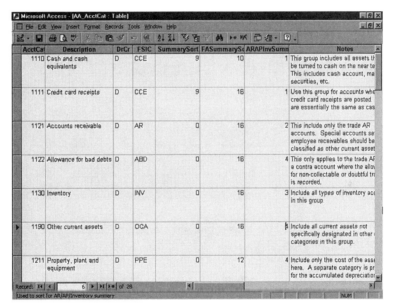

Even if you don't have any accounting software on your computer, a generic database is created, with many database tables into which you can manually enter your own accounting information.

Working with the Report Wizard

The Report Wizard makes it easy to create a variety of standard accounting reports, such as income statements, balance sheets, and trial balances. To activate the Report Wizard, choose Financial Manager, Report Wizard from the Excel 2000 menu bar. The Small Business Financial Manager Startup Screen opens, as shown in Figure C.4.

FIGURE C.4

Click the Report hypertext link to activate the Report Wizard.

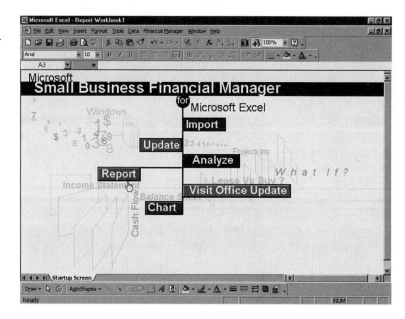

After selecting the Report link, the Create a Financial Report dialog box opens, as shown in Figure C.5.

FIGURE C.5

Choose from seven different reports, and then click Next to proceed.

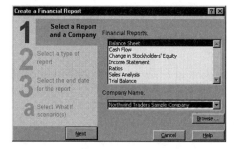

After choosing the type of report you want, the Financial Report wizard asks you to specify which variation you want to use. Figure C.6 shows the two different types of Trial Balances you can create.

FIGURE C.6

The number of report variations depends on the type of report you selected.

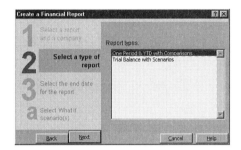

A series of dialog boxes follows, asking for further information. In the case of the sample Trial Balance, the next step in the process requires that you choose the date of the report, as shown in Figure C.7.

FIGURE C.7

Make your date selection and click Finish to create the report.

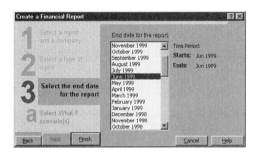

The Report Wizard then completes the report, based on the data that is drawn from your accounting software files. For the purposes of this appendix, use the Northwind Traders database that comes with Office 2000. Their Trial Balance with Comparisons is shown in Figure C.8.

Tip

If you're not sure how you might use the Small Business Financial Manager tools, try running various reports with the Northwind Traders data—you'll have real data to look at, without spending time to set up your own information.

FIGURE C.8

FIGURE C.8

The finished report contains your data in all the right places, along with text and numeric formatting to give the report a polished, professional look.

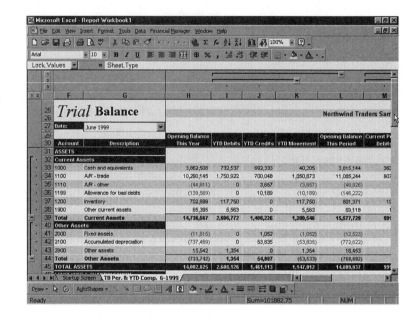

Using the Chart Wizard

Don't confuse this Chart Wizard with Excel's Chart Wizard tool. This wizard offers only business-related charts, and it does the charting for you based on data you add to your database through the Import Wizard. Again, use the Northwind Traders sample database.

To run the Small Business Financial Manager Chart Wizard, follow these steps:

1. Choose Financial Manager, Chart Wizard.

2. Choose the type of chart you want from the Create a Financial Chart dialog box, shown in Figure C.9.

FIGURE C.9

Choose from four basic chart types.

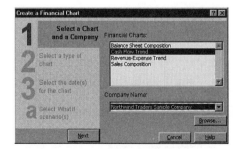

3. Select the database you want to use from the Company Name dialog box, and click Next.

4. Depending on the type of chart you selected, more questions and dialog box options appear in the next step. For this example, you're creating a Cash Flow chart, and you must choose the type of cash flow to include in the chart (see Figure C.10).

FIGURE C.10

How detailed should your chart be? Choose one or all of the options.

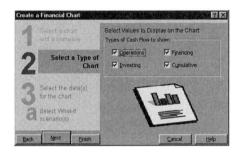

5. Click Next to choose a range of dates for the chart (see Figure C.11).

FIGURE C.11

Your starting and ending dates dictate the time over which the cash flow trend is tracked.

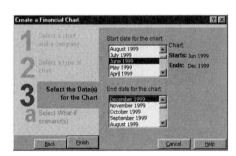

6. Click Finish to create the chart, which appears in Figure C.12.

Selecting an Analysis Tool

The Small Business Financial Manager offers a tool for making decisions such as choosing whether to buy or lease an item for your business. Like the other Small Business Financial Manager tools, the analysis tool asks you a series of questions in a series of dialog boxes. To access this Small Business Financial Manager feature, choose Financial Manager, Select Analysis Tool. The first dialog box is shown in Figure C.13.

FIGURE C.12

The Chart Wizard selects the right kind of chart for the type of data that is being charted. A line chart is selected here to show trends in cash flow over time.

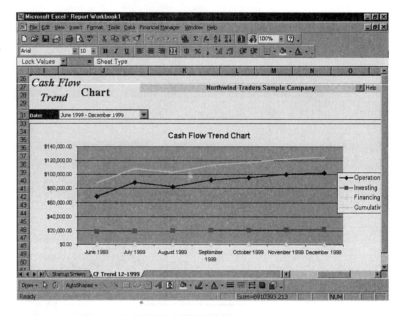

FIGURE C.13

Choose Buy Vs. Lease to ask the Small Business Financial Manager to help you make your decision.

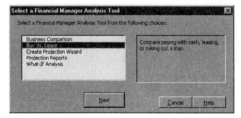

After selecting the Buy Vs. Lease tool, you are asked to give the Small Business Financial Manager more information about your intended purchase (see Figure C.14).

FIGURE C.14

Enter the name, the price, and the tax amount for the item you're considering.

Click Next to proceed to the dialog box shown in Figure C.15. Here, you can give the Buy vs. Lease tool your purchase options—paying cash, taking out a loan, a lease, or other financing options.

FIGURE C.15

Document your purchase/lease options to help the Small Business Financial Manager analyze your alternatives.

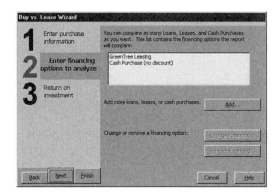

At this point, you can click Finish or Next. Clicking Next takes you to a final dialog box, in which you can specify your tax bracket and any potential profit you'll make from the item (see Figure C.16).

FIGURE C.16

If you don't know your tax rate, or if there is no potential profit, leave the options blank and click Finish.

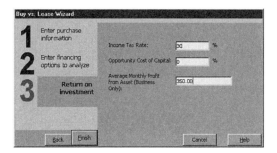

The resulting analysis appears on a formatted worksheet, as shown in Figure C.17. Scroll through the report to view the various calculations, and use the information to make your decision.

FIGURE C.17

Analysis reports are an excellent source of objective information—seeing the numbers on paper can help you make an informed financial decision.

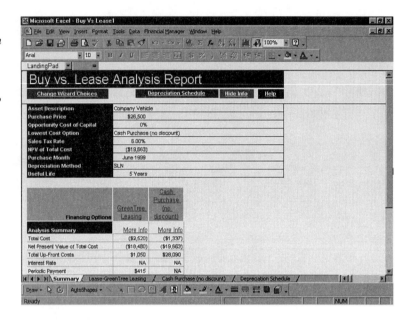

The Business Planner

Not all businesses have an actual business plan, but documentation of a plan for your business can be very useful when you're starting out or when you're going through normal growth phases in the life of your business. The Small Business Tools package gives you a tool for building a business plan, eliminating your need to know how such a plan is traditionally structured. Simply enter the requested information, and let the Business Planner do the rest.

To use the Business Planner, follow these steps:

1. From the Start menu, choose Programs, Microsoft Office Small Business Tools. From the resulting submenu, choose Microsoft Business Planner.

2. The Business Planner window opens, displaying the Personal Interviewer Step 1 (see Figure C.18). The instructions tell you to scroll through the displayed text and answer questions about yourself and your business.

3. Answer each of the questions. Some questions require that you choose one of several options, and others require you to type in text boxes (see Figure C.19).

4. Answer the questions in Step 2 of 3, and click the arrow to proceed to the final Step.

5. After answering the questions in Step 3 of 3, click the arrow again. The Business Planner displays a new window, as shown in Figure C.20.

FIGURE C.18

There's a lot of text to wade through, but you'll find it to be helpful in understanding business plans.

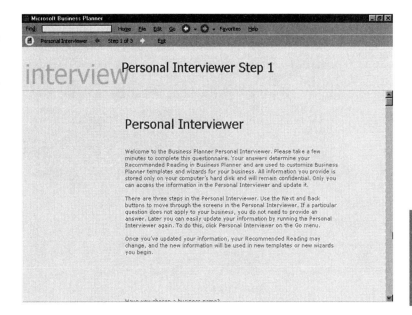

Click here to go back to a previous step

Click this arrow to move forward through the Personal Interviewer

FIGURE C.19

After you've entered your information, click the arrow to move to Step 2 of 3.

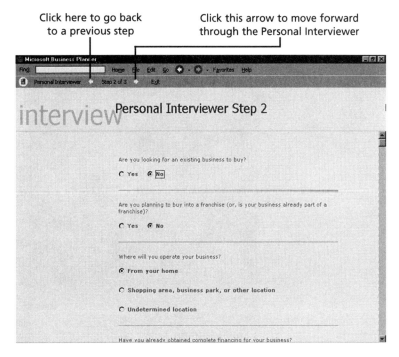

C

FIGURE C.20

Follow each page of the Business Planner to gain more information and to answer questions.

6. Click the business plan wizard hyperlink.

7. The business plan wizard window (see Figure C.21) contains a series of seven hyperlinks. Click the History and Position to Date link to start.

FIGURE C.21

See the list of topic areas about which you'll read informative articles.

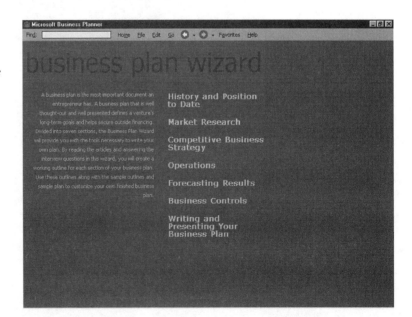

8. Read the first of 15 articles (see Figure C.22) and click the right-pointing arrow to proceed. It's a good idea to read them all, clicking the arrow to move through the articles one by one.

FIGURE C.22

Move through the articles by clicking the right-pointing arrow when you're ready to go to the next one.

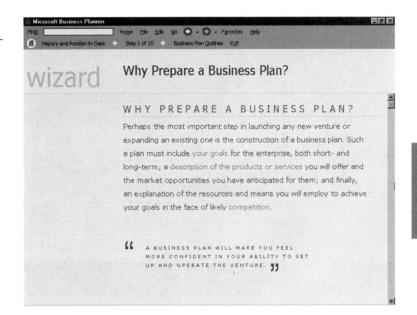

9. At Step 8 of 15, you are asked to name your business plan document in the dialog box seen in Figure C.23. Enter a name for your plan and click Save.

10. Step 8 of 15 continues by asking you to type answers to a series of questions (with intermittent option selections). After responding to all the questions, click the arrow to proceed.

11. At Step 10 of 15, questions about your Management Team are presented (see Figure C.24). Type your responses and click the arrow to move to Step 11 of 15.

12. Articles appear in Steps 11 through 15, at which point you are given a final set of questions regarding your Products and Services (see Figure C.25). Type your responses and click the arrow to proceed.

13. An action plan page appears (see Figure C.26), which includes links to more articles and some Web pages with information that might be helpful to you in growing your business. Click any links that interest you.

FIGURE C.23

Give your business plan document a name and choose a folder in which to save it.

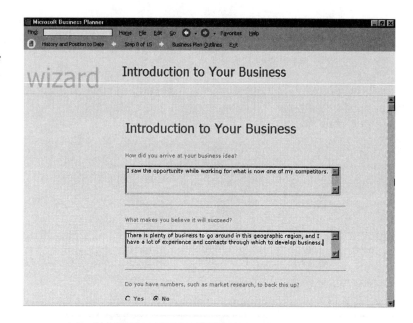

FIGURE C.24

Describe your management team. If you're a very small business, this might be just you.

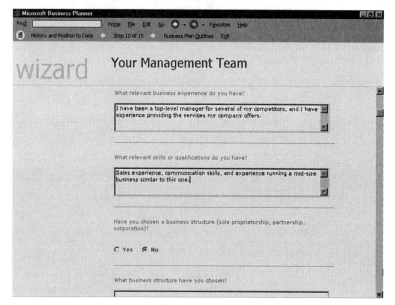

FIGURE C.25

Describe the products you sell or the services you provide.

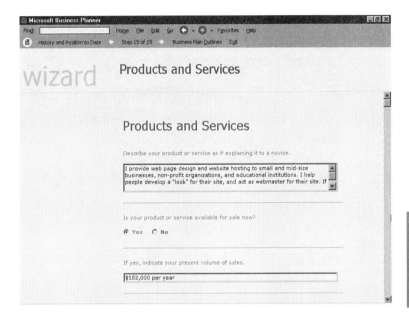

FIGURE C.26

If you still want to know more about business plans, check these internal links and Web sites.

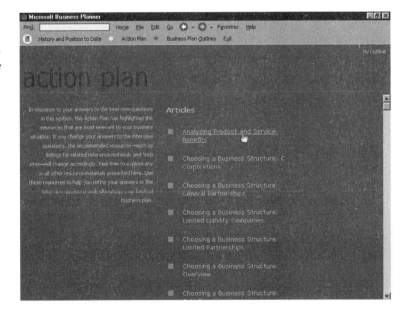

14. Click the Business Plan Outlines button and choose My Outline. An outline that is based on your entries to the questions posed throughout the previous steps appears in a Word document (see Figure C.27).

FIGURE C.27

View the results of your Business Planner labors in the form of an outline.

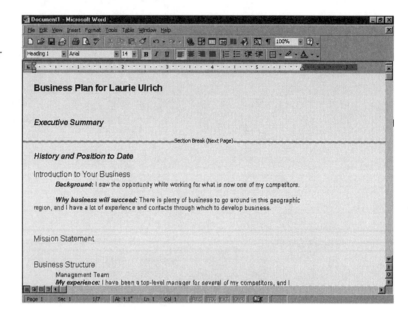

15. Replace the instructional sample text in the outline with your own text. After completing and customizing the outline, you can save and print it as you do any Word document.

Your Business Plan can be used in a variety of ways—as part of a package you supply to the bank or investors, or simply as a reference for yourself to keep things on track as you expand your business. As your business grows and changes, run through the Business Planner again and see how the resulting outline changes to reflect your new answers.

The Direct Mail Manager

If your business does a lot of direct mailing, you might find this Small Business Tools component to be very useful. The Direct Mail Manager performs the following tasks:

- **Imports your address list**—If you've already built an address list in another program, you can access it through the Direct Mail Manager.

- **Verifies your addresses**—The Direct Mail Manager checks for and inserts missing Zip codes, checks spelling, and gets rid of duplicate addresses. The verification process saves you time and supplies by eliminating incorrect addresses and redundant mailings.

- **Prints envelopes, labels, and postcards**—U.S. Postal Service guidelines have been built into the Direct Mail Manager to make sure the output meets Federal requirements.

- **Saves the updated database**—Don't risk forgetting to save the imported and corrected records for your next mailing.

The DirectMail Manager performs these tasks through a Wizard, as shown in Figure C.28.

FIGURE C.28

Import, verify, print, and save your direct mail database with the DirectMail Manager.

To access the wizard, start the DirectMail Manager by following these steps:

1. From the Start button, choose Programs, Microsoft Office Small Business Tools, and then select Microsoft DirectMail Manager.

2. After viewing the list of tasks that the DirectMail Manager performs, click Next to get started.

3. Tell the DirectMail Manager where to find your address list. Click the Browse button to navigate to the folder that contains the list; enter the path and filename into the File box. If your address list is stored in Outlook, click the Outlook Folder option and select the folder (see Figure C.29).

4. Click Next to proceed to the next step, wherein the DirectMail Manager verifies the accuracy of your list and makes sure all your records are unique.

5. After verification, click Next to move on to the Print step. In the Print dialog box, choose the type of printed output you want for your mailing (see Figure C.30).

FIGURE C.29

Select the folder that contains the contacts you've entered with Outlook.

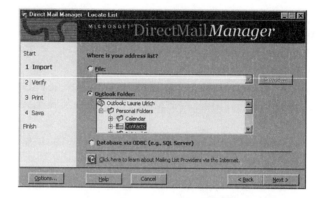

FIGURE C.30

Print the envelopes, labels, or postcards you'll be using for your direct mailing.

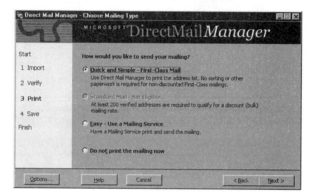

6. Click Next and choose how to save your database. Your options are shown in Figure C.31.

FIGURE C.31

To save you from accidentally losing the changes made during the verification process, you are prompted to save your database.

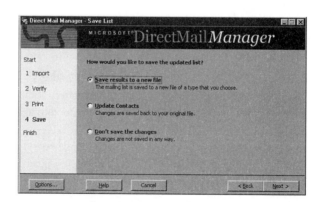

7. Click Next to create a form letter using Word or Publisher, or you can opt to skip this step entirely (perhaps you already have the letter or you're mailing a flyer). Make your selection and click Next.

8. If you chose to create the form letter, the Direct Mail Manager asks you to name your document (see Figure C.32). Click the Create button to build the letter.

FIGURE C.32

Build a form letter that will be merged with your database.

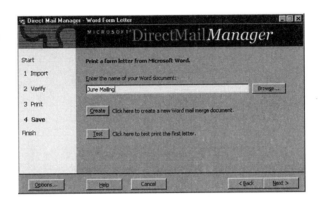

9. Choose the Letter Wizard from the Select a Mail Merge Template, and follow the wizard's steps to create the letter.

After your letter is created, you can place the letters in your Direct Mail Manager-created envelopes and get the mailing out to your customers and prospects. The Direct Mail Manager can be run each time you do a mailing, or just periodically as a means to verify the accuracy of your database.

Tip

In order for the Direct Mail Manager to verify your addresses, it must connect to the Internet and check databases there. If you'd rather skip this step, click the Options button in the lower-left corner of the Wizard dialog box and remove the check mark next to Run Address Verification. This step is skipped, and you proceed to the Print stage.

The Small Business Customer Manager

You don't need to know how to use database software to query your list of contacts for specific records. If, for example, you need to see only your contacts in New Jersey, the Small Business Customer Manager can help you find them. In addition, the Small

Business Customer Manager can be used to pull your contact information from popular accounting applications such as PeachTree, MYOB, and QuickBooks, or you can use your Outlook contacts folder.

To access and use the Small Business Customer Manager, follow these steps:

1. Open the Start menu and choose Programs, Microsoft Office Small Business Tools, and then choose Microsoft Small Business Customer Manager from the submenu.

2. After starting the Small Business Customer Manager program, you are asked to select a database to use for your contacts (see Figure C.33). You can select one of the listed databases or you can click the Browse button to locate your file. For the purposes of this appendix, you'll be using the Northwind Traders sample database, provided by Microsoft.

FIGURE C.33

Choose the database you want to view and edit through the Small Business Customer Manager.

3. Click OK to close the Microsoft Customer Manager dialog box and open the Small Business Customer Manager main program.

4. A dialog box opens, asking for your personal information—name, company name, and so forth. Fill this out and click OK to proceed.

The Small Business Customer Manager opens, displaying the selected database (see Figure C.34). A full set of tools for selecting specific records from within the database is offered, in the form of a menu bar, toolbar, and list boxes designed for use with your particular database.

Click the Find
button to search
for a specific
record based on
key text

Use the Ascending
and Descending
Sort buttons to
change the order of
your listed records

FIGURE C.34

*Click the Narrow Your
Choice and Action list
boxes to view only
those records that
match your criteria.*

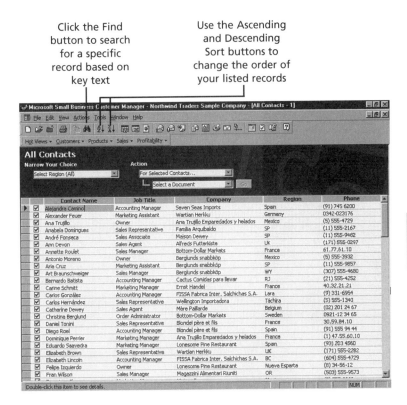

You can insert, edit, and delete records from within the database, and save your changes
before exiting. You can also save your database with a new filename, creating a new version of the database file. The database can be used for direct mailings and reports
through any of the Office applications, such as Word and Excel.

INDEX

Symbols

= (equal sign), formulas (Excel),
180
( ) parentheses (Excel), 182-184
; (semicolon), addressing email
(Outlook), 274
3D formulas (Excel), 191-193
3D view (Excel), 237-238

A

absolute references (Excel),
189-191
Access, 335
Apply Filter button, 367, 374
commands
Apply Filter/Sort (Filter
menu), 367
Column (Insert menu),
356

Copy (Edit menu), 382,
477, 533
Delete Column (Edit
menu), 356, 532
Delete Record (Edit
menu), 357
Export (File menu), 383,
535
Filter (Records menu),
365, 374
Paste Append (Edit
menu), 223, 384
Print (File menu), 373,
380
Run (Query menu),
370-372
Relationships (Tools
menu), 376
Save (File menu), 372
Copy button, 533
data
adding to documents
(Word), 475-478
copying, 382-383
data entry forms, 351-355
Database dialog box, 337

databases
creating, 336
saving, 348
Design button, 373
Edit Relationship dialog box,
377
Excel
data integration, 381-386
databases, 223
Expression Builder dialog
box, 346
fields
adding, 356
creating, 339-341
deleting, 356
input masks, 343-344
naming, 387
ordering, 355
planning, 338-339
primary keys, 339-340
setting data types,
340-341
settings, 341-343
Validation Rules, 346-347
Form Wizard, 352-354
Objects panel
Queries button, 368-372
Reports button, 378

G-H

N

Q

R

ranges (Excel)
  cells
    averaging, 184-186
    borders, 161-163
    Clipboard, 144-146
    copying, 142-146
    counting, 187-188
    dclcting, 141
    deleting names, 147-148
    editing, 141-142
    moving, 142-144
    naming, 146-148
    selecting, 138-139, 178
    shading, 161-165
  noncontiguous, 139
Read flag, email (Outlook), 285
read receipts, email (Outlook), 282-283
receiving email (Outlook), 286-287
Record Macro dialog box
  Excel, 262
  Toolbars button (Word), 257
  Word, 256
Record Narration command (Slide Show menu), PowerPoint, 452
Record Narration dialog box (PowerPoint), 452
recording
  macros
    adding files (Word), 256-260
    errors, 255
    Excel, 260-264
    keyboard shortcuts (Excel), 260-262
    keyboard shortcuts (Word), 255-256
    toolbar buttons, 257-259, 268
    Word, 253-255
  narrations (PowerPoint), 451-453
records (Access)
  adding, 349-351
  deleting, 357-359

editing, 357
fields, 338
  adding, 356
  creating, 339-341
  deleting, 356
  input masks, 343-344
  naming, 387
  ordering, 355
  planning, 338-339
  primary keys, 339-340
  setting data types, 340-341
  settings, 341-343
  Validation Rules, 346-347
filtering, 373-374
sorting, 364-366, 370
records (Excel)
  adding, 205
  consistency issues, 204
  deleting, 205
  editing, 205
  entering, 202-204
  fields, 198
    columns, 199, 216-218
    setting, 199-202
  filtering
    AutoFilter, 210-213
    custom filters, 213-215
  rows, 199
    blank rows, 207
    hiding, 216-218
    sizing, 218
    unhiding, 219
  sorting, 206-210
Records menu commands (Access), Filter, 365, 374
redirecting AutoSum formulas (Excel), 177-178
reestablishing hyperlinks (FrontPage), 543
references, absolute (Excel), 189-191
relationships, tables (Access), 375-378
Relationships command (Tools menu), Access, 376
Relationships window (Access), 376-377
relative addressing (Excel), 189
Reminder Sound dialog box, 315

reminders (Outlook), 311, 315
Remote Mail command (Tools menu), Outlook, 287
removing. See deleting
Reply flag, email (Outlook), 285
Reply to All flag, email (Outlook), 285
replying, email (Outlook), 287-288
Report Wizard (Access), 378-380
Report Wizard (Excel), 618-619
Report Wizard command (Financial Manager menu), Excel, 618
reports (Access), 375, 378-381
requesting read receipts (Outlook), 282-283
Required setting, fields (Access), 342
Review flag, email (Outlook), 285
Rich Text command (Format menu), Outlook, 278-279
Rich Text format (RTF), 291, 466
right-click menus. See shortcut menus
rows
  records (Excel), 199, 207
    hiding, 216-218
    row control buttons, 134
    sizing, 218
    unhiding, 219
  tables (Word), 97
Rows command (Insert menu), 205, 219
Ruler command (View menu), Word, 66, 81
rulers (Word), 71
Run command (Query menu), Access, 370-372
running
  presentations (PowerPoint), 454-456
  queries (Access), 370-373, 387

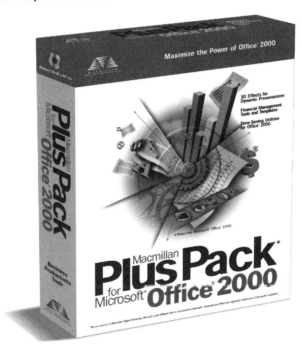

Other Related Titles

FrontPage 2000
Denise Tyler
ISBN: 0-672-31499-1
US $39.99 /CAN $59.95

Microsoft Access 2000 in 21 Days
Paul Cassel
ISBN: 0-672-31292-1
US $29.99/CAN $44.95

Excel Programming
Matthew Harris
ISBN: 0-672-31543-2
US $29.99/CAN $44.95

Outlook 2000 Programming in 24 Hours
Sue Mosher
ISBN:0-672-31651-x
US $19.99/CAN $28.95

Microsoft Power Point 2000 in 24 Hours
Christopher Haddad
ISBN:0-672-31432-0
US $12.99/CAN $19.95

Microsoft Word 2000 in 24 Hours
Heidi Steele
ISBN:0-672-31442-8
US $19.99/CAN $28.95

Microsoft Excel 2000 in 24 Hours
Trudi Reisner
ISBN:0-672-31445-2
US $19.99/CAN $28.95

Microsoft Outlook 2000 in 24 Hours
Herb Tyson
ISBN:0-672-31449-5
US $19.99/CAN $28.95

Windows 95 in 24 Hours, 3rd Edition
Greg Perry
ISBN:0-672-37482-7
US $19.99/CAN $29.95

Windows NT Workstation 4 in 24 Hours
Martin Kenley
ISBN:0-672-31011-2
US $19.99/CAN $28.95

Windows NT Server 4 in 21 Days
Peter Davis
ISBN: 0-672-31555-6
US $29.99/CAN $44.95

www.samspublishing.com

Sams Teach Yourself Windows 98 in 24 Hours
Greg Perry
ISBN:0-672-31223-9
US $19.99/
CAN $ 28.95

Sams Teach Yourself The Windows Registry in 24 Hours
Gerald Honeycutt Jr.
ISBN:0-672-31552-1
US $19.99/
CAN $29.95

Sams Teach Yourself Microsoft Project 98 in 24 Hours
Tim Pyron
ISBN:0-672-31258-1
US $19.99/
CAN $28.95

All prices are subject to change.

By opening this package, you are agreeing to be bound by the following agreement:

You may not copy or redistribute the entire CD-ROM as a whole. Copying and redistribution of individual software programs on the CD-ROM is governed by terms set by individual copyright holders.

This software is sold "as-is," without warranty of any kind, either expressed or implied, including but not limited to the implied warranties of merchantability and fitness for a particular purpose. Neither the publisher nor its dealers or distributors assumes any liability for any alleged or actual damages arising from the use of this program. (Some states do not allow for the exclusion of implied warranties, so the exclusion may not apply to you.)

NOTE: This CD-ROM uses long and mixed-case filenames, requiring the use of a protected-mode CD-ROM Driver.

CD-ROM Installation

Windows 95 Installation Instructions

1. Insert the CD-ROM into your CD-ROM drive.
2. From the Windows 95 desktop, double-click the My Computer icon.
3. Double-click on the icon that represents your CD-ROM drive.
4. Double-click on the icon titled START.EXE to run the CD-ROM interface.

 Note

> If Windows 95 is installed on your computer and you have the AutoPlay feature enabled, the START.EXE program starts automatically whenever you insert the CD-ROM into your CD-ROM drive.

Windows NT Installation Instructions

1. Insert the CD-ROM into your CD-ROM drive.
2. From File Manager or Program Manager, choose Run from the File menu.
3. Type <*drive*>\START.EXE and press Enter, where <*drive*> corresponds to the drive letter of your CD-ROM. For example, if your CD-ROM is drive D:, type D:\START.EXE and press Enter. This will run the CD-ROM interface.